Christmas 1994

THE BOOK OF THE
ARCHERS

———

♫

Dum dee dum dee dum dee dum etc !

All my love,

Martyn
xxx

THE BOOK OF THE
ARCHERS

Patricia Greene, Charles Collingwood
and Hedli Niklaus

MICHAEL JOSEPH
London

MICHAEL JOSEPH LTD

Published by the Penguin Group
27 Wrights Lane, London W8 5TZ
Viking Penguin Inc., 375 Hudson Street, New York, New York 10014, USA
Penguin Books Canada Ltd, 10 Alcorn Avenue, Toronto, Ontario, Canada M4V 3B2
Penguin Books (NZ) Ltd, 182-190 Wairau Road, Auckland 10, New Zealand

Penguin Books Ltd, Registered Offices: Harmondsworth, Middlesex, England

First published in Great Britain October 1994
Second impression November 1994
Third impression November 1994
Fourth impression November 1994

Text copyright © Patricia Greene, Charles Collingwood and Hedli Niklaus 1994

The Archers logotype © 1993 British Broadcasting Corporation

The Archers and *The Archers* logotype are trademarks of the British Broadcasting
Corporation and are used under licence

Typeset in Meridien
Designed and Printed in England by Butler & Tanner Ltd. Frome, Somerset

A CIP catalogue record for this book is available from the British Library

ISBN 0 7181 3849 X

The moral right of the authors has been asserted

CONTENTS

AUTHORS' NOTE

In the preparation of this book we have been fortunate to have been able to draw not only on our own knowledge of *The Archers* as members of the cast for many years, but also on the BBC's extensive archives. Our work became a voyage of discovery for each one of us, and we hope that you will have as much pleasure in reading it as we have had in writing it. We began by piecing together the lives of some of Ambridge's better-known characters, but became more and more absorbed in tracking down those incidental stories and personalities which give the series its rich texture and help make it so real. We increasingly felt that we were uncovering not simply a set of biographical details but also an intriguing picture of the social changes during the decades since the programme began.

We have included as much information on each character as we could in the space available, but our choice has of necessity been selective. We have checked all the facts to the best of our ability. All known details of births, marriages and deaths are included at the beginning of each entry and actors' names are given at the end. In some cases a detail that you might like to know, such as what happened to characters after their disappearance, or a character's surname, has not been included because it is not available – indeed has never been invented. Some characters for whom there are entries, such as Godfrey Wendover and Shane, have never actually been heard; others, particularly in the early years, were played by members of the cast in addition to their normal roles, and many were not credited in the records. In all these cases no actor's name is given at the end of the entry; nonetheless, they are as much part of the programme as characters for whom actors' names do appear. The storylines are up to date at the moment of going to press.

The views expressed on the characters are our own. All characters have their own supporters and detractors and you will not always agree with our assessments; but that is part of the fun, and should lead to some enjoyable discussions among the fans of the programme.

We are grateful to Vanessa Whitburn, the editor of *The Archers*, and her team for allowing us access to the source material and for their help and advice; members of the cast who have assisted us with information; Jerry Johns, Donald Steele and Nick Green of the BBC Press Office at Pebble Mill for their patience as we went through all the photographs we could find, old and new; and Leon Tanner, Louise Page and Chris Hawes, without whom this book would never have materialized.

Patricia Greene, Charles Collingwood and Hedli Niklaus
MAY 1994

ILLUSTRATIONS ACKNOWLEDGEMENTS

The authors and publisher are grateful to Bob Arnold, who kindly loaned the photograph on page 121; and to BBC Picture Publicity for permission to use all other photographs in this book, all of which are BBC copyright, with the exception of that on page 36 which is from the authors' collection.

ADAMS, MR

Sid and Kathy Perks discussed their intended purchase of the Bull in July 1993 with the free-trade manager at Shires Breweries, Mr Adams, in the hope of getting assistance in the form of a loan.

ADAMSON, DOROTHY

b. 14 Jan. 1945; 1 son, 1 dtr

During the fifteen years she spent in Ambridge, Dorothy never played the role of a submissive vicar's wife. With two growing children it was hard to make ends meet on her husband Richard's stipend, so she began to look for part-time employment. Her first job was helping in Carol Tregorran's market garden but in 1976 she left there to work in Borchester at the 'Gear Change' boutique. There was a gear change for Dorothy herself when in October that year she took over the running of the village playgroup.

Busy as she was, she always stood loyally by Richard's side and played as much of a part in church life as she could. She had a surprise windfall when her great-aunt Alice left her a small end-of-terrace house in Felpersham, but it turned out to be worth far less than they had hoped.

After a spell in the village shop she became Dr Matthew Thorogood's receptionist. Unfortunately she was unable to resist the odd careless indiscretion or 'confidential' leak, and it became increasingly difficult for her to combine her two roles, receptionist and vicar's wife. But before she could begin to solve this conundrum, Cyril, Bishop of Felpersham, had suggested that Richard move to a new parish in County Durham. At first Dorothy refused to leave Ambridge, but Richard persuaded her to visit the new parish before they made a final decision. She realized that she was being offered a new challenge and to his great delight she agreed to go. Amongst the flurry of farewells the family were given a lunch at Home Farm and a leaving party at the village hall, where they were presented with a cheque and a rose bowl.

Heather Barrett

ADAMSON, MICHAEL

b. 7 Dec. 1968

Younger child of Richard and Dorothy, Michael Adamson showed promise on the trumpet.

ADAMSON, RACHEL

b. 19 Jan. 1967

When the Adamsons lived in Ambridge in the eighties, their daughter Rachel was in the tennis team and sixth form at Borchester Grammar School, and moved on to Lancaster University where she read English literature.

ADAMSON, REVD RICHARD

b. 15 March 1943; 1 son, 1 dtr

At Christmas 1973, the services at St Stephen's were taken by the new vicar, Richard Adamson. He and his family were the last to come to live in the old vicarage. From his bespectacled appearance he might have been taken for one of the old school, but Richard realized that the church had to move with the times. In 1975, the old house and its grounds were sold. Some of the land went for housing and the Adamsons moved into a new and more manageable vicarage.

To some, Richard might have seemed so holy and conscientious as to make the ordi-nary mortal feel sinful. He ran the scout troop, gave bell-ringing lessons, hatched, matched and dispatched, and was even a Samaritan. But in his spare time, the dog-collar came off and he played cricket and football for the Ambridge teams. As a Samaritan, Richard took many calls from George Barford and played a vital part in helping him overcome his life-threatening drink problem. When the divorced George wanted to marry Christine Johnston in St Stephen's, Richard had the courage to move against the advice of his bishop and go ahead with the ceremony. He saw a church wedding for the couple as a triumphant act of thanksgiving.

Richard tried to counsel Lucy Perks when she found it difficult to adjust to the new relationship between her father Sid and his second wife Kathy but became concerned when she joined his confirmation classes, as he felt that she was doing so for the wrong reasons and that she was trying to anger her agnostic father. When Bishop Cyril asked him to consider taking a new parish in County Durham in 1988 he con-sented, sad to leave Ambridge but looking forward to new challenges. He and his fam-ily moved northwards, onwards and, we hope, upwards.

Richard Carrington

ALDRIDGE, ALICE MARGARET

b. 29 Sept. 1988

Alice was born in 1988, a symbol of Brian and Jennifer Aldridge's attempt to revive their marriage after Brian's affair with Caroline Bone eventually ended. She was called Margaret after her grandmother (Peggy Woolley) and Jennifer nicknamed her 'Duchess'. Like her sister Kate, she became a handful as she grew older, and found all sorts of ways to annoy her father, such as pouring orange juice over his computer disks. While Brian and Jennifer discovered all the disadvantages of having a baby late in life, Jack Woolley threw himself into the role of stepgrandfather with great enthusiasm. He and Peggy accomplished Alice's potty training while her parents were away on a skiing holiday – to the delight of her parents on their return.

Inadvertently Alice did indeed help bring Brian and Jennifer together, when she was four years old. Her half-sister Debbie Aldridge was looking after her when she fell off a gate, gashing her head so badly that she had to go to hospital. As usual it took time to track down her parents, but once they heard the news there was no mistaking the sincerity of their response. Jennifer's renewed determination to help them all be a real family again would have been sweet music to her daughter's ears had she been old enough to appreciate it. Alice was kept in overnight, but suffered no lasting damage and was allowed to go home the next day.

She objected fiercely to attending nursery school in September 1992, but was happy to accompany her parents on a skiing holiday in the winter. This was perhaps not as great a sacrifice to Brian and Jennifer as it might seem, for they went with friends who had a child of the same age and that indispensable accessory, a nanny.

ALDRIDGE, BRIAN

b. 20 Nov. 1943; m. Jennifer Travers-Macy 29 May 1976; 2 dtrs

When Brian Aldridge met Jennifer Travers-Macy in 1975 he resembled one of the heroes in the G.A. Henty novels he enjoyed so much. Dashing and ruthless, he was a gentleman farmer from a naval background and attractively wealthy. He purchased Home Farm with 1,500 acres from the Bellamy Estate in 1975 and had the house converted for him to live in; then he decided that to complete the picture he needed a wife. It didn't take long for Jennifer to succumb to his charms and they were married on 29 May 1976 after her divorce.

The couple have a comfortable lifestyle. They were the first family in Ambridge to have their own solar-powered swimming-pool. Brian has been able to buy the newest and best in farm machinery and add to his land and lifestock as he felt fit. He has always expected Jennifer to play a traditional role in their marriage and never liked the idea of her working, but he has indulged her expensive hobbies. His immediate family has also benefited from his generosity; but Brian can be patronizing, which has got on everyone's nerves, particularly Phil Archer's – once Brian dismissively gave Phil a blank cheque to cover some damage he'd done to Brookfield stock, which Phil found infuriating.

Family has always meant a great deal to Brian, perhaps because both his parents died when he was twenty-eight. It took him time to adjust to his two stepchildren, Adam Macy and Debbie Aldridge, but he never stinted them materially, and paid for their private education. He was delighted when he heard that he was going to be a father in his own right, but couldn't resist teasing Jennifer by telling her that if the child was a boy he would have to be called Ebenezer, as this was a family name. Underlying the joke was Brian's very real desire for a son and heir, and when Katherine Victoria was born in 1977 a trace of disappointment could be distinguished under his delighted response.

The next years were taken up with farming and domestic troubles. Brian was called to an industrial tribunal for unfair dismissal of one of his workers, Jack Roberts; he tried to help Christine when her husband Paul Johnson went bankrupt; his brother-in-law Ralph Bellamy suffered a heart attack; and, most important of all, Jennifer started an affair with John Tregorran, which nearly ruined their marriage. He became restless and dissatisfied, feeling that his life had got into a rut. So when he met up with the allur-

left to right: Brian, Jennifer and Debbie Aldridge (Charles Collingwood, Angela Piper and Tamsin Greig)

ing Caroline Bone at the Hunt ball in 1985 and danced with her all night, he was ripe for change and distraction.

He ran wild risks as he wooed Caroline, taking her out to public places, even kissing her in the Country Park. When Jennifer found out, as inevitably she did, Caroline insisted that they had to part, but Brian found it hard to let her go. Some months later he was still in pursuit; and there was a delightful irony when Christine wanted him to buy a 75 per cent interest in a horse called Two Timer Tootsie – which, when he learned that Caroline rode him, he decided he would.

An accident was to have a major impact on the Aldridges' lives. Brian pushed Joe Grundy out of the way of a cow suffering from 'mad cow's disease' and got struck himself. He was operated on for a cerebral abscess caused by the blow and during convalescence suffered a post-traumatic epileptic fit. He couldn't drink or drive, and the drugs made him drowsy. For a man like Brian such restrictions were unendurable and he found it hard to come to terms with the reality of his condition. Matters weren't helped by Jennifer's fussing or the fact that, despite her tendency to histrionics, she looked after the farm competently while he was in hospital.

In 1992 Brian's desire to manage the farm himself and anxiety about his finances made him interested in the idea of expanding the leisure potential of his estate, and he did some local research. He fished with Jack Woolley and rode with Christine in order to pick their brains, without revealing why, although they had their suspicions. He received an unexpected bonus at this time when his stepdaughter Debbie returned home halfway through her university course because of an unhappy love affair. He has found in her an intelligent and sympathetic companion and his decisions to create a fishing lake and a course for off-the-road riding owe a great deal to her.

The next two years showed Brian at his worst, although with some cause. Roger Travers-Macy, Jennifer's former husband, returned in 1991 to try to resume his role as Debbie's natural father, which made Brian unattractively jealous and possessive. When he learned that Jennifer was sleeping with Roger it was the last straw. A series of escalating rows and recriminations had the effect of making him aggressive and unpleasant to others. Even Debbie didn't escape from the sharp end of his tongue when he expected her to deliver results from the 'Courses for Horses' scheme she had set up. He had money troubles too, and had to put off the opening of the fishing lake. His daughter Kate was disturbed by the family tensions and got herself into difficulties; but when family therapy was suggested he found reasons not to attend the sessions, blaming the situation on Jennifer and expecting her to resolve it. It was not so easy for him to lay all the blame at Jennifer's door when Kate ran away from home in August 1994.

Matters settled into an uneasy truce at Home Farm. Jennifer ended her affair with Roger, and Brian's epilepsy improved so that he could drink an occasional glass of wine. He still twirls his vocal moustache when he meets a pretty woman, but it has become a habit rather than a danger. Despite underlying dissatisfactions, Brian and Jennifer get on well enough, and neither has wanted to end their marriage despite considerable pressures.

Charles Collingwood

ALDRIDGE, DEBORAH (DEBBIE, FORMERLY TRAVERS-MACY AND MACY)

b. 24 Dec. 1970

Debbie is Jennifer Aldridge's daughter by Roger Travers-Macy and was five when her mother married Brian Aldridge in 1976. She got on well with her stepfather, who was generous: among other presents he bought her a pony of her own because he knew she loved riding. Brian wanted his stepchildren to take his name but Roger objected, and the children merely dropped the Travers, and used Macy as their surname. When she was older, however, Debbie called herself Aldridge, which pleased Brian enormously, although she has not as yet had her name changed by deed poll.

When Debbie went to Exeter University to read French and English, Brian and Jennifer thought she was safely settled, but she returned in June 1991, having been granted a sabbatical. Then a mysterious stranger in his early forties arrived, asking about her, and it was clear that Debbie didn't want to see him. He was Simon Gerrard, her tutor in French Canadian literature. They had started sleeping together and she had been on the point of going back to Canada with him when he had left her for someone else. That relationship was now over and Simon wanted to go back to Debbie, who couldn't make up her

mind how she felt. Brian's reactions were less complicated. When he found Simon at Home Farm, apparently manhandling his step-daughter, he threw him out. Furious at Brian's interference Debbie stormed out after Simon, disappearing for a few nailbiting days before ringing to ask to be fetched from Hollerton Junction. Jennifer obliged, but almost wished she hadn't as Brian and Debbie refused to exchange a civil word, each waiting for the other to apologize.

It all blew over and it was a much happier family group that met to celebrate Debbie's twenty-first birthday with lunch at Grey Gables. Once again a stranger asked for her where-abouts, but this time it was her natural father, Rogers Travers-Macy, whom she hadn't seen for years. They made a private arrangement to meet a couple of days later at Nelson's Wine Bar but didn't bargain for Jennifer who, fearful that Debbie was meeting Simon, had followed her there. Jennifer was totally taken aback to dis-cover her former husband. She determined not to tell Brian anything about it, but the cat was let out of the bag when a new car arrived on the doorstep as a present for Debbie from her loving father, Roger.

Jennifer invited Roger to dinner, which Brian spent mainly in the lambing shed, leav-ing Debbie to observe how well her parents were getting on. Deeply and rightly suspicious, Debbie told Roger that she didn't want to see him again and believed him when he said he would keep away. She was soon involved with Brian's ideas for the creation of a course for off-the-road horse riding but could not ignore the peculiar behaviour of her mother, which suggested that she was having an affair. Debbie could guess the name of her lover. She sounded out Brian with her suspicions, and it became clear that he too was aware of what was going on. Debbie's home life became a nightmare as she found herself in the middle of a war between Brian and Jennifer, each looking to her for support. In desperation she told Roger to leave Jennifer alone, and at last he departed from Ambridge, leaving behind him much acrimony.

Elizabeth Archer too had been having a bad time, which drew the girls together. Debbie was very supportive over Elizabeth's affair with Cameron Fraser and subsequent abortion. Their friendship pursues a volatile pattern of its own, but real affection lies beneath everyday jealousies and irritations. Debbie needed all Elizabeth's support after her shattering experience in 1993 when Debbie and her stepsister Kate were held hostage in a raid on the village shop. No one was seriously hurt but Debbie was left shaken and restless. She suffered further trauma the following year with Mark Hebden's death when he drove into a tree in an effort to avoid Debbie and Caroline Bone, whose horses had been disturbed by a speeding car.

To Jennifer's distress Debbie chose not to return to university, and now she works for Brian. She has helped Nelson in his antique shop so successfully that he offered her a partnership which she turned down. Her love life is volatile, and although her name has been coupled with that of Dr Richard Locke they have more cuffs than clinches; whether anything comes of the relationship remains to be seen. In the meantime she got to know Steve Oakley, a contractor helping out during the 1994 harvest.

Tamsin Greig

ALDRIDGE, JENNIFER (NÉE ARCHER, FORMERLY TRAVERS-MACY)

b. 7 Jan. 1945; 1 son by Paddy Redmond; m. Roger Travers-Macy 27 Sept. 1968; 1 dtr; divorced Feb. 1976; m. Brian Aldridge 29 May 1976; 2 dtrs

Jennifer was a bright and bubbly little girl of six when in 1951 her parents, Jack and Peggy Archer, returned to Ambridge from Cornwall. She couldn't wait to grow up and made a precocious fifteen-year-old, staggering on stiletto heels, wearing lipstick and proudly walking out with Gary Kenton of Percy Hood's Farm.

Jennifer went to the West Midland Training College at Walsall, qualified as a teacher in 1966 and found herself a job at Hollerton Primary School. She sold a short story to a woman's magazine and the snobbish Jack Woolley was so impressed that he commissioned her to write a brochure about the history of Grey Gables. Both these events encouraged her talent for writing and an interest in the past history of Ambridge, which have remained with her ever since.

She never had problems attracting men but lost her heart to a farmworker at Brookfield, Paddy Redmond, who went on holiday and brought back a fiancée, Nora McAuley. By then Jennifer knew she was pregnant and that she had to tell her parents. They were hurt and bewildered, and their efforts to accept the situation weren't made easier by her obstinate refusal to tell them the name of the father. Her son Adam was born on 22 June 1967, the same year that Jennifer's first novel was accepted for publication.

Even encumbered with a baby, Jennifer had no shortage of suitors. She married Roger Travers-Macy and had a daughter, Deborah, by him in 1970, but the marriage was not to last. She was busy, working full-time at Grey Gables and writing a thriller as well as looking after her children. Roger was buyer for a firm of antiquarian booksellers and often away, so she moved in with Paul and Christine Johnson at Wynford's Farm, meeting Roger for an occasional unsatisfactory weekend in their Borchester flat. They were finally divorced in 1976, but by then Jennifer had other fish to fry.

Jennifer had met Brian Aldridge at dinner at Carol Tregorran's, and they were at once attracted to each other. They went out for lunch, then a dinner, and wound up at the Royal Show together. He started to give her lessons in golf, and of course tongues, always hyperactive where Jennifer was concerned, started to wag. Her second book, *It's Murder*, had just appeared in bookshops and Brian enjoyed the reflected glory and the fact that people's heads turned when he took her out. It didn't take her long to say 'yes' when he proposed, and they were married at the Borchester Register Office on 29 May 1976, shortly after her divorce came through.

Jennifer thoroughly enjoyed her new lifestyle, but there were strings attached. Brian indulged her materially but he expected her to look good and keep within her allowance. After the birth of her second daughter, Kate, in 1977, she had to work hard to get her figure back, and while she enjoyed owning a swimming-pool it meant that she had to learn how to swim. There were more serious problems. Brian and Adam didn't get on well together and Adam received bad reports from school; she was worried that her brother Tony Archer was showing too great an interest in Libby Jones the milk recorder while his wife Pat was away; and after Paul Johnson's bankruptcy in 1977 she had to offer a temporary home to his wife Christine and their adopted son Peter.

Like her husband, Jennifer has a low boredom threshold and at times her desire for new stimuli has led her into trouble. After the failure of the Two Jays Craft Studio which she set up with Jill Archer in 1978, she told Colonel Danby that she longed for an absorbing job; she and John Tregorran started to work together on an historical survey, and she became absorbed in him instead. When Brian took her flying, she thought she saw the site of a village in Joe Grundy's meadow; she did some research and mounted an exhibition of her findings which was so successful that she and John decided to write *An English Village Through the Ages* – and matters worsened. Brian was fearful of a partnership of a different sort; Jennifer's attempts to smooth things over with a cosy dinner failed miserably when the two men quarrelled over farming ethics and John left before the food was on the table. John and Jennifer afterwards carefully kept their distance.

In 1986, Jennifer was devastated when she discovered that Brian was having an affair in his turn, with Caroline Bone. She allowed Brian to convince her that Caroline was responsible, and tried to believe him when he told her that it was over, but she

Brian and Jennifer Aldridge (Charles Collingwood and Angela Piper)

has felt insecure ever since. They decided to have another baby, hoping that it would bring them closer together, although wary of the risks of Jennifer having a baby in her forties. After an uncomfortable pregnancy it was a relief when Alice, a healthy little girl, was born in 1988, but Brian was bitterly disappointed, as he had wanted a son.

The following year Brian had a bad accident, followed by a post-operative epileptic fit. He became crochety and difficult, but the crisis brought out the best in Jennifer, who was actually heard to say that money isn't everything. This mood, however, was too good to last, and she reverted to her shal- lower self when Roger-Travers Macy came back into her life. Using the pretext of getting to know his daughter, Debbie, now twenty- one, Roger blatantly set out to woo Jennifer once more. She allowed herself to be seduced, not least by the excitement of snatched meetings and near betrayals, but eventually, encouraged by Jill Archer, she told Brian the truth and did her best to put Roger out of her life. It cost her a great deal but she managed it. Brian was able to com- ment wryly that he thought it was over because she was so interested in his fishing project – after John Tregorran it had been oil-seed rape.

With all these extracurricular activities and her contributions to local events and politics Jennifer has been dependent on paid help or her long-suffering mother Peggy to sort out the housework and care of her children, with varying degrees of success. Eva Lenz, a young German girl, came to help out when Kate was little; Betty Tucker came to clean but left abruptly after unwelcome attentions from Brian; and Dawn Porritt, who came to look after Alice, left when they refused her a contract. Even the formidable Mrs Walker refused to work as many hours as Jennifer required, and all Jennifer's attempts to dump Alice on Peggy at the drop of a hat failed when Peggy decided that she was taking advantage of her, which she was. The idea of taking charge of her own life and looking after her home and children herself has always been unpalatable.

It is not surprising that the tensions within the household have been reflected in the behaviour of the children, particularly Kate's. Brian has been less than helpful, blaming Jennifer for everything, and leaving her to attend family therapy sessions with Kate without him; to his surprise Jennifer has persisted with the sessions, showing unexpected courage and tenacity. She was anguished not to hear from her daughter for so long after her abrupt departure from home at the end of August 1994, needing a quality of understanding from Brian that he found difficult to provide.

Brian has been more constructive with Debbie, but has found a companionship with her that he lacks with Jennifer, so that painfully she sometimes feels left out.

Jennifer's plaintive 'Cooee!' can often be heard as she visits her friends and relatives, and there is something poignant in the sound. Selfish and attractive, she has never truly fulfilled her early promise, and despite her wealth and her exotic trips abroad her life seems to have an edge of disappointment.

Ysanne Churchman; Elaine McNamara; Freda Hooper; Carol Lynn-Davies; Angela Piper

ALDRIDGE, KATHERINE VICTORIA (KATE)

b. 30 Sept. 1977

Poor Kate. She hasn't had the best of backgrounds to help create a well-adjusted adolescent, or else an evil fairy was present at her christening party.

She was a placid baby and had more than her fair share of possessions as she grew up, including a pony of her own called Velvet. The first sign that rot had set in was when she refused to let her cousin Helen Archer ride Velvet and had to be forcibly persuaded to 'share'. The concept that it is better to give than to receive had already passed her by.

She went off to Cheltenham Ladies' College in 1988, at eleven years old. A year later she was seen with a gang of unsavoury youths at the Ambridge cricket pavilion. When she started smoking, and then helped sabotage the Christmas tree on the village green, Brian and Jennifer realized that they had a problem on their hands.

Things went from bad to worse as Kate's pleas for attention became more numerous. She announced that she had turned vegan, refused to go to the Pony Club and had her

Kate Aldridge (Susie Riddell)

ears pierced, twice in each ear. Her school had found her equally difficult and when she ran away on her thirteenth birthday it was the last straw: they asked Jennifer to withdraw her. She then went to the newly amalgamated school Borchester Green where she was no happier. Her grandmother Peggy Archer tried to help by asking Bert Fry to find Kate some behind-the-scenes work for the village nativity play, but after watching her posturing and smoking he said that he felt more inclined to give her a good spanking. When Brian discovered that his phone bill was sky high because she was making long-distance calls to a German boy she'd met when skiing, he knew exactly how Bert

felt. So did Tony Archer after she conned him into allowing her to use the phone at Bridge Farm.

Helen Archer was Kate's greatest – possibly only – fan. She was easily enticed to secret meetings in Blossom Hill Cottage (empty after Peggy Archer had married Jack Woolley in 1991). William Grundy was co-opted as messenger boy and after an initiation rite Brenda Tucker was allowed to join the gang. They forced the lock to the attic door, and once inside the children lost no time in excavating Peggy's personal possessions, including a letter hinting at a wartime romance with an American soldier, Conn Kortchmar. Kate and Helen mischievously forged a letter from Peggy to Conn, and then forgot all about it.

Kate became preoccupied with her boyfriend, Warren, driving around with him in his stolen Alfa Romeo and drinking lager at Scandals in Borchester. She banned the others from the cottage and when she found William there she locked him in the attic. Before she could let him out, she and Warren were involved in a minor car accident. William spent a long lonely night before the faithful Helen Archer biked frantically over to release him. Resentful and unrepentant, Kate refused to explain her presence in a stolen vehicle to the police; in spite of this they let her off with a caution. Matters worsened when Conn turned up in answer to the forged letter, causing Peggy two months of confused emotions, none of them favourable towards Kate.

On her school's advice, she saw an educational psychologist who recommended family therapy. She and Jennifer, though not Brian, attended several sessions and tried to come to terms with the problem. Unexpectedly Lynda Snell applied some therapy of her own by inviting her for tea and sympathy, so starting a continuing relationship.

Kate was involved in the dramatic raid on the village shop in 1993 and as much marked by the experience as the other hostages. She had felt proud of letting down the tyres of the getaway van, but afterwards was afraid that she might only have prolonged the raid and endangered Jack Woolley's life. For once Jennifer managed to be in the right place at the right time and shared a rare moment of contact with her daughter when Kate put into words some of her feelings.

More troubles were in store, however. When her GCSE results came out in August 1994 they were as bad as she and her parents expected. She agreed to attend the Borchester Technical College in the autumn for resits and Brian and Jennifer thought the matter settled. Far from it. They should have had their suspicions, since Kate had uncharacteristically offered to help man the riding course. The day after her results, Kate decamped with a few clothes and money stolen from the takings. The police were called in but scaled down their investigation when Jennifer learned that there had been a sighting of Kate. At last Kate got in touch, but made it clear that she did not intend returning home in a hurry.

Kate is as much sinned against as sinning, and Tony was the one who remarked on her resemblance to Mrs P., and if she has enough of those genes within her the chances are that in her own time she will come good.

Henrietta Smethurst; Susie Riddell

ALEX

It's typical of Kenton Archer that he should have formed a business association with Alex, bosun of his first ship. Alex's sharp practices in share dealing caused an investigation by FIMBRA into the investment firm Alex worked for, resulting, in 1989, in his being sacked and the threat of prosecution.

ALISTAIR

Senior partner in the Borchester veterinary practice for whom Robin Stokes works.

ALLARD, JESS

2 sons; d. Dec. 1961

Widower Jess Allard owned his own farm, and formed a milking co-operative with Dan Archer and Fred Barratt which they called Ambridge Dairy Farmers. He was interested in the idea that shared resources could prove cost-effective. Jess did not live long enough to enjoy any profits from the scheme, however, as he died in December 1961, only eight months after it was officially begun.

Max Brimmell

ALLARD, JOE

Joe was Jess Allard's elder son. Although his father had wished his sons to carry on with the farm after his death, Joe decided to sell it. Under the terms of his father's will he had to give first refusal to Ambridge Dairy Farmers, and by arrangement with them he sold it to Phil Archer who then joined the co-operative. Joe left Ambridge in March 1962.

Ralph Lawton

ALLARD, REX

Rex was Joe Allard's younger brother. There was bad feeling between the two brothers when he went out with Joe's fiancée Ruth. He left Ambridge to make a new life for himself when the farm was sold in 1962.

Brian Kent

ALLARD'S FARM

see Hollowtree Farm

AMBRIDGE

The village of Ambridge lies six miles south of Borchester, with the River Am flowing lazily through it. Around the triangular village green, on which there is a pond, are clustered black and white cottages and old brick houses; and the village pub, the Bull, overlooks it. There's no school any more but the village shop remains, outside which is an old-style red telephone kiosk, which Ambridge has been proud to retain, thanks to local support. A similar campaign ensured the retention of the wooden fingerpost on the green when it was threatened with replacement by a modern sign. The parish church of St Stephen's is situated in a slightly elevated position on the edge of the village to the west. Many church and village fund-raising events are held in the village hall. Behind the village's picturesque facade are modern developments such as the council houses east of the green and the 1978 estate of privately owned detached houses known as Glebelands. New arrivals have added their voices to village events but in the main Ambridge is still a farming community.

AMBRIDGE FARM

Ambridge Farm was one of five tenant farms on the Bellamy Estate and the home of Ken and Mary Pound for thirty years. They retired from the farm in 1983 and Mike and Betty Tucker took their place as tenants. Their first job was to make the farmhouse habitable. The Pounds had painted everything brown excluding the kitchen and bathroom, which hadn't been touched for years, and it needed re-wiring and re-plastering. Mike rented 150 acres from the Bellamy Estate and 15 acres from Gavin Fry of Wheathead Farm. By 1985 he had 65 milkers, 35 heifers and calves, and he ran a milk round, but it was still not enough to enable him to earn a living, and he couldn't keep up with his interest repayments to the bank. The bank foreclosed and in January 1986 Mike had to declare himself bankrupt and the Tuckers left. The land was reabsorbed into the Bellamy Estate, and Matthew Thorogood rented the farmhouse and some of the outbuildings which he converted into a surgery.

AMBRIDGE FARMERS LTD

Brookfield, Allard's Farm and Barratt's Farm formed a co-operative venture which started operating in April 1961 under the name Ambridge Dairy Farmers. Phil Archer took over Allard's Farm in August 1962 and the three farms were fully incorporated into Ambridge Farmers Ltd a month later.

AMBRIDGE HALL

Ambridge Hall was built in the 1860s by the Lawson-Hope family as a home for the village doctor. It was originally an ugly house, but its yellow brick has mellowed with age, its wooden shutters lend it style and, set in a now mature garden, it has a certain Victorian charm. There are six bedrooms and a quaint staircase which leads to what used to be the servants' quarters.

The property was left by Charles Grenville to his wife Carol when he died in 1961. Jack Woolley bought it from her in 1968 when she was married again, to John Tregorran, and sold it in 1973 to Laura Archer, who gave it its rather grandiose name. She lived there with her lodger, Colonel Danby, to whom she intended to leave it. However, after her death in 1985 it was discovered that she hadn't signed the top copy of her will, so it was inherited by her next of kin, a niece who lived in New Zealand. The Hall was put up for sale the following year and advertised in *Borsetshire Life* for £160,000. Intriguing rumours spread of all sorts of enquirers – Dutch, Arabs, even a pop star – but in fact it was purchased by incomers Lynda and Robert Snell.

AMBRIDGE VILLAGE SCHOOL

Despite local opposition, Ambridge village school was closed in December 1973. For some time it housed Christine Johnson's playgroup; in 1976 it was converted into a new village hall.

ANDRENE

One of the first waitresses at Nelson Gabriel's Wine Bar in June 1980. Nelson abandoned his patrons to her charmless attentions so that he could attend the races, but returned to a barrage of complaints. She did not last long.

Marian Kemmer

ANGUS

In the days when Phil Archer was Fairbrother's farm manager, the Estate's pedigree Ayrshires were in the care of Angus. He was not altogether happy in Ambridge, since his Scottish family had not wanted him to move south. Christine Archer, on a trip to Edinburgh, visited his relatives and was able to effect a reconciliation. He had a long association with Phil in the running of Fairbrother's farming affairs.

Lester Mudditt; Laidlaw Dalling; Andrew Faulds

ANTROBUS, MARJORIE

b. 1922

Marjorie Antrobus might be described as a game old bird, equally at home in the company of Guy Pemberton over dinner, or singing 'Yellow Submarine' in the back of Eddie Grundy's van.

Before settling in Ambridge, she had led a colourful, adventurous life with her late husband, Teddy. Marjorie has not yet divulged her memoirs, but we know that as well as being a professional soldier, he was also a famous big-game hunter, to which the tiger-skin rug in the hall at Nightingale Farm still bears mute testimony. Marjorie and Teddy lived for some time in Palestine – where she learnt bee-keeping from an Arab neighbour in the shade of an exotic bougainvillaea – and later in Africa. Teddy is buried in Kenya.

On her return to England Marjorie became a successful breeder and exhibitor of Afghan hounds. She and her beloved 'gels' moved into Nightingale Farm in 1985. She was quickly dubbed 'the dog woman'. Though the dogs were usually impeccably behaved, Portia did once misplace 'the quality of mercy' on Jack Woolley's smug bull terrier Captain. Marjorie was horrified when Portia gave birth to nine mongrel puppies. Later, when David and Ruth Archer moved into Nightingale Farm while their own bungalow was being completed, they found one night that Portia had borrowed their bed and given birth to four little Afghans.

Marjorie is a staunch member of the WI. Ambridge first heard her clear enunciated speaking voice a year before she moved there, when she was a visiting speaker at the Ambridge WI. Her subject then had been 'The Colourful World of the Afghan'. Later, she was proud to represent Ambridge at the Albert Hall AGM in 1986, and did not flinch from joining in the discussions on the subjects of, among others, AIDS and Child Abuse. She persuaded the Ambridge branch to boycott the village shop until CFC aerosol cans were withdrawn from the shelves, and stood firm when Jack Woolley tried the desperate compromise of slashing the prices.

Her other contributions to village life over the years include the production of the morality play *Everyman* in Christmas 1986 and in 1992 a spirited wartime revue, *Tickety Boo*. She showed her skills in entertainment too when she purchased an electric organ; she and Ruth Archer won a talent competition at the 1989 Ambridge spring festival singing a Flanagan and Allen song, 'Nice People with Nice Manners'; and her Lady Bracknell in 1990 was superb.

Marjorie has always had a good rapport with the young people of the village: Nigel Pargetter, Usha Gupta, Ruth and Richard Locke all have reason to regard her as a good friend. She has often been a willing babysitter for Sharon Richards's daughter Kylie. She even found herself in competition with Martha Woodford for the job.

But Martha, too, has been at the receiving end of Marjorie's kindness. She spent the night as her guest once, and when she admired the view from the flat, Marjorie told her to 'stay as long as you like'. Marjorie meant by the window, but Martha misinterpreted her and stayed for a fortnight.

Marjorie managed the situation with skill.

She has many friends. She became close to Colonel Danby for a time, and even offered to share her home with him (he gently refused). In spite of this, she has often felt lonely, and unfulfilled. This drove her to answer a small-ad in *The Borchester Echo* ('gentleman farmer seeking companionship'). She was not well pleased when none other than Joe Grundy turned up. But even then, she was sympathetic. She helped him to write to another applicant, and lent him one of Teddy's tweed jackets for the date that resulted. She was happy to dine out with Joe when he came into some money from the sale of his posset pot, and gently insisted that she drive him home in his old van afterwards.

She is a devout, but practical-minded Christian. She has a soft spot for the clergy and works hard for the Church. Richard Adamson and Marjorie were good friends when she lived in Waterley Cross. Jerry Buckle tried to persuade her to go with him to Mozambique, but she turned him down. She was at first rather jealous of Robin Stokes' attachment to Caroline Bone, but was invaluable to him when, after her accident, Caroline was lying close to death in hospital. Her clear words of faith were exactly what were needed in Robin's time of darkness and despair.

Margot Boyd

APRIL COTTAGE

April Cottage and Keeper's Cottage are a pair built by Charles Grenville in 1960 to take the place of older houses affected by the building of a new road through part of his land towards Borchester. Len and Mary Thomas were the first occupants of April Cottage and Martha Woodford the most recent.

ARCHER, ANTHONY WILLIAM DANIEL (TONY)

b. 16 Feb. 1951; m. Pat Lewis 12 Dec. 1974; 2 sons, 1 dtr

Tony was Peggy and Jack Archer's only son and Doris and Dan Archer's first grandson. He was a bright little boy and had a special bond with Walter Gabriel – with the result that at eighteen months he greeted Phil Archer with the words, 'Hello me old pal, me old beauty!' Nothing seemed to worry him; once, when at the age of five he got lost on the beach at Bournemouth, his distraught relatives found him happily singing 'Robin Hood'. As he grew older he lost this cheerful optimism; nowadays Tony is better known for his moaning.

At first all went well for him. Needing help to get started farming, which he genuinely loved, he was lucky enough to win the support of Ralph Bellamy. Tony worked for him while attending classes at Borchester Technical College on day release and again after graduating with distinction from the Walford Farm Institute in Shropshire. Seeing his potential, Bellamy encouraged him to learn his trade, sending him to Cambridgeshire to study crops of Brussels sprouts and following his advice afterwards. There was one drawback, however: Tony's weakness for the fairer sex. He had a succession of girlfriends, for each of whom he felt enduring passion as long as she lasted. When he rushed to Hollerton Junction one day to say goodbye to his latest flame, Jane Petrie, instead of looking after a new cow due to calve, Bellamy was so angry that he fired him. Tony disappeared for a short trip to France while the dust blew over, and then returned to look after Dan Archer's dairy herd at Brookfield. He made it up with Bellamy eventually.

When Haydn Evans offered him a partnership deal in 1973 over Willow Farm, he was glad to accept. He was trying to make a go of it with a small herd of 35 cattle when he became engaged to Mary Weston. She broke it off but Tony was not heartbroken for long as Pat Lewis, Haydn's Welsh niece, had fallen in love with him. Pat proposed to him a mere four days after he heard that Mary was going to marry her boss, and two months later they were married.

By the time they moved to Bridge Farm in 1977 when Jim Elliott, the previous tenant, died, they had a son, John Daniel. In 1979 their daughter Helen was born with a dislocated hip and Pat exhausted herself worrying over her. Tony was working hard and seeing little reward for his efforts. He promised Pat that he would work less and play more, and arranged a surprise supper for her as a treat. But only a couple of weeks later, while he was having a drink with Mark Hebden and Shula Archer in the Bull he started to act very strangely, almost as though he were drunk; and the next day he was rushed off to hospital suffering from tetanus. He'd scratched himself on a rusty nail and typically hadn't kept up with his injections. He made an impossible convales-cent and turned to drink, after which things went from bad to worse. He was irritable and unpleasant; he forgot to secure Pat's chickens and they were killed by a fox; he drove Mike home when drunk and they crashed; and he ran over Marmaduke, Mrs P.'s cat. Event-ually Pat had had enough and left him, taking the children with her. Belatedly Tony came to his senses and managed to persuade her to return, then treated her to a holiday in Corfu which did them a lot of good.

Their decision in 1985 to become organic farmers was one of the best they made, and they've made a go of it (even though Jennifer Aldridge, attempting to help, pulled up their first crop of carrots instead of the weeds). They've learned how to trim back cabbages, remove blackleg from potatoes with seaweed spray and what backache really means when it comes to pulling leeks. When their whole-saler went bust Tony wanted to play the market but Pat insisted on joining the Co-op. He changed his mind when the Co-op's fields-man turned out to be a pretty woman, and Pat wasn't pleased when she learned that he had promised to plant yet more leeks. Pat's homemade organic yoghourt and ice-cream sell well and together they've opened a farm shop which has proved so successful that they've expanded it, overcoming the skul-duggery of Howard Friend, representative of the Borchester Environmental Trust, who, intending to open an organic produce shop himself in Felpersham, tried to use his posi-tion to block their application.

Tony was brought up in a household dominated by forceful women, and it's not surprising that he married another one. But it would be a mistake to believe he is henpecked; he can hold his own with a variety of techniques familiar to family life all over the world, ranging from sulks, emotional blackmail, spitefulness and outright aggression. His relationship with his two sisters, Jennifer Aldridge and Lilian Bellamy, is spiky; all of them speak their mind, generally with disastrous results. He's had fierce quarrels with both of them, especially with Lilian after her husband's death when she had to manage the Berrow Estate of which Tony is a tenant. His vocal disapproval of Jennifer's behaviour is often unintentionally comic, but much of it is hot air, and in fact Tony is as good a brother as any other. Most of his arguments with his mother have been to do with money. It took him a long time to come to terms with Peggy's remarriage (to Jack Woolley) because he was so afraid that she would leave everything to her husband. It never seems to occur to him that there might be something distasteful in his constant harping on a situation that will only come about through her death, but Peggy shows astonishing forbearance with her tiresome and self-centred son.

Tony can often be found of a night propping up the counter at the Bull, sinking a pint of Shires and putting the world to rights, until Pat's familiar call of 'Toneey!' is heard and he's off home, head down, ready for the next disaster.

Philip Owen; June Spencer; Colin Skipp

RCHER, BEN

see Archer, John Benjamin

ARCHER, CHRISTINE

see Barford, Christine

ARCHER, DANIEL (DAN)

b. 15 Oct. 1896; m. Doris Forrest 17 Dec. 1921; 2 sons, 1 dtr; d. 23 Apr. 1986

In 1951, Dan Archer was a struggling tenant farmer, farming the family acres as they had been for generations. In the next forty years agriculture and everything to do with it were to change beyond all recognition. Mechanization was taking over everywhere and he was already beginning to think of getting rid of his working horses, Blossom and Boxer, who for many years had pulled the plough, threshing machine and hay cart.

Dan had retired his horses by 1955, by which time, due to his tenacity and hard work, he had been able to buy Brookfield Farm. He continued to pour his energies into it for the rest of his working life, adding extra acreage when he could, with the result that when he died in 1986 the Archer family had built Brookfield into one of the most successful farming enterprises in the area.

Born in 1896, into an old Ambridge farming family, Dan was the eldest of three sons. He left the village school at thirteen to work on the land with his father. During the First World War, he served in the 16th Battalion of the Borchester Regiment. After his return from the war he courted and won his sweetheart Doris Forrest. They were married in 1921. Theirs was a happy and successful

Doris and Dan Archer (Gwen Berryman and Edgar Harrison)

when foot-and-mouth disease broke out.

This forced Dan to consider a new pattern of farming. With the help and backing of his bank manager, Mr Grant, he decided to build up a new dairy herd from scratch. The cows he chose were Friesians. By 1961 he was able to form Ambridge Dairy Farmers with Fred Barratt and Jess Allard. Dan was delighted when his son Phil bought Allard's Farm in 1962 and joined the firm, now fully amalgamated as Ambridge Farmers Ltd. In 1965, when Fred Barratt retired, Dan and Phil bought his share of the company and it became an Archer family affair.

Dan and Doris also had their fair share of family troubles to sort out. They tried to help their eldest son Jack with his many problems; and when his alcoholism became chronic, they were very supportive of Jack's wife Peggy and the three grandchildren. Dan had the good sense to allow his second son Phil to go his own farming way. They had many a friendly argument about the relative merits of sheep and cows. When Phil's young wife Grace died in a fire, Dan and Doris guided him lovingly through the trauma. They were delighted when Phil remarried and readily accepted his new wife Jill into the family. Their only daughter

marriage: together Dan and Doris were able to face the inevitable ups and downs of farming life.

Over the years, Brookfield suffered from potato blight; a barn burnt down destroying Dan's crop of oats; precious lambs were lost when lightning struck a tree; and the chickens got fowl pest; but, worst of all, in 1956 all his sheep and cattle had to be slaughtered

Christine was encouraged in her various equine ventures; and when she was deserted by her first husband Paul Johnson, Dan stood by her. He was not pleased about her engagement to the divorced, reformed alcoholic George Barford, but family loyalty, as ever, prevailed. He showed more broadmindedness than Doris did when presented with the news of granddaughter Jennifer's illegitimate pregnancy.

Dan was a thrifty man, especially where Doris was concerned. As a present he had her old sewing machine motorized, and it was another sixteen years before he bought her a new one. He was appalled when she bought new lino for the kitchen and a washing machine. But he could also be very generous. When his brother-in-law Tom Forrest was accused of killing Bob Larkin, Dan promised to fight his cause, 'if it takes every penny I've got.' He was always willing to help his old friend Walter Gabriel. When Dan's brother, Frank, died in New Zealand, he accepted his strident sister-in-law Laura into Brookfield without too much complaint.

Not for Dan's workers the horror of being thrown out of their tied cottages at the end of their working lives: he rehoused them. They fondly called him 'Boss' and he, in turn, looked after them. He could sometimes be sentimental: in 1958 he went to the trouble of tracing his old shire horse Boxer to reunite him with Blossom, so that they could pull the hay wagon carrying Letty Lawson-Hope's coffin.

Dan Archer enjoyed a joke, a jar, his pipe, his skittles, his fishing and shooting, singing in his rich bass baritone and good plain country cooking. He disliked pyjamas, political chicanery on the parish council (of which he was a member) and pigs.

In 1958 Doris began her campaign to persuade Dan to retire. Eleven years later, at the age of seventy-three, he announced that he would go into semi-retirement and redistribute some of his Ambridge Farmers Ltd shares among his children. Then he and Doris moved into Glebe Cottage. He continued to work at Brookfield, but in his time he had seen a revolution in farming and was feeling increasingly like a back number.

Doris Archer died in 1980, a year before their diamond wedding. Dan was devastated. But sheep were still grazing on Lakey Hill, which helped to comfort him a little. Once again he tried to persuade Phil to increase the flock, abetted by grandson David, but soon saw the sense in Phil's refusal.

He was being driven home after tea at Brookfield by his granddaughter Elizabeth Archer, when he saw a sheep in trouble. He made her stop and went to its aid, but the effort was too much for him: he had a sudden heart attack and died in his ninetieth year.

Harry Oakes; Monte Crick; Edgar Harrison; Frank Middlemass

ARCHER, DAVID THOMAS

b. 18 Sept. 1959; m. Ruth Pritchard 15 Dec. 1988; 1 dtr

As the heir-apparent to Brookfield, David has had a long struggle to prove himself to Phil Archer. The similarities between him and his father are as great as their differences. Just like the young Phil, David has often rushed in where others feared to tread.

Though he was bright, he was not keen on school work and looked forward to the long holidays from boarding school when he could help his father and grandfather on the farm. It was suggested that with a bit of effort he could get A-levels in maths, economics and geography and become the first Archer to go to university, but much to Phil's irritation he failed maths. Vowing to re-take his maths and pass, David came home to Brookfield in 1977. For a year he assisted his father, played football and cricket for the village, and followed Michele, the glamorous New Zealand sheep-shearer wherever she went. She was a tantalizing distraction and David failed his maths again. Phil and Jill were worried sick that he would sacrifice his whole future in Ambridge for the sake of the lovely Kiwi, but to their relief Michele was a wanderer and wandered off into pastures new.

Having given up all hope of going to university, David was relieved to be accepted by the Royal Agricultural College in Cirencester in 1978. After his two-year course, it was back to Brookfield again. Here, to his delight,

left to right: Phil, Jill, Ruth and David Archer (Norman Painting, Patricia Greene, Felicity Finch and Tim Bentinck) with Pip Archer

Phil put him in charge of the pig unit while Neil Carter was away. But David still had a lot to learn: not noticing that three sows were due to pig, he put only two in farrowing pens. When the third sow gave birth and rolled on her litter, a frantic David had to rush to Phil for help.

When David celebrated his twenty-first birthday on 18 September 1980, his future was still not clear. (His parents hoped that it wouldn't be with Jackie Woodstock.) In November Brian Aldridge employed him to help with the early lambing, but when three lambs died because of the time David was spending with Jackie, Brian saw red. And when Jackie repaid David's devotion by dropping him, David decided that he had no option but to get away for a year. He went to stay with Kees, a friend he had made at Cirencester, on his small family farm just north of Amsterdam.

On his return to Ambridge in 1983, he treated himself to a five-year-old red Triumph Spitfire – and fell for Sophie Barlow. Their courtship was far from smooth, but by 1986 it began to look as if farmer David was about to marry dress-designer Sophie. David approached his parents about being made a director of Ambridge Farmers Ltd but they turned him down on the grounds that if his marriage to Sophie failed she might take half his share of the farm. David was furious at the implication that his marriage might fail, although the closer the wedding came, the more the couple began to have doubts themselves. Phil tried to appease him by replacing the Spitfire with an XR3i but nothing could ease the hurt of not being made a family director. David decided to cut loose, bought

a new suit and applied for a job as manager of the Berrow Estate. He didn't get it.

It steadily became clear that Sophie wanted a life in London rather than in the lambing shed. She finally broke down in Felpersham cathedral as they were discussing their last-minute plans with the Dean and the wedding was cancelled.

Then on 17 June 1987 came a more terrible blow. David was cutting down the branch of a tree with Jethro Larkin. The branch fell on Jethro Larkin, causing a fatal haemorrhage. David was distraught and felt that it was all his fault. When Clarrie told him she felt no bitterness about the accident, he was much comforted but the whole incident had a profound effect on David.

Had it not been for the accident, David might never had met Ruth. Needing a replacement for Jethro, Phil decided to employ a student to take his place. David was not at all keen on appointing a girl, but a girl it was and Ruth Pritchard was her name. His nose was put even more out of joint when his elder brother Kenton returned to Brookfield after years abroad and Phil and Jill made a great fuss of the prodigal's return. In want of consolation and needing to talk to someone who knew just how hard he worked at Brookfield, David went to see Ruth at Nightingale Farm. He was surprised by just how comforting she was but it was a long time before anyone except Mrs Antrobus knew of their fondness for one another.

Jill and Phil realized how upset David was about Kenton, and they decided that now was the time to make David a director. He felt as if he had found a four-leafed clover. He could hardly believe it when he saw his name on the farm cheque book. Now, with more money and more responsibility, things began to move fast. Ruth took him home to meet her parents and by the end of September the two of them announced their engagement and hurried and joyous arrangements were made. It was a woman, Deaconess Carol Deedes, who pronounced them man and wife on 15 December 1988.

David missed his new bride dreadfully when she returned to Harper Adams College at the start of the new year but he was soon busy helping out at Home Farm in the wake of Brian's accident. When Ruth did come back to Ambridge for the weekend or holidays, they had to live at Brookfield and this was not easy. How they jumped at the chance when Brian offered to rent them a cottage while Ruth did her one year's practical study at Home Farm and a new bungalow was built for them in the farmyard at Brookfield.

When Ruth was busy lambing, the hours were long and arduous. A piece of pork pie and a salad for her tea on a dark winter night just wouldn't do. And Ruth told David so. Soon she had him running her baths and running after her generally, but she looked after him in her turn and together they learned the realities of being a working couple.

Inevitably there were delays over the building of the bungalow, and when Brian needed his cottage for another farm worker, the pair moved back into Ruth's old flat at Nightingale Farm. It was better than Brookfield but far from ideal. The last straw was when their treasured wedding presents were stolen, most of them still in their boxes.

David called the police. DS Barry arrived somewhat the worse for drink, and when he made facetious remarks about newly-wed couples, it was too much for David and he manhandled Barry out of the flat. Finally the bungalow was finished and David and Ruth could at last shut their own front door.

In June 1991 Ruth learned that she had passed her exams with flying colours and for the next two years the pair of them put into practice all they had learnt at their respective colleges. Though they now had their own bungalow, there were still frictions at Brookfield. When Elizabeth announced that she was pregnant by Cameron Fraser, the quick-tempered David was all for sorting him out there and then. He had exactly the same response to the squatters in Rickyard Cottage. Ruth, who, to David's delight, was by now expecting their first child, was more sympathetic. While David was away visiting a friend in Sussex, Ruth had a fall walking on Lakey Hill. Although Ruth had badly bruised the base of her spine, the pregnancy was unaffected. A guilt-ridden and solicitous David dashed back to Ambridge to find everything totally under control. Philippa Rose Archer was born on 17 February 1993. David adored her from the first moment. Phil couldn't understand why they had called her Philippa. He would have preferred a family name. David had to point out that Philippa was as close as they could get to Philip.

Much as he loved his daughter, it cannot be said that Pip, as the baby quickly became known, was a silent baby and David found it difficult to get used to the broken nights. She had arrived in the middle of lambing and David was found asleep in all sorts of unlikely places. (You have to be tired to drop off in a cold lambing shed when Bert Fry is talking to you!) David assumed that Pip would be christened in the Archers' family gown. He couldn't understand why Ruth wanted Pip to wear her family gown for the christening, in preference to the one he had worn. A tactful Usha Gupta saved the day by presenting Pip with a new gown of her very own.

As Pip grows, so do David's ambitions for Brookfield. He is always looking for ways to expand the farm and was disappointed when he was unable to rent extra land from Nigel Pargetter. Nowadays he is more likely to be able to see things from his father's point of view. The two of them still have their disagreements, and now that Phil is over sixty-five, there is surely one brewing about when he will step down and let his son take over at Brookfield.

Gordon Gardner; Nigel Carrivick; Timothy Bentinck

Archer, Doris (née Forrest)

b. 11 July 1900; m. Dan Archer 17 Dec. 1921; 2 sons, 1 dtr; d. 27 Oct. 1980

Doris Forrest was brought up to do as she was told. She was the only daughter of Squire Lawson-Hope's gamekeeper William Forrest and his wife Lisa. Like many country girls of her generation she would have thought herself lucky to get a job up at the Hall, first as a kitchen maid, and then as a personal servant to the Squire's wife, Lettie.

But then she fell in love with a young tenant farmer by the name of Dan Archer. They were a devoted couple from the beginning. Soon they married and Doris began her life at Brookfield Farm as wife, cook, dairymaid, nurse and mother to their children. It was in some ways just as hard as her former life: money was scarce and life not always easy. But she truly loved it. Now she was able to make her own decisions and choices. She and Dan may have been deeply in tune with each other (in life as in the duets they sang together) but they were both strong individuals. There was love in the home, laughter, too. But their children were allowed to grow in their own way.

Doris brought them up to distinguish good from bad, to respect Christian principles and know the value of hard work. Though she did everything she could for her children, and was always there for them when they needed her, she never meddled unduly. Even when her son Jack fell victim to alcoholism she still believed in him and hoped and prayed for the best. She bore his death with fortitude, and also that of daughter-in-law Grace when she met with her tragic accident. When her granddaughter Lilian's husband Nick and Christine's husband Paul both died before their time, she was with them in their sadness. There were tears as well as laughter at Brookfield. She was immensely proud and fiercely protective of her family. Doris might always have been taught to 'know her place', but she was delighted when she and Dan were able to afford to send Philip and Christine to grammar school.

There is no truth in the rumour that, in order to be elected president, she tried to bribe members of the WI with jars of her preserves and bottled fruits – she had simply

Doris Archer (Gwen Berryman)

den, but with little effect. She loved her garden and made it bloom. When arthritis finally defeated her desire to dig and plant, she found Bernard Hill to help out. Dan's male pride was piqued and Bernard had to go.

House decoration was usually initiated by Doris, too. Dan would try to help, with sometimes disastrous results. But her colour schemes could be eccentric: she once painted the kitchen scarlet and grey, as Dan was known to remind her from time to time.

She tried her hand at most things, but it has to be said that the internal combustion engine defeated her. She was far more at home in a pony and trap.

Her family, and the village and people of Ambridge were Doris's life. Within those boundaries she found plenty to interest her, was even something of a gossip (especially when keeping company with her great friend Mrs Perkins) and was always ready with help for anyone who needed it. She was discovered dead in her armchair at Glebe Cottage, by her granddaughter Shula, one October day in 1980. Her many friends were shocked and saddened. Dan was for a long time lost without her. Doris was in many ways typical of her generation of countrywomen, and embodied many of their strengths and virtues. But farming has changed out of all recognition since her day.

Gwen Berryman

made too many and was giving them away. But Ambridge WI would certainly have been lost without her. Her cakes and pastries were legendary. She was a willing volunteer for any good cause. She planted trees, knitted for the Arthritis Council, organized cottage-garden contests, and, of course, was a stalwart of the church flower rota.

She went regularly to church and, something of a traditionalist, she was shocked when the vicar allowed her widowed daughter Christine to marry the divorced George Barford at St Stephen's. We can only speculate what she would have made of the idea of women priests. Certainly, she could never stomach the new Series Three communion services of the Church of England. She went to evensong instead.

Farmers don't waste their time growing flowers, Dan Archer would say. Doris nagged and chivvied him to take an interest in the gar-

ARCHER, ELIZABETH

see Pargetter, Elizabeth

ARCHER, FRANK

b. 1 June 1900; m. Laura Wilson;
d. 30 May 1957

Ben and Dan Archer's younger brother Frank was born at Brookfield, but left the family fold for New Zealand where he settled, married Laura Wilson and remained till his death.

ARCHER, GRACE (NÉE FAIRBROTHER)

b. 28 Sept. 1930; m. Phil Archer 11 Apr. 1955;
d. 22 Sept. 1955

Beautiful Grace was an only child. Her widowed father George had made a fortune in plastics, bought a farm in Ambridge, and began to play the role of gentleman farmer. Grace fell readily into hers: that of the beautiful, pampered daughter of the estate, star of the tennis courts, target of the county's most eligible young men. She loved all of it. Happiest when she was the centre of everyone's attention, Grace learned to be expert at manipulating events to put herself into exactly that position.

She had a volatile nature and her rapid changes of mood and decision could be infuriating. In February 1952, she begged Phil Archer to let her manage the poultry in Jane Maxwell's place, then promptly forgot to feed them. In the same year she played matchmaker to her father and Helen Carey and then was jealous when they decided to marry that Easter. She turned down Clive Lawson-Hope's proposal of marriage, but was furious when he withdrew it. She would frequently play off one boyfriend against another, but as soon as they sought romance elsewhere she wanted them back.

Grace loved horses. She put up the money for the riding school she founded with Christine Archer in May 1952. It started in a small way, with just one or two horses. Then, when Christine and Grace discovered Grey Gables, they expanded operations. But here as elsewhere in her life Grace's carefree attitude created problems: she would dash off on an impulse and buy a totally unsuitable horse, or, much to Chris's frustration, sometimes fail to put in her fair share of hours.

When she first took an interest in her father's new estate manager, Phil Archer, they both had romantic interests elsewhere, Grace with Alan Carey, Phil with a succession of local girls. Their friendship deepened, but when Phil first asked George Fairbrother for Grace's hand in September 1952, he was aghast to find that she had money of her own. He resolved to earn the £2,000 he thought necessary to hold his own, which he reckoned would take about five years. Grace was not thrilled and said she wouldn't wait. Shortly afterwards, she went to Ireland, ostensibly to train horses. Phil proposed to her properly on 8 September 1954. They married soon after.

Marriage softened Grace, and she would have liked to have had children with Phil. George Fairbrother made Phil a director of the estate. Phil arranged a celebratory dinner party at Grey Gables with Carol and John Tregorran and Reggie and Valerie Trentham. Grace went back to her car to look for a lost

ear-ring and saw to her horror that the stables were on fire. Impulsive as ever, she
dashed in to try to save Christine's horse
Midnight. A burning beam crashed down on
to her lovely head. She died in Phil's arms on
the way to hospital, on 22 September 1955.
Midnight was saved.

Monica Gray; Ysanne Churchman

ARCHER, HELEN

b. 16 Apr. 1979

Daughter of Pat and Tony Archer, Helen was
born with a dislocated hip. She had to wear
a special harness for the first three months
of her life and had three-monthly checks
until it was established that she could walk
normally.

Helen has inherited her family's love of
horses and riding. She helped Christine
Barford at her stables, rode her cousin Kate
Aldridge's pony when allowed and by the
time she was eight her dream was to have a
pony of her own. Tony produced Comet for
her. He was fat, hairy and unshod, but Helen
loved him. Christine lent her a saddle, Kathy
Perks bought her a pair of boots from a charity
shop and Lynda Snell gave her a tweed jacket,
a cast-off from her stepdaughter Leonie. Helen
was in seventh heaven. Other members of the
Pony Club laughed when they saw Comet,
but she ignored them. Christine, impressed
with her determination and skill at riding,
offered to buy Comet and give her a lovely
little chesnut instead, but, loyal to her first love,
Helen wasn't having any of it.

Only a year later Comet came to a sad

end. Helen mistakenly put him in the grain
store for warmth where he binged on Tony's
wheat and became very ill. The vet washed
his stomach out and he survived but Helen
was unable to ride him again. He was then
found gorging in a field of lush spring grass
with acute laminitis, and he had to be put
down. Although Helen was told that he was
in the horse hospital all her instincts told her
that he was dead, and she never quite forgave her parents for lying to her.

Lured in her early teens by her cousin
Kate Aldridge, in 1991 Helen passed some
pleasantly illicit hours in Blossom Hill
Cottage drinking cider, smoking and reading
the lonely hearts column in *The Borsetshire
Echo*. Finding an old letter to Peggy Woolley
hinting at a wartime romance with someone
called Conn, the two girls wrote to him, forg-
ing Peggy's signature. The game was up
when Conn arrived in Ambridge in person.
That, coupled with Kate's desertion for her
boyfriend Warren's embraces, completed
Helen's disillusionment. She has led a quieter
life for some time now.

Frances Graham

ARCHER, JACK

*b. 17 Dec. 1922; m. Peggy Perkins 17 July
1943; 1 son, 2 dtrs; d. 12 Jan. 1972*

The eldest son of Dan and Doris Archer, Jack
lived his life on a knife edge. A deeply insecure man, he sought solace in compulsive
gambling and in alcohol. In the end, they
were to destroy him.

He met the cockney Peggy Perkins when

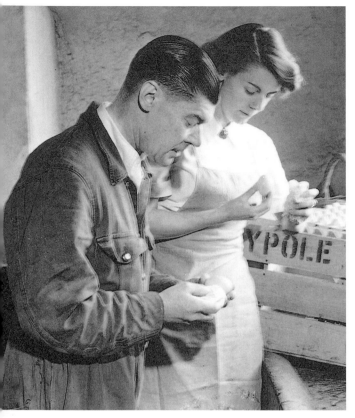

Jack and Peggy Archer (Denis Folwell and Thelma Rogers)

he was in the army. It was one of those wartime romances. They married in 1943 and their daughter Jennifer was born to them in 1945. Two years later, Lilian arrived, by which time the war was over and they were running a smallholding back in Ambridge. In 1951 their son Tony was born.

But when an old army chum Barney Lee turned up with a plan to set up a farm in Cornwall, Jack, ever the rolling stone, uprooted the family and went with him. They were back before anyone in Ambridge had had time to notice they'd gone. Apparently Barney had taken a dangerous

shine to Peggy and Jack had hustled her and the family away.

Working by day at Brookfield and learning the tricks of the licensee's trade at the Bull by night, Jack was too busy at first to notice that Barney was back in the neighbourhood. When he found out that his 'pal' had been hanging round Blossom Hill Cottage and Peggy, Jack walked out of the house, but was persuaded to return by his sister Chris and brother Phil. Jack and Peggy kissed and made up.

After this, things should have gone smoothly. Jack was finally offered the licence of the Bull in December 1952, but as early as the following autumn he had become restless. He upset Peggy by telling her that he would like to return to the land. He felt trapped behind the bar at the Bull and began hitting the bottle. The brewery issued an ultimatum: either the licence must be transferred to Peggy or they were out. Jack felt a total failure, and suffered a mental breakdown. On the advice of a psychiatrist he was admitted into the county hospital for treatment. He stayed there, under sedation, for four months, until, somewhat improved, he came back to the family and the Bull in time for Christmas.

The death of Grace Archer in 1955 had a sobering effect on Jack. He knuckled down to his new job as foreman at the local market garden (Peggy was now in sole charge of the Bull) and for a time enjoyed his work. In March 1959 Jack and Peggy had the opportunity to purchase the Bull outright. With the help of a generous loan from Aunt Laura Archer, the pub was theirs.

Laura invested more money in the Bull in 1964 and Jack and Peggy were able to build an extension with a flat where Laura came to live. By then the children were teenagers, and Jennifer in particular seemed to find the opposite sex something of an attraction. Jack was possessive and protective of her. He was furious when she got involved with Paddy Redmond and had an illegitimate child by him in 1967.

Jack and Peggy decided that they needed a break, and embarked on a cruise with the Barratts. The high life suited Jack, when he could have it. But it was his downfall, for of course it exacted a price. By the time they returned, Jack had started drinking again, and was now in the grip of another compulsion: gambling. By February 1968 his health was being seriously undermined by alcohol. He no longer felt up to working even short hours. He tried to keep his drinking from Peggy, but the effects were all too apparent to everyone. His liver began to pack up, and in July 1971 he entered a clinic in Scotland for urgent treatment. He never left: at the tragically early age of forty-nine he died there on 12 January 1972.

Denis Folwell

ARCHER, JENNIFER

see Aldridge, Jennifer

ARCHER, JILL (NÉE PATTERSON)

b. 3 Oct. 1930; m. Phil Archer 16 Nov. 1957; 2 sons, 2 dtrs

'And now I'll show you the fifteenth use to which this very versatile little household gadget can be put.' Phil Archer was in Mitchells department store in Borchester when he heard this energetic sales pitch and watched attractive blonde Jill Patterson demonstrate a House Drudge. He'd already seen her at the church fête and was delighted to have this opportunity of engaging her in chat, arranging to meet her at the Borchester show. A month later he proposed to her on New Street station, Birmingham. It was 1957, when a woman was expected to marry and look after her husband and family. Jill did this admirably, but soon found that fifteen uses simply weren't enough.

It must have been hard for sister-in-law Christine Archer, who couldn't have children, to watch Jill pod them like peas. The twins, Shula and Kenton, were born in 1958, David in 1959 and Elizabeth in 1967. Jill was the perfect wife and mother, even managing the farm when Phil won a six-month world tour as a prize in a competition. She has always been in demand by the WI, WRVS, the parish council and by anyone who wanted someone responsible to take on a job. She has involved herself in local struggles, fighting to keep the village school, for Borchester Grammar School to go comprehensive and for a gypsy site to be established in Borchester. Eighteen years later she was fighting Phil to allow squatters to remain at Rickyard Cottage, strong as ever in her sense of social justice.

Jill and Phil have stayed together and been faithful to each other. They've had their ups and downs, but each has played the role expected of them; and together they are at the heart of Ambridge, just as Dan and Doris Archer were in their day. Jill has always

Phil and Jill Archer (Norman Painting and Patricia Greene)

staying with David and his wife Ruth. The Ambridge grapevine was soon gossiping furiously but no one could really believe that Phil and Jill would part. It was left to Ruth to rescue the situation. She engineered a meeting between the two on Lakey Hill, and in a touching scene they resolved to make more time for each other. Eventually her farm holiday scheme did so well that Brian Aldridge envied her the success of her 'diversification' and even Phil had to admit that it was an integral part of the farm economy.

Jill's children have been a source as much of anxiety as of delight. She was unhappy when Kenton went into the merchant navy, and worried about his health when he returned to Ambridge. His symptoms reminded her of her own collapse in 1976 when she was found to be suffering from myxoedema, a thyroid deficiency; in Kenton's case his final blood test revealed that he had an over-active thyroid gland. She would like him to return from Australia to settle down, but he shows no signs of fitting in with her wishes.

His twin, Shula, has turned out more satisfactorily after a turbulent childhood and angst-ridden adolescence which exhausted her parents. It was a relief when she married dependable Mark Hebden. Jill grew fond of her gently spoken son-in-law and was saddened by his tragic death. She has been a tower of strength for Shula throughout her

known how to handle Phil. Their occasional rows have been minor, and one of their most dramatic disagreements was over Jill's bed and breakfast guests in 1991: after a sleepless night due to a crying baby Phil stormed out of Brookfield and refused to come home,

difficulties and their relationship is very close.

Jill has a soft spot for Elizabeth, the spoilt baby of the family – which made it all the harder when Elizabeth fell in love with Cameron Fraser and had an abortion without telling her mother. Jill was devastated: she felt as though her grandchild had been murdered. It took her a long time to come to terms with what had happened and begin to like her daughter again. Hers has been a peculiarly poignant situation with one daughter desperate to have a baby and the other determined not to have hers. It says a lot for their upbringing that the girls still like each other.

Jill has been delighted that David wanted to farm, but there's been friction between Phil and David, as there was between Phil and Dan, and she's had to smooth things over. Her relationship with Ruth got off to an uneasy start. Ruth was prickly, independent and most importantly the first qualified farmer's wife in Ambridge. When Jill wanted to go shopping she preferred to work on the farm. She didn't care about housework and couldn't cook, and they didn't have much in common. After the couple moved into their bungalow there were some embarrassing moments when Jill walked in on them bearing casseroles of good will. Even when they changed the locks she wanted a spare key and Phil was in the unenviable position of being the one to tell her that she was becoming a music hall joke. She was hurt, but took it on board with common sense and she and Ruth now have a much better understanding.

Growing older has been no easier for Jill than for anyone else. Brookfield was lonely when the children fled the coop, but Phil still needed her attention. In 1991 he had to have a hip replacement, and became so bad-tempered that Jill insisted that he have the operation done privately; nor did she let up afterwards when he tried to get out of the exercises he was supposed to do. But despite everything it was a contented couple who lay in bed watching *Casablanca*, listening to the bells of St Stephen's ring in the New Year of 1992 and pretending to be out when Mark and Shula called.

For many Jill is the wife and mother everyone would like to have. Her failings, such as they are, spring from love and concern. Her arm must often ache from putting the kettle on for endless cups of tea and sympathy. As she has matured she has become a force to be reckoned with and has tackled difficult situations with great tact and courage. When Brian started to thrust his attentions on an unwilling Betty Tucker it was Jill who called his bluff and threatened that if he didn't stop she would move the Tuckers to Woodbine Cottage and tell everyone why. He stopped. And one of the scenes the village will never forget was when she told Lynda Snell publicly and humiliatingly exactly what she thought of her. But such scenes are rare: in the main Jill moves through Ambridge with dignity, warmth and an infectious giggle.

Patricia Greene

ARCHER, JOHN

Dan's father, tenant farmer at Brookfield, married to Phoebe.

ARCHER, JOHN BENJAMIN (BEN)

b. 27 May 1898; m. Simone Delamain 1928;
d. 2 Aug. 1972

John Benjamin Archer, Dan's younger brother, was usually known as Ben. In the twenties he emigrated to Canada 'under a cloud': Dan had discovered that he had been paying court to his fiancée Doris. So familiar had the pair become that he called Doris Dot and she called him Johnnie. For a while all family ties were cut.

Then the family heard that he had become big 'in oil' and had in 1928 married a woman named Simone Delamain, who died only a year later.

It was Laura Archer who invited Ben to return to Ambridge in 1969. The two had met years before when Ben was visiting New Zealand (while Laura was living there). He could stay for only a few days as he was on a business trip. His family in England realized that they hardly knew him and when he died shortly after his return to Canada there was little grief.

Humphrey Morton

ARCHER, JOHN (JACK)

see Archer, Jack

ARCHER, JOHN DANIEL

b. 31 Dec. 1975

John Archer believes that the world is his oyster and so far he hasn't been too disillusioned. He's an ambitious young man who is always looking for a new way to make a fast buck. His entrepreneurial streak is not always appreciated by his parents, Pat and Tony, who have found themselves bailing him out on more than one occasion by feeding his pigs or selling his frozen pork. Things did once backfire on John when, having failed his driving test, he asked Tony to chauffeur him and his mobile disco to a party, John was horrified when Tony started dancing and reliving the high life of the sixties. Not surprisingly, John made sure he passed his test second time round.

John Archer (Sam Barriscale)

Though he was always practical, John did not initially think of farming as a career but as he grew older he became more interested in helping around the farm. Tony enjoyed having his help, particularly as he didn't have to pay for it, but both parents encouraged him to get as many qualifications as he could.

This was one of the reasons why Peggy Archer contributed to his fees so that he could go away to Brymore School. The other was that she, like Pat, was worried about his growing involvement with Sharon Richards who was living with her baby Kylie in a caravan at Bridge Farm. Even though he was only fifteen, John was determined to make Sharon, who was three years his senior, look at him twice. In a desperate attempt to impress her he blew £200 of his savings on a new suit and took her out to Nelson Gabriel's Wine Bar, only to be humiliated by Nelson's refusal to let him buy Sharon a drink as John was under age. John hoped that Sharon would shed a tear when he set off for Brymore but all she could say was that she'd miss having him to empty the caravan toilet.

When John came back from Brymore, Tony was expecting his son to help out at Bridge Farm; but John, enterprising as ever, asked Brian Aldridge if he could work at Home Farm for a year. From Brian, John learned about intensive farming. It was a complete contrast to his parents' organic farm and John was impressed by the profits that Brian was making from the Common Agricultural Policy. But John was keen to jump on the organic band-wagon when it suited him. Realizing that if he raised weaners as 'Conservation Grade Pork' he could make more money out of them, he immediately applied for 'Conservation Grade', much to the disgust of Pat, who thought it was a catch-all phrase. It was all-out war between Eddie Grundy's turkeys and John's pork as to which would grace the Ambridge dinner tables at Christmas 1993.

As John matured, so did his relationship with Sharon. Celebrating John's victory in the Single Wicket competition, they discovered that the gap in their ages mattered even less than before. Pat and Tony, alarmed by the way things were developing, could only look on in horror and hope that John knew what he was doing. For his part, John continues to tolerate his parents and will bless them with his presence as long as it suits him, which is clearly not going to be for long.

Sam Barriscale

ARCHER, KENTON

b. 8 Aug. 1958

Kenton Edward Archer to some extent takes after his irresponsible Uncle Jack. He is probably closest to his twin sister Shula, even if at first glance they would seem to have little in common.

Kenton promised a great deal: star pupil at Borchester Grammar School, he showed no sign of any interest in farming. Instead, at sixteen, he became a cadet in the merchant navy. Following his training at Southampton, he informed the family that he wanted to become a navigation officer. He began on cruise ships and moved on to oil tankers and paid only fleeting visits home. Letters arrived

left: Kenton Archer (Graeme Kirk)

at Brookfield from all over the globe. But Ambridge all but lost touch with him.

He came home on a short leave for the funeral of his grandfather Dan on 28 April 1986. He was touched by the genuine warmth and feeling the family expressed towards him. Two years later, Jill received a letter: Kenton was on his way home again, this time for good. His brother David felt resentful of this prodigal son, particularly when, equipped with a new XR3i Cabriolet (latest model of David's own car), he began to lay siege to the local girls including, to David's fury, his fiancée Ruth. But he needn't have worried. Kenton wasn't really serious about her, or about anything else for that matter. He was far too interested in flashing his money around, gambling, getting drunk at the Bull. Phil got him to promise to help

him on the farm, but he was unreliable, inefficient, lazy. He did manage to heal the rift with David, and was best man at his wedding to Ruth, although he was late for the rehearsal and went to the wrong church on the day itself.

By Christmas 1988, the family were becoming very concerned about Kenton. He was losing weight rapidly, feeling weak and listless, obviously frightened by the series of blood tests he was having. There was even an unfounded whisper of AIDS around the village. To everyone's relief, an over-active thyroid gland was diagnosed, a condition controllable by drug treatment.

His behaviour was harder to control, particularly his handling of other people's money. In business with his ex-naval friend Alex, Kenton came perilously close to serious trouble. He and his partner had been selling foreign stock without registering with FIMBRA, which was a serious matter and the Securities Investment Board looked long and hard at his affairs. He narrowly escaped a prison sentence.

So, after a narrow escape like that, what did Kenton do? He got involved in antiques. Phil became concerned that if Kenton were to stay at Brookfield permanently, the farm wouldn't be able to support three families. In August 1989, Phil decided, along with his son and daughter-in-law Mark and Shula, to help Kenton buy Nelson's antique shop. Kenton moved into the flat above. Mark thought it only fair that Kenton should pay him £400 a month in rent in place of the interest he and Shula would have gained on the money they were investing in him. Kenton accepted Mark's terms.

The business didn't thrive. Kenton travelled the country in search of priceless antiques and filled the shop with over-priced bric-à-brac. Perhaps Kenton felt his fortune was round the next corner; but the shop failed. Mark, for his sister's sake as much as anything, generously bought him out, and with this capital Kenton became partners with Nelson Gabriel. Some thought they deserved each other. Within a short time Nelson felt that he didn't deserve Kenton. Nigel Pargetter and Elizabeth Archer, too, tried to help and encourage him, but when Kenton organized an auction at the village fête, he accepted goods that had been stolen, and found that some of them were Ruth and David's wedding presents; the writing was on the wall.

Kenton was never one for putting down roots. When he left with his parents to attend a family wedding in Australia, at first he stayed on to support his father, who had fallen ill. But few people were surprised when only Phil and Jill came home. Kenton had decided to stay. So there he is, down under, still searching for that pot of gold on the other side of the world.

Judy Bennett; Simon Gipps-Kent; Graeme Kirk

Archer, Laura (Aunt Laura, née Wilson)

b. 29 Aug. 1911; m. Frank Archer;
d. 14 Feb. 1985

It was typical of Laura Archer that after the death of her husband, Frank, in 1957 she should up roots and emigrate from New Zealand to start a new life in Ambridge. Phil Archer was given the job of going to meet her off the plane at London airport and Laura arrived to take the whole Archer clan by storm.

She had only been at Brookfield for a few days before she began to give her brother-in-law, Dan, advice about the way in which he should run his farm. As far as Laura was concerned there was very little difference between farming in Borchester and farming in South Island, New Zealand. She had plenty of money and proposed that she should invest it in the farm. It came as a surprise to her when Dan turned her offer down. But she was still determined to stay in Ambridge.

In February 1958 she moved into a cottage of her own. Already, in its own subtle way, Ambridge was beginning to change her: the teetotaller who had arrived had begun to brace herself with the odd drop of brandy during the damp English winter. She was consistent in her generosity, however, and in May she proposed to Jack and Peggy Archer that she should help them buy the Bull by lending them up to £4,000. They gratefully accepted. Five years later she invested further in the Bull, and moved into a flat in the extension that her money enabled them to build. But she didn't live there long: already by the following year she had bought and moved into Barratt's Farm.

Laura did not like to be left out of anything that was going on. She was to be found on most committees and organized anything that needed organizing. In her time she was a parish councillor, a church warden, organizer for the Over Sixties, president of the WI and leading light of the Ambridge Protection Scheme (thwarting Jack Woolley and Ralph Bellamy's development proposals).

Not all Laura's campaigns were successful. Despite her continual harassment of all and sundry, in 1974 Ambridge failed in its bid to become Best Kept Village (although it came second the following year). She did manage to save the only surviving elm tree in Ambridge, however. When she saw contractors on the Old Vicarage site in 1975 about to cut it down, she summoned helpers from the Ambridge Protection Society who faithfully mounted guard. In the end it was discovered that the contractors had mistaken their instructions and they were not supposed to fell the elm. Victory drinks all round. Alas, the tree died from Dutch elm disease the following year and in her sadness she decided to set up a 'Plant a Tree on the Village Green' scheme. Her plans to scoop the publicity for the tree-planting rebounded when Doris Archer appeared at the centre of the photograph in *The Borchester Echo*. She was even less pleased when she realized that the caption under the photograph called her 'Miss Laura Arch'.

She was completely unsuccessful at learning to drive and employed first Roger Travers-Macy and then Helen Fairlie as her chauffeurs. When she could no longer afford a chauffeur she took to cycling round the village.

In 1973, she bought Jack Woolley's former home which she renamed Ambridge Hall. It was a large house which had been built for the village doctor in the 1860s and she soon found its upkeep expensive. The situation was slightly eased in 1976 when Freddie Danby moved in as a paying guest. He was soon calling her Laura. Together they attempted to save money by embarking on a self-sufficiency scheme which involved cheese-making, home brewing, damson-bottling, herb-growing and keeping livestock. The last was not successful. Danby's piglet became a pet called Edric; a broiler chicken from Neil Carter was nursed back to health and named Superhen; and a favourite duck was called Jemima. So many village pond ducks found food and favour at the house that Laura and Freddie privately dubbed it Duckingham Palace.

Practical and pragmatic, courageous and proud, she refused marriage to Colonel Danby when he tentatively proposed in 1980 and their lives went on as before.

Laura died of heart failure in 1985 after a short illness. She had made a new will leaving Ambridge Hall to Freddie but the original had gone missing and the copy had not been signed. Her great-niece Judy Wilson from Australia inherited and Freddie found himself homeless.

It's ironic that, when Laura's home was sold, one of its new occupants should be the almost equally formidable Lynda Snell.

Gwenda Wilson; Betty McDowall

ARCHER, LILIAN

see Bellamy, Lilian

ARCHER, MARGARET (PEGGY)

see Woolley, Peggy

ARCHER, PAT (NÉE LEWIS)

b. 10 Jan. 1952; m. Tony Archer 12 Dec. 1974; 2 sons, 1 dtr

Though Pat came from Wales, she was far from being a demure Welsh miss, and if, when he married her in 1972, Tony Archer thought he had found someone to warm his slippers he must have soon been disillusioned. He should have been warned by the fact that it was she who proposed. After that he has hardly been able to call his soul his own, and she has been more than a match for his tendency to gloom, his resentment of his mother and sisters for being better off than him, and his weakness for the ladies.

On a practical level Pat is the perfect farmer's wife. She loves farming as much as Tony and has never shirked hard work at Bridge Farm. Five months after the birth of her first son, John, in 1976 she could be found hay-making and was in charge of the calf-rearing shortly after that. It is not recorded whether she gave up the captaincy of the Ladies' Football Team, but if she did it could only have been because she was busy reading *Spare Rib*. She has stood up fearlessly for what she believes in on a number of occasions, over both serious and trivial issues. She spoke up for George and Christine when they wanted to be married in church after George's divorce. She was one of the first to try to help Susan Carter when she was accused of helping her brother after he raided the village shop; Susan, sensitive to patronization, was less than grateful, but Pat's concern and warmth were never in doubt.

Tony's generally chauvinistic reactions to her beliefs have only made Pat more determined. Never a supporter of CND, he took a dim view of her attendance with the Adamsons at the Peace Service in memory of Nagasaki. His horror when she told him she was taking the children on a CND march, his irritation when she ordered the *Guardian* instead of the *Daily Express* and his complete incomprehension of some of the courses she has been on, with titles such as 'Women as Economic Units' have always provided a great deal of amusement for outsiders if not for themselves: few people can remember when Pat and Tony last had a good laugh.

When her daughter, Helen, was born in 1979 with a dislocated hip, for the first time in her life Pat couldn't cope. She fussed over Helen and neglected John, and when she realized this fussed over both children. She became depressed and vowed that she wouldn't have another baby, giving Betty Tucker her baby clothes. A holiday in Wales with her mother cheered her up, but she and Tony had mixed feelings when she discovered that she was pregnant again. After the birth of Thomas in 1981 Pat and Tony were at odds and constantly bickering. Ripe for a fling, Pat attended classes in Women's Studies at Borchester Technical College and fell in love with her lecturer: dark, handsome and soon-to-be-divorced Roger Coombes. She started to wear eye make-up for the first time and had her hair cut, but Tony didn't notice. He never knew how close his marriage came to collapse.

As Pat has grown older her more excessive feminist views have changed, not because she has mellowed but because she has been so busy. For of the partnership it is she who has been most successful. In 1988 she found an outlet for their organic yoghourt and butter with a London delicatessen and in 1989 received an invitation to the Women of the Year lunch. Over the next couple of years she expanded the dairy and developed organic ice-cream. This led to some conflict with Tony, who wanted to be a farmer not a dairy manager, but that was as nothing to the scene he made when Pat turned down the offer of a deal for

Pat Archer (Patricia Gallimore)

the ice-cream with Underwoods. She explained to Tony that she couldn't bear the fact that it would mean the ice-cream going out with the Underwoods' label instead of Bridge Farm's. At first he seemed to understand, warming to her feminine emotionalism as he saw it, even kissing her in public,

44

and waited for her to come to her senses. But when he realized that she meant it and that all that potential income was not to be theirs all hell let loose. Fortunately they had to bury their differences in order to set up the farm shop, and later to fight for its expansion. They also had to worry about John, who had been caught with his shirt off at Sharon Richards's and was showing more interest in her than in his future.

That Pat makes a loyal friend is a further irritation to Tony, particularly when it interferes with his own routine. Kathy Perks fled to Bridge Farm when Sid Perks chucked her out of the Bull, and Pat refused to turn her away; she invited Sharon and her baby Kylie, tenants of Pat and Tony's caravan, to stay at Bridge Farm too when Kylie had a cough; Thorkhil, the Danish student who had come to help on the farm, was already staying there. Tony complained that his farm was turning into a hostel for the homeless but as usual Pat ignored him, and helped Sharon to move into her new council house and Kathy to find a counsellor.

Pat has been a breath of fresh air to the other Archer womenfolk with her forthright opinions, common sense and determination to support the equality of women and champion the underdog. Her marriage has weathered over the years into an acceptance of what can't be changed, which makes Pat and Tony's moments of sympathy towards each other all the more meaningful. Pat's uncharacteristic tears when John left for Brymore School were mopped up by an unusually gentle Tony, and lent a warmth to their partnership which is often missing.

Patricia Gallimore

ARCHER, PHILIP WALTER (PHIL)

b. 23 Apr. 1928; m. Grace Fairbrother 11 Apr. 1955; m. Jill Patterson 16 Nov. 1957; 2 sons, 2 dtrs

From the moment Philip Archer enrolled at the local farm institute it was obvious that he was going to be a different sort of farmer from his father. Dan's farming education had been entirely practical, but the old methods were changing. It was more important that Phil could mend a tractor than look after a working horse. Inevitably father and son came into conflict over their farming methods and it took a long time for Phil to realize that whatever the theory was, the practicality could be very different. Phil had a hot temper and they both had a stubborn streak, so it could take them a long time to make up after a disagreement.

When Phil and his brother, Jack, were growing up at Brookfield it was accepted that the farm would be able to provide a living for both of them, any family they might have and their parents Dan and Doris. Thirty years later, with mechanization and the introduction of the milk quotas, it would be a very different story and Phil agonized over what would happen if Kenton wanted to take up farming, for he knew that Brookfield couldn't support both David and Kenton.

On leaving the farm institute, Phil disappointed Dan by going to work as an estate manager for George Fairbrother. He quickly fell in love with his boss's daughter, Grace, but she was more interested in the brooding Alan Carey. Phil went out with other girls in an attempt to make Grace jealous but succeeded only in hurting them in the process. Then, in 1952, Grace condescended to become Phil's girlfriend. When he asked her father for her hand in September he was shocked to discover that Grace was a wealthy woman in her own right. Proudly he said that he couldn't marry her until he made £2,000 of his own. Grace, finding that it could take five years for him to make that amount, told him that she wouldn't wait. Phil was shocked, as he felt that he was doing the honourable thing, but by now he was used to Grace's capricious temper, and stoically set out to make £2,000 from breeding pedigree pigs.

In 1954 Phil proposed to Grace when she returned to Ambridge after a year in Ireland. She said 'yes' and both families waited to see if the headstrong pair would finally make it to the altar. They did, and were married on 11 April 1955. It looked as if, whatever their ups and downs, they had a long married life ahead of them. Together they began to look forward to having a family, something that Grace had been totally against before her marriage. Then when George Fairbrother made Phil a director of the whole Fairbrother Estate, their future seemed assured. They decided to celebrate at Grey Gables. There was a fire at the stables and Grace, without thinking of the possible consequences, rushed in to save the horses. A burning beam fell on her and she died in Phil's arms on the way to hospital.

Numb with grief, he struggled to come to terms with what had happened. Dan and Doris tried in vain to comfort him. They expected him to give up working for the Estate and return to Brookfield. But he decided to stay on and continued to live in Coombe Farm, the home he had shared with Grace. He threw his energies into improving the Estate but, realizing that his father was getting on, helped out at Brookfield when he could. It was Phil who supported Dan when his herd had to be slaughtered after an outbreak of foot-and-mouth disease in 1956.

Then suddenly Phil was in love again, this time with Jill Patterson. Completely the opposite of Grace, unselfish, generous and loving, Jill was exactly the woman Phil needed. They married in 1957 and set up home in Coombe Farm, where their first three children were born. When Charles Grenville bought the Estate from George Fairbrother in 1959, Phil began to think about acquiring some land of his own. It was beginning to look as if Dan would never invite him to be a partner at Brookfield.

Dan finally asked Phil to join Ambridge Farmers Ltd in 1962 and he leapt at the chance. The family moved to Allard's Farm, which they renamed Hollowtree. The development of Ambridge Farmers Ltd brought father and son into much conflict. Phil wanted to increase the dairy herd and modernize the milking parlour, whereas Dan wanted to increase the number of sheep. Phil's view prevailed and he began to build up the herd by selective breeding, although in 1984 he was disappointed when the introduction of milk quotas meant he had to reduce his herd.

There were other frustrations along the way and Phil began to urge Dan to think about retirement. At last Dan and Doris announced that they were moving to Glebe

Cottage. Phil prepared to take over the farm-house and the farm but he soon discovered that he and Dan differed about what they meant by retirement and eventually Phil was forced to admit that his father still had a lot to contribute to the running of the farm.

Both his parents' deaths hit Phil hard. It had begun to seem as if they would go on for ever. Dan's death in 1986 landed him with a huge inheritance tax bill. Though he hated the idea of selling land to pay it, Phil realized that he had no other option but to sell off 55 acres of Willow Farm.

Though they have had difficulties, Phil and Jill's marriage has stood the test of time. On the whole she has managed to deal with his obstinacy and hot temper without getting involved in confrontation, but Phil knows that his wife can dig her heels in, as she did over the squatters at Rickyard Cottage. Robin Stokes had to intervene before the matter was resolved.

Phil found his children's teenage years difficult to deal with. His daughters' various boy-friends exasperated him, particularly Nigel Pargetter; but when Phil realized that Nigel truly loved Elizabeth he was happy to give his blessing to their marriage. And though the death of Shula's husband Mark stirred up many painful memories, his support towards her was

unwavering. Whilst he may sometimes have found his daughters difficult, he has found his sons incomprehensible. Expecting both Kenton and David to want to join him at Brookfield, he was surprised when Kenton announced that he was joining the merchant navy and when David chose to work for others rather than Ambridge Farmers. Jill had to remind Phil that he hadn't always worked for his father, and that his relationship with David was a case of history repeating itself.

Always used to being fit and active, Phil found it very frustrating when he had to have a hip replacement in 1991. He was in

Phil Archer (Norman Painting) and Grace Fairbrother (Ysanne Churchman)

such pain that Jill insisted that he should have the operation done privately. For a year he was unable to participate fully in the running of the farm and was forced to hand over much of the hard labour on the farm to David, his wife Ruth and Bert Fry.

Unlike many farmers, Phil has a lot of interests outside Brookfield. He is a magistrate – a fact that is not always appreciated by the Grundys; plays the organ at St Stephen's and the piano for pantomimes; and spends many happy hours leaning over the gate into the orchard at Brookfield, scratching the backs of his Middle White sows – the only animals on the farm that Phil gets sentimental about. One of them, Freda, was given several reprieves before being sent for slaughter, but eventually the practical farmer won through. When Freda no longer paid her way, Phil could no longer keep her.

Norman Painting

Archer, Philippa Rose (Pip)

b. 17 Feb. 1993

'Pip', daughter of David and Ruth Archer, was born at the Borchester General Hospital with a touch of jaundice, weighing 8 lb ½ oz. Her return home from hospital coincided with lambing time and the ensuing chain of broken nights thoroughly upset her parents, but after a period of adjustment matters improved.

Surprisingly, Bert Fry became one of her favourite attendants, to the annoyance of her great-uncle Tom Forrest, who felt subtly challenged but didn't know what to do about

it. They were both present at her christening party and had more than their fair share of the orange and Cointreau madeira cake baked by her doting grandmother, Jill Archer. Pip looked enchanting in a silk christening gown donated for the occasion by Usha Gupta and a lacy shawl knitted by Marjorie Antrobus.

Archer, Ruth (née Pritchard)

b. 16 June 1968; m. David Archer 15 Dec. 1988; 1 dtr

Ruth Pritchard, nineteen years old, from Northumberland, only daughter of Heather and Solly Pritchard, came to Brookfield as an agricultural student in July 1987. She was looking for some practical experience before starting at Harper Adams College in Shropshire. The year before she had been farming on a kibbutz in Israel. In Ambridge, she lodged at Martha Woodford's cottage. The contrast could hardly have been sharper.

She was enthusiastic and eager to please. Sometimes David Archer and, to a lesser extent, his father Phil were inclined to exploit this. She was left to her own devices rather too often, and naturally she made mistakes. She contaminated a whole milk load, failed to spot a cow with bloat and killed Mr Wendover's runner beans with careless spraying. What's more, she failed her first tractor proficiency test and limped painfully round the village after a cow had stood on her foot. Poor Ruth: what a start! Her enthusiasm and confidence were at a low ebb. And when Phil got Bert Fry in, only two months before her departure to college, she felt a total failure and unwanted at Brookfield.

Away from the farm, life wasn't always easier. Martha was kind to Ruth, but smothering. When Martha suggested an evening of whist with Colonel Danby and Mrs P., for her to get to know more people, Ruth, feeling that she had to escape, left. Martha was hurt and confused.

Life with Mrs Antrobus at Nightingale Farm, where she moved next, was far more to her liking. Despite the gap in their ages, Ruth and Marjorie Antrobus soon became firm friends. Ruth was even a little sad when in September 1988 she had to pack up and set off for college. Only Marjorie had been allowed to share the secret of Ruth's love for David Archer.

Kenton's triumphant return to Brookfield a month earlier had made David resentful, and one evening at Nightingale Farm he had confided these feelings to her. She had listened sympathetically and the consolation she offered made him realize how slow he had been in realizing his affection for her. They soon made up for lost time. They announced their engagement and their desire for a Christmas wedding.

Ruth's mother fell ill, so it was left to Jill to make the hurried arrangements. Her future mother-in-law was shocked by some of Ruth's wishes. She didn't want to take the name Archer, for instance. And she didn't want bridesmaids. The reception had to take place in the village hall and, what's more, she was to be married by a woman priest and wear a dress that could later be dyed and worn to parties. And so she did. Her dress

was stunning: in a thirties style, ivory silk, with headdress and veil. At the reception, her father, normally a timid man, gave a witty speech about the joys of being a toilet-roll manufacturer. The day was a great success. But, try as she might, Ruth's attempt to retain her maiden name failed. Everyone called her Mrs Archer, and that was that. She moved into Brookfield.

But after the wedding a difficult period followed. She was David's wife, certainly, but she was also a young farmer, and she wanted to farm. She wasn't in the least interested in taking on the traditional role of farmer's wife. Jill found this hard to understand. When Ruth came home one night with fish and chips to eat with David in front of the telly, Jill brought them a casserole. Ruth was furious. She suddenly felt a longing for her former life, and for Northumberland. None of this was easy for David either. But then things changed for the better.

David was offered the foreman's job at Home Farm, and Steve Manson's house, and Ruth was going to be able to do her year's practical work there too. Ruth thanked Phil for all the help he'd given her in getting her started, but relations with Jill remained awkward. David was torn between them at times. Ruth felt shut out from the Archer clan. She was grateful to have her trusted friend Marjorie Antrobus to confide in.

David was unhappy at Home Farm and in time returned to Brookfield. Ruth was worried that this might affect her placement with Brian Aldridge, whom she admired as a farmer, but she needn't have worried. That season she prepared the lambing pens and worked tirelessly as the lambs were born.

When lambing was over, she was exhausted, but fulfilled.

Brian rather spoiled the fun. He was getting a new foreman and needed the cottage, and with their bungalow far from ready it was back to the flat at Nightingale Farm for David and Ruth. From Ruth's point of view, it was better than Brookfield. But she and David had their doubts, as they lay on the floor while Marjorie's dog Portia nursed her pups on their bed. She had several arguments with Bill Knowles, Brian's new foreman, whom she instinctively mistrusted, and was heartbroken when their wedding presents were stolen from the flat.

But then, little by little, her smile came back. First, Ruth's grandmother's watch, presumed stolen, was found, and, to her amazement, the cutlery, some glasses and a table lamp, all wedding presents, turned up at Kenton's auction at the village fête. Two months later the bungalow was ready at last, and Marjorie Antrobus suggested a party, so that wedding presents could be replaced by house-warming ones.

But even in their new home, Jill was constantly interfering, rearranging the cupboards and furniture and interrupting delicate moments of intimacy with steaming hot casseroles. The final straw came on David's birthday. Jill assumed they would dine at Brookfield. Ruth had other plans: a romantic candlelit dinner in Borchester. Driving back, happy and contented, Ruth and David noticed lights in the bungalow. Surely not another burglary? No, a midnight visit from Jill, bearing a birthday cake. This time she'd gone too far. Both Ruth and David told Jill that her interference in their lives must stop.

Bill Knowles continued to bring Ruth problems, too. He gave her only menial tasks at Home Farm, and Brian Aldridge backed him up, telling Ruth that she was, after all, 'only a student'. But he had reason to be grateful to her when she discovered that Bill Knowles, along with the fertilizer rep, had been cheating Brian of hundreds of pounds. Bill was sacked on the spot.

Ruth passed out of Harper Adams with flying colours in June 1991. At last she was beginning to feel at home in Ambridge. By now her share of the work at Brookfield had increased and she was given more responsibility, especially on the dairy side. David nicknamed her 'the Great White Dairymaid'. But Ruth felt that she was underpaid and asked Phil for a rise. He refused, but did offer her and David a 60 per cent share of profits.

Everything began to fall into place. Even Ruth's relationship with Jill improved, and in May 1992 Ruth was able to comfort her in her distress over Elizabeth's abortion. Soon after, though, Ruth herself became pregnant, and, after sharing the news with Phil and Jill, she and David dashed north to inform her own delighted parents. On their return the Archers clan gathered in the Bull to celebrate. It was hard for Shula to summon up a smile, and Elizabeth, arriving late, offered cold congratulations. But mostly there was great joy.

During her pregnancy, Ruth had to ease off work, but still found time first to suggest, and then to organize and implement a most successful feed co-operative. Phil, Brian, Tony and Joe Grundy all got involved, to Ruth's great satisfaction. Here were men listening to her, a woman, taking her ideas seriously, treating them with respect.

Winter, and the birth of her baby, approached. Philippa Rose Archer, to be known universally as Pip, was born on 17 February 1993. Ruth's parents hurried down to see their granddaughter. Pip was a demanding child from the beginning and Ruth had to supplement her own breastfeeding with a bottle. Within a month she was back on the farm, but soon she had to admit that a full milking rota was too much for her, both at work and at home.

Ruth's self confidence grew, and she began to assert herself more within the Archer family. At last it seemed that Ruth and Jill could find ways of getting on better together. Uncle Tom Forrest gave Pip a sapling to grow strong and tall beside her.

Ruth Archer is one of the new generation of women on the land. She has fought hard for the right to be treated as an equal. And will go on fighting for it.

Felicity Finch

ARCHER, SHULA

see Hebden, Shula Mary

ARCHER, SIMONE (NÉE DELAMAIN)

b. 1900; m. John Benjamin (Ben) 1928; d. 1929

French-Canadian wife of Ben Archer. Her death within a year of their marriage drove him to drink.

ARCHER, THOMAS (TOMMY)

b. 25 Feb. 1981

Third child of Pat and Tony Archer, usually called Tommy though he prefers to be known as Tom. He goes to Borchester Green School. Tony is already hopeful that he will become a farmer.

ARCHER, TONY

see Archer, Anthony William Daniel

ARKWRIGHT HALL

Even in its heyday seventeenth-century Arkwright Hall was not a masterpiece of architecture. With large rooms, it is solidly built; the priest hole, discovered in 1959, is one of its few attractions. Now it has fallen into disrepair and is an empty shell awaiting restoration.

Charles Grenville bought it in 1959, and turned it into a community centre under the supervision of John Tregorran. A general purposes committee was formed, chaired by Doris Archer, with Joan Hood and Jimmy Grange representing the teenagers. The centre opened in 1960 and was especially popular with young people as it was equipped with a soundproof room for rock and roll. It served many useful functions, but the youth activities often generated controversy with the noise and nuisance they created.

On Grenville's death in 1965 it was bought

by Jack Woolley, who began a series of improvements to create a leisure centre and appointed Sid Perks to run it. Jack's schemes proved to be more ambitious than the demand justified – he had hoped to install a swimming pool convertible in winter to a dance hall and to carry out a complete redesign of the gardens – but the centre closed in 1967 after just a year of operation. In 1970 he reopened Arkwright Hall as a field study centre where, under the direction of Robin Freeman, Gordon Armstrong built up a wildfowl sanctuary on Arkwright Lake. After Freeman moved on in 1974, it became clear that the activities did not warrant such a large establishment and the grounds were absorbed into what became the Country Park. The house remained unoccupied and fell into disrepair.

ARMSTRONG, GORDON

A burly young bachelor from Newcastle with a liking for the countryside, Gordon Armstrong made a strong impression on the girls when he first came to Ambridge in 1971. Jack Woolley had taken him on for a year's trial as assistant keeper to Tom Forrest, and he stayed at the Lodge. He soon fell in love with the au pair at Brookfield, Michèle Gravençin, and became unofficially engaged to her, but she went home to France never to return. He wined Angela Cooper and dined Trina Muir, chatted up Jane Dexter and took a shine to Susan Harvey, but in spite of their many charms decided that marriage was not for him.

He enjoyed his job and worked hard. When his position was confirmed the following year he was given the responsibility of building up the numbers of wildfowl for the field study centre, which put his considerable knowledge of wildlife to good use. After Tom Forrest's retirement he was promoted to head keeper. He played a number of sports, and was secretary of the bowls team at the Bull as well as captain of the Ambridge Wanderers football team.

Two years later he felt the need for a change of scene. His intermittent romance with Trina Muir finally came to an end when she went home to Scotland and decided to stay there without telling him. Dispirited and sorry for himself, he accepted the post of head keeper to Lord Netherbourne and left Ambridge.

Gordon Gardner; Tom Coyne

ARNOLD, DOROTHY

see Sinclair, Dorothy

ARNOLD, TED

Ted Arnold and his sister Dorothy came to Ambridge when he was appointed by Charles Grenville to take over as manager of the market garden after the departure of the Howells in 1961. A year later Jack Woolley offered him work at Grey Gables looking after the gardens and greenhouses, but he succumbed to temptation there and stole money from Jack and from Laura Archer. Put on probation early in 1963, he left to live in Borchester.

Brian Kent

ARTHUR (ART)

Tony Archer wasn't much impressed with the work put in at Bridge Farm by his YTS trainee, Art, when he took him on in 1986. After he was found unconscious with hypothermia due to working in mid-winter without proper clothing, Pat Archer looked after him and his work improved. At the end of his year's training, Pat tried to persuade Tony to keep him on, but by the time she'd convinced him Art had found a job as assistant herdsman near Waterley Cross.

ASTY

Julia Pargetter stung her son Nigel when she compared him unfavourably with Asty. She had met Asty abroad on one of her exotic holidays, and brought him to Lower Loxley in 1991 to redesign her suite. He encouraged her to part with a lot of money for his grandiose schemes. Nelson Gabriel, himself no stranger to sharp practices, warned her that Asty was part of an antiques ring, colluding to buy, among other things, her valuable antique bed at well below its true value. Julia, bewitched by Asty's pretensions, dismissed the accusation; Nigel assessed him as a 'nasty little freeloader'.

ATKINS, AMOS

d. Jan. 1955

Amos Atkins was an unpleasant piece of work and a bad farmer. His cows were sorry-looking creatures and people were reluctant to buy them. Dan Archer did not like having him as a neighbour, especially after Amos threatened him off his land with a gun.

He was looked after by his niece Audrey, a shy timid girl. It was typical of Amos that he spread a false rumour about Jack and Phil Archer's romantic intentions towards her.

In 1955 when Amos set gin-traps in open fields, Simon Cooper, Tom Forrest and Jack went to talk to him about them. They found Amos dead at the foot of the stairs.

Wortley Allen

ATKINS, AUDREY

Audrey Atkins, a very timid girl, was employed as housekeeper to her Uncle Amos. She was forced to work very long hours for very little pay. Sick of the treatment, she ran away and was employed by Helen Fairbrother. After the death of her uncle in 1955, £300 appeared to be missing and it was generally thought that she had taken it while settling his affairs. The money was later discovered by Len Thomas behind a loose brick in Amos's kitchen. The find exonerated Audrey completely.

Pauline Seville

ATKINS' FARM

Old Amos Atkins gave up the tenancy of Coombe Farm and bought Wagstaff's farm when it was auctioned at the Wheatsheaf in Hollerton in January 1954. He moved in immediately with his niece Audrey in

January, but died the following year. Dan Archer bought it into Brookfield and let the farmhouse to Len and Mary Thomas.

ATKINS, PIGGY

Atkins, the Penny Hassett butcher in the fifties, followed the old tradition of pig-sticking used by his father 'Old Piggy' Atkins in the thirties. He was a great friend of Joe Grundy. He and his wife Rosie seemed an unremarkable couple, but when many years later Percy Jordan bequeathed to Walter Gabriel an album of photos of Rosie, all taken after her marriage, it raised the possibility that she might have had more to her than had ever been suspected – certainly by Piggy!

AVRIL

Tony and Pat Archer's discovery in 1988 of an outlet for their yoghourt in a London delicatessen didn't prove to be the route to prosperity they had hoped. Avril, the manager, made life difficult for them with fluctuating orders and constant pressure to force their prices down. She insisted that she must be their exclusive outlet, which meant they couldn't even sell to their local milk round. The loss of her custom after only a few months didn't prove too great a blow.

B

BAGGY

Baggy lives with his girlfriend Sylvia and an indeterminate number of children. Unmarried, unwashed, he wears an earring and works as a garage mechanic. Together with Snatch Foster, he is almost permanently banned from the Bull, but drinks to excess in the Cat and Fiddle. (His drunkenness had severe repercussions in 1988 when he imbibed too much of Joe's cider whilst beating for Brian Aldridge's shoot, and drove the birds the wrong way.) Friend of and bad influence on Eddie Grundy, he is unwelcome wherever he chooses to visit.

In 1981 Baggy lent Eddie money to make a demonstration record. Anxious at its late return he went to Grange Farm and threatened Joe Grundy. Clarrie chased him round the yard with a kettle. (She later gave Eddie the money to repay the £250 debt.)

It was against Joe's better judgement that he asked Baggy in 1983 to repair the track to Grange Farm. Baggy arrived in a multi-coloured double-decker bus with Sylvia and assorted children, among them Aslan,

China, Sunshine and Buttercup. Because the bus was a bit overcrowded they put up a teepee. It was still there a month later and so were the holes in the drive. Joe told them to get out, which they did, knocking down the gate on their way.

In August 1991, a mysterious 'corn circle' was discovered in a Grange Farm field. No one was surprised that Eddie tried to take advantage of the event by charging sightseers; he even got a local historian excited about it. Elizabeth Archer, then working as a reporter on *The Borchester Echo*, planned an all-night vigil but couldn't keep it; yet Clarrie told her that she had seen lights shining in the fields. Off went Elizabeth to investigate. Her suspicions were aroused when she realized that the shape of the flattened crops resembled horns, and confirmed when she found Baggy's video library card. Eddie and Baggy were revealed as the perpetrators of one of Ambridge's most successful hoaxes.

BAGLEY, HAROLD

Harold had ambitions to get on to the parish

council in 1955 but was discouraged from standing by Walter Gabriel and Tom Forrest. Their arguments were technical, but their motives may have had more to do with Harold's tendency to be ill-tempered and argumentative. He particularly had it in for Dan Archer who he was convinced was depriving the public of their footpath rights at Brookfield.

Lewis Gedge

BAGSHAWE, MRS MABEL

Crusty, deaf old widow Mabel Bagshaw is believed to be still alive living in Felpersham. She had a long feud with Mrs P. over the death of her budgie, convinced that Mrs P. had poisoned it. In 1983 everyone had to repress a smile when she got left behind in Weston on an OAP outing and had to find her own way back by train.

BAILEY, MAX

When sixteen-year-old Jennifer Aldridge went on a school skiing trip to Switzerland in 1961, she was soon attracted to one of the ski instructors, Max Bailey. She lied about her age and gave him her home address; but when her mother, Peggy Archer, read one of his letters she was alarmed by its implications.

Max was a student studying engineering and his skiing job was only temporary. He lived with his father in Wolverhampton, and it wasn't long before he came to visit Jennifer at the Bull and started taking her out. He caused a family upset the following year when he took her to France for a fortnight against her parents' wishes.

Although the romance was short-lived Jennifer kept in touch with Max. She turned to him and his father for refuge during the Christmas of 1966, when she knew that she was pregnant but didn't know how to break the news to her family.

Alaric Cotter

BANHAM, MRS FREDA

Headmistress of the village school until it closed down in 1973, when she left Ambridge.

Nancy Gower

BANISTER, MR

Nigel Pargetter's tenant at Old Court Farm, Lower Loxley, who died in October 1988.

BANNISTER, MR

The solicitor employed by John Tregorran to represent Gregory Selden, who rejected his help.

BARCLAY, FAY

Christine Archer worked till 1952 at Borchester Dairies with Fay, whose ill-timed gossip about Chris's previous boyfriends ruined a promising romance between Chris and Vivian Kennedy the following year.

BARFORD, CHRISTINE (NÉE ARCHER AND FORMERLY JOHNSON)

b. 21 Dec. 1931; m. Paul Johnson 15 Dec. 1956; 1 adopted son; m. George Barford 1 Mar. 1979

Christine was the youngest child of Doris and Dan Archer, and the apple of Dan's eye. She had numerous boyfriends, and one proposal, from Clive Lawson-Hope, before meeting Paul Johnson and marrying him in 1956. Until then her first love had been horses, and when Paul met her she was running a riding school with Grace Fairbrother and spending most of her spare time riding in competitions.

Three years into their marriage Paul told Christine that he had no intention of playing second fiddle to a horse. A selfish, restless man, he never understood the comfort Christine found in the undemanding affection of her horses, or the extent of her generosity. Whenever he was in financial trouble, which was quite often, Christine would sell horses to help him out - a sacrifice he seemed to take as his due. It never occurred to him that she should have the freedom to explore her undoubted talents; in that respect she suffered from being a wife in the pre-feminist era of the fifties. In 1957 she came third at Richmond, second at the area finals at Dagenham, and second again in the Foxhunter competition at the Horse of the Year Show. She might have achieved great things in the sport.

A great sadness in her life was her inability to conceive, which formed a special bond

Christine Archer (Lesley Saweard)

between her and her niece Shula Hebden when she had similar problems. She and Paul adopted a boy, Peter, but she would have liked her own child; she must have felt a pang when she saw how far advanced science had become when Shula needed help. In Christine's day fertility drugs had come on to the market but she and Paul felt that they were too risky.

Paul held down a variety of jobs, abroad as well as at home, and at first Christine went with him. Eventually she stayed in Ambridge looking after Lilian's riding stables, running a playgroup and becoming involved in the local scene. Paul's restlessness extended to women and matters came to a head when he admitted having had an affair with his boss's PA, Brenda Maynard. Christine patched things up, but everything fell apart again when he pursued yet another rainbow which he thought would solve all their problems. By now he was back in Ambridge as acting manager at Grey Gables, and attended an innocuous sales conference in London. When he returned home his head was filled with the wonders of fish farming, and he became obsessed. He booked contractors, raised money on the house, and didn't take out insurance. Disaster struck in the first month when leaves clogged up the pump, preventing the water from being filtered. The situation was a nightmare for Christine. Creditors clamoured for payment, their bank accounts were frozen and even the telephone was disconnected. Her family did what they could to help, and touchingly Doris asked her niece Jennifer Aldridge to sell a Victorian brooch given to her by Mrs Lawson-Hope so that Christine could buy things for Peter.

Paul took the car and disappeared. He sold it to realize cash so that he could escape abroad. (Christine was still paying the monthly instalments.) Brian Aldridge tracked him down in Hamburg and Christine went to see him. She realized that to all intents and purposes her marriage was over. Her home had to be sold to pay off debts and Christine and Peter moved into the farmhouse at the Stables. There was irony in its name, 'Onemomona', the Maori word for 'Home, Sweet Home': for Christine the next months were anything but sweet. She was trying to persuade Paul to come back to face bankruptcy charges when he died in a car accident on the autobahn.

Unexpectedly the person who helped her most was George Barford. With his common sense and, because of his own experiences, a true understanding of what she had been through, he gave her a warmth and companionship she had missed for years.

Her family were horrified: not only because they felt that the relationship had come too soon after Paul's tragic death, but because at the time George was still married. However, two months later his divorce came through and he proposed. Now the family was upset because Christine wanted to be married in church and when the vicar, Richard Adamson, put the matter to the vote at the parish council, chiefly composed of Archer relatives, they voted against. Adamson decided to ignore their recommendation and his bishop, and there was an unpleasant scene when Phil Archer tactlessly told Christine that she had lost Adamson a job as rural dean. At this stage she had many quarrels with Phil, who was worried for her and at the same time felt that George was not good enough for her.

Phil would have been surprised to learn

that George felt the same way. He was very aware of their difference in station and uncomfortable with playing the gamekeeper to Christine's Lady Chatterley. Christine had no such doubts and they married in 1979, the bride wearing a gown of cream and old gold satin, with Tom Forrest as best man.

George and Christine make an unlikely couple, but they get along. George has mellowed with age and Christine, freed from the mesmerizing spell cast by Paul, has grown more confident. There have been difficult times – with Terry Barford, George's son, who nearly drove him back to drink; with George when he poisoned Robin Stokes's dog Patch by mistake; with Brian when she thought his plans for diversification would threaten her livelihood – but she has survived them all. Her voice suggests welly boots and Barbour jackets, someone who has lived in the country all her life and intends to continue to do so.

Pamela Mant; Lesley Saweard; Joyce Gibbs; Lesley Saweard

Barford, Ellen

m. George; 1 son, 1 dtr; divorced. Sept. 1978; m. 1979

Ellen was George's first wife who, though separated from him, didn't give up hope of their getting back together. He left her in 1970, but four years later she turned up unexpectedly at the Lodge, where he lived, to beg him to return, but he wouldn't listen. She played on his feelings of guilt about their children, Terry and Karen, and he was the first person she turned to when Terry ran

away from home aged fifteen and was put on probation for breaking and entering a store. She was angry when Terry decided he wanted to live with his father after he left school, and when he got into trouble again she was determined that he should live with her. This he did, after he completed his sentence at the detention centre near her home. Having refused George a divorce for many years on the grounds of being a Roman Catholic, she found it convenient to change her mind when she wanted to remarry in 1978, freeing George to marry Christine Johnson.

Penelope Shaw

Barford, George Randall

b. 24 Oct. 1928; m. Ellen; 1 son, 1 dtr; separated 1970; divorced Sept. 1978; m. Christine Johnson 1 Mar. 1979

George Barford arrived in Ambridge to take up the post of Jack Woolley's gamekeeper on 9 April 1973. His gravelly voice, laced with a country burr, was instantly attractive but he was a man who kept himself to himself and did not suffer fools gladly. It wasn't until September that PC Drury learned that he'd once been in the police force; and it took the love and curiosity of a good woman, barmaid Nora McAuley, to bring down more of his barriers. He'd intrigued her from the moment they met, particularly as he kept her at arm's length, but it was some months before she discovered that he was an alcoholic and that he was separated from his wife of ten years, Ellen. Such was Nora's devotion

George Barford (Graham Roberts)

prised when Nora returned to the Bull. Once there, however, she discovered she was pregnant. George said he would stand by her but tragedy struck when Nora had a miscarriage. She moved back with George, and there followed the most peaceful period in their difficult relationship. He became more sociable, took Nora out and even thought about joining the bell-ringers.

Further pressures came when George's son Terry, to whom he was very attached, came to visit him and Nora while on probation for stealing. A year later, then sixteen, Terry came to live with them for good. He started to drink and, finding him drunk in one of the hides on Arkwright Hall lake, George was so upset that he managed to talk to him about his own problems with alcohol – a difficult thing for such a private man to do. Unfortunately, although impressed, Terry could not mend his ways; and after driving a stolen car whilst drunk wound up in a detention centre. George responded with great dignity to a situation that must have been especially galling to an ex-copper, and was touched when Terry apologized for getting into trouble.

It was a great relief to him when Terry decided to join the army in 1978. By then George's relationship with Nora was over: it petered out sadly when she started work at Horton's canning factory, found a more easy-going lover and left George to live with him in a flat in Borchester. This would have been more of a blow had George not already got to know Christine Johnson, although not with

that, despite his suicide attempt in April 1974 and his refusal to see her when she visited him in hospital, by May she was looking after him at home at the Lodge and determined to stay.

His inability to talk about his deepest feelings, and his periods of withdrawal, made him a difficult partner and no one was sur-

romance in mind. George was a keen cornet player and it had been Chris who suggested that he play a cornet solo for the Hollerton silver band at the village fête a couple of years previously. Then when she moved into the Stables he had called to see if she needed any help. She found herself confiding her anxieties over her husband's bankruptcy case; and it was to him she turned when she learned of Paul's death.

George's divorce came through in September and by March 1979 he and Christine were married with six men forming a triumphant archway of bugles and the reluctant approval of the Archer family, who felt that they made an ill-assorted pair. His marriage to Chris has mellowed him (although he is sensitive to having married out of his class and never knows what to say to Phil).

George knows his job and doesn't take kindly to change or criticism. He gets on well with Tom Forrest and has a soft spot for Eddie Grundy, even though he's the bane of his life when it comes to poaching. He clashes with Jack Woolley almost as a matter of habit, but by and large runs things his own way. The most touching difference between them concerned Captain, Jack's beloved and very spoiled dog. George looked after Captain while Jack was having his pacemaker fitted, and as usual brooked no nonsense, giving him the first discipline he'd had for years. Far from resenting this, Captain kept running back to him after Jack's return – a strain on any friendship. Three years later Captain went missing for the last time and George found him dead under Terry's old bed.

George was persuaded by Lynda Snell to stand in opposition to Jack Woolley for the seat of chairman on the parish council, and won it. He made an excellent chairman and was soon absorbed in the problems of low-cost housing. His refusal to give Sharon Richards, a single parent and known to him, preference on the housing list, and his help to her in filling in her application form, show at once his integrity and his humanity.

Obstinate and proud, George always tells the truth as he sees it. The only occasions he has swerved from this principle have been to do with his own strong emotions and the need to save face. Alongside Tom Forrest he represents the old country values, and remains reassuringly immovable in the face of change.

Graham Roberts

BARFORD, KAREN

b. 4 June 1962

Younger child of George and Ellen Barford.

BARFORD, TERRY

b. 18 June 1960

Terry has given his father George Barford a hard time over the years. It wasn't altogether his fault. His father had left home when Terry was only ten, and he hardly saw him after that. He ran away from home to London in 1975 and was put on probation for breaking and entering a store. Alerted by friends in the police, George went down to talk to him. He came to visit George in

Ambridge and got casual work there when he left school at the age of sixteen. He never really settled down and Nora McAuley was the first to notice that he had started drinking. His troubles came to a head when Terry foolishly stole a car, drove it into a telegraph pole while drunk and then assaulted the police officer who found him. George was horrified, but was later touched when while at home on bail Terry said he was sorry. He was sentenced to three months at a detention centre. After that he went back to live with his mother.

In 1977 he joined the army, the Prince of Wales' Own Regiment of Yorkshire, which pleased George, who felt that Terry was following a Barford family tradition. He didn't adjust easily to his father's remarriage, but did his best to be civil to Christine. The attractions of Caroline Bone drew him back to Ambridge, and he fell heavily in love, but when she insisted on keeping their friendship light he was disappointed and cut leave to return to camp. The army seemed to do him good and he became a lance corporal in 1980 and a corporal in 1984.

When, in that same year, he had an accident in Berlin and needed an operation for a blood clot under the skull, George flew out at once to Berlin to be with him, even though he hated flying.

Terry remained in the army for a further five years, until after a stint in Northern Ireland he'd had enough. He came back to Ambridge with a vague idea of becoming a gamekeeper. Brian Aldridge took him on as a trainee under Tom Forrest, then paid for him to attend a gamekeeping course at college. But he couldn't cope with civilian life or the kids who nicknamed him 'Rambo' and he dropped out. One evening Christine found him wandering in the middle of the road, on his way home from the wine bar. The next day Terry was gone. He wrote a nasty letter to Christine, blaming his father and his parents' divorce for all his problems, and they didn't hear from him again until three months later, when he rang them from Berlin to say that he was with a mate and working in a bar.

Paul Draper; Jonathan Owen

BARLEY, MRS

Nanny to Richard Grenville, sacked in 1963 by his father Charles Grenville because of her neglect of the child.

BARLOW, MR

In 1960 Walter Gabriel bought Parson's Field adjoining Mrs Turvey's garden. When he permitted Jack Archer to dump scrap on his land, it looked so ugly that in desperation Mrs Turvey bid him £120 for the lot. She found out why Walter was so smug over the transaction when she tried to sell the scrap on and discovered that it was worthless. So she summoned the aid of Mr Barlow, who came to see Walter pretending that he was a contact man and bid him £50 for any scrap he had available. Walter was soon on Mrs Turvey's doorstep to buy back his precious metal. It took some time for him to realize that he had been fooled.

Gordon Walters

BARLOW, SOPHIE

When David Archer said he was 'spending the night at Steve's', little did his parents guess that he meant Sophie Barlow's. The two of them had met at a Young Farmers' social in 1984 and David was soon besotted by the lisping red-head.

When she was introduced to life in Ambridge, Sophie quickly made many friends. Such was her charm that Phil Archer regrew a beard when she said she preferred him with one.

After graduating from college, Sophie embarked on a career as a fashion designer but David wanted her as a farmer's wife and proposed. Sophie accepted without thinking the matter through: she was too busy designing outfits for a fashion show at Grey Gables. The show was such a huge success that Sophie had to employ members of the WI as seamstresses to fulfil all the orders she had taken. Her clothes were also spotted by a representative from a London fashion house and Sophie was offered a job designing clothes for chain stores.

At first she was hesitant about whether she should accept, but it was a chance she just couldn't turn down. She moved to London and realized that she was a city rather than a country girl. While they were discussing wedding plans in Felpersham cathederal, in tears she told David that she wanted to call off the engagement in order to concentrate on her career. Success had given Sophie Barlow new-found confidence.

Moir Leslie

BARLOW, TIONA

Flamboyant mother of Sophie Barlow and a lover of the arts, especially painting and drawing.

BARNABY, HUGO

Hugo Barnaby arrived in Ambridge in 1968 to unwind and think. At first he stayed with his cousin John Tregorran. The two had a lot in common: Hugo was a fine-art dealer and shared John's interest in the past. He liked Ambridge and decided to rent Glebe Cottage from Doris Archer. There he settled down to write a book and a television play. He was so involved with his writing that when he was offered a lucrative lecture tour of America, he suggested John go in his place. This upset John's wife Carol but Hugo was more than happy to look after her in John's absence.

Hugo won the admiration of many of the farmers in the area when he wrote an article defending British factory farming. His premise was that factory farming in this country was well regulated by law and that animals were ill-treated abroad. Given his attitude to factory farming, it's surprising that he became interested in tree preservation; and that he was so keen he even encouraged the local schoolchildren to take part.

In 1969 John was offered another lecture in the States, which he had to turn down because Carol was pregnant. He suggested that this time Hugo should go in his place but

Hugo Barnaby (Michael McClain) and Peggy Archer (June Spencer)

Hugo took umbrage. He felt that John was trying to force him to leave the village because there had been gossip about Hugo and Carol. Hugo declined the trip and decided he would be better off advising Jack Woolley about furniture for the newly acquired Grey Gables. He also helped Brigadier Winstanley prepare an inventory of his furniture on the understanding that should he come to sell, he would give Hugo first refusal.

By the time he left on his next visit to the States and Australia, things were better between Hugo and The Tregorrans. He asked them to look out for a house for him to buy and in 1969 he bought Nightingale Farm from the redoubtable Lady Isabel Lander. She liked the urbane ex-public-school man and invited him to spend Christmas with her in Sussex.

Hugo turned Nightingale Farm into a Rural Arts Centre, but the venture did not last long and soon he was off on another trip to America. News reached John and Carol that he had become engaged in Boston and they thought he would settle down in America. A year later he was back, after breaking off his engagement; he was cagey about why. But when John again went off lecturing, Hugo was quick to pay court to Carol, without success. He decided it was time to turn his back on Ambridge for good and set off to build a new life in America.

Michael McClain

BARNES, MANDY

Mandy Barnes was a chiropodist based at Borchester Health Centre who visited Dan Archer and Walter Gabriel early in 1983. She thought Dan's feet 'remarkable', though she never explained why.

BARRATT, BETTY

Quiet, nervous and very houseproud, Betty was Fred Barratt's wife. She had lost her baby daughter when she was only a few months old and to her great regret had no other children. She found it difficult to talk to others and would have been lost without the help of Doris Archer, who befriended her. She persuaded Betty to join the WI, with the result that she gradually got to know some of the villagers.

The Barratts went on several holidays with Doris and Dan Archer which Betty much enjoyed, although she was always anxious about the amount Fred drank when they were away. A gentle, unassuming woman, she was not very practical, and when she tried to help in the office at Ambridge Dairy Farmers she soon got into a muddle and had to stop.

When Fred first talked of retirement she longed to move to a cottage near the sea, but when the time came, in 1965, they bought Laura Archer's cottage in the heart of Ambridge. Fred became increasingly unpleasant, drinking too much and slandering their friends and acquaintances, which upset Betty. She admitted to Dan that she knew that Fred had been having an affair for the past two years, and neither of them was surprised when Fred disappeared from home. Dan found him working in Borchester, but Betty decided to continue to live alone in Ambridge. She had financial security because she owned some property which Fred had bought in her name and, freed from the constraints of his presence, she found she could enjoy the occasional cigarette and small sherry.

Brenda Dunrich

BARRATT, FRED

Owner of his own farm, Barratt's Farm, Fred was active in local affairs in the fifties. He made himself thoroughly unpopular as chairman of the local branch of the National Farmers' Union with his views on the inefficiency of local farmers, but he had ideas about how to improve matters. He interested Dan Archer of Brookfield and Jess Allard of Allard's Farm in the idea of combining the dairy side of their farms with his, and in 1960 they agreed to form a co-operative. They consulted the NFU and by December Fred and Jess had already moved their cows into the new milking parlour built at Brookfield. Ambridge Dairy Farmers was officially launched on 5 April 1961.

After Jess Allard died, Phil Archer, farm manager for the Grenville Estate, bought his farm in 1962, renaming it Hollowtree Farm and joining Ambridge Dairy Farmers. By the end of the year Phil, Dan and Fred agreed on the complete amalgamation of the three farms, now to be known as Ambridge Farmers Ltd.

Fred had health problems and took early retirement in 1965. Laura Archer bought his farm, renting its 100 acres to Ambridge Farmers Ltd, and Dan and Phil agreed to buy out his interest in the co-op in instalments. Fred and his wife Betty moved to Laura's cottage in the village, but he missed farming and started to drink too much and to gossip. He annoyed everyone with his slanderous comments about the involvement of Nelson Gabriel and Sid Perks in a mail-van robbery, until Jack Woolley threatened to show Betty proof of a past affair unless he kept quiet.

In March 1968 Fred left his wife and disappeared from home. Dan found him in Borchester, working in a greengrocery which he now owned. As surly as ever, he claimed that he had left because Jack Woolley and Ralph Bellamy had encouraged him to buy land which was now useless since their development scheme had been turned down. In fact he had bought the land in Betty's name and he was angry because she refused to allow him to sell it. Dan knew that there was also another woman in the background, but held his peace. The Barratts remained apart.

Tommy Duggan

BARRATT'S FARM

In 1961 the dairy side of Fred Barratt's farm was amalgamated with Allard's Farm and Brookfield to create Ambridge Dairy Farmers. Allard's Farm was bought the following year by Phil Archer and by the end of 1962, he, Dan Archer and Fred Barratt had agreed to the complete amalgamation of the three farms, to be known as Ambridge Farmers Ltd.

Poor health forced Fred Barratt into retirement in 1965, so Dan and Phil agreed to buy out his interest in the company. Fred sold Long Field, a meadow alongside Arkwright Hall, to Jack Woolley, and the remainder of the farm to Laura Archer, who leased 100 acres to Ambridge Farmers Ltd and retained a small amount of land and the farmhouse, which she called 'Onemonoma', the Maori word for 'Home, Sweet Home'.

Lilian Archer's riding school was begun in the grounds in 1967, and when Laura moved to the more imposing Ambridge Hall in 1973, Lilian, by then married to Ralph Bellamy, bought the property, renaming it the Stables.

Christine Johnson joined Lilian in running the riding school and took it over after the Bellamys left Ambridge in 1975. Three years later she moved into the house. When she married George Barford they decided to make it their home, and there they have remained.

BARRY, DS DAVE

Detective Sergeant Dave Barry never got his man. He spent a long time trying to prove that various dubious items which appeared in Nelson Gabriel's antiques shop were stolen, but much to Nelson's amusement he never succeeded. Though he did point out to Lynda Snell that a table she had purchased from Nelson for £2,000 was a fake, there was nothing he could do about it.

Ambridge didn't have a village bobby after PC Coverdale left and in 1984 the Police House was put up for sale. Dave, who was offered a discount because he was in the police force, decided to buy it. By default he became Ambridge's semi-resident policeman. In his spare time he began (tastelessly in the eyes of most villagers) to redecorate his new house. He became involved with Kathy Holland after he went to investigate the theft of a video recorder from Borchester Grammar School. Their relationship lasted two years; then Kathy decided she preferred the more dependable Sid Perks.

Dave did his best to serve the local community but was never popular. When he was drawn to play against the Deputy Chief Constable in a golf tournament at Grey Gables, Eddie Grundy, his caddie, was quick to tell everyone that Dave had played badly in order to ingratiate himself with his boss. Worse was to follow later that evening, when at the post-golf party, a drunken Dave passed a crude aside about Caroline Bone to Jean-Paul. *Entente cordiale* broke down and a vulgar brawl took place as the Frenchman defended Caroline's honour.

When Kathy's marriage to Sid entered a sticky patch, Dave was flattered to listen to her tales of woe. Their attraction for each other was rekindled but the strain of infidelity soon proved too much for Kathy and she ended the affair.

They say a policeman's lot is not a happy one – and so it was for Dave. He sank into depression and soon became so dejected that he even sought out Nelson's shoulder to cry on. (How the worm had turned.) Eventually he decided that the best thing he could do was move out of Kathy's orbit. In September 1990, he put the Police House up for sale and set off for St Albans.

David Vann

BARTLETT, MR AND MRS

Borchester teachers Edward and Joan Bartlett lived over the village shop in the seventies.

BARTON, ALAN

What Alan Barton did for a living, nobody knows; but what he did in his spare time was chase the girls – normally girls who were already attached. This did not make him hugely popular, particularly with Paul Johnson when Alan took a fancy to Christine. Even in the late fifties such men existed.

Richard Statman

BATES, PC ALBERT

Bates took up his post as police constable of Ambridge in 1964, accompanied by his wife, who gave birth to their son in October. They were joined in Ambridge by his parents, who rented Rickyard Cottage for a year before returning north. Bates left Ambridge for Borchester when he was promoted. PC Drury replaced him.

Ralph Lawton

BATES, NORMAN

Jennifer Aldridge was relieved when Brian Aldridge announced in October 1990 that he'd hired some help, but less impressed when she found that he meant a chauffeur, Norman Bates. By the following June, he was forced to make economies and Bates had to go.

BEARD, MRS

Mrs Beard was the nanny employed by Ralph and Lilian Bellamy in 1973 to look after their son James when Lilian had to go into a nursing home. There were difficulties from the start, when she offended their housekeeper Mrs Blossom. She insisted on being called 'Nanny Bellamy' and was so strict that Ralph Bellamy dismissed her only four months later.

BEDDOES, RONNIE

A mysterious man of independent means, Ronnie Beddoes came to the Bull as a temporary manager while Jack and Peggy Archer were in Italy in June 1956, and stayed for three years. He was fully trained, and a tower of strength behind the bar. He was also unmarried and, to Jack's annoyance, he found Peggy enticingly attractive. The family were relieved when Jack Woolley offered him the manager's job at Grey Gables. He did well there but before long this rolling stone moved on. No one ever knew where.

Harry Littlewood

BEDFORD, MR

Representative of the Borsetshire County Planning Office consulted by Carol Tregorran about the opening of the farm shop in the converted stables at Ambridge Farm in 1974.

BEECHAM, TIM

When Debbie Aldridge heard that Tim Beecham had been asked to be the best man at the wedding of Nigel Pargetter and Elizabeth Archer, she put her foot down.

She didn't fancy being chief bridesmaid under such circumstances; she knew that Tim had been responsible for some of the worst practical jokes that had happened in and around Ambridge. (This cavalier has wooed a string of girlfriends, who have been impressed – perhaps mesmerized – by the bright orange walls in his Borchester flat.)

It was Tim who, in 1984, sprayed the statue of Prince Albert in Borchester with gold paint. He was also responsible for the legend 'Elizabeth Archer wears thermal vests', which appeared on the wall opposite Borchester magistrates court in 1986. When he was prosecuted for this, Mark Hebden tried in vain to defend him. Tim was fined £200 with £200 costs but what annoyed him most was being banned from Brookfield by Phil Archer.

Nelson Gabriel's Wine Bar was witness to many of Tim's excesses. It was there that this irrepressible rogue and Nelson had a bet on how long Elizabeth's vow of chastity would last. When Nigel got to hear of it he was so furious that he punched Tim on the nose. And Tim ended up paying £100 towards the cost of his wild participation at David Archer's stag night party. But though they all remain good friends and meet occasionally for a night on the town, there was a general sigh of relief when Debbie won her point, and Nigel decided that he would find another best man.

David Parfitt; Tim Brierley

BEESBOROUGH, MANDY

Mrs Beesborough, attractive Pony Club instructress from Lower Loxley, came face to face with the Aldridges when Kate took up riding and the Pony Club Christmas rally was staged at Home Farm in 1987.

The sight of this gorgeous red-head, whip in hand with tight jodhpurs and boots, was nearly too much for Brian and his wealth was an obvious attraction for Mandy. She began to appear at Home Farm too often for Jennifer's comfort and the last straw came when Brian took her to the races with him on the day Jennifer gave birth to Alice. Jennifer pulled hard on Brian's lead and called him to heel, making sure Mandy was sent packing. Mandy remounted, pulled hard on the bit and rode off back to where she belonged.

BEGUET, MARIE-CLAIRE

Marie-Claire Beguet was one of the town-twinning delegation that came over from Meyruelle, France, in 1993. She stayed at Home Farm and was in danger of overdoing the *entente cordiale* with Brian Aldridge, impressing him in pretty, broken English with her understanding of cricket. She had played it on the beach while on holiday in Brighton as a young girl, she remembered. (On those pebbles? *Peut-être que non.*)
Juliette Mole

BELL, FRED

A farmer from Waterley Cross, who in 1974 delivered secondhand timber to Hollowtree pig unit for Phil Archer. There had been an outbreak of swine vesicular disease on his farm and the infection was carried to one of Phil's pigs, which meant that they all had to be slaughtered.

BELL, HENRY

Agent for Mr Knockholler, who inspected the Fairbrother Estate on behalf of his client when it was put up for sale in 1958.
William Avenell

BELLAMY, ADMIRAL

d. 1964

Ralph's father, Admiral Bellamy, having sold his grand house to Squire Lawson-Hope in 1955, left Ambridge and spent his remaining years gazing out to sea with a headful of naval memories.
Fred Yule

BELLAMY ESTATE

see Berrow Estate

BELLAMY, JAMES RODNEY DOMINIC

b. 30 Mar. 1973

Born 30 March 1973, with a silver spoon in his mouth, James, only son of Lilian and Ralph Bellamy, went to live in Guernsey with his mother. People say he has her looks; certainly, he is tall, handsome and very sporty. And rich as well.

BELLAMY, LILIAN (NÉE ARCHER, FORMERLY NICHOLSON)

b. 8 July 1947; m. Lester Nicholson 26 May 1969; m. Ralph Bellamy 3 Sept. 1971; 1 son

Lilian seems to have lived her life in a minor key with an abiding air of sadness: by the age of thirty-three she had been widowed twice.

Her early childhood was spent in the shadow of her brilliant older sister Jennifer, but in 1961 when her parents, Jack and Peggy Archer, gave her a pony, she at last found something at which she could shine. She spent every moment she could riding and soon realized that all she wanted to do was work with horses. In 1965, she was thrilled to help Valerie Woolley run the rid-ing stables at Grey Gables. She found the work satisfying and a year later enrolled at a riding academy near Felpersham, with a view to running her own stables before long. Twelve months later her dream came true when, disenchanted with Valerie's way of doing things, and helped by Laura Archer's, she enrolled her first pupil at her own sta-bles, which consisted of three horses and four ponies. With Lilian's enthusiasm, busi-ness quickly improved.

The following year a young Canadian pilot officer, Lester Nicholson (known as Nick), came to the stables for a ride. Although Lilian had had boyfriends before, Nick was the first one to make her feel there might be room for something in her life other than horses: she fell blissfully in love. They were married in May 1969. Unfort-

Lilian Bellamy (Elizabeth Marlowe)

unately by this time, Nick had been invalided out of the Canadian Air Force because of ear trouble and soon after the wedding Lilian and her beloved Nick flew to Canada so that he could receive urgent treatment. In March 1970, the unthinkable happened. While in hospital, Nick fell downstairs and was killed.

Lilian bravely returned home and resumed her work at the riding stables. Towards the end of this ill-fated year, the mature Ralph Bellamy asked her if she would act as hostess at a dinner party he was giving. She did – and began to enjoy herself in Ralph's company. He too was interested in horses and Lilian began to ride his horse, Red Knight, in point-to-point races. After she won the ladies' race, Ralph, flushed with their joint success, proposed to her. Lilian asked for time to think about it and ten days later said 'yes'. Most of Ambridge was shocked that she was getting married so soon after Nick's death and to a man who was twenty-two years older.

After an autumn wedding and honeymoon in Venice, the following three years were perhaps the happiest and most secure of Lilian's life. With the help of considerable backing from Ralph, she built up the stables into a first-class indoor and outdoor riding school. Shula Archer would never have become the gifted rider she was, without Lilian's excellent teaching. Ralph supported her through the premature death of her father Jack and it was a great delight to them both when Lilian gave birth to their son, James, in 1973.

A minor heart scare for Ralph brought this period of Lilian's life to an end. The Bellamys decided that they must leave Ambridge for somewhere with an even slower pace of life. Ralph found a manager for the estate and

Lilian arranged that Trina Muir should stay on as stable manager, while Christine took on the instruction at the riding school. It was with some regret that Lilian set off for a long summer cruise round the Mediterranean. They were distressed when they learned that while they were away their favourite horse, Red Knight, had to be put down after a riding accident. Lillian's links with Ambridge lessened still further when she decided to settle in Guernsey with her husband and son and only came back on occasional visits to see her family.

She found it harder than she had expected to adapt to her new life and soon became bored. By 1978, the marriage was under great strain and Lilian was drinking heavily. Ralph's health deteriorated: he had a major heart attack and died in January 1980. Once again, Lilian had to cope with death and bereavement far from home.

She spent the next ten years drifting as a rich, sad, unfulfilled widow. Ralph had left her and James well provided for and Lilian spent his money on luxury holidays, unsuitable men and alcohol. Though she occasionally returned to Ambridge, it was obvious that she thought of Guernsey as her home. In 1989 she decided to sell the Bellamy Estate, despite objections from various members of her family; the only property she retained in Ambridge was Blossom Hill Cottage. Peggy hoped secretly that one day she would return.

Nelson Gabriel, one of her few remaining friends in the village, tried to persuade her to invest in his wine bar when she came back to Ambridge to attend Peggy's wedding to Jack Woolley. She turned him down and went back to the Channel Islands, having outstayed her welcome at Home Farm. She was still drinking heavily and had become something of a family embarrassment.

By 1994 her son James was a grown man and needed somewhere of his own to live. Lilian decided to sell Blossom Hill Cottage in order to buy him a flat in London. She left Peggy and Shula to deal with the sale and continued to live out her lonely life in Guernsey.

Margaret Lane; Elizabeth Marlowe

BELLAMY, RALPH

b. 26 Feb. 1925; m. Lilian Nicholson 3 Sept. 1971; 1 son; d. 18 Jan. 1980

To all intents and purposes, Ralph Bellamy was the last squire of Ambridge. He inherited a large estate from his father Admiral Bellamy and, with a great deal of ruthlessness and business acumen, rapidly increased it. His acquisitions were impressive. With Jack Woolley as his partner he took over the Grenville Estate in 1965. When it came to the land he was a real gentleman farmer, keen on horses, running a shoot and building up vast beef and dairy herds. His interests weren't just concerned with farming: in 1969 he bought Paul Johnson's motor company. Those that dealt with him knew that he could be ruthless.

His money made him attractive to a number of women, including Valerie Woolley. He did not hesitate to enjoy a secret, amorous partnership with her, even though she was married to his business partner. Ralph himself did not marry until well into his forties. His wife was the recently widowed Lilian

Nicholson. Though much younger than he was, Lilian shared his passion for riding. They married and moved into the Dower House.

When his son and heir, James, was born in March 1973, Ralph was delighted. In keeping with the tradition in which he'd been brought up, he employed a nanny to look after James but sacked her when he decided that she was too strict for his little pride and joy. A reluctant Lilian had to give in to her lord and master's insistence that she cut down on the time she spent working at the Riding Stables in order to concentrate on bringing up their son.

Then came the news that Ralph had a heart problem and should take things more easily. He decided to move somewhere warmer with a slower pace of life. And so they did. In 1976 he bought a large house on Guernsey. For once in his life, Ralph had made the wrong decision. He and Lilian were both too ambitious to be trapped on a tiny island with nothing to do, and they drank and fought until Ralph's failing heart could no longer support his squire-like frame: he had a massive heart attack in 1979. He died three months later. Lilian was left a rich widow with a seven-year-old son. Friends and tenants paid their last respects at a memorial service in St Stephen's on 31 January 1980. The squire of the Bellamy Estates was no more.

Jack Holloway

BENSON, JIM

Jim Benson worked on George Fairbrother's farm under the management of Phil Archer in 1951. He was a shy man who so hated to be thanked that when he repaired and painted Walter Gabriel's tractor he delayed its return to avoid Walter's gratitude. On the rare occasions that he lost his temper he was explosive, as Helen Fairbrother found out at the Yewlden ploughing contest. Alf Grundy had used his tractor and left it in such a bad way that it refused to start; when Helen started to make polite enquiries as to what was wrong, Jim gave her such a blasting that Fairbrother got to hear about it and promptly gave him the sack. It took Helen's intercession to get Jim his job back.

Jim had other problems too, which he confessed to Phil. His half-brother Stan had stolen some money and cigarettes from the NAAFI and had been hiding in Copley's spinney for two months. Jim and his wife Mary had done their best to feed him, but the situation was getting too complicated. Phil gave him the fare to go and see Stan's commanding officer, and in the end Stan gave himself up.

Jim would have liked to have struck out on his own, but it was never to happen. When Fairbrother sold up, Jim stayed on to work for Charles Grenville, who put him in charge of the dairy stock in 1960.

Ronald Baddiley; Monty Crick

BENSON, MARY

Jim always said that Mary was too good-hearted for her own good, but he said it kindly. Before their marriage, she had gone out with both Jim and his half-brother Stan at the same time and an awkward situation arose when Stan went AWOL from the army

in 1951 and stayed in hiding near the Bensons. Mary looked after him as best she could but was upset when he tried to kiss her, and very relieved when he gave himself up.

She knew how anxious Jim was to buy some land and set up independently, but didn't think he had the wherewithal to do it. In 1955 Dan Archer was in a quandary. Jim put in an application for the tenancy of Amos Atkins's cottage and asked Dan to withdraw his application to give him a better chance. But Mary asked Dan to do no such thing. In the end Dan listened to Mary and the tenancy went to Brookfield.

It was a good job that Jim was a tolerant man. When Charles Grenville offered the Bensons a brand new cottage in 1960, Jim had to turn it down. He explained that Mary was terrified of insects and wild life, so Grenville, with a raised eyebrow, allowed them to remain where they were.

June Spencer

BENT, SUE

When Polly Mead, barmaid at the Bull, went to work at the Regency Hotel, Borchester, in 1965, she was replaced by Sue Bent whose beehive hairdo and overpowering Californian Poppy scent upset the regulars. Her main claim to fame was that she had once known Ralph Bellamy in Cambridgeshire and thought he was dishy. This was not enough to keep her in Ambridge, however, and when less than a year later Polly wanted to come back to the Bull, she was happy to exchange jobs.

Linda Polan

BENTLEY-JONES, JONATHAN

Jason the builder's discovery of a piece of fourteenth-century pottery in the churchyard of St Stephen's in 1992 brought the county archaeologist Bentley-Jones to Ambridge. His curiosity was aroused by talk of ancient timbers discovered under the bell tower two years earlier when the clock weights had fallen through the floor. His investigations revealed that the timbers were of Saxon origin, but they were in such a poor state that he decided, to the relief of the vicar Robin Stokes, that they should be suitably protected and left in peace.

BERROW ESTATE (FORMERLY BELLAMY ESTATE)

The land of Squire Lawson-Hope, principal landowner in the Ambridge district in the fifties, now forms the major part of the Berrow Estate. The Lawson-Hopes sold up in 1954 to George Fairbrother and the Bellamy family. Subsequently, Fairbrother's property was acquired by Charles Grenville, who sold a large part to Ralph Bellamy in 1965.

When in 1975 Ralph Bellamy, now fifty, wanted a new direction in his life, he decided to break up the Estate and leave Ambridge. His Estate, like the Squire's before him, was of such significance to the village that any prospect of change was viewed with great suspicion and anxiety. Untroubled by such considerations, Ralph sold off 1,500 acres to Brian Aldridge, with which he established

Home Farm, and 1,000 acres to Mr Barnet, who set up the Blossom Hill Estate. Ralph elected to keep the Dower House and the remaining 1,000 acres which he renamed the Berrow Estate. This Estate consisted principally of five tenant farms (Ambridge Farm, Grange Farm, Valley Farm, Red House Farm and Bridge Farm), two dairy units (Sawyer's Farm and Heydon's Farm) and 110 acres of woodland. Andrew Sinclair managed the Berrow Estate in Bellamy's absence, and Joby Woodford was responsible for general maintenance. The Dower House was let to Mr Lucas, a retired solicitor, and Christine Johnson took over the management of the Stables from Lilian Bellamy. Peggy Archer was told that she could stay at Blossom Hill Cottage, of which she was the tenant, for as long as she liked.

Ralph and Lilian went off on a cruise to work out what they wanted to do next, eventually choosing to settle in Guernsey. Ralph died there in 1980 and ten years later Lilian decided to sell the property to raise capital for ventures with her new partner. Rumours spread like wild fire: that the Estate was to be broken up and sold separately, that an Arab prince had bid for it, that a buyer had arrived in a helicopter. It was almost an anti-climax when smooth-talking Cameron Fraser finally purchased the Estate intact in July 1990. By the following year heads were being shaken gloomily over pints in the Bull as the regulars discussed their anxiety that the Estate had fallen into the wrong hands. The revelation that he had been a crook and a swindler was no surprise to them. This time no one was sorry when the Berrow Estate was put up for sale again, in October 1992.

It was bought by Guy Pemberton, a distinguished widower with first-hand experience of farming. He fast became a highly respected member of the local community, unwittingly filling a village role that had lain vacant since Ralph Bellamy left.

BIGSBY, MAJOR AUSTEN

Faced with finding a speaker at short notice for the WI in October 1975, Mary Pound asked Major Bigsby, who spoke at length on 'Patagonia and the Patagonians' – a far cry from their usual fare. He was to spend the night at the Bull, but talked so late with Ken Pound at Ambridge Farm that he found himself locked out. An irritable Sid Perks let him in, only to find that he couldn't get back to bed because the Major was still in full flow.

Arnold Peters

BLAKE, SUSAN AND BLAKE, MRS

Fourteen-year-old Susan Blake was nearly at the end of her tether when she tried to steal a chicken for her ill mother's Christmas lunch in 1959. Fortunately for her, Ned Larkin and Jack Archer saw what she was trying to do and told Doris Archer, who responded with her usual generosity by organizing a hamper from the villagers. They arranged for Mrs Blake to go into hospital early in 1960, while Susan was cared for by Tom and Pru Forrest. Charles Grenville provided a happy ending to this episode by sending mother and daughter on a month's holiday.

Carol Lynn-Davies and Margery Field

BLOSSOM AND BOXER

Blossom and Boxer were the last pair of working horses at Brookfield and Dan Archer's favourites. Dan sold Boxer reluctantly in the early fifties and put Blossom out to grass. They were brought out of retirement to pull the hay wagon that was used to carry Letty Lawson-Hope's coffin when she died in 1958.

BLOSSOM HILL COTTAGE

Blossom Hill Cottage is a thatched cottage with a sunny outlook and welcoming appearance. It has two bedrooms and French windows lead out of the sitting-room. Mike Daly fell in love with it and bought it from Squire Lawson-Hope in 1952. After Mike's abrupt departure in September there were a number of tenants, including Marjorie Butler and John Tregorran, before Ralph and Lilian Bellamy bought the cottage for £6,500 in 1971. They let it to Lilian's mother, Peggy Archer. While she lived there, in 1982 it was burgled and the following year it was badly damaged by fire. After making essential repairs Peggy took the opportunity to have the cottage plastered and redecorated. After she moved into the Lodge in 1991, when she married Jack Woolley, the cottage remained empty until it was used without permission by Peggy's granddaughter, Kate Aldridge. Kate made a duplicate key and used the cottage as a base for illicit smoking and drinking with her cousin Helen Archer until found out.

In 1994 the cottage was bought by Borchester solicitor Usha Gupta, Mark Hebden's former partner.

BLOSSOM, ROSE

d. April 1986

Mrs Blossom was for many years house-keeper to Brigadier Winstanley. After his death in 1971 she moved to a bungalow in Manorfield Close, where she had a special dispensation from the 'no pets' rule so that she could continue to look after Amber, the Brigadier's golden retriever.

Idleness did not suit her and by September she was working for Ralph and Lilian Bellamy as housekeeper. She felt that they made a big mistake when they hired Mrs Beard as nanny for their baby son James in 1973, as she thought Mrs Beard far too strict. There were ructions in the household and Mrs Blossom felt the effects of Mrs Beard's sharp tongue. When Bellamy asked Mrs Beard to leave, his housekeeper for one was delighted.

When the Bellamys left Ambridge in 1975 Mrs Blossom stayed on at the Dower House and looked after their tenant Arnold Lucas until he left in 1979. She enjoyed a quiet retirement and died in April 1986.

Anne Offord

BLOWER, CLARA

Clara Blower was Joe Blower's empty-headed sister. After the sale of his farm in 1955 they had money to spend, and she 'put on airs' and bragged to Jack Archer that she had bought a £98 television set.

BLOWER, JOE

Joe Blower was a tenant farmer on Squire Lawson-Hope's estate, an old friend of Dan Archer and fond of nothing more than to be arguing with Walter Gabriel – the pair would bet on anything. His sister, Clara, lived with him. After some bad luck with his pigs and a poor harvest he tried in 1955 to raise more capital but couldn't. He decided, to the village's surprise, that he had had enough of farming. He sold on the tenancy of his land without consulting the Squire, who was furious but didn't contest the matter.

Joe spent the money on a new car and arrived at the Bull 'dressed like a dandy' to take Mrs P. for a drive. Much to Walter's fury he also took her to the pantomime and gave her a new clock for Christmas in 1955. When the money ran out he left Ambridge.

Leslie Bowmar

BLOWER'S FARM

see Kenton's Farm

BONE, CAROLINE J.

b. 3 Apr. 1955

Capable, independent and immaculately dressed, Caroline Bone came to Ambridge in

1977, accompanied by a Great Dane, Leo. Her forebears are aristocratic: she is related to Lord Netherbourne through marriage and has many aristocratic friends. Although she trained in cookery and hotel management in Lucerne and Paris, she happily took a job at the Bull as a part-time barmaid. It wasn't to last long.

She travelled first to Acapulco and then back to Bristol, where she opened a wine bar with some friends. When it failed, Sid Perks took her back at the Bull and gave her the chance to introduce cordon bleu dishes in the new wine bar. But pub life wasn't really Caroline's metier. Shrewdly, Jack Woolley offered her a job as hostess at Grey Gables, and an apartment there. Caroline agreed to Jack's terms and moved in 1979. She's been there more or less ever since.

She has tremendous flair for the job, professionalism and charm; and, above all, she enjoys it. She has brought in innovations: her riding weekends have been a great success and her introduction of *nouvelle cuisine* to the restaurant has put Grey Gables on the culinary map. Perhaps the achievement which most pleased Jack Woolley was when she arranged for the 1984 Borsetshire NSPCC gala dinner to be held at Grey Gables and persuaded its patron, her friend the Duke of Westminster, to attend in person. Then the Duke announced that the president of the NSPCC would be in the area and would like to attend. Caroline had only hours to prepare for the arrival of HRH the Princess Margaret. As Jack flapped, Caroline simply got the situation under control and the visit was a great success.

After a while, Caroline became restless at Grey Gables. She was about to leave for Switzerland when Jack spotted the danger, stepped in and promoted her to restaurant manager. He would have done anything to keep her, thinking of her more as a surrogate daughter than an employee. She became general manager in 1988.

Caroline has always been restless in her emotional life, too. Brian Aldridge, with whom she'd had a flirtation two years earlier, met her at the 1985 Hunt ball, and they took up their affair with renewed passion. What with Brian's ice-cold denials and no one ever believing Tony Archer when he told of various sightings, it seemed that Caroline might drift in to being Brian's mistress for the foreseeable future. Until in June 1986, when, while out riding, Caroline was thrown into the road outside Grange Farm and nearly run over by Eddie Grundy. Injured and shaken, she was carried into the farmhouse and the doctor was sent for. Dr Poole happened to be unavailable, and it was the locum, Dr Matthew Thorogood, who called. He was exactly the loyal, dependable man she needed at the time. They were attracted to each other, in spite of Brian's jealous fury, and Caroline moved into Ambridge Farm with Matthew, though keeping a room at Grey Gables.

Tongues were quick to wag: Caroline and the doctor were accused of living in sin. Neither of them found the situation easy and their complicated working hours meant that they often hardly saw each other for days at a time. When Matthew suggested that they went to Florence for the weekend, Caroline jumped at the chance to spend some time with him. She was not happy when she heard that Shula and Mark Hebden had been invited too. Matthew suggested that they buy a house together and they tried to buy Willow Farm. When the deal fell through, Caroline realized that she felt relieved. The relationship with Matthew cooled and Caroline moved back to Grey Gables to wait for Mr Right to come along.

That summer, Shula and Caroline decided to get fit, but the Grey Gables outdoor swimming-pool was far too cold for a daily dip. They bribed Higgs, Jack's chauffeur, with a packet of tobacco to turn up the heating and had a glorious swim. When Jack discovered that this little exercise had left the hotel with no oil and no water he was furious with Caroline and insisted that the pool was to be for the use of guests only in future. The swimming-pool fiasco did, however, sow the seeds of a brilliant idea: the health club at Grey Gables.

Caroline's friendship with Shula has certainly stood the test of time. When they first met they had many things in common – their age, their single status and their passion for horses and riding. And though circumstances may have changed, the bond between them remains.

After her lack-lustre affair with the doctor, Caroline was ready for something more glamorous. And when Cameron Fraser arrived on the scene it looked as if he would be the man to provide it: racing at Ascot, grouse shooting in Scotland, no expenses spared. For most of 1990 Caroline was happy simply to enjoy herself with him and watch as he had the Dower House redecorated. But as the New Year approached things began to disintegrate. Despite Caroline's insistence

that she must be at Jack and Peggy's wedding on 1 January 1991, Cameron was angry that she wouldn't spend Hogmanay with him in Scotland. He solved the problem by going without her.

Then, while Jack and Peggy were on their honeymoon, Jack's beloved dog Captain died. Caroline agonized over how she would break the news but Cameron could only talk about his own problems. She began to realize that she was being taken for granted. When he began to flirt with Elizabeth Archer at a dinner party that Caroline had been invited to host, she decided that enough was enough and called the whole thing off. She watched from the sidelines as Cameron proceeded callously to break Elizabeth's heart. Whatever may have happened between them, Caroline was as shocked as the rest of the village when she heard that Cameron had disappeared along with the £60,000 which he had persuaded her to invest (though she eventually got most of the money back).

With her usual resilience where men are concerned, Caroline took herself off for a holiday white-water rafting on the Zambezi. It looked as if she would settle for life as a career woman. That was until she became friends with Robin Stokes. He was kind and considerate in a way that her other boyfriends hadn't been and for a long time seemed to be content to be just a friend. But despite differences over faith (Robin was a non-stipendiary minister and Caroline an agnostic) feelings between them began to deepen. Soon Caroline could be found at the Vicarage helping Robin when his children came to stay. Caroline could not believe that Robin did not want a sexual relationship with her. She invited him to a performance of Bach's Christmas Oratorio in Birmingham, the plan including an overnight stay. Religious guilt prevented Robin from making love to Caroline. She was hurt, confused and humiliated. And for a while, in spite of Robin's attempts to explain, things were difficult for them.

Their love of animals brought them together again. When Robin's dog Patch was fatally poisoned, Caroline generously bought a Jack Russell puppy to replace him. The following day Caroline's beloved horse Ippy was stolen. Together she and Robin tried to find the missing horse, to no avail. Eventually Caroline proposed to Robin and he accepted. Since this was to be Robin's second marriage, the Church insisted that they should go to counselling together. Caroline agreed – she wanted to know just what she would be letting herself in for as the wife of a minister. After a few hiccups, Robin's sons, Sam and Oliver, seemed happy to accept Caroline as a stepmother, and everybody looked forward to a wedding early in 1994.

Days before the wedding, Caroline decided to go for a ride in order to relax. A car overtook at speed, the horse shied and Caroline was thrown. Mark Hebden, who was driving in the opposite direction, swerved to avoid her and drove into a tree. Mark was killed and Caroline went into a lengthy coma. The wedding was cancelled. Robin and his parishioners prayed for her to come round, which eventually she did.

That was just the beginning of a long and slow recovery period. It was months before she was able to go back to work. While convalescing, Caroline had a chance to think long and hard about her impending marriage. She decided that she could not go through with it. Much as she loved Robin, she did not share his faith. Once again, Caroline put on a smile and got on with her life.

Sara Coward

Bonnetti, Craig, Colin and Lee

In 1988 Pat and Tony Archer decided to treat themselves to a new kitchen. They found what they wanted, a pine suite called 'Old Albion', and their kitchen fitters, the Bonnetti brothers, promised faithfully to deliver it and install it in time for Christmas. Mike Tucker stripped out the old kitchen in readiness, but no one turned up, and Pat had to manage without a kitchen throughout the festive season. By January Pat and Tony were getting desperate, but all they could learn was that Craig, the brother who did the fitting, had disappeared, taking with him their van and all the tools. Worst of all, it turned out that his two brothers Colin and Lee only delivered units and had no idea how to install them.

Pat and Tony called Mr O'Hara and Eddie Grundy to help, and eventually the kitchen was sorted out to everyone's satisfaction. At that point Craig returned, furious to find the job finished. He had spent an illicit weekend with his girlfriend, and then been so afraid of facing his brother Lee's disapproval that he had gone on to spend Christmas with their parents in Macclesfield.

Brian Aldridge, who had helped sort out the electricity when it proved too much for Mr O'Hara, got rid of Craig in double-quick time, but he was still shouting for his money as he went out of the door. Pat and Tony were thankful to put the entire episode behind them.

BOOKER, HARRY

Harry Booker left the army motoring pool to come and live with his parents-in-law, Ken and Mary Pound in 1973. He hated farming and would not help them. Things became very strained. When Ken arranged a job at the garage for him, Harry, who was mad about cars, would not accept it.

Though he did not get on with his in-laws, Harry did get involved with the life of the village. He was an excellent sportsman and captained both the football and cricket teams. Once Laura Archer press-ganged him into taking the WI keep-fit class, which ended in disaster when he made them do squat thrusts in time to 'Stars and Stripes'. When it became clear that there was little for the young people of Ambridge to do, he set up a youth club.

In 1974 he jumped at the opportunity of driving the new post bus and although he and Marilyn were living in Penny Hassett he came in day-to-day contact with Ambridge, delivering post, newspapers and groceries. Walter Gabriel and Laura were his unfortunate passengers on the day of his most heroic drive. Robbers armed with iron bars had set up a road block, so he took to the fields and escaped them, driving over ground too rough for them to pursue him. The mail was saved, though Laura's false teeth were broken in the process.

He became more and more involved with cars and driving. He drove the school bus until there was an unfortunate breakdown.

Harry was the only adult on the bus and was faced with the choice of going for help or staying with the children. He went for help and got back just in time to see a child who had got off the bus almost struck by a car. When the school disciplined Harry he decided to resign. He went into the secondhand car trade and had the usual hits and misses.

In 1980, succumbing to their rural surroundings, he and Marilyn tried their hand at raising chickens. It was not a success.

A bad back forced Harry to resign from the Ambridge cricket team in 1983 and this, together with the phasing out of the post bus have meant that he and Marilyn now confine their interests to Penny Hassett.

Alex Johnston; Gareth Armstrong

BOOKER, MARILYN (NÉE POUND)

b. 1951

Marilyn Booker was not overjoyed at having to return in 1973 with her husband Harry to her parents' rather drab farm after he came out of the army. A year later they moved to their own place in Penny Hassett.

She was in favour of Borchester Grammar School going independent, but she was less pleased when she discovered that the fees were too high to send her daughter Lisa and son Robert there, even though she was augmenting the family income by assisting in the farm shop. She showed true flair at upholstery class and had to take over a sofa from the less gifted Jill Archer, who rewarded her with a present rather than the hoped-for cash.

She showed a caring side to her nature

when she helped with the administration of the Talking Newspaper project.

BORCHESTER

Six miles north of Ambridge is Borchester, the county town of Borsetshire, founded in Roman times and a substantial market town since the Middle Ages. It is the principal commercial centre for the people of Ambridge, visited for its banks, shops – Underwood's department store seems to have been there since time immemorial – and entertainments. The centre of the town remains attractive, if increasingly congested, but the northern approaches have been changed beyond recognition with the building of a bypass road with its inevitable crop of industrial buildings and out-of-town stores.

BOX, CHARLIE

Silas Winter, Walter Gabriel and their great friend Charlie Box used to go poaching and mole-trapping together in the old days. But when Charlie died in 1982 he was missed not for these activities but for his mastery of bingo calling. He was a hard act to follow. Sid Perks tried, disastrously, Dorothy Adamson did her best, but it was Aunt Laura who came up trumps.

BOYD, RICKY

When Joan Hood promised Ricky Boyd that Tina Paget would be at the Borchester Palais

one Saturday night in 1960 but she failed to turn up, Ricky confronted Tina threateningly in John Tregorran's shop. He got more than he bargained for when she hit him with an antique paperweight. It was a wise rejection. Within a year he was in jail: he and two friends set fire to one of Charles Grenville's barns, and when tackled by Walter Gabriel and Sally Johnson Ricky had knocked out Walter and threatened Sally with a knife.
Leslie Dunn

BRADSHAW, MRS

Live-in housekeeper for the vicar, Revd Ridley, when he returned to Ambridge late in 1955.

BRAITHWAITE, MR

Solicitor for the Johnson family in 1960 when Paul Johnson was working for Charles Grenville's Octopus Trust Ltd.
William Avenell

BRAMMIDGE, HEATHER

Heather Brammidge was a keep-fit instructor in Lyttleton. In 1974 she popped over to Ambridge WI to put the ladies through their paces.

BRETT, STEPHEN

Defending counsel for Ricky Boyd and his

friends, when they were charged in 1961 with setting fire to Charles Grenville's barn.

Max Brimmell

BRIDGE FARM

Bridge Farm is one of several tenant farms in the Berrow Estate, 170 acres in extent, with a late Victorian red-brick farmhouse of no particular distinction. Pat and Tony Archer have been there since the death of the previous tenant, Jim Elliott, in 1977. Whereas Elliott was a beef and arable farmer, the Archers have concentrated on dairy farming.

They began there with the milking herd and hens they'd had at Willow Farm, but in 1984 started a plan to produce organic vegetables. The Soil Association permitted them to use the organic food symbol on their carrots and potatoes in the following year, and despite seeing little return for the first years, they have never looked back. By 1989 the Co-op was collecting their vegetables twice a week and they also supplied organic vegetables to the village shop. Pat has expanded the dairy, where they produce organic ice-cream, butter and yoghourt under the Bridge Farm label; and they opened a farm shop in 1992 in which to sell their produce.

Earlier that year they were offered the freehold of Bridge Farm, valued at £160,000, but they turned it down. They felt that it would tie up too much of their capital, and in any case as theirs was a succession tenancy, they knew that when the time came their son John would be able to take over the farm in his turn.

BRIGGS, ANN

Mrs no-good Anne Briggs, with her no-good husband and no-good son, rented Rose Cottage from Sid Perks in 1976. They paid no rent and when Sid applied pressure they were gone. Sid won a court order for their rent but, of course, it was no good. They had vanished.

BRIGGS, PETER

Peter Briggs was an animal feed salesman who worked for a firm in Borchester. He brought his family from two damp rooms in Penny Hassett in 1976 to the cosy warmth of Rose Cottage, but he did not want to pay Sid Perks rent for it. Sid threatened him with a court order but they vanished – what's more, taking everything with them but a table, a sofa and the hall carpet.

BRIGGS, STEPHEN

Son of Peter and Ann Briggs, Stephen was four when his family came to Ambridge in 1976 for a short while. He just had time to be caught stealing from the village shop before vanishing with his parents one moonlit night.

BRINKLEY, SARAH

The Aldridges and Sarah Brinkley's parents, John and Hazel, know each other through their children, who play together. Sarah probably saved Adam Macy's life in 1977 by getting help for him when he was bitten by an adder during one of their rides on Heydon Berrow.

BRODDY, BRI

Bri Broddy was the son of Enoch Broddy. Like father, like son: he was a bamboozler.
Kenneth Shanley

BRODDY, ENOCH

Enoch Broddy and his son Bri came from Walsall. They were con men. Among the many they beguiled was Mrs P., whom they coaxed into parting with her valuable Act of Parliament clock for just £100 in 1980. Peggy Archer, horrified, contacted PC Coverdale, but what could he do? They had paid for it, after all. But a close eye was kept on the Broddys – too close, they felt, so they decamped to con elsewhere.
John Baddeley

BROOKES, MR

Phil Archer's portly, food-loving bank manager took every opportunity to dine his clients at the Feathers in Borchester. Phil, Jill and Peggy Archer sensibly repaid him with a lunch at Brookfield, at which he agreed a loan to enable Phil to purchase part of Willow Farm in 1983.

BROOKFIELD

The Archer family had been farming Brookfield for many years as tenants of the Lawson-Hopes when in 1917 Dan Archer, at the age of twenty-one, succeeded his father in the tenancy. The farm was then 100 acres. He bought Brookfield outright when the Lawson-Hope Estate was broken up in 1954 and created Ambridge Farmers Ltd with his son Phil and Fred Barratt in 1962; Dan and Phil bought out Barratt's interest on his retirement in 1965.

In the sixties the partnership made a number of further purchases and in 1983 Phil, by then the active partner since Dan's retirement, added to the acreage when he bought some of the Willow Farm land when Haydn Evans sold up. After Dan's death in 1986, Phil had to sell off 55 acres to pay the tax bill, but in 1993 he was able to buy a further 7 acres at a good price when Matthew Thorogood sold the part of Willow Farm that he had bought as an investment. Now the partnership consists of Phil and his son David, and Brookfield is a mixed farm of 469 acres.

The old brick and timber farmhouse dates back to the sixteenth century and is in the centre of one of Ambridge's four medieval open fields (West Field, Lakey Hill Field, East Field and Brook Field). Besides being a working farm, Brookfield is a family home where over the years changes have been made in and around the farmhouse. In the early sixties Nigel Burton converted a loft in one of the barns into a flat; and the garden was completely replanned by Carol Tregorran, enabling Doris Archer to plant the roses she loved so much. Phil and Jill Archer installed a new kitchen in 1982, and three years later in 1985 added a second bathroom. The primitive plumbing system meant it could only go in their daughter Elizabeth's room. She spent £300 on coral pink tiles and towels, which irritated Phil enormously.

Jill made a significant contribution to the diversification of Brookfield when in 1990 she started offering farm holiday accommodation which, despite Phil's scepticism, proved very successful.

In 1990 a bungalow was built for David and Ruth Archer by the river. There was an initial set-back when their builders went bankrupt and disappeared with the windows and a lorry-load of bricks, but eventually the work was completed. Tom Forrest gave them a horse chestnut tree as a gift (a charming gesture he repeated when their daughter, Philippa Rose, was born and he gave her a sapling).

Brookfield provides a comfortable if not luxurious lifestyle for the Archer family and epitomizes a rural way of life that seems to be increasingly rare.

BROWN, BETTY

Dan Archer thought Jim Brown's precocious seventeen-year-old daughter Betty 'a fast piece'. He was so unnerved when she coaxed him to drive her home after a skittles match in 1955 that he insisted that Jack Archer should come along too.

BROWN, CHARLES

Sid Perks went to work for Charles Brown, a pig farmer at Paunton Farm, outside Ambridge, in June 1967. Charles revealed that he was in fact a professional gambler, hiding with his brother from a gang of thugs demanding protection money. An unsuccessful criminal, he had the bad luck to be recognized by an ex-police sergeant and arrested for an earlier offence. He was later charged with a mail-van robbery (in which Nelson Gabriel was involved) when the van was found hidden under the hay bales at Paunton Farm.

Geoffrey Lewis

'BROWN', FAY

Fay was Charles Brown's accomplice, who posed as his wife at Paunton Farm while they set up a mail-van robbery in 1967 with Nelson Gabriel.

Linda Polan

BROWN, JIM

Owner of the garage at Penny Hassett in the fifties and father of Betty.

BROWN, MICHELE

When the shearers arrived at Brookfield in 1976, they brought with them an independent, extrovert girl from New Zealand. The daughter of an important New Zealand sheep-farmer, Michele Brown was working her way round Europe, shearing sheep and taking any other jobs she could get. Her tales of life down under reminded Laura Archer of home, and for a while she grew very nostalgic. When Michele left Ambridge for a holiday, a restless Shula Archer was allowed to go with her.

On her return, Michele took a job as a waitress at Grey Gables where her outspokenness alarmed Jack Woolley. She told him a few truths about his staff and went on to say that they should be represented by a trade union. If he hadn't appreciated her capabilities he would have sacked her on the spot, but when the time came he even helped her to renew her visa. While working at Grey Gables, she shared Neil Carter's flat at Nightingale Farm on strictly platonic terms. David Archer was enchanted by her. One day he missed harvesting at Brookfield because he was so busy mooning over her. Phil Archer was furious and it came as a great relief to him and Jill when they heard at the end of 1977 that Michele was leaving, via London for America.

BRYDEN, PC GEOFF

Geoff Bryden took over from PC Randall as village bobby in 1955. Not only was he keen on his job; he also made it his business to get to know the villagers informally. He had the grave responsibility of dealing with all the enquiries relating to the shooting of Bob Larkin by Tom Forrest in 1957. He was eventually promoted and transferred to Borchester in 1964.

John Dexter; Geoffrey Lewis

BUCKLAND, EVE

John Tregorran played matchmaker when he persuaded Norris Buckland's twin sister, Eve Buckland, to stay on in Ambridge (where she had been staying with her twin brother Norris on an exchange with Revd Ridley) and help look after Revd Ridley on his return to Ambridge at Christmas 1955. Revd Ridley, however, saw through the plot and in any case needed no such assistance. Eve rejoined her brother in London.

BUCKLAND, REVD NORRIS

Overworked in London, Norris Buckland exchanged places with Revd Ridley in the spring of 1955. He upset the parishioners with his outspoken sermons and alienated Ben White when he put a cricket ball through his window. The exchange had limited success and Revd Ridley was warmly welcomed back the following Christmas.

Harold Reese

BUCKLE, REVD JEREMY (JERRY)

b. 10 Jan. 1938

Jerry Buckle was vicar of Ambridge for two years, but before he left in 1991 he had certainly made his presence felt.

He started life in the army, and indeed was a lieutenant in the Grenadier Guards in Nairobi where his distinguished father worked in government. Quite suddenly, though, he became a pacifist, resigned his commission and returned to England with his wife, Frances. She tragically developed cancer and died. It was then that Jerry decided to enter the Church.

A man of the world, Jerry rarely flinched

from a problem. Many of his older parishioners, such as Tom Forrest, resented his political sermons and 'green' alternative views. He appealed more to the young and less privileged, such as the Carters and the Grundys. In 1989 he made a brave, defiant act of Christian generosity when he scandalized many people in Ambridge by inviting the homeless Clive Horrobin and his pregnant girlfriend Sharon Richards to live at the vicarage. He continued to stand by Sharon and her daughter Kylie when Clive deserted them. Even though things were difficult at the vicarage, he was still not keen on Sharon and Kylie moving into a caravan.

Jerry was fortunate to have one true friend in Ambridge, Marjorie Antrobus, who had known him in Kenya. It was she who taught him bee-keeping. But his new hobby did not last long: at the end of 1990 Gerry was offered an opportunity to go back to Africa – to Mozambique – on a missionary trip and he accepted. He offered Marjorie a chance to go with him but she declined and after the appropriate jabs and mouthfuls of malaria tablets he set off alone.

When he got there, Gerry realized that that was where his duty lay. He wrote to the Bishop asking to be relieved from his duties in Ambridge. His ex-parishioners, led by Marjorie, have done what they can to support his continuing work in Mozambique.

Michael Deacon

Bull, The

The Bull is the most famous inn in Borsetshire, where eavesdropping on conversations is to get to know most of what is going on in Ambridge.

Peggy Archer and her husband Jack obtained the licence of the Bull in 1952 when Sam Saunders retired after twenty years in the job. They moved in the following January. With Jack's weakness for drink it wasn't an ideal career move and by November the licence was transferred to Peggy because of Jack's 'dilatoriness'. In 1957 Stourhampton Brewery took over the Bull; they sold it two years later as a free house, asking £5,300. With financial help from Laura Archer, Jack and Peggy bought it. When in 1972 Jack died and the Bull became too much of a responsibility for Peggy, she offered its management to Sid and Polly Perks.

Alongside the traditional darts matches and quiz evenings, and the bowls on the green at the back, there have been daring innovations: the Steak Bar opened by Sid and Polly Perks in 1972, with glass-topped tables and pink chrome benches; the fruit machine of 1982, optimistically entitled 'the Golden Plum', which Sid rented from Nelson Gabriel and which obsessed Tom Forrest; Sid's plan for taped music in the bar which sadly fell by the wayside when he found out it needed a licence; and the music nights of 1993 which raised the profits but brought down the ceiling, or at least some of the plaster. Life in the Bull is never dull.

Several times Peggy contemplated selling it, but it wasn't until 1993, secure in her second marriage, that she felt she could let it go. She gave Sid and his second wife Kathy first refusal as she had always promised. At first it looked as though he couldn't raise the necessary sum but Guy Pemberton came to his rescue and they went into partnership.

BULL FARM

Mr Martin, owner of Bull Farm, emigrated with his son and married daughter in 1974. When the farm was auctioned in three lots at the Drum and Monkey in Borchester, Phil Archer was interested in acquiring some of the land adjoining Brookfield. He was pleased to purchase 35 acres for just under £20,000. The farmhouse was withdrawn at £42,000 and wasn't sold until the following year when a businessman, Charles Harvey, moved in with his family. A Mr Hopkins from Hollerton bought 10 acres for development, but planning permission was turned down. Tony Archer was able to turn the situation to his advantage and rent the 10 acres for £100 a year on the understanding that he would vacate at short notice should planning permission be given at a later date.

BURTON, JOAN (NÉE HOOD)

b. 1941; m. Nigel Burton 8 Sept. 1964; 1 dtr

Joan was the youngest daughter of Percy and Betty Hood. A bright girl, having passed her GCSEs successfully, she starred in the Ciné Club's first film in 1957.

Her mother was impressed with Dusty Rhodes, son of a surveyor in Hollerton, and encouraged Joan to go out with him. But Dusty tried to involve Joan in a series of petty thefts for which he was responsible. Her refusal to join him so maddened him that on one occasion he pushed her out of his car after stealing her handbag containing the Youth Club funds. Jimmy Grange (on whom she had a crush) took her to PC Bryden to make a statement.

In 1959 the Hoods left Ambridge to return to the Borders. Jimmy seemed indifferent to her departure but nevertheless she absconded from home to see him. Her uncle Doughy sent her home with Rita Flynn as her escort. But the lure of Jimmy was still strong. She returned once more to Ambridge, ostensibly on holiday, but really looking for a job. Carol Grey obliged, and offered her office work at the market garden. In 1962 she got a new job at the Grenville Estate where she met Nigel Burton. After a turbulent courtship she married him. Dan Archer employed her part-time in the office at Brookfield after the birth of her daughter Juliet.

Nona Blair; Esma Wilson

BURTON, JULIET

b. 7 May 1965

Juliet Burton is the daughter of Joan and Nigel Burton.

BURTON, NIGEL

m. Joan Hood 8 Sept. 1964; 1 dtr

Nigel Burton took over from Jimmy Grange as farmhand in charge of the dairy at Brookfield in 1961. Doris Archer was annoyed at his request for a key to his bedroom, which he insisted on cleaning himself and keeping private. She was mollified when she discovered that he was sending £1 a week home to his widowed mother.

Janet Sheldon and he enjoyed a relationship for a while, but her continual breaking of dates became too frustrating for him. He obtained permission from Dan Archer to convert the loft over a barn into a flat, which he occupied for three more years. After a stormy courtship, he married Joan Hood in 1964. Paddy Redmond, who had been his contemporary at college, suggested that Dan might employ him in his place. The Burtons took over Thornton Farm. In 1965 a daughter Juliet was born.

Bryan Kendrick

BUTANE, RICHARD

Friend of Mark Hebden, and a regular at the Appletree on Sunday evenings, Richard Butane gave Mark and Shula Archer the experience of their lives in 1980 when he showed them Borsetshire from a hot-air balloon.

St John Howell

BUTLER, AMY

Amy Butler came as the new barmaid to the Bull in 1960. She caused tongues to wag by cooking for Dan Archer and Nigel Burton at Brookfield while Dan's wife Doris was in Newmarket visiting her daughter Christine, in hospital after a riding accident. The rumours owed more to the tendency of the village to gossip than to any real cause for suspicion. Amy spent seven more uneventful years in Ambridge before leaving in 1969.

Patricia Gibson

BUTLER, MARJORIE

When Jane Maxwell departed from Fairbrother's in February 1952, Phil Archer had to find another poultry girl to take her place. He reported that the new recruit, Marjorie Butler, had first-class qualifications but was 'no oil-painting'. Poor Marjorie, feeling that people saw her only as an accessory to the poultry and the pigs, set about improving herself. She had a perm and bought new clothes, and rather to everyone's surprise her efforts paid off. Some months later, she was seen courting a young chap called Ginger Green and she persuaded Phil to employ him.

Then one weekend Ginger mysteriously disappeared. The awful news that he was a married man reached Marjorie's ears and she was devastated. Against everyone's advice she clung obstinately to the hope that Ginger would leave his wife and come back to her. She gave in her notice and went to Ginger's lodgings, convinced that if he saw her again he would realize how much he loved her. It was too late. Ginger and his wife had left the night before. Marjorie trailed back to her own digs, certain that Ginger had made the mistake of a lifetime. She packed her bags and left Ambridge, a sadder but not wiser woman.

Kathleen Canty

CALDER, VANCE

At the suggestion of Dick Raymond, whom he met in Malaya, Vance Calder came caravanning to Ambridge in 1952. His welcome among Dick's friends was soured when he casually revealed to Christine Archer that Dick had become engaged overseas.

CALEY, DR

The doctor at Borchester General Hospital who dealt with Adam Macy's adder bite.

CAPTAIN

Jack Woolley's sentimental yet genuine love for Captain, his Staffordshire bull terrier, knew no bounds. He spoilt him almost to the point of ridicule.

When Jack was having his pacemaker fitted in 1988 George Barford looked after Captain, giving him a great deal more discipline than he'd been used to. When Jack returned, Captain kept running back to George.

It was sad and ill-timed that Jack should be away on his honeymoon when Captain died in 1991. Jack was broken-hearted when he heard the woeful news that Captain had gone missing for the last time and had been found dead by George Barford. Perhaps it was Jack's absence that caused the old dog to breathe his last, for undoubtedly Captain was fond of his old master.

Captain was buried in an oak coffin with brass fittings near the golf course at Grey Gables on the route of one of his favourite walks. Kenton Archer provided a headstone which read, 'Well done, thou good and faithful servant.' Tissues were in order as Jack made a farewell speech in honour of his canine friend at a memorial service for him.

In the pub afterwards Jack bought drinks for the few who had paid their last respects and, on leaving the pub, realized that for the first time he had not put his hand into his pocket for Captain's lead.

CAREY, ALAN

Alan Carey was widowed Helen Carey's son, who came with her in 1951 (he was then twenty-four) to stay with their friend Squire Lawson-Hope. Alan was an excellent tennis player, fond of birdwatching and a good carpenter. He had been with the tanks in Korea, where he had been badly shot up, and suffered the additional horror of watching his twin brother, Rex, burned alive. Grace Fairbrother found his brooding presence deeply attractive and felt that she could help him conquer the neurosis bequeathed him by the war – which she did, though indirectly. Repairing her car, he had a narrow escape when it slipped off the ramp. Grace was more frightened than he was, and he suddenly realized that an onlooker might be more terrified than the person actually experiencing the event: perhaps his brother Rex had not been as frightened as he had thought. A load was lifted off his shoulders and he became brighter – and fell in love with Grace. He proposed to her but was turned down, and became depressed once more. His spirits improved when he visited friends in Yorkshire and met Ann Fraser, who became his fiancée. He brought her to Ambridge for the Whitsun wedding of Helen and Mr Fairbrother in 1952.

Dudley Rolph

CAREY, HELEN

see Fairbrother, Helen

CARMICHAEL, JEAN

At a WI talk by Mary Weston in 1974, Mrs Carmichael heard references to her brother Ben Truscott which she thought libellous and reported to him, setting off an unhappy legal dispute.

CARTER, CHRISTOPHER

b. 22 June 1988

When Christopher's mother, Susan, first saw him she was horrified: her baby had been born with a unilateral cleft palate and hare lip. Despite his beautiful blue eyes and shock of black hair, she could not overcome the revulsion she felt towards him. Her husband Neil did everything he could to resolve the situation but it was not until Christopher's palate was successfully operated on that Susan could bring herself to wheel him round Ambridge.

Christopher is close to his elder sister Emma and they spend a lot of time playing together. After the raid on the village shop by their Uncle Clive, Susan was mortified to find them playing 'shop raiders'.

Christopher was greatly affected by his mother's imprisonment in 1993. It was disconcerting for the five-year-old to be left without his mother and he found it difficult to cope with a variety of different carers. Not surprisingly when his mother returned home he refused to leave her side; and he had to be led away sobbing when he went back to school at the start of the summer term.

CARTER, EMMA

b. 7 August 1984

Emma Carter has had many problems in her young life. Daughter of Neil and Susan Carter, she was born a month prematurely and had to go into an incubator for several days. Her parents' desire to take her home was then frustrated by an outbreak of baby jaundice. It was a relief when they could finally tuck her up in her cot in the nursery they had painted cream and decorated with a coloured frieze.

After her shaky start things seemed to go well until she started primary school at Loxley Barratt. Suddenly she started crying and dashing from the room. There was also a problem at home where she had begun to wet the bed. Eventually, urged on by Neil, Susan took her to see a psychologist. It became clear that Emma had been very upset when her parents' attention was concentrated on her younger brother, Christopher.

The situation slowly began to rectify itself but for a long time Emma was fearful of spending the night away from home in case she had an 'accident'.

Always a sensitive child, she was very upset when her mother was sent to prison and she refused to visit her. Her 'punishment' of Susan continued after she returned home; for a long time Emma remained cold and distant.

Emma likes pretty clothes and attends Brownies and dancing classes. Her appearances in various village shows have often brought tears to her parents' eyes. They are both very proud of her.

Jane Collingwood

CARTER, NEIL

b. 22 May 1957; m. Susan Horrobin 25 Feb. 1984; 1 son, 1dtr

Neil was a born pig man, but few in Ambridge recognized this talent at first. Nor had he any idea of it himself, being a town boy who fell in love with the country. He was born in Oxfordshire, moved to Birmingham with his mother and at sixteen was apprenticed to Ambridge Farmers under an agricultural training scheme. He left the city and got lodgings with the Woodfords.

To begin with, he created some havoc at Brookfield. He overturned a tractor, failed his proficiency test and wasn't brilliant at getting up early on winter mornings. Some blunders were more serious, as when he left a gate open between two pig pens and the animals attacked each other. One pig was lost on that occasion, and Phil was very angry. But he recognized that, if nothing else, Neil was a tryer. Jethro Larkin gave him lectures in the draughty barn over lunchtime sandwiches, Phil Archer continued to persevere with his raw apprentice and Neil began to learn from his mistakes. Both Jethro and Phil had grown to like the lad. By the end of his training he had become a positive asset to Brookfield and Phil kept him on.

He was a good footballer, and was invited to play for Borchester United, but by this time he'd decided that farming was his life.

He had also acquired a motor-bike, and was helping Martha with her shop deliveries. He helped out in the Bull in the evenings. But he got into trouble when his then girl-friend Sandy Miller planted her 'reefers' in his pocket at a party. Although he was found guilty of possessing drugs and had to do community service, he gamely didn't inform on her. But he'd gained the (perhaps unfair) reputation of being something of a tearaway. He went out for a short time with Ellen Padbury, who became 'Miss Ambridge 1977'. He took Eva Lenz out once or twice to dances, much to the annoyance of PC Coverdale.

He was engaged for a time to the barmaid Julie who used to jog around the village in a shocking pink tracksuit and wear startling miniskirts at the Bull. Their wedding date was set, but the vicar, Richard Adamson, tried to persuade Neil to think again. His misgivings were borne out when Julie two-timed Neil with PC Barry and Neil broke off the engagement.

But Shula Archer broke his young heart. He drove a tractor into a tree once while he was waving and grinning at her. Jethro laughed when Neil spilled slurry down a new anorak he'd worn to impress her. Shula gently explained many times that they could only be friends, and, painfully, after years of trying, he accepted the situation. They still went to dances together, when other partners let them down, and they have over the years become firm friends.

Neil Carter (Brian Hewlett)

There were other girls in Neil's life, but the one he was eventually to marry was Susan Horrobin. Susan took a fancy to Neil when she won the prize pig, Pinky, at the Ambridge fête. She hated it, but Neil built a pen for it and turned up with bagfuls of pignuts for the animal. In return, Susan helped Neil out with his hens. At first Susan made all the running, inviting Neil out to the pictures and chatting him up in the Bull. One Christmas, Susan gave Neil an expensive initialled wallet. He'd only bought her a box of chocolates and, shamed, he took her on a bargain-break holiday to London and a posh hotel. When Susan announced she was pregnant, Neil 'did the decent thing' and proposed to her there and then. They married in February 1984. Neil was living at the time in the flat at Nightingale Farm, and Susan moved in and their daughter, Emma Louise, was born there in August; but when their landlord Hugo Barnaby wanted to sell the property the Carters received £4,000 compensation money and moved into No. 1 The Green. Neil was reluctant to live so close to his in-laws, the irresponsible Horrobins, but finally agreed to take out a mortgage and buy the house. They lovingly decorated it and gave it a new front door.

Neil and Susan acquired a smart van and had 'Willow Farm Fresh Eggs, Neil and Susan Carter' painted on the side, but sadly the hens contracted salmonella and had to be slaughtered.

Pigs were Neil's passion. In his time working at Hollowtree, he discovered a real empathy and feeling for the animals, something he's always had in common with Phil Archer. In times of stress they can both be seen scratching their pigs' backs and confiding in them.

Bill Insley and Neil embarked on a farm sharing scheme at Willow Farm. Bill died suddenly, but a grateful Neil discovered that he was heir to the barn and eight acres of land there. Now he could house his animals on his own land. He kept a set of wellingtons and overalls at Willow Farm and at Hollowtree, so as not to cross-infect animals at either farm.

Christopher John Carter, their second child, was born in June 1988 with a unilateral cleft palate. Neil has always loved and cared for his children. When Emma started bed-wetting, he was the parent who calmed and comforted her. He likes playing with the children and found the time to make a dolls' house for Emma (Susan made the dolls for it). It was largely for the family's sake that Neil reluctantly took on the job of animal feed salesman, at Susan's urging, and gave up his job at Hollowtree. But he insisted on keeping his own pigs.

When in 1993 Susan was imprisoned for helping her convict brother Clive, Neil once more had to cope with the disturbed children. He did his best to lighten their bleak Christmastime.

After Susan's release from prison, Neil was confused at her behaviour. She was reluctant to talk about her prison experiences, kept her feelings bottled up and accused Neil of being unfaithful to her. Maureen Travers had attempted to take advantage of Neil's loneliness when Susan was inside and had pressed her attentions on him. Neil might have been tempted, but he stayed faithful to Susan. He was alarmed when Susan took it into her hands to confront the devious Maureen. Slowly Susan and Neil began to talk to each other openly about the trauma of Susan's imprisonment and its implications for them both, and to get on with the remainder of their lives as best they can.

Brian Hewlett

CARTER, SUSAN (NÉE HORROBIN)

b. 10 Oct. 1963; m. Neil Carter 25 Feb. 1984; 1 son, 1 dtr

Susan started life with her mum, dad, four brothers and one sister in an overcrowded council house on the village green, but she always longed to better herself.

She began to be noticed when she was nineteen and Sid Perks gave her a full-time job behind the bar at the Bull. Tom Forrest thought she was 'nice and fresh-looking'. Mark Hebden noticed that she was pretty. But Susan noticed, and only had eyes for, the young Neil Carter.

In 1983 Susan won Pinky the pig at the village fête. Susan never cared for the animal, but Neil built a shelter for it, brought it nuts from Brookfield, sprained his ankle chasing it and accepted her help in return for feeding his hens. Love began to bloom. On a bargain-break weekend in London (she'd never been before) she informed Neil that she was pregnant, and they decided to marry. When he heard of her pregnancy her father threatened to disown her, but he came round in time to be at the wedding, which took place on 25 February 1984. The bride wore a heavy imitation-silk dress 'just like

Susan Carter (Charlotte Martin)

Lady Di's, only white'. Eddie Grundy was best man and there followed a hearty reception at the village hall, which was not even spoiled by Susan's brothers scoffing all the vol-au-vents. Jack Woolley's dog Captain had already had a good chew at the wedding cake.

Baby Emma was born a month early and Susan was desperately anxious when she had to go to a special baby unit. A few years later, Christopher John Carter was born with a shock of black hair, blue eyes and a cleft palate and hare lip. Once more Susan's baby was taken away from her. Susan reproached herself, guiltily convinced that she was in some way responsible for Christopher's appearance. After the successful operation on the baby's face, she over-compensated for her earlier feelings, concentrated all her affection on Christopher and began to neglect Emma. Emma started wetting the bed.

A demon for work, Susan weeded carrots and picked potatoes at Bridge Farm, pulled pints at the Bull, served in the shop, helped Neil with his livestock and kept the house clean and tidy. She was delighted when she got a job at the Berrow Estate office. Cameron Fraser noticed her potential and suggested that she learn computer skills. She was going up in the world. She persuaded Neil into getting himself a white-collar job as a feed salesman. She enjoyed extending her social range and was flattered to be offered sherry by Lynda Snell. They took out a mortgage, bought their council house and became houseowners. Susan was proud to be the first Horrobin to do so, and celebrated with scampi and chips and a new Georgian-style front door.

She might be socially ambitious, but Susan never turned her back on her own. She gave a home to her brother Clive and his pregnant girlfriend Sharon Richards, caring for her and for her baby Kylie when Clive walked out. Clarrie Grundy and Betty Tucker have always found her to be a good friend. In the village, she has a reputation for kind-heartedness.

Clive traded shamelessly on her good heart. When he was a fugitive after the armed robbery at the village shop, he used emotional blackmail to make her shelter him. She was arrested and tried for the offence of seeking to pervert the course of public justice, convicted and sent down for six months. She absconded to attend Mark Hebden's funeral, and a further ten days were added to her sentence after a fight with a fellow prisoner afterwards. Prison was traumatic for her. When, having served her time, she came home, she couldn't bring herself to talk about it. To make matters worse, she became convinced that Neil had been having an affair with Maureen Travers while she'd been inside. He was able to convince her otherwise and she had a violent confrontation with Maureen. They have tried desperately to put it all behind them; but they have had to work very hard to repair the damage to their lives and their relationship.

Charlotte Martin

CARTWRIGHT, ELIZABETH (LIZ, NÉE ALDRIDGE)

Visiting the Aldridges in 1977, Brian's sister Liz proved to be opinionated and tactless about the running of Home Farm. Jennifer began to feel that Liz knew more about the estate than she did herself, and resolved to be better informed in future.

CARVER, MARTIN

Agricultural valuer Martin Carver planned to spend a quiet night at Grey Gables on his way to a valuers' convention at Stratford-upon-Avon in 1992, but his room had been double-booked. Offered a bed by Joe Grundy, he thought his problem solved; but he found himself cornered in a discussion of Joe's tax problems. He told Joe that a realistic valuation of his cows would help – Joe had estimated them at about half their value – and in exchange for the room agreed to write a letter to the tax authorities. But faced with the offered room and its singular smell, he left in haste and accepted an alternative offer at Brookfield.

CAT AND FIDDLE, THE

The Cat and Fiddle is Ambridge's alternative pub, though it's not in fact in the village. It's not quite in the class of the Bull, but some of the older clients took refuge there to escape landlord Sid Perks's music nights at the Bull in 1993. When Eddie Grundy is periodically banned from the Bull, he makes his way to the Cat and Fiddle and joins his cronies Baggy and Snatch Foster.

CATCHER, ELSIE

Appointed head of the village school in 1927, Elsie Catcher taught there for forty years until her retirement in 1967. She was irreverently nicknamed 'Old Mousetrap' by her pupils, who used to call after her, 'Once round Elsie Catcher, twice round the gasworks!' She belonged to the Ornithologists Club in Borchester and played the organ in the church. In 1951 she was secretary to the parish council. Whatever her pupils may have thought of her, she was sufficiently attractive to make Peggy Archer jealous when she helped her husband Jack Archer look after the children while Peggy was in hospital in 1953.

A retirement party was held for her on 25 July 1967 in the village hall, at which she was presented with a handsome cheque by Phil Archer – a kindly gesture on his part as on one occasion she had told Jill that Shula was a backward child.

Thelma Rogers; Mary Wimbush

CATCHPOLE, ROBIN

Robin Catchpole was arrogant, shallow and an undoubted ladykiller. He joined *The Borchester Echo* as a young roving reporter and roved straight into Shula Archer. He declared his love for her, as he did with all girls, but Mark Hebden, her boyfriend, was having none of it.

While on the *Echo*, Robin covered many a local news item until he left Ambridge in 1982 to work on a fringe magazine in London. Sighs of relief all round.

Edward McCarthy

CATTERMOLE, SUSAN

By 1973, Susan Cattermole, courtesy of her husband one understands, had had seven children and she left them unattended many a night to drink in the Cat and Fiddle. What is more, she was a thief. Angela Cooper, who then ran the village shop, caught her with her hands in the till. This took the pressure off Martha Woodford, her assistant, who until then had been the number one suspect. Ambridge (in fact the world) is better off without the likes of Susan Cattermole.

Penelope Shaw

CAVENDISH, DR DAVID

Dr David Cavendish was in advance of his time. In the fifties he was regarded as something of a crank. As early as 1955 he urged Carol Grey to grow organic fruit and vegetables, arguing in favour of plenty of muck rather than fertilizers. He persuaded Ben White, the baker, to make bread in accordance with his own special recipe, and told Jack Archer that he based his medical philosophy on the need for freshly grown food.

Cavendish's diet didn't prevent him from being extremely irascible at times. He objected vigorously to John Tregorran's proposal to hold a fair near Manor House which the doctor had bought from Squire Lawson-Hope in 1955, and shouted at people bathing in the Manor lake, which he also considered to be his property. He was very much attracted to Carol Grey, but for a time his name was linked romantically with Eileen Rawlings, whose brother Peter was one of his patients. His financial situation was disastrous and worsened when he tried to realize his dream that health care should be within the reach of all. In order to establish a health centre at Manor House he borrowed money from Eileen and Peter's parents as well as £3,000 from John Tregorran, who became a shareholder. It wasn't enough. In 1956 he asked George Fairbrother to name his price for Manor House and left Ambridge without saying goodbye to anyone but Carol, his dreams evaporated and leaving behind him a trail of debts.

Geoffrey Lewis

CHARLIE

When Nelson Gabriel was depressed after the sale of his antiques shop in 1989, Jack Woolley gave him Charlie, a spaniel pup, to cheer him up. The gift proved to be a mixed blessing. During their first year together Charlie left a trail of damage, driving Mrs P., his next-door neighbour, to putting down pepper to keep the dog out of her garden. A course of training with Mrs Antrobus brought some measure of control but Nelson's patience has often been tested.

CHUBB, LT PAUL

One of Caroline Bone's most glamorous boyfriends, local boy Paul Chubb was six foot two and a pilot in the Fleet Air Arm. When not in the sky, Paul would whisk Caroline off for the weekend in Walberswick, Suffolk, at a cottage lent by an understanding friend. In 1984 he had eyes only for Caroline; but by 1985 his eyes had wandered and he left Caroline to marry a younger girl called Philippa.

CLARKE, FRED

While Fred Clarke was barman at Grey Gables in the seventies, he interested Sid Perks in the racing pigeons which he bred. He also found himself in demand each year at Christmas, arranging the lighting for the pantomime.

CLIFFORD, BILL

Bill Clifford was a probation officer who saw Terry Barford once a month while he was on probation in 1976. He was sympathetic and soon managed to establish a rapport with Terry when he told him that he supported Derby County FC. When Nora McAuley alerted him to the fact that Terry had started to drink he handled the matter well, reassuring Terry's father George Barford that he would try to get to the root of the problem before taking further action. However, Terry took the matter out of his hands when he stole a car and was sentenced to three months at a detention centre.

John Baldwin

CLINT

Clint is Jason's builder's mate. In 1992 he and Jason upset Martha Woodford, Sid Perks, and Clarrie and Joe Grundy by 'bullfighting' with bones found in the churchyard while he and Jason were digging a trench for a new lavatory. Clint and Jason protested to the outraged villagers that they were not human bones.

CLINT

One of the Grange Farm turkeys, Clint was selected by Eddie Grundy to be kept separate from the rest and fattened for the family's own Christmas dinner in 1989. William Grundy christened him and became so attached to him that he let him out of his pen and saved him from his intended fate. Eddie and Clarrie Grundy weren't pleased at having to make do with a frozen turkey.

COBB, HARRY

Once a general handyman for Ralph Bellamy, Harry Cobb was a retired widower and grateful for part-time work at the Bull in 1969. He helped with the heavy work but occasionally he served at the bar, and took over entirely when Jack and Peggy Archer had a holiday. Romance flowered for him when he mended Mrs P.'s leaky tap, and he entrusted her with one of his most closely kept secrets, that he dyed his hair. Encouraged by her response he bought her a mina bird for her birthday, but kept it for himself when she preferred Walter Gabriel's gift, a pet budgerigar. In 1971 he began to suffer from bronchitis, and went to live on the south coast to see if his condition would improve in a sunnier climate.

Charles Leno

COLEMAN, GEORGE

Tom Forrest's assistant on the Bellamy Estate, George Coleman was appointed underkeeper during Tom's imprisonment in 1957. He moved on six years later to work in Staffordshire.

George Walters

COLLARD, GRAHAM

Graham Collard joined Brookfield as a cow-

THE BOOK OF THE ARCHERS

man in 1977. He and his wife Val, who worked at the local canning factory, lived happily with their young family in Rickyard Cottage until 1991. When Ruth Archer left college a place on the farm had to be found for her and, though Phil Archer was genuinely sorry to have to lose him, the family came first and Graham was made redundant. Fortunately, he found a new job at a Hollerton farm. Jill Archer organized a farewell get-together for him at the Bull.

CONWAY, CLARICE

Clarice Conway met Doughy Hood when he was a seaman and his ship was berthed at London Docks. They had exchanged letters when he was at sea. One day in 1958 she arrived in the village carrying a letter which she avowed 'hinted at marriage'. Rita Flynn tore the letter from her hand and fought Clarice off, much to Doughy's relief.

Gwen Muspratt

COOMBE FARM

In 1953 George Fairbrother bought Coombe Farm from Squire Lawson-Hope and Amos Atkins gave up his tenancy of the farm to take a smallholding next to Brookfield. Phil Archer, Fairbrother's farm manager, transferred his pig-breeding scheme to Coombe Farm and developed a herd of Herefords there. When his daughter Grace married Phil, Fairbrother rented the farmhouse to them for £1 a week. After Grace died in 1955, Phil continued to live there on his own.

The following year the farm was converted into two dwellings to provide a home for a new stockman and his wife, Mr and Mrs Rodgers, who came to look after the Herefords.

When Phil took Jill Patterson out for supper one evening forgetting that it was the second anniversary of Grace's death, he told her about the tragedy, and together they went to pick some flowers at Coombe Farm and took them to the churchyard. After their marriage in 1957 their first three children were born at Coombe Farm. It was with regret that the young family moved to Allard's Farm in 1962.

COOMBES, ROGER

Pat Archer met Roger Coombes at Borchester Technical College in 1984 when she was going through a bad patch with her husband Tony Archer. Separated with two children, he was the lecturer for her course in Women's Studies. For the first time Pat had found someone who shared her beliefs and she became very involved with him. His divorce came through in September but he seemed doubtful about whether he and Pat had a future together. They were seen together in the Feathers and a friend of Dorothy Adamson's who also knew Roger told Dorothy all about the relationship. Richard Adamson had a quiet word with Pat, who eventually broke off the affair.

COOPER, ANGELA

see Evans, Angela

COOPER, BESS

Bess, wife of Brookfield farm worker, Simon Cooper, came from a large family in Hollerton. The Coopers moved into the smallholding owned by Dan Archer in 1952 while their cottage was being refurbished. Bess liked it so much that she didn't want to leave. At one stage she persuaded Simon to find out if Dan would sell it to them, but it was a dream never to be fulfilled. Although Bess thought Dan was a fair employer she agitated for Simon to set up on his own. He never managed it and in 1956 his health began to fail. He could no longer keep up with his work at Brookfield or on the smallholding, and he had to retire. They moved into a cottage closer to Ambridge where Simon died the following year. Bess left Ambridge and went to live with one of her sisters.

Pauline Seville; Gertrude Salisbury; Peggy Hughes

COOPER, JIM

Farmhand of Fred Barratt's in the sixties, at the time when Ambridge Dairy Farmers was coming into operation. Fred showed his commitment to the co-op when uncharacteristically he allowed Jim to help at Brookfield (one of the farms in the co-op) when Jimmy Grange had an accident.

COOPER, SIMON

'No one should cry about death,' Simon Cooper once said. 'If you go one way then you ain't worth crying about and if you go the other then you're a darned sight better than if you'd stayed alive.'

Simon worked as farm labourer at Brookfield and from 1952 lived at the smallholding with his wife Bess. Always straightforward, he enjoyed a pint, and a game of dominoes or darts and was a mean skittler, too. He had a good sense of humour and amused himself by gently baiting Walter and Mrs P. But he was also sensitive and could easily take offence. When he thought that Dan Archer suspected him of fiddling the books, he walked out of Brookfield in a

left to right: Phil Archer (Norman Painting), Simon Cooper (Eddie Robinson), George Fairbrother (Leslie Bowmar) and Dan Archer (Harry Oakes)

huff. Nonsense, of course. Dan only wanted an accountant to set up a balance sheet for the smallholding, as he was running it at a loss, but it was some time before Simon could face Dan again and ask him for his old job back. Dan was delighted and Simon worked on at Brookfield, always with his hat on, until back trouble forced him to retire in 1956.

Eddie Robinson

COOPER, STAN

Stan Cooper was a widower from the Black Country who had retired early from engine driving because of bronchial trouble. In 1972 Jack Woolley employed him to run the village shop and do a bit of barbering on the side. His daughter, Angela, helped him by running the post office side and doing some ladies' hair-dressing. In September he was badly scalded when he knocked the steam cock while driving the *Empress of Ambridge* during its inaugural trip on Jack Woolley's Ambridge Park Railway. He recovered in hospital where Jack arranged for him to have a private room. Stan thanked him but said he'd rather be in the general ward and have the money instead.

The business struggled to make a profit and Stan had to take a job serving petrol at Bellamy's garage, leaving his daughter to run both shop and post office with help from Martha Woodford.

When, to Stan's dismay, Angela announced she was marrying local farmer, Gwyn Evans, and emigrating to Canada he was unable to cope with the upheaval. He soon left Ambridge

and Jack asked Martha Woodford if she would take over in the shop.

Geoffrey Lewis

CORBEY, DICK

Peggy Archer was sufficiently impressed with Dick Corbey's efficiency as a temporary manager of the Bull after Jack Archer's death to ask him to stay for an extra three months, but her judgement proved to have been at fault. He was not greatly liked by the regulars, and rumours began to emerge that he had a shady past and was known under other names. When he disappeared, taking some of the stock, and was caught by the police in Manchester, he tried unsuccessfully to implicate Peggy in the theft. At his trial he exonerated her and pleaded guilty. At Laura Archer's suggestion, Peggy let the Bull to Sid and Polly Perks – a much happier arrangement.

Geoffrey Lewis

COVERDALE, EVA (NÉE LENZ)

b. 10 Mar. 1959; m. James Coverdale April 1980

If Eva Lenz expected to spend her time in Ambridge improving her English and looking after the children at Home Farm, she was much mistaken. The blonde, brown-eyed, nineteen-year-old German au-pair soon had young men buzzing round her like bees round a honeypot. She received romantic interest from Nick Wearing and Neil Carter; but the person who was really desperate to win her was Eddie Grundy.

He could not believe his luck when he found her stranded by the roadside one dark November evening in 1979, but Eva was terrified when he tried to lure her in a forceful manner to accept a lift in his JCB. Wasn't she pleased that PC James Coverdale arrived on the scene? He sent Eddie packing and escorted Eva back to Home Farm where he was soon a regular caller. Though Jim was not liked by many in the village, Eva felt differently about him. There was a strong bond in the fact that they were both outsiders and Jim soon popped the question. Her parents were furious at the news of her engagement and Eva had to fly home to the Fatherland to persuade them to approve. They did so only grudgingly and she scurried miserably back to England and to Jim in the Police House. When Eddie discovered they had spent the night there together, he took his revenge on Jim by reporting what had happened to his sergeant. Jim received a roasting. When Eva discovered that it was Eddie who had betrayed them she angrily tipped a pint of bitter over his head. Eddie finally understood just how she felt about him.

Jim and Eva were married in April 1980. The newly-weds were a tactless pair and found it hard to be accepted by the village. It came as a relief all round when they left for Plymouth the following year.

Hedli Niklaus

COVERDALE, PC JAMES

b. 1948, m. Eva Lenz April 1980

When Jethro Larkin and Eddie Grundy couldn't produce shot-gun certificates, PC James Coverdale immediately confiscated their guns until he had seen the relevant bits of paper. It was typical of his pedantic way of enforcing the law. He infuriated Eddie still more in 1980 when he insinuated that he had been poaching deer in the Country Park; for once, Eddie was completely blameless. He warned Eva Lenz for riding a bicycle without lights. Even though he fancied her, he found it impossible to turn a blind eye.

Once the law took Jim by surprise. He bought some damsons from Freddie Danby's roadside stall, and it gave Jack Woolley great pleasure to point out that the stall had been erected without the necessary permission. For once, James Coverdale wasn't on the case.

His lack of tact was legendary in the village – he had a way of upsetting the locals – and many people were surprised when he and Eva Lenz became lovingly engaged (and subsequently married). There was a universal sigh of relief when Jim announced that he was moving to Plymouth to join the CID. Eddie magnanimously urged Sid Perks to collect for a leaving present, but, not surprisingly, people were reluctant to contribute, especially as in the few weeks before he left, Jim managed to upset almost everyone by issuing reprimands over any number of trivial indiscretions.

Finally, a grudging farewell party took place for the man who was Ambridge's last village policeman. Jim had too much to drink and departed for Plymouth with a well-deserved hangover.

Leon Tanner

CRABBE, MISS

Ben White and Miss Crabbe were gossiping about Jack Archer's unsuitability for taking over the Bull when they were disturbed by a knock at the door. The subject of their conversation reeled in, smelling of brandy and demanding to use the phone. He said that he'd been given the brandy medicinally after being involved in an accident, but Ben and Miss Crabbe didn't believe a word of it. Ben, whose nephew Malcolm White had also applied to run the Bull, made it his business to report to PC Randall and Mr Fairbrother that Jack was drunk at the time of the accident. Jack weathered the gossip and was appointed licensee the following month, December 1952.

Vera Ashe

CRAIG

see Lisa

CRAWFORD, MR

Mr Crawford was an industrialist and owner of the mineral rights on land belonging to George Fairbrother and Squire Lawson-Hope. Fairbrother invited him to Ambridge in 1951 to enlist support for his plans to mine ironstone (to which there was much opposition in the village) but Crawford fell in love with the village and refused to co-operate, so the scheme fell by the wayside.

CROW, MR

Jack Woolley's legal adviser in the sixties.
William Avenell

CROWTHER, AUDREY

An old chum of Mrs Antrobus's turned up in Ambridge in 1990 and took a shine to Jack Woolley, much to Peggy Archer's annoyance. She needn't have worried, as Jack's taste never ran to women covered in dog hairs and partial to the occasional nip from a bottle tucked in the handbag.

CRUMPS, THE

After Mr Banister's death in October 1988 Nigel Pargetter had no shortage of offers for the tenancy of Old Court Farm. Tony Archer and Brian Aldridge wanted more land and David and Ruth Archer hoped to find a place of their own. But they were all disappointed. Nigel decided to rent it to the Crumps, a deserving family already tenants of his on an adjacent holding which they were finding too small to be viable.

CZORVA, BARONESS

The shapely, mysterious Baroness Czorva crept secretly into Ambridge in the 1950s, told secret agent Mike Daly that he was expected elsewhere and together they crept out again.

Brenda Dunrich

DALY, MIKE

'Me friends call me Moike,' Mike Daly told Squire Lawson-Hope as he negotiated a price for Blossom Hill Cottage in March 1952, which should have been enough to alert Ambridge that he was not all that he seemed. Irish and twenty-eight, he could charm the birds off the trees, and he had come to Ambridge to write thrillers. It turned out that his own life story was more thrilling than anything he had yet written, although he tried to keep it hidden.

Mike made friends with Walter Gabriel and Mrs P. and provided Christine Archer with a shoulder to cry on when Dick Raymond left her for South East Asia. They were all curious about him – especially when he suffered an attack of malaria and Mrs P. found an MC medal while doing some cleaning for him – but smilingly he refused to answer any of their questions.

Reggie Trentham started spreading rumours that Mike was in fact a Major John Smith of the Pay Corps, who had been cashiered for embezzling funds. Mike was having tea with several of his friends at Blossom Hill Cottage when, uninvited, Reggie swept in, followed by a glamorous stranger. There was a sudden hush when Reggie introduced her as Mike's fiancée, Valerie Grayson. Clearly Mike recognized her, but that was all his friends were destined to learn as he asked them to leave. It wasn't until a week later, when Dan and Doris Archer allowed him to invite them all to Brookfield, that he gave them the full story.

He had joined the army and found its discipline irksome, longing to work on his own initiative. He was dropped into occupied France before the invasion with instructions to contact the Resistance and annoy the German High Command whenever he had the opportunity. This course of action soon landed him in Dachau concentration camp where life was made very unpleasant for him. It was decided that he could only get out by 'dying'. A pro-British German officer certified him dead and committed his body to a medical research outfit, and a corpse did indeed arrive there, although it was not Mike's. He was smuggled home to England under the name of Major John Smith, thereby keeping up the pretence of his 'death' and prolonging his usefulness. After a spell in hospital to recover from his unpleasant experiences, he was cashiered as Major John Smith to arouse the interest of enemy agents. At this point Valerie, also working for intelligence, posed as his fiancée. It was a far cry from the usual everyday story of country folk.

Reggie Trentham, who had gone out with Valerie, was very jealous to learn that she was engaged to 'Major Smith', which is why he had been so spiteful to Mike. Valerie remained in Ambridge, having found work with Mr Fairbrother. Ambridge romantics coupled Valerie's name with Mike's, but he preferred to remain a bachelor and she eventually married Reggie.

Grace Fairbrother and Christine offered Mike a partnership in their riding school, but he turned it down as he thought other work was in the offing; and indeed before the year was out he was suddenly called away.

An element of mystery still surrounded his character when he returned to Ambridge a couple of years later and asked Valerie to come and work for him on a special mission. She refused. A Baroness Czorva made contact with him and told him that 'a certain party' was waiting to see him, and once more he packed his bags.

John Franklyn; Michael Collins

DANBY, LT-COL. FREDERICK (FREDDIE)

b. 1 Nov. 1912

In 1976, Colonel Frederick Danby arrived in Ambridge looking for a place to stay for at least a month; he was to stay for many years.

An ex-army officer (he had served in Burma with the Gurkhas under General Slim) he had recently found employment as local representative for a national charity. Laura Archer offered to provide him with bed and breakfast at Ambridge Hall, which together with dinner at the Pickwick Grill promised to be an ideal arrangement. Freddie quickly found that eating out every night was a drain on his limited resources and started looking for a house to rent. When Laura found out, she quickly offered to provide him with an evening meal (except on Thursdays when she was busy with the Over Sixties). Although it took Freddie some time to bring himself to call her Laura, the two of them settled into amicable domesticity. In the winter they would sit by the fire reading – he his thrillers and Laura her travel books – or listening to his Sousa marches. In the summer they played croquet, which quickly became a bone of contention between Freddie, who was a cunning player, and Laura who was quite unaware of the rules.

Ambridge suited Freddie well: he was a country man at heart. A life of hunting, shooting and fishing was beyond his means but he enjoyed the odd pigeon-shoot with Tom Forrest. He had a streak of a performer in him and the village enjoyed his performances of Baron Stoney-Broke, an ugly sister, and Everyman in Laura's production of a morality play. He donned top hat and tails to be MC at the Edwardian evening held at Grey Gables in 1976.

He was not a proud man, and when he lost his job as a charity organizer he was quite happy to go down to the job centre and get himself work as a forecourt attendant at Wharton's Garage. When an outraged Laura put a stop to that, Jack Woolley employed him as steward at the Grey Gables golf club. Jack was displeased when Freddie refused to dress up for a visit from Lord Netherbourne: even more so when he learned that they were old friends. When Laura was ill, he happily took charge in the kitchen. Poor Laura became heartily sick of curry.

When their finances became tight, Freddie and Laura tried their hand at self-sufficiency. They had some luck with vegetables but soap-making proved beyond them. None of the animals they raised ever made the cooking pot – Freddie was too sentimental for that.

In 1980, aware that their friendship was putting Laura's good name in jeopardy, he tentatively suggested marriage. It came as a relief when she refused.

Because of the loss of her will, after Laura's death he became homeless. He moved into the bungalow in Manorfield Close where Mrs Blossom had lived. The local widows quickly seized the opportunity to bring him scarves and madeira cake. Overwhelmed by their attentions he drove away to stay with an old army chum in Bristol. It is to be hoped that he arrived safely; his ill-luck with secondhand cars had become legendary.

Norman Shelley; Ballard Berkeley

DANCER, BOB

'Ton-up boy' from Hollerton who put a lighted firework under a pensioner on Bonfire Night 1962. No one was sorry when his motor-bike was later found on fire. The culprit was never found – but the word went round that Laura Archer might have had something to do with it.

Patrick Connor

DARREN

On behalf of the WRVS, in 1981 Jill Archer organized holidays in and around Ambridge for deprived children, and Darren spent a week in the summer with her. He was a Liverpool boy, eleven years old, son of a housebreaker and with a brother in prison and rather out of his depth at Brookfield. Of all the people in Ambridge he might have got to know, it was Joe Grundy he befriended, but his stay was not long enough for Joe to be able to pass on too many rural dodges.

Judy Bennett

DEEDES, REVD CAROL

Deaconess who advised and married Ruth and David Archer.

Angela Thorne

DELAMAIN, SIMONE

see Archer, Simone

DEMETER AND PERSEPHONE

Ambridge was not surprised when Lynda

Snell decided to provide her own goats' milk by buying two goats in 1989, nor when they were christened rather more classically than most village animals. What did surprise was that she persisted with them against all the odds and, in her idiosyncratic way, cared for them successfully.

DENHAM, MR

Christine Archer bought an excellent saddle cheaply from Mr Denham in 1976. He was anxious to be rid of everything that might remind his daughter of her stolen horse and its likely fate as horsemeat.
William Eedle

DERWENT, VIRGINIA

Nicknamed 'the ice maiden', Virginia Derwent brought glamour to Ambridge in 1983 when she came to visit Caroline Bone with whom she had taken a cordon bleu cookery course in Paris. Rich, blue-eyed and beautiful, she had a brief fling with David Archer.

DEXTER, JANE

When a shrewd and attractive PR woman arrived at Grey Gables in 1977 to help Jack Woolley with a conference, he was immediately attracted to her. Jane set up a meeting in London between Jack and a prospective manager and he seized the opportunity to wine and dine her, ignoring her protests that they were just business associates. Jack's chauffeur Higgs mischievously spread a rumour that the two of them were in Paris.

Persuaded by Jack to become his agent for the conference business, Jane began to spend a lot of time at Grey Gables. Soon Gordon Armstrong was vying with Jack for her attentions – but Jane wasn't interested in either of them. After Jack missed the Jubilee tree-planting in order to spend time with her he realized that he had made a fool of himself and Jane decided that it would be better if she concentrated her energies in London.
Eileen Barry

DICKSON, MRS EILEEN

The post of warden at the Field Study Centre was for a married man, so when Robin Freeman's wife left him late in 1973, he feared that he would lose his job. The Field Studies Council decided to bend the rules and allow him to remain as long as he employed the very efficient Mrs Dickson as the Centre's housekeeper and matron.

DOCTOR

see also Cavendish, Dr; Locke, Dr Richard; MacLaren, Dr; Poole, Dr John; Thorogood, Dr Matthew; Vyce, Dr Aloysius

In the early days Ambridge had a doctor with whom everyone was familiar, but whose proper name was never used. He diagnosed Mike Daly when he had an attack of malaria, referred Phil Archer to a specialist in 1952 with a suspected cataract, and treated Peggy Archer for diphtheria. He was unmarried, kept bees and shared a friendly rivalry with Jack Archer in growing chrysanthemums, occasionally winning prizes. He retired in the fifties.

Eddie Robinson; John Franklyn; Ronald Baddiley; Peter Wilde; Robert Mawdesley; Eric Skelding

DOWER HOUSE, THE

Ralph and Lilian Bellamy, who owned the Dower House as part of the Bellamy Estate, moved into it after their Venice honeymoon in 1971. Since the Bellamys were extremely wealthy, their house made an obvious target for thieves. On one memorable occasion, George Barford spotted strangers hanging around the place, and caught them in the act of whisking valuable items into a removal van. Fortunately he had the good sense to summon Tom Forrest and Harry Booker and didn't tackle them on his own.

When Ralph and Lilian left Ambridge in 1975, the Dower House was let to a retired solicitor, Arnold Lucas. There were many tenants over the years, but the house was empty when Lilian asked for the key so that she could have a last look at it before selling it to Cameron Fraser alongside the rest of the Berrow Estate (as it was called by then) in 1990.

Fraser lived there briefly before his sins found him out and he had to flee the country. There was a great deal of village interest when his possessions were auctioned. Shula Hebden was impressed with many items, but Nelson Gabriel insisted that they were all fake; and Jill Archer kept well away, feeling that the whole process was macabre.

When Guy Pemberton bought the Estate in 1993, he had the Dower House done up before moving in. It didn't take him long to get the measure of his tenant farmer Joe Grundy, and when Joe insisted that his peeling wallpaper was the Estate's responsibility Guy neatly fobbed him off with paint and wallpaper left over from the redecorations.

Once more looking lived in and well tended, the Dower House has regained its rightful standing in the village.

DOWNES, MONICA

Wealthy girlfriend of Roger Travers-Macy who asked him to join a group holidaying in Jersey in 1967. He wanted Lilian Archer to go with them, but she refused.

Jane Rossington

DRURY, BARBARA

Barbara Drury was a typist in an insurance office before her husband's job brought her to Ambridge in 1975 and during the thirteen years she spent in the village she constantly missed the bustle of city life.

Barbara was reluctant to take an active role in the village, blaming her 'difficult position' as wife of the local policeman, Colin Drury. Despite being an excellent dressmaker, she refused to lend her talents to help make costumes for a revue. And it was a surprise for many when she became a staunch supporter of Riding for the Disabled. John

Tregorran charmed her into typing his pamphlet on *Ambridge Twenty-five Years Ago*; but she was never happy in Ambridge and no one was surprised at her joy when her husband received an urban posting. His promotion was an added bonus.

Ysanne Churchman

D RURY, PC COLIN

PC Drury (who took over from PC Bates on 5 June 1967) had his 'patch' increased to include Penny Hassett and almost as far as Hollerton. To enable him to cover the area, he was given a panda car. He was still primarily a village bobby and knew people by name. With his wife Barbara he lived in the Police House and entered village life as much as his official position would allow. Colin cheered for Ambridge Wanderers football team and supported local fêtes, where in 1976 he won the sack-race. When he went to Willow Farm to collect his prize of a dozen eggs he decided he would take the opportunity to test the brakes on Tony Archer's trailer. The brakes were so efficient that the eggs slid off the seat and were smashed. It was perhaps justice, as it transpired that Colin had won the race by cheating.

Though he took his duties seriously, Colin was not always officious. When he attended the opening of the Youth Club and noticed Shula driving a car before she had passed her driving test he decided that a warning was enough.

His detection skills were good. When Tom Forrest was hoaxed into leaving his pheasants unattended so that they could be poached, Colin realized that the tricksters would probably strike again. As soon as he heard that the poachers had tried the same trick on Ken Pound, Colin took up guard in Ken's hen-house and caught them in the act. But there was one big mystery he couldn't solve. £500 was found stuffed down the side of an old armchair in Walter's shed. Aware that the mail-van robbery was still not settled, Drury challenged Nelson Gabriel. Nelson admitted that the money was his, but insisted that he had hidden it in the chair as a surprise present for his father. PC Drury could not disprove the story.

He did his best to keep the peace in Ambridge, but once overstepped the mark by suggesting that Dan Archer form a vigilante group to discourage robberies from the church. When his superiors heard about this, Colin was severely reprimanded. Though Colin enjoyed village life, his wife Barbara did not. In the thirteen years she spent in Ambridge she made few friends and was keen to return to the bustle of city life. Colin finally gave way to her persuasion and took a town posting where he was promoted to sergeant.

John Baddeley

D UPONT, MISS

While Miss Dupont enjoyed getting to know Jack Woolley when her school party from Borchester visited Grey Gables in 1979, her pupils were grudgingly entertained by Tom Forrest and George Barford, with the aid of ferrets supplied by Joe Grundy. Jack's interest was rapidly quenched when he found that the boys had covered the animals' box with his jacket, making it reek of ferret.

DYER, ALICE

Blind since the age of three, Alice Dyer, Bess Cooper's little niece, wanted to learn the piano. Her parents could not afford one. Secretly, her uncle Simon Cooper and her father Edward scraped together every penny they could, bought a piano and led the little girl into their front room on Christmas Day in 1951 to receive her present. She was overjoyed.

ECCLES, ELVIS, MADONNA AND MARILYN

In the spring of 1993, a peacock appeared at the Bull. Sid Perks, the landlord, christened him Eccles. He and his wife Kathy were so taken with Eccles that, when he disappeared, they arranged to get three more from Lower Loxley Hall. These were named Elvis, Marilyn and Madonna. They did not prove to be the success that Eccles had been, for there were complaints about their aggression to the customers and damage to neighbours' property. All three came to sad ends: two were found in the village pond and the third was run over after a rowdy night at the Bull. Fortunately, in his own good time, Eccles reappeared and decided to take up residence.

EDDIE

Agricultural student helping at Brookfield during 1975 while Jethro Larkin was off with a broken leg.

EDWARDS, MR

Employer of Len Thomas until January 1955, when after a row Len gave in his notice.

EDWARDS, PERCY

Entertainer Percy Edwards, famed for his animal and bird impersonations, was the celebrity guest at the 1963 Christmas concert in the village hall.

EKLAND, BRITT

When William and Edward Grundy entered a children's competition for tickets to *Aladdin* in Birmingham, their father Eddie discovered that the prize included a meeting with the star, Britt Ekland. He wasted no time in putting in several entries himself, in the boys' names, and found himself the winner. A beer during the interval of the pantomime, a glass of champagne backstage afterwards and, not least, an extreme attack of nerves all combined to ill effect, and he had to make an undignified exit, while the rest of the family enjoyed their meeting with Britt. The village heard of the encounter often from Eddie – though in a rather different version, usually beginning, in smug tones, 'Me and Britt ...'

EL DORADO

Walter Gabriel's junk yard, El Dorado, opened in Felpersham in November 1961 next door to the pet shop in which he and Mrs Turvey were partners. It failed to live up to its ambitious name and lasted less than two years.

ELLAND, JAMES

James Elland was the local bank manager in 1972. Ralph Bellamy wanted to buy land in Wales and needed a loan. It was not forthcoming – he was that sort of bank manager.
John Baddeley

ELLIOTT, JIM AND MEG

Jim was the tenant farmer of Bridge Farm, and he was nearing retirement when in 1977 he died in Borchester General Hospital after a heart attack. He left behind him a widow, Meg, and a grown-up son and daughter. The Elliotts had been well liked in the village but their activities had been restricted by the poor state of Jim's health. However, many people turned up at his funeral and in accor-

dance with her husband's wishes Meg arranged with Sid Perks to give them all a drink at the Bull, in Jim's memory.

Meg decided to live near her son, and left Bridge Farm as soon as she could to enable the new tenants, Pat and Tony Archer, to move in.

ELLIS, HAROLD

No one knew why Harold Ellis put up with the treatment he received from his employer, Bert Gibbs, in the seventies. Local speculation was that Bert 'had something on him'; certainly the only favour Harold ever received from him was free transport to work.

ELPHINSTONE, MRS

One of a group of parishioners, including Mrs P., who spoke out strongly against the use of the Series Three communion service at St Stephen's in 1976.
Patricia Greene

ESCOTT, DAVE

Dave Escott was an unscrupulous business-man who got to know Peggy Archer when he was staying in the Bull in 1974. He told her that he was an interior design consultant with his own company, Escott Design Service, and that he would decorate the Ploughman Bar free of charge to promote his business. Peggy found him attractive and agreed to the idea, although when he urged her to become his business partner she resisted the temptation. Alarm bells began to ring when he offered her money to recommend him to all her friends, and she was horrified when he sent her a cheque after Jack Woolley offered him work at Grey Gables. She immediately sent it back, but the situation aroused Jack's interest and he found out that Escott was an undischarged bankrupt with an unregistered company. After a few words from Jack, Escott found it expedient to disappear, leaving a cheque to pay for his stay at the Bull. It bounced. Peggy did not pursue the matter, though she was not particularly grateful to Jack for his interference, as she felt that she could have managed Escott perfectly well on her own.

Charles Collingwood

EVANS, ANGELA (NÉE COOPER)

The Coopers – Stanley and his daughter Angela – arrived in Ambridge in 1972 to run the village shop for Jack Woolley. Angela looked after the post office section, and soon became a familiar sight in the village buzzing around on her scooter as she delivered the papers. She had an unpleasant experience when she was assaulted on her way home one October night in the same year, but she managed to escape and the man responsible, a stranger to her, was caught and arrested. Her life took a turn for the better when she fell in love with Gwyn Evans. For Gwyn's sake she tried to protect the reputation of his scapegoat brother Dylan when she discovered that he had stolen £20. She even sold her precious scooter to repay the money. She was more than delighted to see Dylan leave Ambridge shortly afterwards.

Gwyn and Angela wanted to get married, but obstacles were put in their way. Haydn Evans, Gwyn's father, wanted Gwyn to settle down at Willow Farm and felt that Angela was far too flighty and would interfere with his concentration. Stanley Cooper didn't like Gwyn at all and thought Angela could do better for herself. Such well-reasoned opposition had predictable results: in April 1973 the couple eloped. They were married by special licence and emigrated to Canada.

Elizabeth Revill

EVANS, DYLAN

Dylan Evans arrived unexpectedly in Ambridge in 1972. He was the no-good son of Haydn Evans and brother of Gwyn. His time in Ambridge was mercifully brief but he left a trail of debts behind him.

Donald Houston

EVANS' FARM

see Willow Farm

EVANS, GWYN

Gwyn's father Haydn Evans bought 100 acres north of Lakey Hill specially for Gwyn in 1972, but Gwyn shocked him by falling for Angela Cooper, marrying her and moving to faraway Vancouver. His marriage, one gathers, was rocky at times. Gwyn became a townie and worked in a shoe shop.

John Ogwen

EVANS, HAYDN

Haydn Evans's principal reason for buying Willow Farm in 1972 was his son, Gwyn. But the Welsh boy soon fell in love with Angela Cooper and the two decided to emigrate to Canada. The farm was too big for Haydn to manage on his own and he offered Tony a partnership. Tony jumped at the chance (and ultimately married Haydn's niece, Pat).

When Martha Woodford moved to Ambridge he bought her cottage in Penny Hassett. He loved the place and, determined to give it a Welsh name, called it 'Haford' (or 'haven', in English). Walter kindly offered to carve a nameplate for him, but when Haydn caught Mrs P.'s eye, jealous Walter was far from amused. Back came the plaque and Haydn was furious: it read 'Hallog',

meaning polluted. Happily their petty squabble was soon over and a sign reading 'Haford' went up on Haydn's door.

When Tony and Pat married in 1974 Haydn decided to leave them to run the farm and bought the garage from Ralph Bellamy. He ran it successfully for several years. At the same time he was heavily involved with village life. He was a member of the parish council, captain of the bowls team and had even succeeded in creating the Ambridge Chorale. As retirement approached he began to think more and more of returning to Wales. In 1981 he sold up in Ambridge and returned to the land of his fathers.

Charles Williams

EVANS THE MUCK

When Tony and Pat Archer decided to turn to organic farming in 1985, Tony found a useful source of help and advice in a Welsh farmer known as Evans the Muck.

FAIRBROTHER, GEORGE EDWARD

1 dtr; m. Helen Carey 17 April 1952; 1 son

George Fairbrother very nearly changed the look and character of Ambridge altogether.

After making a small fortune from plastics this widower bought a farm in the village in 1951 and settled in with his daughter Grace. The accidental discovery of ironstone on his land fired his imagination and he immediately set in motion plans to mine the ore, unaware of how contentious these plans would appear to other Ambridge landowners. Ambridge remained agricultural only by the timely intervention of Squire Lawson-Hope, who proved to the owner of the mineral rights, Mr Crawford, that it would not be in the majority of folk's interests to develop iron at the expense of farming. George protested that parochial Ambridge had become old-fashioned and was only slowly brought round to dropping his industrial plans and getting on with being a gentleman farmer.

Grace was the indulged and only apple of his eye until, fishing one day in his trout stream, he realized that he had become captive to the charming Helen Carey. They were married in 1952 and a year later a son, Robin, was born.

Although he was pleased to officiate at children's sports events and on one occasion introduce Gilbert Harding at the church fête,

Grace and George Fairbrother (Ysanne Churchman and Leslie Bowmar)

George and Helen Fairbrother (Leslie Bowmar and Joy Davies) with Robin Fairbrother

he was primarily a forward-looking energetic businessman. With the able help of Phil Archer (whom he made a director), his estate grew to be more than 1000 acres. His farming interests embraced high-yield land, broiler chickens, breeding and showing pedigree cattle, and a packaging business. At one point Carol Grey remonstrated with him

about 'trying to organize the whole village to his particular needs'.

His high-handed attitude involved him in some minor legal battles. He was fined 10s. with 8 guineas costs at Borchester petty session for shooting a racing pigeon; charged by PC Bryden with setting fire to gorse on Lakey Hill without a licence; and fined £8 for allowing his Ayrshire cattle to be infected with warble. When his help was needed, though, he gave it. When Tom Forrest was accused of manslaughter, George paid for his defence. After hesitating on the advisability of Grace running a riding school, he finally relented and gave her his wholehearted support. He reacted in the same way to her pursuit of Phil Archer, whom she married in 1955. Even after her tragic death later that year he involved Phil in his long-term plans.

In 1959 he sold his house and land to Charles Grenville and he and his family quietly left the village.

Leslie Bowmar

FAIRBROTHER, GRACE

see Archer, Grace

FAIRBROTHER, HELEN (FORMERLY CAREY)

m. 17 April 1952

Helen Carey, a pleasant and well-mannered widow aged forty-two, arrived in Ambridge in 1951 with her son Alan to stay with her old friend Squire Lawson-Hope.

From the upper middle classes, Helen enjoyed a glass of dry sherry, cubbing, playing the piano and croquet. George Fairbrother and she met socially and their friendship soon turned to love. Apprehensive at first of George's daughter Grace, she nevertheless shyly accepted George's proposal of marriage and settled in the village. Her stepdaughter made Helen's position difficult to begin with but with her well-bred tact and sensitivity, Helen won Grace's favour.

A visit to her London doctor, ostensibly because of migraine, confirmed that she was soon to have a child. In 1953 Robin was born, to his father's delight and his mother's relief. Alan's child was born in 1956, making her a grandmother.

A lady of her time, she did not concern herself directly with her husband's business affairs, but worked behind the scenes on his behalf; nor did she flinch from censuring him for his high-handed attitude to his employees. She persisted in her support of Jim Benson when Fairbrother sacked him for rudeness to her, admitting that she had goaded him with her insistent questions, and winning his reinstatement; and she kept an eye on Mary Jones as she struggled to care for her ill father.

After Grace's untimely death in 1955 Helen was a comfort to George, sensibly reminding him that life had to go on.

Helen was sad to leave Ambridge after the house and land were sold to Charles Grenville in 1959. She returned to make final preparations for Grace's memorial window at the church. Fifteen years later she came on a visit from Kenya to Carol Tregorran.

Joy Davies

FAIRBROTHER, ROBIN EDWARD

b. 6 Feb. 1953

Robin Fairbrother was the son of Helen and George Fairbrother, and half-brother to Phil Archer's first wife, Grace. He and his family left the village when he was a little boy.

Elizabeth Archer met him in 1987. By then thirty-four years old, he was a wine-importer and owned a house in the Dordogne. Elizabeth couldn't understand Jill's refusal to invite him for dinner. The truth was that he revived far too many painful emotions for Jill, including a dormant jealousy of Grace. Just when Jill started to mellow sufficiently to invite him to lunch, Elizabeth guiltily broke the news that he had a wife, and although separated he still saw her. Robin's wife was a hospital registrar working in London and when he disappeared for a week Elizabeth feared the worst. He didn't answer her calls and refused tea at Brookfield. When Elizabeth caught sight of him at Nelson's Wine Bar, he had no choice but to explain that he didn't want to see her again because he was trying to save his marriage. She dashed her glass of wine into his face.

FAIRLIE, HELEN

Miss Fairlie was engaged as a chauffeuse-cum-housekeeper to Laura Archer after Roger Travers-Macy left in March 1966. For some years she worked quite happily in this domineering lady's employ until she was sacked when Laura decided that she could no longer afford to keep a car.

FARM SHOPS

In 1973 Carol Tregorran suggested to Ken Pound that they should go into partnership and open a shop. She wanted an outlet for the sale of fruit and vegetables from her market garden and wondered if he would be interested in a similar outlet for his dairy produce.

They got permission from Ralph Bellamy to convert part of the stables at Ambridge Farm into a shop which was opened on 7 April 1974. It did very well until threatened with closure by the local planning authorities, who said that it interfered with local trade and caused a traffic hazard. Carol and Ken pleaded their cause and in the end the authorities gave way.

Carol withdrew from the partnership in 1976 and the shop was closed when Ken and Mary Pound left Ambridge in 1983. The following year Mike and Betty Tucker, who were then renting Ambridge Farm, made a brief attempt to resuscitate the shop as Betty's Barn. Mike thoughtfully rigged up a bell to ring in the kitchen every time a customer arrived at the shop, but Betty found running to and fro exhausting, and by the end of July it was shut for good.

At the end of 1992 Pat and Tony Archer opened a farm shop at Bridge Farm to sell their organic produce. It was so successful that they immediately applied for permission to expand and, despite local opposition and the duplicity of Howard Friend, a potential competitor, were allowed to go ahead.

FEATHERSTONE, HENRY

Henry Featherstone owned a bookshop in partnership with John Tregorran and later Roger Travers-Macy, who persuaded him to print a catalogue of his old books for circulation to collectors. In the spring of 1969 he planned to go to live with his married daughter, who lived in Scarborough.

Ralph Truman

FELPERSHAM

Ambridge lies seventeen miles west of the cathedral city of Felpersham. The city has a hospital, Crown Court, repertory theatre and cinema as well as a prison and a dry ski slope. St George's Day is celebrated there each year with a procession of floats called 'the Riding of St George' and a variety of other festivities.

FENNER-BROCKMAN, DUNCAN

On one of his Home Farm shoots in 1989, Brian Aldridge was as usual anxious to impress. All went exceptionally well until Duncan Fenner-Brockman demanded a better position and took offence when Brian sent Tom Forrest to suggest he swap with someone else. This was not the personal attention to which he felt entitled and he stormed off.

FERGUSON, MR

The bank manager with whom the Archer

family met to discuss ways they might sort out the financial problems surrounding Paul Johnson late in 1977.

FERGUSSON, SHEILA

Jill Archer met Sheila Fergusson at her French classes at the Borchester Technical College in 1977. Sheila was a lively extrovert who, with her assumption that husbands could survive on their own while their wives had a good time, swept aside some of the cobwebs in Phil and Jill Archer's marriage. She persuaded Jill to go to Paris with her for a three-day break, and to Jill's amazement Phil raised no objection. This may have been due in part to the fact that Sheila fascinated him. When she rode up to tea at Brookfield on her son's motor-bike, he couldn't take his eyes off her or her eye-catching clothes and enjoyed her bubbly conversation.

Sheila wanted to extend the holiday by another ten days and Jill kept Phil on tenterhooks over whether she would or not. In the end three days were quite enough in Sheila's company and Jill came home exhausted. She hadn't learned another of Sheila's tricks – how to get extra booze through the customs – but Sheila generously gave Phil a litre of Cointreau as his share of the spoils. As generous in her conversation, she dropped Jill in it by describing the fun they'd had with Henry and Clive from Scarborough, as well as with André, Gaston and Maurice. Phil didn't feel that there was safety in numbers and it took Jill some time to smooth down his ruffled feathers.

Linda Polan

FISHER, LOUIS

When Jean-Paul went to work at Nelson Gabriel's Wine Bar in 1990, following a disagreement with Jack Woolley at Grey Gables, Nelson invited *The Borchester Echo*'s famous food critic Louis Fisher to sample Jean-Paul's latest culinary creation. Nelson was astounded when no review appeared in the paper and accused Jack Woolley, proprietor of the *Echo*, of spiking the review in spite. He didn't believe him when he denied it.

FLETCHER, DEREK AND PAT

Pat and Derek Fletcher were first-time buyers of one of the houses on Jack Woolley's new development at the Glebelands in 1979. They didn't enjoy living in the country, particularly when they found Susan Carter's pig Pinky, who had escaped from his pen, asleep in their kitchen. They were very irritated when the environmental health inspector found no cause for complaint and shocked to discover from the housing department that pigs could be kept as pets on council property. Their troubles didn't stop there. Nigel Pargetter managed to sell them a fishpond, which was in fact a paddling pool. He and Shula Archer filled it one night, singing at the tops of their voices and waking up half Glebelands. The Fletchers went off on a golfing holiday to recover.

FLYNN, RITA

Rita Flynn was an Irish girl who came to

work for Doughy Hood in the fifties and lived in a caravan on his ground. She divorced her husband, who had been in prison in Aberdeen for robbery and violence. A warm-hearted creature, she flirted with Phil Archer and was pursued by others. Doughy grew very fond of her and, despite her protestations, made a will in her favour. In 1961 she announced her engagement to Michael O'Leary and they went to Ireland at Easter.

June Spencer

Forrest, doris

see Archer, Doris

Forrest – foster children

see Martin, Johnny and Stephens, Peter

Forrest, prudence (pru, née harris)

b. 27 July 1921; m. Tom Forrest 26 Sept. 1958

When Pru Harris worked at the Bull in the early fifties, Tom Forrest grew used to seeing her attractive figure behind the bar. Everyone in Ambridge knew long before Tom that Pru was the right girl for him, but he didn't propose until February 1958. By September they were married, but already Pru was showing signs of ill-health. Shortly after their wedding a patch on her lung was discovered and she had to spend six months in a sanatorium.

In 1960 the Forrests decided to foster two small boys, Johnny Martin and his friend Peter Stevens, and Pru had her hands full looking after them as they grew up. An excellent cook and gardener, she managed to win no less than fifteen first prizes in the Ambridge flower and produce show in 1985, to the annoyance of all her rivals.

When Sid and Polly Perks took over the Bull in 1972, they realized that they couldn't afford two barmaids. Pru was very upset when they asked her to leave. But the cloud had a silver lining, for Phil Archer urgently needed help at Brookfield in Jill's absence, and when Jill returned two months later, she asked Pru to continue as housekeeper. Pru did so happily for several years. Her life took a new direction in 1976 when Tom retired as Jack Woolley's head keeper and was asked to manage the new garden centre opening at Grey Gables, with Pru as his assistant. She continued to work there when Tom moved on to take charge of Woolley's fishery a year later.

The Forrests suffered a major upheaval in their lives together when in 1991 Pru had a stroke and was taken to hospital. After her return home she was discussing the harvest supper when she had another stroke, more serious than the first. Despite all the signs to the contrary, Tom was convinced that she would make a full recovery, but Pru needed specialist care that he could not supply. She now lives in a nursing home called the Laurels, with a comfortable room of her own and a view from the window which embraces Lakey Hill.

Mary Dalley; Judi Dench

Forrest, Thomas William (Tom)

b. 20 Oct. 1910; m. Pru Harris 26 Sept. 1958

Tom Forrest became a gamekeeper like his father before him. His knowledge of country life and lore is vast and like his sister, Doris, he never wanted any other life than that of rural Borsetshire. In his time he has been employed by Squire Lawson-Hope, George Fairbrother, Charles Grenville (who built him the new Keeper's Cottage in 1960), Ralph Bellamy and Jack Woolley, who gave him a silver tea-set when he retired in 1976.

His hours as a keeper were often long and arduous as he battled to keep poachers and other vermin away from his game. He didn't take holidays and it was not until 1970 that he had Boxing Day off. Though he had many good friends in the village and the door at Brookfield was always open for him, his life was an essentially lonely one.

Then, as executor of her mother's will, he got to know Pru Harris, who was working as a barmaid at the Bull. Tom began to spend more time at the Bull, but his mind was not always on his dominoes. Then Bob Larkin arrived in the village and began to make advances towards Pru. It was obvious to all that Tom was very upset and angry.

One night while stalking poachers, he accidentally shot and killed one. It happened to be Bob Larkin and he was arrested on the charge of manslaughter. Most of the village stood by him: they couldn't believe Tom could be guilty. When he was acquitted there was a triumphal return to the village. Walter Gabriel organized a silver band and the car Tom was in was pulled through the streets. He proposed to Pru in February 1958 but it was five months before they were married, as Tom wanted to get his pheasant chicks hatched and put under cover. The couple were married quietly in September 1958.

A month later he was on his own again:

Tom Forrest (Bob Arnold)

a shadow had been found on Pru's lung and she had to go to a sanatorium for eight months. He was delighted to see her back and they settled down to cosy domesticity. Unable to have children of their own they fostered Peter Stephens and Johnny Martin. Both boys had come from a children's home and could sometimes be naughty and wayward. But Tom and Pru persevered and by the time Peter and Johnny left Ambridge, they were hard-working young men.

Tom retired as Jack Woolley's head keeper in 1976 and managed Woolley's new garden centre instead, with Pru as his assistant. But the profits didn't satisfy Jack; so he brought in an expert, Jim Bolton, to improve matters, and asked Tom to manage the fish farm – a job that appealed to Tom. When Gordon Armstrong left in 1978 he was also able to help with the keepering once more. In 1989 Brian Aldridge asked him to act as a full-time gamekeeper for Home Farm but Tom, then seventy-nine, had to refuse – although he has occasionally helped Brian prepare for a shoot.

At home, Pru was content to go on filling the shelves at Keeper's Cottage with her jams and jellies while Tom toiled in the garden. Between the two of them over the years they have won almost every prize at the Ambridge flower and produce show, many of them several times over.

In 1991, Pru had a stroke. Tom was determined that he should look after her at home but when a second stroke left her speechless he was forced to let her go into a nursing home.

Age and loneliness have taken their toll on Tom. He has become rather truculent, as Jill Archer found when he went to stay at Brookfield after breaking a bone in his ankle, slipping on Clarrie Grundy's highly polished floor, but essentially the old Tom remains. He still has a lovely singing voice which is heard at most village events and his rivalry with Bert Fry over who has the best garden is undiminished. He has had to retire as a churchwarden and is no longer the leader of the bell-ringers but his staunch Christian faith still sustains him.

George Hart; Bob Arnold

FORSYTH, MR

When Sid Perks had trouble in 1977 with his tenants, the Briggs, Tony Archer recommended that he should consult his solicitor, Forsyth. He explained that the Briggs were protected tenants under the Rent Act and as they had a small child the court might well find in their favour. However, he was willing to give them a month's notice on Sid's behalf and tell them that a court order would be served if the rent wasn't paid in seven days.

FOSTER, BRUNO

b. early 1989

Son of Snatch Foster, godson of Eddie Grundy – God help him!

FOSTER, JOHN

The land commissioner who came to Brookfield in 1958 to discuss Dan Archer's plans for the co-operative.

FOSTER, MRS

Secretary of the Borchester Goat Society, who advised Betty Tucker when she started to keep goats in 1975 and found her two pedigree goats to start her herd.

FOSTER, SNATCH

Snatch Foster is one of Eddie Grundy's friends. They usually meet in the Cat and Fiddle because he has been banned from the Bull since 1976. (The ban was for life, but has frequently had to be repeated, as Snatch hasn't taken it too literally.)

Snatch named his baby son after the boxer Frank Bruno and wanted him to be baptized. The vicar, Jerry Buckle, planned a joint christening for Bruno with Alice Aldridge, despite everything the Aldridges could do to make him change his mind. The ill-matched double splashing was as embarrassing as they had feared – but because Alice screamed and Bruno behaved like an angel.

FRANCES (FRAN)

Phil and Jill Archer were worried when in 1988 they found out that their son David was seeing a divorced woman. Frances was an old friend of Caroline Bone's and formerly a nurse in Felpersham, but they felt that the fact that she was thirty-three and had two children made her an unsuitable girlfriend. They were much relieved when she told David that their relationship was over, as she preferred her independence to becoming a farmer's wife.

FRANKLIN, BASIL

When Basil Franklin and Nelson Gabriel came out of the RAF in 1961, they started a light engineering business together in Borchester.

Donald Scott

FRASER, ALAN

This handsome and steel-eyed fitness fanatic was a hard man. At eighteen he joined the Parachute Regiment. Some say he was in the SAS. Later he became a courier and then a bodyguard. It was said that Fraser was not his real name – a dark horse, indeed.

He had been in Venezuela with Nelson Gabriel for a time. He came to live at the Lodge in 1981 and became romantically linked with Caroline Bone. He possessed few belongings, made frequent trips abroad and seemed unlikely ever to settle down, although Caroline would loved him to have done so.

He spent Christmas with her and together they saw in the New Year at a party at Brookfield. But at the end of January he left Ambridge to fetch a low-loader from the Middle East and was never seen again. Poor Caroline!

Crawford Logan; Peter Wickham

FRASER, ANN

When Grace Fairbrother turned down his proposal, Alan Carey went to visit friends in Yorkshire, where he met Ann. They fell in love and became engaged. He brought her down to meet his mother, Helen Carey, on the occasion of her wedding to George Fairbrother in 1952, and then they returned to Yorkshire.

Noreen Baddiley

FRASER, CAMERON

b. 31 Oct. 1954

Cameron Fraser arrived in Ambridge in 1990. He had bought the Berrow Estate and, on moving into the Dower House, he spent a small fortune modernizing it. He gave every appearance of a man of sophistication and wealth who lived life to the full. His easy manner and gentle Scots brogue suggested sensitivity and kindness. The exterior was convincing enough to attract Caroline Bone, who, recovering from her relationship with the rather dull Matthew Thorogood, was ready for some excitement.

With Fraser, she found it, more, in fact, than she'd bargained for. At first the social whirl took her happily away, but then doubts began to creep in. To his estate workers he was good news, playing the country squire to the hilt, exuding charm all over the place, and assuring everyone (via Shula Archer in the Estate office) that their jobs were safe and that nothing would change. His only enemy was Brian Aldridge, and he was simply jealous because of Caroline.

Within six months, though, things began to change. Perhaps he just stopped trying to please. When Shula was absent because of her ectopic pregnancy, Caroline was infuriated by his callous attitude towards her best friend. He angered Caroline further by announcing that he'd be in Scotland for Hogmanay that year, and therefore unable to attend Jack and Peggy Woolley's wedding at Grey Gables. What's more, he failed to see why she felt she couldn't go with him. By the time he returned, warning bells were starting to ring in Caroline's ears and she was having serious doubts about the man. For a time, they blew hot and cold with each other. But then Caroline wanted out.

Elizabeth Archer, on the other hand, wanted in. Following some outrageously flirtatious behaviour, she stepped into the shoes that Caroline had left. Soon she was blindly, desperately in love with Cameron.

Back in the Estate office, Cameron had let the mask slip. After her marriage to Jack Woolley, Peggy resigned without regrets, relieved to escape his rudeness. Shula clashed with him too, over his abrasive style. They disagreed about who should have Ivy Cottage when its tenancy was reviewed, and in the ensuing row Cameron threatened to remove his Estate business from Rodway & Watson. Shula retorted that she would be happy to move off the account, but Cameron was forced to eat humble pie when, unable to find a suitable replacement, he had to ask Shula back. She agreed only when he promised not to interfere with her work.

Serious trouble was to follow. Poor Mike Tucker lost an eye working for Fraser. He showed no concern whatever, apart from worrying about the legal implications. With pressure mounting, he got drunk at Nelson Gabriel's Wine Bar and let a few indiscreet revelations slip out. Apparently, ten years earlier he had done a six-month stretch in prison for fraud. He was anxious to avoid another brush with the law at all costs, and in this instance succeeded as the charge was brought against his farm manager, Geoff Williams, who was fired.

Nigel Pargetter's fondness for Elizabeth

Cameron Fraser (Delaval Astley) and Caroline Bone (Sara Coward)

Financial problems were closing in on Fraser. By April 1992 his company in Scotland was on the verge of going bust. More and more investors were demanding to know about their savings. Fraser had, in fact, been embezzling his clients' money, reinvesting it, and was in the process of losing the gamble.

Fraser had to buy time. He flew back to Scotland, breaking a date with Elizabeth, and phoning her with promises of a holiday. Their future together needed careful planning, he said. Elizabeth allowed herself to be reassured. On his return she met him once more and the two of them drove off down the M40 apparently to begin their holiday. Elizabeth talked constantly of their baby. Cameron listened in silence. He pulled into a motorway café and they ordered a meal. Then he told Elizabeth to wait. Fifteen minutes later, he had not returned. Nervously she asked the waiter to check the toilets. He told her that he'd seen Fraser driving away at speed. Cameron had gone for ever.

Poor, pregnant Elizabeth – abandoned by the man she loved so much. She had an abortion. The people of Ambridge, including Caroline and Marjorie Antrobus, who had invested several thousands of pounds with Cameron Fraser, and Elizabeth, who had invested a great deal more than that, were left to pick up the pieces and regret the day he had come into their lives.

Delaval Astley

FREDA

Freda was a Middle White sow who came to Brookfield in 1987 after Dan Archer's old

infuriated Fraser (Elizabeth enjoyed being dizzy piggy in the middle). He took her to dinner, away for weekends, showered her with presents. He was her Prince Charming. But in May 1992 the carousel of fun and laughter came to an abrupt halt: Elizabeth was pregnant. When she told him that she wanted to have his baby, she was badly shaken by his off-hand, unconcerned reaction. So what? – have an abortion, he told her.

friend Jim Palmer had a heart attack and asked Phil to look after her. She was pregnant and Phil's son David was concerned about the possibility of cross-infection with their own pigs. Phil agreed that Freda could go to Nightingale Farm where David's girl-friend Ruth could care for her. Mrs Antrobus gave a warm welcome to the sow and to the litter that soon arrived; but her dogs and the piglets proved to be incompatible, so they had to return to Brookfield. Looking after Freda, Phil developed a soft spot for her, which made him reluctant to send her to market. To the unsentimental David's disgust, Jill encouraged Phil to keep her. But when on Christmas Day in 1991 Freda produced a litter of only three piglets, Phil had to accept that her time had come. She went to market in February. He was saddened at her departure but took comfort in the two piglets he kept and named Milly and Molly.

FREEMAN, ROBIN

Robin Freeman was a botanist who in 1970 was appointed warden of the Field Study Centre at Arkwright Hall, where he lived with his wife Zoe. They were an unhappy couple; their marriage had been scarred by the death of their only child, and his experiences as a Japanese prisoner of war. Zoe didn't settle down well in Ambridge, and suffered from fits of depression. Her problems eventually overcame them both and she left Robin in July 1973. He was worried that he would have to leave his post, as it had been advertised for a married man, and the Field Studies Council asked for his resignation.

Dan Archer told him to fight the decision, and Jack Woolley came to his aid. Eventually he was able to stay on with an appointed housekeeper, Mrs Dickson.

Peggy Archer asked for his help when Jack Woolley started to pursue her too rigorously, but her plan rebounded when Robin became equally attentive. In the end she used her work at the Bull as an excuse to keep both men at bay.

After starting a dig in Jiggons Field, which had Anglo-Saxon connections, Robin decided to accept an academic post elsewhere and left Ambridge in October 1974.

Peter Kenvyn

FREEMAN, ZOE

Zoe was the wife of Robin Freeman who was appointed warden of the Field Study Centre in 1970. They had had a child who died in infancy and she had never fully recovered, suffering from fits of depression and erratic behaviour. She consented to attend the psychiatric unit at Borchester General Hospital, but seemed to find more comfort in her friendship with Alan Nicholas, an itinerant guitar player.

When Jill Archer was away in London, Zoe called unexpectedly on Phil Archer, ostensibly to tell him that Alan was a bad influence on Tony Archer. Six days later she turned up once more and Shula Archer discovered her kissing Phil passionately. When Phil told Robin what had happened Robin confessed his fear that Zoe was a nymphomaniac. He confided his troubles to Peggy Archer and when Zoe turned up at the Bull with another man in tow, Peggy gave instructions that she was not to be served. Zoe left Robin and Ambridge for good in July 1973. This was one of the rare instances when the local community failed one of its members.

Margot Young

FRIEND, HOWARD

When Pat and Tony Archer submitted plans for expansion of their farm shop to the local planning committee, they were disconcerted when their application was turned down, especially when they learned that unexpected objections had been raised by the Borsetshire Environment Trust, headed by Howard Friend. Tony revised his plans in accordance with the Trust's recommendations and resubmitted them, but the planning committee deferred its decision and a preservation order was slammed on a beech tree he had intended to cut down in order to enlarge the shop entrance. His suspicions were aroused when Mike Tucker told him that Howard Friend was opening a shop near Felpersham which would be selling organic produce, and confirmed when Lynda Snell explained how Friend had approached her to obtain information about Bridge Farm and its future prospects.

Tackled by Tony about the integrity of his actions Friend remained enigmatic, and when planning permission was finally granted he condescendingly told Tony that his plans for his own shop would be unaffected.

Geoffrey Whitehead

FRY, ALISON

Wife of Gavin Fry, Alison is a friend of Betty Tucker's. Her children often play with Roy Tucker.

FRY, BERT

b. 1936

When Shula Hebden told her father that one of the tenanted farms on the Berrow Estate was being taken over, and that the foreman was being made redundant, Phil Archer was delighted. This meant that Bert Fry was available.

Phil was looking for a farm worker, and, with Ruth Archer leaving to go back to college, the timing was perfect. Bert had an enviable reputation in the district as a highly skilled and experienced man, with a natural understanding and sensitivity towards the land. Jill Archer was also in need of a cleaning lady, and Bert's wife Freda was ready to help out. Bert and Freda moved into Woodbine Cottage, and by the summer of 1988 became an integral part of Brookfield Farm.

Bert has won honours locally at a number of ploughing matches, and when he beat David Archer shortly after he came to Brookfield, it was felt that justice had been done. He has a facility with words, and can often be heard making up sayings and rhyming couplets. Elizabeth Archer thought they should be shared more widely and engaged Bert to write a weekly special for

Bert Fry (Roger Hume)

The Borchester Echo. So gladly did he respond that, apart from driving Elizabeth nearly mad, his relentless outpourings became a great success. The local television company became interested, and the thought of media stardom rather went to Bert's head. He felt patronized, however, when a smart producer made him take off his pink shirt and dark suit and wear rough peasant clothes for the programme instead. Even Lynda Snell had to draw the line when Bert produced a poster for her production of *The Importance of Being Earnest*, which read 'featuring TV personality Bert Fry'.

He had two cats, Tinker and Pickle, and when Bert was suffering from a touch of writer's block, Ruth suggested he write a column on cats. Tinker arrived home with a rat, and jogged Bert's memory. Once he'd owned a cat with false teeth, he said, but it was hopeless at ratting.

Life in Woodbine Cottage suited Bert and Freda fine, but in 1990 a poll tax demand arrived. Jill helped him with the forms, but it was Freda's contribution that worried Bert. He sold his beloved old Wolseley, bought a Granada and began running it as a taxi for his brother-in-law, Alfie. The taxi earnings enabled him to pay off Freda's poll tax and he was content.

Once he drove David to the end-of-term ball at Harper Adams College. He was supposed to drop off David, load up with Ruth's belongings and drive back to Ambridge. Ruth would bring David back in her car the following morning. Bert, having delivered David, took himself off for a wander round the college kitchens. It was hot and he was thirsty. Seeing a large jug of fruit cocktail, he quaffed it down in large, grateful gulps. It was rather more alcoholic than it looked, and Bert had to be put to bed in Ruth's room while she and David danced the night away.

Bert is a regular churchgoer, proud to be made deputy churchwarden and the official winder of the church clock. It was a frightening moment when, showing William Grundy the workings of the clocktower, a large weight crashed to the floor, narrowly missing the heir to the Grundy dynasty. Bert was mortified. By way of apology, he gave William a pot of Freda's rowan jam. Clarrie was uncertain whether to eat it or rub it on William's chest.

For a man in his fifties, Bert is in fine physical shape. When, in order to attract new members, the health club at Grey Gables offered the first free membership to the winner of the fittest man competition, Bert won hands down. A modest man, he took a little persuading before he felt brave enough to use the luxurious facilities on offer. He finally plucked up courage and went to sample the sauna. He found himself sharing the steam with Lynda Snell and Jennifer Aldridge. Poor, pink Bert! He didn't know where to look.

Sometimes he gets the wrong end of the stick. When he overheard Phil and David discussing getting rid of Freda, he was terribly worried. Freda not wanted at Brookfield any more? Phil realized what had happened and explained: it was Freda the pig that had to go, not Mrs Fry.

Bert and Freda have a traditional marriage, but Bert showed that he could be a 'new man' when it came to babies: he was the one who could calm little Pip Archer down in his strong arms, when a spot of emergency babysitting was needed.

They are by now an integral part of life at Brookfield, and in Ambridge, too. Bert is a link with a past kind of farming that is rapidly vanishing. Long live Bert Fry – even his rhyming couplets.

Roger Hume

FRY, FREDA

The overall winner of the 1990 flower and produce show, Freda Fry is a celebrated, old-fashioned cook. Her jams, cakes, pastries and pies are all mouth-watering as Bert can testify. Butter, cream, sugar and eggs are amongst her chief ingredients and she has no time to spare for anything that smacks of *nouvelle cuisine*. Not surprisingly, Freda didn't take kindly to being told that the meals she provided at the Bull contained too much fat.

A spotless housekeeper, Freda is always in demand to clean but she has enough on her plate with Brookfield and the Dower House.

Freda is a real treasure. Bert is justifiably proud of 'his' Freda and is careful to guard her reputation. When she went to work at the Bull, he insisted that it be behind the scenes because he didn't want men ogling her.

FRY, GAVIN

Gavin Fry lives with his wife Alison and their children on the Glebelands estate. He is a touch flash: a souped-up Capri type. He owns a small 20-acre farm above Hassett Hill.

GABRIEL, NELSON

b. 1933; 1 dtr by Nancy Tarrant

When Cameron Fraser's possessions were auctioned at the Dower House in 1992, Nelson Gabriel discreetly let it be rumoured that the furniture was fake reproduction. He then scooped the pot by buying it himself and selling it on at a handsome profit. A typical Nelson Gabriel manoeuvre, it has to be said, and one which he would certainly seek to justify in his deep, sardonic, world-weary voice. His has been a history of double-dealing, brushes with the law, high hopes, many disappointments and failures. Though he has mellowed to some extent, settled down and become part of the fabric of Ambridge life, he is a leopard who has no intention whatever of changing his spots.

Nelson served out his National Service in the RAF, although he never actually flew a plane, being a member of the ground staff. In 1961 he wanted his father Walter to invest £3,000 in a light engineering business he planned to set up in Borchester and Walter sacrificed the last of his football pool winnings to help – a fool to himself, as Mrs P. was not slow to point out. Four years later Nelson forged the signature of his co-director, Toby Phillips, on a contract which could not be completed without extra capital. Carol Grenville and Paul Johnson saved the day by buying up his business, for which he was not visibly grateful. Unabashed, he was soon partnering Toby Stobeman in his betting shops, living in a luxury flat and wining and dining Jennifer Archer.

He whisked Walter off on a cruise, but he had an ulterior motive: it was all part of his secret plan to mastermind a mail-van robbery. Walter returned alone, leaving Nelson to join him by charter plane at a later date; but his plane was reported missing, and Nelson presumed dead. At first Walter's obstinate refusal to believe the news prevented him from breaking his heart, but three months later Dan Archer brought him a packet of money and a letter forwarded from the pilot at Nelson's request should anything happen to him. While Walter grieved, his son was actually alive and well, tossing back Scotch at Paunton Farm (out-

Nelson Gabriel (Jack May)

side Ambridge) while finalizing his plans for the robbery with phoney pig farmer Charles Brown, who knew him simply as 'Boss'. One of Nelson's saving graces is that beneath his smooth veneer lies a measure of incompetence, coupled with an enviable ability to escape the consequences of his actions. Not only did the robbery fail; his fingerprints were found on a bottle of Scotch in Paunton Farm and he was tracked down by Interpol and hauled before the Borchester magistrates. He was finally brought to trial at the Assizes, but managed to get himself acquit-

ted. Walter was over the moon, and was rewarded by another cruise – a pleasant change from visiting his son in prison.

After all this excitement, Nelson kept his head down. He bought Hollowtree Farmhouse for conversion into flats, but was soon away again. No one ever quite knew where he was or what he was doing, which drove Walter to distraction, although Nelson did keep an eye on his father, taking him on holiday an buying him a colour TV. He would be staying one minute at Grey Gables, the next at the Bull. You could usually tell the state of his affairs by the car he drove.

By 1980 he wanted to be based in Ambridge. He bought an old warehouse in West Street, Borchester, and converted it into a wine bar in the twenties' 'speak-easy' style. The following year he bought the vacant premises next door. He wanted to set up a sauna and massage parlour with Caroline Bone as manageress and Clarrie Grundy as chief masseuse; but rural Borsetshire was not yet ready for that. Reluctantly he decided to go in for antiques instead and Lilian Bellamy went into partnership with him. The opening day of his new antiques shop was somewhat marred when Walter fell off a chair 'renovated' by Eddie Grundy. Matters were soon to get worse. Some months later DS Dave Barry, not normally renowned for his ability to get his man, arrested Nelson for handling stolen goods. It turned out that Nelson had been buying items from a Thomas Guthrie in Glamorgan whose real name was Mackelvane and who was a thief. Barry thought that Nelson was part of a ring, and with a leap of hitherto unsuspected imagination claimed that Peggy Archer and Lilian Bellamy were also part of the conspiracy. The case was dropped for lack of evidence, but it had serious repercussions for Nelson in that Lilian pulled out of her partnership with him just when he was relying on her to take over full financial responsibility.

The next couple of years were bleak for Nelson, despite all his clever wheeling and dealing. He even had to descend to renting Sid Perks a clapped-out fruit machine, optimistically dubbed 'the Golden Plum', for £25 a week. When he waited for a delivery for the wine bar from J.T. Wholesale Importers,

it never arrived. The owner had also run into hard times and had solved it by running off with most of his customers' cash. Unable to afford to buy in more stock, Nelson had no choice but to close the wine bar and do what he always did in times of emergency: disappear.

Eventually Nelson was tracked down by Walter who persuaded him to come back to Ambridge. Walter said that he would go into partnership with him, and with money from the sale of property in Lanzarote and the supreme sarifice of exchanging his Jaguar for a Cortina Estate, Nelson was ready to open the Wine Bar again.

Fate had another trick in store. On a sunny June day in 1986 an attractive young girl turned up at the Wine Bar and Nelson froze when he heard her first words, 'Hello, Dad!' Her name was Rosemary Tarrant, and she was his daughter by one of his first girlfriends, Nancy Tarrant. He had known that Nancy was pregnant, but not that he was the father; he was not sure that he knew how to handle his new status. This was made harder still when Rosemary revealed that she was training as a police cadet. Rosemary came to live with her father at Honeysuckle Cottage for a while and generally they got on well together, although Nelson was not impressed by her boyfriends. He had always enjoyed the company of women and was disadvantaged by knowing precisely what Rosemary's boyfriends would be getting up to. When Peter, an ex-boyfriend of hers, came to spend the night at Honeysuckle Cottage he fled for refuge to Mrs P.'s.

Walter died in 1988 and left a big hole in his son's life. 'He was the sweetest man I knew,' commented Nelson; and it was that sweetness which had guided Nelson and prevented him from the worst excesses of his chosen way of life. When the lease was up on the Wine Bar and he couldn't renew it without cash, he decided to put the antiques shop up for sale, eventually selling to Kenton Archer (despite his liking for stripped pine). He felt sad and old. Mrs P. died, sharpening his sense of the end of an era, and he heralded in the new decade in a thoughtful and gentle vein.

It was Kenton who restored Nelson to his more acerbic self. Kenton's business had not thrived and Nelson took him in hand. He found a property in the Old Market Square in Borchester and set up a partnership with Kenton, who was his natural disciple; Nelson saw in his youthful attempts at conning a reflection of his own more masterful techniques. Then Nigel Pargetter's mother, Julia, swept on the scene and Nelson inexorably, delightfully, found himself almost falling in love, just when it had appeared that he had nothing left to hope for in that quarter. Their relationship is fraught and dangerous, but with his Humphrey Bogart hat on Nelson is ready for anything.

Nelson continues to run his wine bar and antiques shop, tempering his natural cynicism with wit and occasional acts of unexpected generosities.

Jack May

GABRIEL, ROSEMARY

see Tarrant, Rosemary

GABRIEL, WALTER

b. 25 Aug. 1896; 1 son; d. 3Nov. 1988

Walter's voice, said Dan Archer, sounded like a rusty nail being shoved through the bottom of a cocoa tin. He was a rascal, but had such a great benevolence and love for mankind that it was impossible to be cross with him for long. 'Hello me old pal, me old beauty,' he would cry, and everyone would cheer up. Many years later, in a moment of rare intimacy, he confessed to Mrs Perkins that he mispronounced words so as to make people laugh; he wasn't always as guileless as he appeared.

To begin with, his farm was a village disgrace and he was sometimes drunk. He was brought up short when Squire Lawson-Hope put his farm under supervision, and saved by Mrs Perkins, who loaned him £400 to put it to rights, which he did. By 1953 he was telling Jack Archer that he was going to propose to Mrs P., but he was put off when Jack laughed and said that he was only after her money. Secretly a romantic, Walter was so shocked that his motives might be misconstrued that he ducked the issue – and so began the longest courtship ritual in Ambridge history. It took him seventeen years to pluck up courage to propose again, but Mrs P. turned him down. He was a jealous lover and constantly checking on her other suitors. They came and went – or in the case of her second husband, Albert Perkins, came and stayed – but Mrs P. was always true to Walter in her fashion. She was his loyal friend and mentor, and often gave him the sharp end of her tongue; but she looked after him devotedly for many years. In his turn he rewarded her with gifts, some more acceptable than others. She wasn't happy on one occasion when she returned home to find that he had rotovated her garden as a surprise, as she had just sown her seeds. Christmas of 1976 was memorable because he plucked up the courage to steal a kiss. Mrs P. was outraged and refused to speak to him or to go to the Woodfords for New Year's Eve if he was going to be there too. Desperate to make it up, Walter hit on the brilliant notion of being the first across the Woodford threshold in 1977. He turned up at ten p.m., champagne at the ready, only to watch his hopes for forgiveness dissolve when he pulled the champagne cork and it hit Mrs P. in the back of the neck.

The other love of his life was Nelson, an unsatisfactory son in the eyes of everyone but his father. Nelson added a dash of sophisticated glamour to Walter's life. He took him on exotic holidays; but he made him pay for them with endless loans and constant anxiety about his shady business activities. Nelson did love his father, though, and made sure that he was looked after, particularly after he opened the Wine Bar in Borchester in 1980.

In 1957 Walter gave up his farm and moved into Honeysuckle Cottage, buying a minibus and becoming the village carrier. He was full of zest, brimful of ideas for helping the village and schemes to bring him in enough money to get by. He was Father Christmas in a Borchester store; he made bags with wooden curtain rings as handles to sell; and he was part-owner of a pet shop with Mrs Turvey for a while. He bought a junk shop in Hollerton, and when that shut opened another in Ambridge with a stuffed gorilla called George as signpost. He and Ned Larkin clubbed together to buy Parson's Field, adjoining Mrs Turvey's garden. They tried several schemes to make money, and in the process annoyed her and seemed unperturbed when nothing came of them.

Walter was musical and could play the euphonium well, which went down a treat at the annual carol-singing party at the Manor; but the coach horn he took to blowing at vital moments in cricket matches was less popular. He managed to repair an auto-glockenpolyphon for Jack and Peggy Archer, although it's unlikely that he could have spelled it. He loved tinkering with machinery and bought himself a steam engine. Jack Woolley lent him a shed so that he could work on fitting it to a traction engine and the entire village turned out to watch its maiden voyage from Honeysuckle Cottage to the Bull. He was a great supporter and initiator of village activities, forming the White Elephant Society to help raise funds for the Youth Club, and organizing outings for the Over Sixties; and no one ever forgot the occasion when he bought an elephant called Rosie with her baby, Tiny Tim, to appear in the Ambridge summer festival. Things happened when Walter was around: as when the giant marrow he'd grown for a competition exploded in his hand. He was generous and full of good intentions which didn't always pay off. When he had an unexpected win on the races he bought a video recorder and proudly invited Mrs P., Mrs Bagshawe, Pat Archer and her children to a private viewing of *Snow White and the Seven Dwarfs*. Unfortunately it turned out to be the adult version. The rest of the villagers were all queuing up to watch videos at Walter's house after that.

He liked to help his friends, and to repay them when they helped him, but with his track record it was not surprising that Doris Archer was apprehensive when he came to stay after his roof blew off in 1977. She said

cake. She knew he had meant well.

He was a marvellous wood carver, and his presents were always in demand. He made Dan Archer a rocking-chair which was so popular that everyone wanted one, and he became sick of carving them; he nearly fell into the same trap with the rocking-horse he carved for Christine Johnson's adopted son

Walter Gabriel (Chriss Gittins)

he could come only if he promised not to 'help' her, but it was a vain hope. Determined to show his gratitude, Walter scoured her non-stick saucepans because he thought they were burnt; then he thoughtfully fitted new door handles the wrong way round on all the doors of Glebe Cottage because Doris had difficulty turning them. The long-suffering Doris baked him a special

Peter. When in 1978 Jill Archer and Jennifer Aldridge got together to create the Two Jays Craft Studio, some of his carvings were put on display. They were reviewed in a local paper and he was so taken with the description of his skills that he set up Walter Gabriel Country Crafts in competition. When he discovered that he would have to pay more rates the idea petered out.

Walter had a great sense of history and loved Ambridge. He was very excited when he discovered the foundations of the original manor house with its old water-mill on his land. When Jill suggested that that might make him Lord of the Manor, he immediately promised to give the village green to the villagers if that was the case. It wasn't.

In his later years Walter was sensitive about his age, and thought a lot about his death, particularly when Dan, his closest friend, died. He chose his plot against the south wall of St Stephen's graveyard where all the other Gabriels were buried, told his friends that he would like a commemorative seat on the village green and chose his epitaph: 'All the beasts of the forest are mine; and so are the cattle upon a thousand hills.' His ninety-second birthday party was held in the function room at the Bull, and Sid Perks made him a freeman, promising that from then on all his 'specials' would be free, which highly delighted Walter. During the party he was heard to say, 'I'm going on for ever!' But of course he couldn't. Three months later he contracted pneumonia and died quietly one night. He was buried where he had requested and Amos Hebblewhite took his funeral service. He left his fishing rod to Phil Archer, a silver snuff box to Tom Forrest, love spoons to Shula Hebden and a little Dresden shepherdess to Emma Carter. But to Mrs P. he left nothing, but memories.

Robert Mawdesley; Chriss Gittins

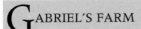

GABRIEL'S FARM

see Wynford's Farm

GADSBY, HAROLD

Mrs Bagshawe's nephew who lived in Felpersham in 1967 and had a herd of 400 pigs.

Arnold Peters

GARAGE

The history of Ambridge's garage is typical of many of the services that used to exist in every village but now are rarely to be seen. The garage had been the smithy, and at the time Paul Johnson bought it from Wainwright in 1967 had none of the facilities taken for granted today. Paul set about modernizing it, putting in a canopy, a self-service pump, a toilet and a small coffee bar. But these innovations did nothing to improve business and he sold it to Ralph Bellamy, who soon closed it. It reopened in 1972, only to be sold again to Haydn Evans three years later. He kept it going until 1985 when it closed for good. Since then, petrol and services have had to be found further afield, at Wharton's garage, about five miles out of the village, or on the Borchester bypass.

GARLAND, BERT AND ANNIE

Bert Garland was a local farmer who, in 1961, caused trouble for Paul Johnson over a tractor deal when a discrepancy in the accounts led to Johnson's resignation from Charles Grenville's company. Annie, Bert's downtrodden wife, showed unexpected strength of character when she insisted that she would go to the police unless he admitted that the irregularity had been his doing. He sent Johnson £100 with his apology, but by then it was too late to make amends.

Reg Johnston and Joy Davies

GARNETT, MR

The examiner who failed Polly Perks when she took her driving test in 1976.

GARONNE, MADAME DENISE

Charles Grenville brought Madame Garonne to Ambridge as his housekeeper when he arrived in 1959. She seemed efficient, if indiscreet – she let slip that she had seen Carol Grey leaving Blossom Hill Cottage late one night. The story was true: Carol had been seeing home a drunken John Tregorran. But there was more to her than efficiency and a careless tongue. In December Ambridge discovered from *The Borchester Echo* that it had been nursing a diamond smuggler in its bosom.

Irene Prador

GASCOINE, JIM

One of the Bridge Farm cows went missing in August 1990, and was found in distress by Jack and Peggy Woolley. They called Martin Lambert, the vet, but Jim Gascoine was acting as his locum and came out instead. He couldn't save the cow but ensured that her calf survived.

GEMMELL, LUCY (NÉE PERKS)

b. 12 Dec. 1971; m. autumn 1994

Lucy Perks was only eleven years old in 1982 when her mother, Polly, died in a road accident, after which she missed her terribly. The tragedy was to have far-reaching consequences, in both the shaping of her personality and the development of her relationship with her father, Sid Perks. They comforted each other and became very close; so when in 1986 Sid started to fall in love with Lucy's schoolteacher, Kathy Holland, it was hard for Lucy to bear. Her reactions showed in her behaviour, which became disturbed: she played truant from school, started to smoke and even stole chocolate Santas from the village shop. All in all it was a confused young girl who attended Sid and Kathy's wedding in April 1987, and who left flowers on Polly's grave, accompanied by a card with the poignant message, 'Goodbye Mum.'

Lucy's complicated emotions found an outlet in championing a variety of social causes, and her vociferously stated opinions aroused mixed feelings among the villagers, depending on whether they agreed with her or not. She broke into the milking parlour at Brookfield and sabotaged the milk, as she thought that Brookfield was running tests for BST; it was lucky for her that Phil Archer, respecting the integrity of her views, if not approving her actions, did not press charges. When he heard of the incident, Sid was speechless, Lucy unrepentant. Then she decided that she wished to be confirmed, although the vicar, Richard Adamson, felt that this sudden conversion had more to do with rebellion against her father than with love for God. However, she prevailed and was confirmed in 1988. After their talks together Richard felt that Lucy needed professional help and arranged for her to meet a friend of his who was both vicar and counsellor, but Lucy was not yet ready to confront her problems and didn't turn up.

Lucy passed her GCSEs and Kathy encouraged her to try for university. She studied for her A-levels at the sixth-form college in Borchester, bought a 'roadie' and worked part-time in a health food shop. She was still preoccupied with ecological issues and when she heard about Operation Raleigh in 1989 she enthusiastically put herself up for it. She wasn't to know that she would hate every minute of the selection weekend or suffer the indignity of being turned down. She tried to pretend that everything was wonderful, but a friend let the cat out of the bag and she wept. But she wasn't put off for long. Soon she was demonstrating once again, this time against circuses. Poor Kathy, on duty for St John Ambulance the same night as the demonstration, sneaked in at the back praying not to be seen.

By now Kathy and Lucy had called an uneasy truce, and Lucy began to realize that Kathy could be a useful ally sometimes in her arguments with her father. Lucy passed her A-levels and it was settled that she would go to Nottingham University to read environmental science in the autumn. In the meantime she worked at a crisis centre in Borchester. She knew that her father found it hard to understand her ideals, and sensed his pain at her growing independence; so when she started sleeping with Hal, one of the other helpers at the centre, she tried to keep it from him. In the end Kathy told Sid the truth and the strained atmosphere at home drove Lucy firmly into Hal's arms.

Her own concerns paled into insignificance, however, when Sid disappeared on Valentine's Day in 1991. At first she was frightened that she was responsible; but her native shrewdness asserted itself and she realized that Kathy was far more likely to be the cause, and Lucy had her own ideas about what had been going on. She asked Kathy outright whether she was having an affair with Dave Barry, and took Kathy's silence as evidence of guilt.

Hurt and angry, she grudgingly helped Kathy to keep the Bull going until Sid's return, sure that she would hear from him eventually. When her father rang her she arranged a secret meeting with him in Birmingham and succeeded in persuading him to come home. Father and daughter were united in their detestation of Kathy: one of Lucy's proudest moments was when Sid publicly ejected Kathy from the Bull, telling her never to return. Thereafter she seized every opportunity to prevent Sid and Kathy from achieving any sort of reconciliation. But she was no match for the healing virtues of time. Nearly a year later she took an early-morning cup of tea to her father and was shattered to see Kathy's head on the pillow beside him. Baffled and betrayed, she returned to university, aware that her father was putting someone else before her for the first time she could remember.

Lucy didn't come back until the summer,

and then only because she was in debt. The long-suffering Sid and Kathy (Kathy under protest) cancelled a much-needed holiday to give her the money she required, and having got what she came for she returned to Nottingham early. Since then communication has been rare, and Sid has had to depend upon the occasional letter or phone call. She even broke the news of her impending marriage on the telephone, which upset him enormously. Her fiancé was Duncan Gemmell from New Zealand, and Sid and Kathy went out for her wedding in the autumn of 1994 – Kathy secretly relieved that her stepdaughter would be living so far away, Sid desolate.

Tracey-Jane White

GERRARD, SIMON

In 1991 a stranger appeared in Ambridge looking for Debbie Aldridge. He was a forty-year-old Canadian widower, a visiting lecturer whom she had met at university, who wanted her to go back to Canada with him. Her stepfather Brian Aldridge threw him out of Home Farm, and although Debbie was furious at first, she realized that the relationship had no future.

Garrick Hagon

GIBBS, ALBERT THOMAS (BERT)

Bert Gibbs was a lugubrious man. He and his wife came 'from away' in the fifties and bought Meadow Farm. He got it for a good price and was soon able to pay off the mortgage. It was rumoured that his sour temper resulted from the untimely death of his only son years before.

He read the newspapers, listened to the radio and watched a good deal of television, yet managed to be misinformed about most of the current issues of the day. This led him into many arguments.

Bert also had a passion for litigation. He lost his battles with *The Borchester Echo*, which, he said, had erroneously used his name in a story about effluent; and against Richard Adamson, who had let down an electric wire across a public footpath on Bert's land. One of Bert's cows strayed over the path, ate a plastic bag and died on Lakey Hill. The cow wasn't insured (Bert was 'between policies'). He joined the National Farmers' Union, but it couldn't help him when his diesel tank collapsed, spilling its noxious contents all over his yard.

Patriotically, he gave an ox for roasting on the village green for the Jubilee celebrations. When he shot one of Jack Woolley's deer which was trespassing on his land, he gave a haunch of venison to Phil and Jill Archer 'for good advice and help'.

In 1979 he retired, sold the farm (Phil bought 30 acres) and left the district.

Graham Rigby

GILPIN, MR

Jack Woolley's solicitor referred him to Mr Gilpin of Williams, Gilpin & Williams, divorce specialists, when Jack and Valerie Woolley were thinking of ending their marriage early in 1974.

GIUSEPPE

Italian Giuseppe arrived as the manager at Grey Gables in 1977 and was there until 1982.

GLEBE COTTAGE

Built in the 1840s, Glebe Cottage is a small house next to St Stephen's Church with mellow bricks and a particularly pretty country garden. Letty Lawson-Hope left Glebe Cottage with its four acres of land to Doris Archer for her lifetime; Doris let it to Ned and Mabel Larkin in 1963, and then to Hugo Barnaby in 1968. In the early seventies she and Dan Archer bought the freehold from the Lawson-Hopes for £2,000. It made a delightful retirement home for them where, despite Dan's reluctance to accept his withdrawal from farming, they found great contentment. Doris died peacefully there. She willed the cottage to Dan for his lifetime and it then passed to her granddaughter Shula Hebden, who went to live in it with her husband Mark.

Shula and Mark renovated the cottage extensively, but their plans for rethatching the roof had to be postponed when the builders discovered a colony of wild bats. Since bats are a protected species, the work had to wait until they moved on.

After Mark's death in a car crash in 1994 Shula remained there on her own.

GLEBELANDS

Jack Woolley bought a stretch of land near the village green from Ralph Bellamy in 1978. He wasted no time before submitting plans for a housing development to be called Glebelands, which aroused strong opposition in the village.

The planning officer agreed to a group of houses being built, each of which might sell for £30,000, so Woolley had a considerable investment to protect. When the parish council voted against the proposed development he insisted on calling a parish meeting where full support was given. Work started on the building under the stern surveillance of Laura Archer and Colonel Danby, who told Jack nicely but firmly that they were determined to see to it that the approved plans were followed to the letter.

By 1979 the development was finished and only one house had not been sold before completion. Glebelands did not prove the eyesore the villagers had feared, and has now become a familiar part of Ambridge.

GLOVER, DEBBIE

When Debbie Glover worked at Carol Grey's market garden in 1957, Carol found her difficult to deal with and was glad when she left to find work at Tony Stobeman's bookmaker's office. Her home life was unhappy and at Christmas Walter Gabriel found her crying in the church because she and her mother were on their own and short of money. Walter had just won a hamper in a draw, and he gave it to Debbie telling her that she had been the winner. Undeceived, she didn't forget his kindness and the following spring when she learned that he was

looking for a new dog, she found him one.
Esma Wilson

GOODMAN, MR

When Nora Salt was thinking about divorcing her husband Greg, Jack Woolley suggested she see his solicitor Mr Goodman. Ironically two years later he was himself seeking similar guidance.
William Avenall

GOODMAN, LADY MERCEDES

'I've seen softer skin on a crocodile handbag,' said Sid Perks when treated to a glimpse of Lady Mercedes topping up her tan at the Grey Gables health club. Lady Mercedes is the Spanish-born wife of Sir Sidney.

GOODMAN, SIR SIDNEY

Sir Sidney's knighthood was for services to industry; his enterprises included canning factories in Borchester and Spain. The Spanish connection dated from his time fighting for General Franco in the Spanish Civil War. His social engagements around Ambridge usually involved business in some form, whether entertaining Spanish suppliers to a dangerously chaotic shoot, or being entertained by Brian and Jennifer Aldridge in the hope that he would get involved in canning their venison. Rising blood pressure and a heart attack in 1989 did not appear to soften his tough approach to life: when Usha

Gupta acted for his factory workers in 1991, he ensured that her firm lost a large contract with a developer friend of his.
Roger Hume

GOODWAY, GERRY

Amiable agricultural contractor Gerry Goodway has often helped the local farmers. He became a particular friend of Tony Archer's, acting as his best man and godfather to Tony's son John Daniel.

GRAHAM, FRANCES

The popular Borchester librarian often used to be seen in Ambridge with the mobile library in the seventies. She was friendly and attractive but disappointed several potential suitors when they discovered that she was already married to a marine biologist called Eric.
Catherine Crutchley

GRAINGER, JIM

A fellow engineering cadet of Kenton Archer's, Jim Grainger came from Devon. When Kenton visited him there in 1975, they took the opportunity to go out with Shula Archer and Maggie Price who were already down there on holiday.

GRANGE FARM

Joe Grundy and his family have been tenants

at Grange Farm for several generations. Built on eighteenth-century foundations, it's a mixture of crumbling brick and cracked rendering, with a wild area outside which Clarrie tries to cultivate from time to time as a garden. It's one of the smaller tenant farms on the Berrow Estate, so Joe and Eddie Grundy don't feel much motivated to attend to its upkeep.

It has always been a question of make and mend with the Grundys; Eddie's wife Clarrie very rarely gets anything new in the way of equipment or furnishings. Joe did once buy her an old twin-tub washing machine so that she could throw out his old mangle, and the parlour got a carpet but it was put together out of offcuts. She was thrilled when they planned a new bathroom suite in 1989, but rather disillusioned by the time Joe and Eddie had botched it together.

In addition to their cows, sheep and cereals, Joe and Eddie are always full of schemes to add to their income, but find it difficult to get any backers as Ambridge knows them too well. Joe tried to sell mineral water but his clients objected to its brown colour, and Eddie dreamed of breeding maggots but Clarrie put her foot down in time. Their annual venture into Christmas turkeys is always fraught with problems and even Clarrie's bed-and-breakfast enterprise was short-lived.

GRANGE, JIMMY

This rather confused young farmworker, a headstrong teenager, was apprenticed to Dan Archer in 1957 and spent all his spare time in a skiffle group in Borchester. He was prone to keeping bad company, easily upset and quick to throw a punch.

In 1960 he developed a crush on Carol Grey. She had shown an interest in his music but Jimmy had mistaken her attentiveness for affection. When Doughy Hood's rival firm, Hollerton Bakeries, tried to steal his business, Joan Hood attempted to sabotage the Hollerton bakery vans and implied that Jimmy had helped her. Carol tackled him at once, and he told her that he would never forgive Joan for 'coming between them'. One look at Carol's shocked face brought home to him his embarrassing blunder. He didn't trouble her again.

In his short time at Ambridge, Jimmy's behaviour had been partly responsible for the closing of the Teenage Club at Arkwright Hall and he had been accused of stealing the Youth Club funds. Clearly, he still had a good deal of growing up to do – which he left to do elsewhere.

Alan Rothwell

GRANGE, MABEL AND WILL

Will, an industrial draughtsman, went with his wife to Brookfield in 1957 to discuss the possibility of their son Jimmy being apprenticed to Dan Archer.

Peggy Hughes and Lewis Gedge

GRANT, MARILYN

When Jack Woolley started the New Curiosity Shop in 1963, he took on Marilyn Grant as assistant to Dawn Kingsley. However, the shop didn't do as well as he had expected, so in the autumn he sold it to John Tregorran, who was able to expand his own shop into it. Marilyn's fate is not known.

GRANT, MR

After the loss of all the Brookfield's cloven footed stock to foot-and-mouth disease early in 1956, Dan Archer went to Hollerton to consult Mr Grant, the bank manager there, about raising money to re-establish the dairy herd.

GRAVENÇIN, MICHÈLE

Jill Archer was delighted when Michèle Gravençin started work as au pair at Brookfield in 1970. So were Ambridge males: she went out with Tony Archer before becoming unofficially engaged to Gordon Armstrong. Sadly for Gordon, whose love life never ran smoothly, Michèle had to return to France when her mother became seriously ill. She remained there after the death of her mother, and Gordon never saw her again.

Lorna Phillippe

GRAYSON, VALERIE

see Woolley, Valerie

GREEN, GINGER

In 1952 Marjorie Butler, the poulty girl, persuaded Phil Archer to give her boyfriend

Ginger a job on the Fairbrother Estate. Ten days later Phil was taken aback when a girl called Helga arrived on the doorstep and announced that Ginger was her husband. Ginger did not turn up for work the following Monday, and by curious coincidence Grace Fairbrother's engagement ring also disappeared. Paul Johnson, who knew the story, caught a glimpse of Ginger at Borchester station and threatened him with dire consequences if he didn't tell the truth. Ginger capitulated at once and led him straight to Helga, who reluctantly handed back the ring.

Nothing daunted, Marjorie still wanted Ginger, and, ignoring the wise advice of Helen Fairbrother, decided to follow her heart's fancy. Sadly she arrived at his digs too late. The birds had flown.

GREEN, SELINA

Selina lived in a council house near the Horrobins. She entered her baby daughter Cheryl for the Beautiful Baby competition at the village fête in 1983.

GREENBOW, MRS

Mrs P. went to look after her former neighbour in London, Mrs Greenbow, when she had an operation in 1973.

GREENWOOD, IVAN

Ivan was for many years the cowman at

Sawyer's Farm on the Berrow Estate. He retired at the end of 1991 when Shula Hebden suggested to Cameron Fraser that he should have Ivy Cottage at a reduced rent, to which Cameron agreed. Unfortunately, Shula gave Ivan the good news too soon. Cameron then changed his mind and Shula had the embarrassing task of informing Ivan that he couldn't have the cottage after all.

GRENVILLE, ANN (NÉE PRESCOTT)

m. Harvey Prescott 20 Apr. 1963

Ann Prescott was working as a junior partner in a gown shop in London in 1961 when she was invited by Carol and Charles Grenville to spend Christmas with them. She re-met an old friend, Harvey Grenville, after an interval of seventeen years and suddenly started to look for a shop near by. Fortuitously she discovered premises near John Tregorran's antiques shop and moved in. She smoothed Harvey's brow, dismissed his feelings of inferiority and married him. After a while, when her husband showed signs of wanting to return to the excitement of the Foreign Office, she firmly but gently refused to leave her shop and they stayed in Ambridge.
Heather Canning

GRENVILLE, CAROL

see Tregorran, Carol

GRENVILLE, HARVEY REDVERS ST JOHN

m. Ann Prescott 20 Apr. 1963

Harvey Grenville was a distant cousin of Charles Grenville who came to stay at the Manor in 1961. Previously with the Foreign Office, he now seemed to be at a loose end. Persuaded by Charles to take over as warden at Arkwright Hall, he occupied a flat there. The next year he moved on and became supervisor of the Fairbrother Estate department and forestry section.

In the meantime, he had met an old friend, Ann Prescott, and they had fallen in love. In 1963 they married. By now Harvey was itching to return to the Foreign Office, but, ever the gentleman, deferred to Ann's wishes to stay. His behaviour, however, became mysterious. To explain it, this shadowy character told his wife that he had been working with the police in connection with some robberies in the district.

The death of his cousin Charles in 1965 shocked him. He had been best man at his wedding and was godfather to his son Richard.

When Ralph Bellamy took over the Estate, Harvey was given notice to quit. He and Ann moved into a suite at Grey Gables, the cost of which was to be borne, he hinted, by his new and unnamed employer.
Ronald Baddiley

GRENVILLE, OLIVER CHARLES

m. Carol Grey 18 Sept. 1961; d. 21 Jan. 1965

In 1959 Charles Grenville strode into

Ambridge to take over the Fairbrother Estate. His family had been landowners for three hundred years and he had inherited their tenacious genes. He had farmed extensively in Africa and toured the world. He was thus equipped with advanced ideas. These were put to good use when he acquired controlling interests in Octopus Ltd, Grenville Enterprises Ltd, Melville Agricultural Machine Co., Borchester Animal Foodstuffs Co. and South Midlands Farm Contracting Company.

Not surprisingly, the Estate ran more efficiently than it had before. He was fair but firm with his employees. When Christine Johnson sought his advice on her husband's business problems, he would not help. Nor would he sell her the horse Tuppence, even though he acknowledged that she rode him well, because he wanted it trained as a racehorse. He knew the value of delegation and when he lost the staunch Phil Archer, he quickly replaced him with the reliable Andrew Sinclair. Later, he insisted that his wife Carol should get a manager for her market garden.

He summoned his housekeeper Madame Garonne, the house was redecorated and he planned fruitful business dinners *chez lui*. When this mysterious Frenchwoman disappeared, he had no hesitation in requesting Carol Grey to play hostess for him, nor in sending her away before dinner when he considered her job was done.

Then, pausing from business, he saw that Carol was desirable and eligible. It was a singlehanded and speedy courtship, in part held in Holland where they were examining new farming techniques. They married in 1961.

Theirs was a good marriage. Carol was able to confess her unhappiness at the theft of some old love letters from John Tregorran to this clear-headed man without rebuke. Nor had he flinched when she had earlier confessed her unconventional parentage. He welcomed John Tregorran as a friend and was pleased that his bride Janet was married from the Grenville home. His cup of happiness was filled when Carol became pregnant. In joyful anticipation of a son, he put the child's name down at his old public school and purchased education insurance. A son Richard was born in 1962.

Tragedy struck in 1963 when his car crashed, killing his passenger Janet Tregorran. He coped well with his own serious injuries and in the following year, equipped with a false leg, he sped off for new business ventures in America. Liking what he saw, he sent for Carol and told her that he would like to sell off his interests in Britain and settle there. She unsuccessfully tried to dissuade him. She returned meantime to Ambridge and a year later received a sad letter. Charles had succumbed finally to a germ which he had picked up in the East but which had lain dormant for years. He had suffered a haemorrhage and was dead.

In his will he left the house, an annuity and three companies to his wife and the rest to his son Richard.

Michael Shaw

GRENVILLE, RICHARD CHARLES

b. 13 Dec. 1962

Richard Grenville's father died in 1965

before his third birthday but he was cared for by his mother Carol and later by his stepfather John Tregorran. He was upset by John's long absence in America and showed disturbed behaviour at his school (also attended by young David Archer). His housemaster, Rupert Marshall, understood the reason behind the boy's petty pilfering and did not seek to expel him. He made a complete recovery when he heard that John was coming home. The family had jolly holidays in Turkey in 1976 and America in 1980 after his A-level year.

John Offord

GREY, CAROL

see Tregorran, Carol

GREY GABLES

Grey Gables is a late Victorian mock-Gothic mansion set in fifteen acres of graceful lawns and gardens. Surrounded by a large country park with its own golf course, outdoor swimming pool and indoor leisure complex, it also has extensive conference facilities.

It was already a country club when Reggie Trentham took it over in 1951 and ran it with his wife Valerie. It had a good restaurant, was a popular function centre and its stables were run by Grace Fairbrother and Christine Archer. Phil Archer and Grace held their wedding reception there in 1955, and five months later they were there again having dinner when they saw that the stables had caught fire. Grace died tragically, bringing one of the horses to safety.

When Reggie sold out in 1962 Jack Woolley bought the property, planning to turn it into an exclusive holiday centre for tired business executives. His was the brain behind all subsequent developments at Grey Gables, and his inexhaustible energy and marketing skills have brought about its success. Much of its current reputation depends on the clever management of Caroline Bone and the excellent cuisine of its chef Jean-Paul.

GRIFFITHS, ELAINE

A rep for a mid-Wales dairy which sold organic milk, Elaine came to Bridge Farm in 1989 seeking supplies. For once Lynda Snell was in Tony Archer's good books when she met Elaine there and lavished fulsome praise on Pat and Tony Archer and their produce. She then whisked Elaine off to the Bull, still singing Pat and Tony's praises. The poor woman never stood a chance. She found herself agreeing to buy the Bridge Farm milk, and arranging collection before she could have second thoughts.

GRIGGS, ALBERT THOMAS

When Albert Griggs was fined for effluent dispersal in 1975, *The Borchester Echo* mistakenly reported his name as Albert Thomas Gibbs. Bert Gibbs was outraged, claimed that his reputation had been ruined and said that he was going to sue, but the matter was settled out of court.

GROVE, BASIL AND VALERIE

Basil, attractive, thirty-three, and with a wife who didn't understand him, was irresistible to Christine Archer when she worked for him at Borchester Dairies. He had a fling with Christine in 1951, but made it up with his wife Valerie soon afterwards, to the great relief of Doris and Dan Archer who had watched their daughter's infatuation with some anxiety.

Michael Ford and Pat Driscoll

GRUNDY, ALFRED GEORGE (ALF)

b. 13 Nov. 1944

Alf Grundy was a credit to his father Joe's upbringing. Everyone knew that he was a poacher, although he was never caught, and at an early age he became past master at slipping packets of chocolate out of Woolworths. He loathed farming and left home the moment he could, working at a variety of jobs until he followed his younger brother, Eddie, into the scrap metal business at Gloucester. He was soon hauled up before Gloucester magistrates and charged with receiving stolen copper wire, but his luck held and he was acquitted. Shortly afterwards he was caught breaking and entering and sent to jail. On completion of his sentence, he turned up like a bad penny at Grange Farm in 1986. Clarrie Grundy was at first well disposed to her brother-in-law but soon changed her mind when she discovered that he had stolen from her son William's

moneybox and had left the farm taking her husband Eddie's car stereo with him.

Terry Molloy

GRUNDY, CLARRIE (NÉE LARKIN)

b. 12 May 1954; m. Eddie Grundy 21 Nov. 1981; 2 sons

Clarrie Grundy is a Cinderella without a fairy godmother.

Her parents were Jethro and Lizzie Larkin; her sister Rosie lives in Great Yarmouth with her husband Denis. Clarrie, a bright girl, left school with several CSEs and went to work for a travel agent. In 1976, after being made redundant, she was reduced to working as a domestic help at several houses in Ambridge. Jill Archer at Brookfield found her a willing and helpful worker, who was better at cleaning than cooking. But Clarrie soon improved her cooking skills by taking lessons from Caroline Bone. She is still best described as 'a good plain cook', though she's not averse to a touch of garlic of a hint of ginger here and there.

Clarrie was never slim and food was always to be her downfall. In 1979, wanting to better herself, she gave up cleaning and went to work full time at the Bull in the Steak Bar. (She still works part-time at the Bull today.) She couldn't resist the chips and soon resorted to eating chocolate slimming biscuits in a desperate attempt to lose weight. In the end they made her so miserable that she cooked and ate an entire fruit cake at one sitting.

Perhaps it was working for Sid and Polly

Clarrie Grundy (Rosalind Adams)

her out for a Chinese meal and their courtship began.

When Clarrie's mother died in 1980, she had to explain to Eddie that she thought they should see less of each other, at least until her father had recovered from the worst of his grief. Eddie didn't seem to mind.

News of Lady Diana Spencer's engagement to HRH the Prince of Wales in 1981 made Clarrie feel sad. Her own prince seemed to be so far from reach. A proposal of marriage seemed imminent, but it was interrupted by a phone call inviting Eddie to make a demonstration Country and Western tape with the famed Jolene Rogers. The tape was made with money borrowed from Eddie's friend, Baggy. But stardom did not beckon Eddie, and Baggy soon wanted his money back. Clarrie, who had received £500 from her mother's insurance, offered to repay her darling's debt if he would marry her at last. Eddie succumbed but it was Clarrie who had to buy the engagement ring, white gold with a single ruby.

Clarrie began a new diet for the sake of the wedding dress, which was to be Victorian-milkmaid-style with a lace ribbon trim which Clarrie had decided to make herself; but, faint from lack of food, she had to call on Polly and Caroline to help with the sewing. The Ambridge 'wedding of the year' took place at St Stephen's church on

Perks in the Bull kitchen which made Clarrie decide that the kitchen at home in Woodbine Cottage should be modernized. To Jethro's horror, Clarrie approached his employer Phil Archer and asked him to contribute to the improvements. The old range and the copper for boiling were to go and a new fridge was to be installed. It was Eddie Grundy who came to do the work. Though he and Clarrie had grown up in the village together, Eddie suddenly saw Clarrie with new eyes. He took

Saturday 21 November 1981. Jethro grudgingly gave his daughter away, Rosie was matron of honour and Eddie's brother Alf was best man. 'All things bright and beautiful,' sang the congregation. Eddie came up trumps: he was only ten minutes late arriving. After the reception held at the Bull Clarrie left with her new husband for Torremolinos. She was on cloud nine.

On their return to the bridal suite at Grange Farm, which had new blue curtains and a matching bedspread, Clarrie came down to earth with a bump: her father-in-law Joe Grundy had filled the room with tatty old furniture. It was an early lesson for Clarrie. From now on, it would be her continual struggle to keep the farmhouse at Grange Farm neat and tidy.

When her first baby was on the way, Clarrie spent £28 on rabbit-patterned wallpaper for the nursery, and bought a tiger mobile and a teddy. Pat Archer lent her maternity nightdresses and baby things. Clarrie ordered clothes and sheets from a catalogue. Eddie, sick of all these expensive preparations, rowed with his wife and stormed out. Clarrie, left on her own, fell down some steps and, frightened of losing the baby, was rushed to Borchester General Hospital. A remorseful Eddie was soon at her bedside. They kissed and made up.

Their son William was finally born two weeks late on 9 February 1983, weighing 8 lb 14 oz. The birth was difficult and Clarrie vowed to have no more children. But by the following January she was pregnant again. When William began to hide under the table, Clarrie put it down to insecurity about the coming baby. 'No, he's just playing Doggy,'

replied his complacent father. Edward's birth was no more straightforward than William's. Clarrie was in Great Yarmouth, helping to nurse Rosie's husband, when she went into labour and her second baby was born there on 28 September 1984.

When Jethro was killed in a farm accident at Brookfield in 1987, Clarrie was distraught. David Archer apologized for the accident and Clarrie was forgiving. Heartbroken, she gave Jethro's thornproof coat and thermos flask to Neil Carter and set herself to preparing the wake.

She inherited her father's dog Gyp and when he came to live with the family at Grange Farm, the cunning Clarrie taped her father's post office savings book to the bottom of Gyp's basket to stop Eddie getting his hands on it. But, generous as ever, out of the £5,000 she inherited from her father, Clarrie bought presents for everyone and loose covers for the parlour. She paid the balance into a savings account for the boys but, inevitably, this was later plundered to buy a 'new' van for Eddie.

Since her marriage, Clarrie has had to work all available hours. Every year it falls to her to feed, pluck and disembowel the Christmas turkeys. Once she lost her precious wedding ring and had to search through all the turkey innards, only to discover it in the soap dish. In 1984 when Eddie and Joe decided that there was money to be made from the health food business, it was Clarrie who ground the flour. The venture was not a success. The Grundy's 'Huntsman' variety of wheat did not make good breadmaking flour. Clarrie ended up using it for flapjacks.

An excellent seamstress, Clarrie and her needle have often been called upon to save the day. She has stitched many a costume for the pantomime, but her finest hour came when she made the gowns for Sophie Barlow's fashion show at Grey Gables in 1986.

Holidays from Grange Farm have been few and far between. In 1990 Clarrie went on a coach trip to Jersey. The driver, Austin, was smitten by her charms. He pursued her with Christmas and Valentine cards. Eddie was driven by jealousy to have himself tattooed. Clarrie was unimpressed.

She persuaded Eddie to consider buying a farm in France, and with a tent in the back of the van they set off across the Channel. Their plans for a farm of their own soon evaporated but Clarrie returned to Ambridge a confirmed Francophile. It was largely due to Clarrie's persistence that Ambridge was twinned with Meyruelle in the south of France and she was part of the first delegation from Ambridge to visit. There she surprised herself by making a speech that was judged *formidable*; she now feels well able to address WI meetings. Her interest in French cuisine was abetted by her friendship with Jean-Paul at Grey Gables, though not appreciated at Grange Farm. Eddie soon suspected, wrongly, that Clarrie's interest in Jack Woolley's chef was more than just culinary and she was mortified when Eddie punched him in the face. Jean-Paul grudgingly accepted Eddie's apology for his *crime passionel*. To this day Clarrie's pudding is to be found on the dessert menu at Grey Gables.

Male chauvinism still rules the roost at Grange Farm but by now Clarrie knows just how to deal with it. To sum her up in her own words: 'If you want a job doing, ask a busy woman.'

Heather Bell; Fiona Mathieson; Rosalind Adams

GRUNDY, EDWARD GEORGE (EDDIE)

b. 15 Mar. 1951; m. Clarrie Larkin 21 Nov. 1981; 2 sons

Slow to learn basic skills, Eddie Grundy could not walk until he was two and a half years old. But he soon made up for lost time. He enjoyed neither school nor Sunday school. He was quick to learn one vital lesson: 'If the gamekeeper don't catch you, it ain't poaching.'

He went to work at Hollerton Plant Hire in 1977 but was sacked for fiddling and was forced to return home to Grange Farm to work for his father Joe for a mere thirty pounds a week to milk their remaining twenty cows. But by now Eddie had other dreams: of being a Country and Western singing star – and of impressing the delectable Dolly Treadgold. They were soon engaged, but Dolly proved to be a flighty fiancée. Eddie called off the wedding with one day to spare.

It was in 1980 whilst he was hired to knock out the old range in the Larkins' kitchen (which was destined to decorate Nelson Gabriel's Wine Bar) that Jethro's daughter Clarrie came to his notice. He invited her to his cellar-saloon at Grange Farm, which was decorated with stampeding bison. Here he wooed her with sad Country

left to right: Eddie, Joe, William and foreground Clarrie Grundy (Trevor Harrison, Edward Kelsey, Philip Molloy and Rosalind Adams)

and Western love songs that reduced her to tears. Just as he was about to propose to her he was interrupted by a phone call inviting him to make a demonstration tape with Jolene Rogers, the lily of Layton Cross. Bad debts resulted. Clarrie lent him money with one condition attached – marriage.

Domesticity soon began to pall after their marriage in 1981. When their first child was on its way, Eddie took £10 of Clarrie's 'carpet money' and went to Gloucester for a binge with his elder brother Alf. Neil Carter had to fetch him home in the middle of the night: Clarrie had fallen down and been rushed into hospital. She was in danger of losing the baby, but all went well. On 9 February 1983 Eddie was presented with his first-born son William. At that moment, he almost grew up a little.

Grundy *père et fils* have an interesting political view on property. Socialist when it comes to tools: equipment anywhere in Ambridge is for the use and good of all, especially the Grundys. When it comes to money, a more despotic rule prevails: winner takes all (or as much as he can get away with). Joe, a wily and seasoned warrior, is usually the victor.

In 1991 a premium bond worth £5,000 in Susan Grundy's name was selected as winner after her death. Joe had practised his late wife's signature and the non-transferable cheque was theirs. In anticipation of such wealth, Eddie persuaded Joe to part with £500 funeral money and bought a dress for Clarrie. He promised he would not tell his brother Alf. Emotional blackmail was used on Clarrie to open a building society account in the name of 'S. Grundy'. The deed was nearly done when Clarrie was spotted by Jill Archer in the building society office. Guiltily Clarrie fled from the scene and returned the cheque to the authorities. But Eddie had already spent the money Joe had given him. Later Joe intercepted a message from Cameron Fraser about Eddie's wages for some baling work: they were waiting to be collected from the Estate office. Joe paid them into his own building society. Scores were even.

There is a long-standing feud between Grange Farm and Brookfield. As a neighbouring farmer, Phil Archer is only too aware that Eddie and Joe's lackadaisical farming practices could well endanger the Brookfield stock. This is particularly apparent over the question of sheep-dipping. In 1991 Joe was fined £2,000 with £200 costs for using a watering can instead of immersing his sheep in the dip bath. Eddie discovered that David Archer had been the informer and declared renewed war on the self-righteous Archer clan. The following year the law changed but the debt remains.

Eddie and Joe have always favoured ferrets as pets over domestic animals, giving their pet ferrets names such as Mathilda, Belle, Tex, Fergie, Sabrina and Mrs Archer (a female ferret is a jill). Once when rats invaded the house from the turkey shed, the ferrets were let loose indoors. Clarrie was furious. Many a rabbit has found its way into the Grundys' cooking pot with the help of these ingenious animals. Sometimes, though, as was the case when Eddie was tenderly initiating his son William into the art of poaching, the ferret will eat the rabbit in its hole and cannot escape until it has been digested. Then its owner must either dig for it or wait until it emerges. Patience and vigilance against gamekeepers are then required. Where his ferrets are concerned, Eddie has both these attributes, or at least a ready line in excuses when apprehended.

A powder-blue Capri with an air-horn and a nodding ferret in the back window is Eddie's prized possession. It once sported a CB aerial bearing a Confederate flag, but this was snatched off by a monkey on a family trip to a safari park. Money inherited by Clarrie from Jethro went into a newish van: Dodge-type painted with sunsets, flames and flowers. Eddie sees this as 'ideal for gigs' but owns that it's not much use for taking stock to market. Clarrie uses it to take William and their second son, Edward (born in September 1984), to school.

Eddie certainly has a sense of humour. He was the only person in Ambridge who found Lynda Snell's video on litter louts funny, even though he was shown leaving an oil can on the village green.

Eddie is a jack-of-all-trades, at least in his own eyes; there are few jobs at which he will not have a go. But he is an erratic craftsman. When he and Clarrie won a bathroom in a competition in 1993, Eddie and Joe installed the bath and the rest of the plumbing and then had to build the bathroom walls round it. It was a shame that the light was the wrong side of the wall and Clarrie had to bathe by candlelight. Flushed by his success, and with a certain amount of blackmail, he persuaded Lynda Snell to agree that he should do the work on the water cascade in her low-allergen garden. However, Lynda and Eddie differed on the definition of a cascade. Eddie has still not received payment for installing his version of the Trevi Fountain.

Determined to play his part in the village cricket team, Eddie painted his wellingtons white and borrowed a pair of trousers from Jean-Paul. They disintegrated in bleach and he was forced to buy some old whites from Nigel Pargetter. A ball hit him 'in an uncomfortable place' but he achieved victory for the team by catching another ball in his hat. The catch was disallowed. When selected to play nowadays he plays at twelfth man.

A skilful darts player, Eddie has played for the Bull and the Cat and Fiddle, holders of the Bellamy trophy (a Viking warrior in brass).

Eddie's bull-horn hat makes frequent appearance at village concerts along with his repertoire of Country and Western songs. He also fancies himself as an actor, though he had mixed feelings about being cast as Mac the Sheep Stealer in the 1992 nativity play. The year before when rival productions of Aladdin were mounted in Ambridge, performances were planned for different evenings. Eddie joined both casts. But there was a hitch and he found himself expected to play Wishee Washee in both pantomimes at the same time. Velcro added to his costumes, silver-painted wellingtons used for both characters, split-second timing and a fast car should have saved the day. Eddie's brain, however, could not cope with such speedy transitions and the scripts became intermingled. He received a standing ovation.

Eddie still dreams his dreams of stardom. There are signed photographs from both Britt Ekland and Anneka Rice on his workshop wall and a letter from John Peel (unsigned) returning some cassettes.

Trevor Harrison

GRUNDY, EDWARD JNR

b. 28 Sept. 1984

Second son of Clarrie and Eddie Grundy, Edward was born in Great Yarmouth and weighed 8 lb 4 oz. He narrowly escaped being christened Barry after Barry Manilow. A placid baby, 'happy just sitting', he had lots of black hair and a beloved teddy bear.

He loathed school just as much as his elder brother had done (and his dad). One school morning he went missing: he had fallen between the bales whilst playing in the barn. Mike Tucker, Neil Carter, Joe and Eddie had to shift 1,500 of them to find him. Then they had to put them all back. He dropped his teddy when they hauled him out, and was inconsolable. So the whole procedure had to be repeated.

He loved visiting the pantomime in Birmingham and meeting its star, Britt Eckland, when William (with a little help from his father) won a colouring competition. He is kinder than his brother: he lent William £2 out of his moneybox for his trip to Meyruelle – though when Elvis the peacock from the Bull tried to bite Edward, his brother vowed revenge for the attack.

GRUNDY, JOE

b. 18 Sept. 1921; m. Susan; 2 sons

As he'll tell you himself at the drop of a pint, Joe Grundy should be a millionaire by now. But three things have always got in the way.

One is cash-flow. Another is his son, Eddie. But, above all, he believes, it's the curse of the Archer family that has always foiled his plans – as when David Archer reported him for not dipping his sheep. (Everyone knows that he'd given them a perfectly adequate sprinkling with a watering can.)

He has quick mind, sure enough, and it teems with ideas for making a fast buck. Sometimes they even come off. He made a handsome profit pulling customers' cars out of the mud at Carol Tregorran's pick-your-own fruit scheme, and letting his land for Auto Cross with parking extra (£1 for a car and 50p for a motorbike) pulled in a bob or two. He did a deal with the foreman of the Borchester Bakery for biscuit crumbs to give to his two prize porkers. Equally successful was the 'White Bedsock' pop concert; and his cider apples, including Taylor's, Bulmers' Norman and Sweet Coppin, do well. His Kingston Black cider is very potent. Cyril, Bishop of Felpersham, an abstemious man, once sampled it on a visit to Grange Farm. The Bishop became so engrossed that Higgs, who'd chauffeured him there, grew tired of waiting, and Joe had to drive him back to Grey Gables in the back of his van.

In fact, alcohol plays an important part in the Grundy saga. Clarrie once noticed that sugar was mysteriously vanishing from her kitchen, only to discover that Joe was secretly concocting his lethal home brew. He and Eddie have been banned from the Bull and the Cat and Fiddle on more than one occasion. Walter Gabriel and Tony Archer were also banned from the Bull for supplying the Grundys with drinks in the garden. Joe had to replace a piano that belonged to the Bull

Joe Grundy ((Edward Kelsey)

tles of champagne he and Eddie consumed with Tom Forrest, also at Grey Gables – perhaps the fact that they knew they intended to leave Tom the bill made it taste sweeter. Calvados, provided by Jean-Paul for a French evening at the Bull, was more to Joe's taste. And he does occasionally enjoy whisky, as long as it's someone else's.

Joe inherited the tenancy of Grange Farm from generations of Grundys. His wife Susan came from religious parents. Joe was distraught when Susan died in 1969, and often invokes her memory, in a lugubrious voice – though he was not above trying to persuade Clarrie to forge her name in an abortive attempt to claim a premium bond prize.

As a farmer, Joe would say that he was dogged by ill-luck. When Susan died in, Joe was left with two unruly boys to bring up. Neither showed any interest in the farm and by 1977 Eddie was scraping a living in Borchester, dealing in scrap metal, and Alf had left home. Disenchanted, Joe let things go to rack and ruin, and raised no objection to Eddie allowing Hollerton Plant Hire to use Grange Farm as a depot. Machinery was strewn about the farm until Mary Pound urged him to shift it before the rating officer, alerted by his neighbours, came to reassess his rates. His bad luck didn't stop there. The following spring he had a bad attack of flu, half his cows were found to be infected with tuberculosis and doomed to slaughter, and as if that were not

when it was ruined by Eddie's unfortunate stomach upset. When his daughter-in-law Clarrie was seized by the idea of moving the family to France, Joe tried drinking wine, but he couldn't take to it, though he did graciously accept the free half-bottle that Jack Woolley provided at Grey Gables on the one and only occasion that the rent cheque was paid on time. And he enjoyed the two bot-

enough, his favourite ferret Turk was killed in a trap. He felt he couldn't go on. Eddie was moved by his father's plight and, not wishing to lose his inheritance, told him that they would fight on together. Which they did, and two years later the farm was re-registered for milk production.

Joe's son Eddie was now a permanent fixture at Grange Farm. The wedding planned in 1979 between Eddie and Dolly Treadgold did not take place, despite the fact that Joe had spent good money on curtains for the parlour, swept out the turkey sheds, draped some borrowed bunting about the place and invited half the village to the reception. But Clarrie proved more steadfast. Joe said the suit he wore for that wedding was new, but everyone else thought it looked exactly like his old one. He laid down a new carpet in the parlour (made from different offcuts) and Mrs Eddie Grundy moved into the farm. Joe agreed that the place needed a woman's touch.

Clarrie is an excellent cook, except that she keeps finding new reasons for economy drives and lentil dishes, forcing Joe to sniff for a decent meal elsewhere. Once when he heard that Martha Woodford was cooking tasty suppers for Bill Insley, he pointedly (and poignantly) asked at the shop for tinned steamed puddings to be added to Clarrie's shopping list. Martha took the hint and Joe got invited to supper, but she drove a hard bargain. A wonky bird table was delivered for mending, along with a shelf for her porch, and then her bicycle. Jennifer Aldridge found Joe a willing raconteur for her oral history project, but for some reason he would always turn up at lunchtime, much to her husband Brian's irritation. Joe was hardly happier

when Clarrie began to experiment with French cuisine. He is firmly a meat-and-potatoes man, and often calls to mind the late Susan's steak-and-kidney pies. It was one of life's cruel ironies that, at a harvest supper competition, Joe won the poor man's meal of rice, while Brian Aldridge won the rich man's casserole.

Joe regards himself as a religious man. St Stephen's lost him to the Methodist Chapel in Little Croxley in 1984. Soon after, he could be seen going round the pubs collecting 'for the little boys in Africa'. He became very drunk and tumbled into the River Am. Nigel Pargetter and Dave Barry pulled him out. He did once have a vision in which his father came to him in a dream to tell him that there was spring water on the farm. Out came the dowsing stick, but, try as he might, Joe couldn't get a twitch out of it. The farm was cursed, Joe said. But Joe and Eddie, too lazy to go further afield, had buried a dead calf in Clarrie's garden and she told them that there would be no tea until they'd removed it – and lo! even as Joe dug a new hole, water gushed forth. 'It's a miracle,' he cried, but the miraculous effects did not last long. Cameron Fraser authorized them to bottle the water and they had no doubt that there was a market, but Joe couldn't afford bottles or labels. Another scheme died for lack of funds. Other people felt that the water's brown colour might have proved a drawback, too.

But he does stand to make some money out of the Common Agricultural Policy. He has eight and a half acres for set-aside, and a 'green' meadow was discovered on his land, with a profusion of wild flowers on it. He has already received cheques from SSIS.

He generally keeps healthy, except when farmer's lung strikes, which it does from time to time. Then Joe takes to his bed, while Eddie has to get up early and milk the cows.

The sale of his posset-pot has refired his ambition for a loving friendship. He brilliantined his hair and took Marjorie Antrobus out to dinner, graciously accepting her offer to pay for the two bottles of Rioja, and to drive him back home in his van.

Reg Johnstone; Haydn Jones; Edward Kelsey

Grundy, Susan

m. Joe Grundy; 2 sons

Susan Grundy was Joe Grundy's wife and mother of Alf and Eddie. She came from religious farming stock. Her mother never spoke to Joe again after the wedding. There wasn't a honeymoon.

A good wife and mother, she made steak-and-kidney pie every Saturday for twenty-eight years. Her bitter marmalade with fine strips of rind was just to Joe's taste.

On the first fine day of spring in 1969 Joe found her collapsed on the scullery floor. She lies in St Stephen's churchyard.

Grundy, William

b. 9 Feb. 1983

Firstborn of Clarrie and Eddie, William Grundy was two weeks overdue and weighed 8 lb 14 oz. By no means a placid baby, he suffered from colic, slept for only three hours at a time and his poor mother was on the verge of hitting him.

He was christened wearing a Victorian gown, a present from his godmother Caroline Bone. Godfathers Sid Perks and Neil Carter gave him a christening mug and an initialled napkin ring. Eddie gave his son a small-sized cowboy hat.

He took his first steps on his first birthday, beating his father by eighteen months.

William started at Loxley Barrett Primary School and hated every moment. Clarrie became so worried that she went to spy on him in the playground at lunchtime. He stole a little girl's apple and made her cry. Clarrie was relieved to see that he seemed able to look after himself.

Though he says that he doesn't want to become a farmer, he has a way with animals. After nursing Sooty the jackdaw back to health, he started a menagerie: he looked after a fox, a badger, a pet newt, a rabbit, a turkey and a collection of animal skulls. He charged the children money for the privilege of looking at his collection. He trained Eddie's Limousin steer from a calf, handling it better than his father was able when it stampeded with him at the Borchester show in 1992, facing manfully up to its departure for slaughter a few months later.

He is, in fact, becoming a budding entrepreneur, in the tradition of his dad and grandad. He was discovered selling sweets to Mike Tucker, whose cholesterol-low diet expressly forbade them. He tried to sell his dad's rally car plates at the side of the road, when told of their potential worth by Bert Fry, with whom he is on friendly terms (even though he has been known to nick his apples). And he tried to sell garden snails to Jean-Paul, the chef at Grey Gables.

He did steal Tom Forrest's strawberries once, and Mike Tucker's milk; and he has had a go at Clarrie's larder and his brother Edward's piggy-bank. On such occasions Clarrie reprimanded him (usually with the back of her hand) and when possible made him recompense his victims out of his pocket money.

But Clarrie became over-protective when her son was imprisoned in Blossom Hill Cottage by Kate Aldridge. Kate's father Brian then took him into custody for poaching. Clarrie was able to obtain his release by reminding Brian of his own daughter's former naughtiness.

Mrs Antrobus gives him piano lessons.

When a dead pea-hen was found in Clarrie's freezer, William admitted to killing it with his catapult but claimed in his defence that the bird had attacked his younger brother Edward. The family hushed up the discovery and buried the corpse.

William's interest in live animals revived in the summer of 1994 when he set up a menagerie of wounded and orphaned animals at Grange Farm and Clarrie worried when he took to charging other children for viewing them. The entrepreneurial streak of the Grundy clan had obviously come out in Eddie's son and heir.

Philip Molloy

GUINNESS, BASIL (LOFTY)

Christine Archer was miserable when her boss, Basil Grove, ended their affair in 1951, so went to Edinburgh for a holiday to try to forget him. There she had the good fortune to meet Lofty, a Scottish man in his mid twenties who wanted to be a farmer. She suggested he should come to Ambridge to find out more about a farmer's life, but he never took up her suggestion, although he did send her a Christmas card that year.

Rikki Fulton

GUPTA, USHA

Originally from Uganda and trained in London, Usha Gupta took nearly a year to adjust to English rural life, finding the slow pace of Ambridge a culture shock.

Arriving in 1991 as Mark Hebden's new partner, Usha was eager to prove herself, and when the local hunt caused havoc among Neil Carter's pigs, she urged him to claim for compensation. Neil said 'no': he didn't want to make a fuss because he might lose some of his egg accounts. She found such timidity hard to understand. What's more, she found Mark's wife Shula's nervous attitude towards her hard to understand. Shula was wary: she hadn't wanted Mark's partner to be a woman anyway, especially an attractive one such as Usha. But gradually, following a beer in the Bull with Neil and Bert Fry, supper with the Archers at Brookfield and a talk to the WI on the Indian way of life (and some sound advice for Sharon Richards over a drink in the Wine Bar), Usha's adoption into the local neighbourhood was accomplished.

Her own family hadn't helped. From the start, they had opposed the partnership. A large family from near Wolverhampton, their constantly negative vibrations caused Usha distress. But it was good that she was able by now to unburden her problems on Shula with whom she had become friends – as she had, too, with David and Ruth Archer; indeed, David tried to match Usha with his brother Kenton, but really that was a non-starter.

It was Ruth, though, with whom she identified most. She cherished their friendship and was touched when Ruth asked her to be godmother to her baby. It was impossible, as Usha is a Hindu, but she was pleased when she was invited to make the first symbolic cut of the christening cake.

Mark's sudden death in 1994 altered Usha's situation yet again. She has found herself alone, obliged to settle the affairs of her late partner and his grieving wife. Hard though it was, she managed to achieve this. She felt at home in Ambridge now – especially since, having bought Blossom Hill Cottage, she has made her home there too.

Sudha Buchar; Souad Faress

GWILLIAM, MR

Mrs Turvey was infuriated with the sound and smell of Walter Gabriel's pigs in Parson's Field in 1960. She contacted the authorities, who sent Mr Gwilliam to explain to Walter that he would have to get rid of the pigs unless he followed rigorous instructions. Walter got rid of the pigs.

Graham Rigby

HAIMES, SANDRA

Sandra Haimes replied to a PO box address in response to a 'gentleman farmer' advertising in a lonely hearts column. He was Joe Grundy. In 1987 Sandra and her son Jason visited Grange Farm for the weekend. She was surprised to discover that the man she hoped might be her spouse was merely a tenant at the farm and was hurt when Jason got locked in the coal cellar. She pursued Joe no longer.

Gillian Goodman

HALL, MR AND MRS

The Halls camped at Brookfield in the summer of 1956 with their son Leslie. Mrs Hall, a kindly soul, thought that Dan Archer's wife had died, and cooked him faggots and peas to keep him going; in fact Doris Archer was on holiday. Leslie got to know Christine Archer, who took him to a horse show which he thoroughly enjoyed, and she introduced him to the Hoods. He told them that he was going to take his A-levels, and tried to persuade Joan Hood to do the same. When the Halls' tent caught fire, Christine and Dan helped put out the blaze and as there was no room at the Bull, Dan took them in at the farm for the night and enjoyed another of Mrs Hall's magnificent meals. He lent them some rick canvas for the rest of their stay to save them having to buy a new tent, but was so grateful for the meals that he was most unwilling to accept any payment when they left a few days later.

Philip Garston-Jones

HAPGOOD-HARMAN, MR

Hapgood-Harman was editor of *The Borchester Echo* until his retirement in September 1976, when he was replaced by Simon Parker. Jack Woolley brought him back to hold the fort for a couple of months in 1977, when Parker and Woolley were at odds, and again in 1978 when Parker left for Kathmandu.

HARDING, GILBERT

Television personality Gilbert Harding opened the village fête in 1952. Mrs P. was worried that if he bought one of her lavender bags she wouldn't know where to put herself, but it proved an unnecessary anxiety.

HARE, GENERAL SIR BORTHWICK (BUNNY)

Bunny Hare escorted Mrs Antrobus to the Ambridge barn dance in 1987. Colonel Danby recognized him as his former commanding officer, and treated him with the greatest respect. The atmosphere became less formal when Bunny took over the calling from Nigel Pargetter.

Bernard Brown

HARPER, MISS

Sid and Polly Perks were impressed with their daughter Lucy's teacher, Miss Harper, when they met her at a parents' evening in 1976. Attractive and friendly, she told them that Lucy was doing very well in spite of being the youngest in the class.

Jane Rossington

HARRIS, MISS

Miss Harris was a lecturer at Borchester Technical College. She brought her students to help clear the village pond in 1974. They were thrilled to discover a silver rose bowl which turned out to belong to Grey Gables and had been stolen in the robbery of 1973.

HARRIS, PRU

see Forrest, Pru

HART, ALICE

The domestic bursar at the Field Study Centre, Alice Hart got married in 1974 and went to live in Penny Hassett.

HARVEY, CHARLES AND JEAN

Early in 1975 the Harveys bought Bull Farm. Charles Harvey was a wealthy and capable accountant.

His wife Jean was determined to make her presence felt and in no time at all, riding rough-shod over any opposition, was reorganizing fundraising for church restoration, organizing the village fête and flower show (scooping prizes as she went), the WRVS and meals-on-wheels. Before moving to Ambridge she had been president of her WI and made it known that she would like the post again. She may still be waiting. Otherwise, her efforts were met with success and her energies were welcomed by the village, although her bossiness caused caustic comment. Laura Archer and she became good friends, perhaps having much in common.

Charles was the 'mystery benefactor' of the floodlit game in Borchester when Ambridge

Wanderers had their victorious replay match against Jephcott in 1976.

The Harveys enjoyed a six months' trip to Singapore in 1986.

Victor Lucas and Patricia Gibson

Harvey, Dr

Phil Archer's eye problems led him in 1952 to Felpersham Infirmary where Dr Harvey operated on him for a cataract. He also dealt effectively with Phil's touch of self-pity: if Nelson could win the Battle of Trafalgar with one eye, he told him, Phil could certainly farm 400 acres.

Lester Mudditt

Harvey, Jean

see Harvey, Charles

Harvey, Susan

Susan Harvey came to live at Bull Farm with her parents in 1975. An extrovert blonde girl who enjoyed riding her horse and playing in the ladies' football team, she appeared in a revue sketch with Brian Aldridge, played the piano for Tom Forrest at a harvest supper and was Prince Charming in the local panto.

A few eyebrows were raised at her friendship with Gordon Armstrong.

Harvey, Trevor

Trevor Harvey had just completed a food technology course in 1989 when he came to work part-time for Pat and Tony Archer in 1989. He infuriated Sid Perks by lending his 'roadie' to Sid Perks's daughter, Lucy, of whom Sid was very protective.

The Heatons

Sharon Richards was overjoyed when the Heatons moved out of their council house on the green in 1991 and it was offered to her. It meant that for the first time she could provide a proper home for her daughter, Kylie.

Hebblewhite, Revd Amos

The vicar of Darrington officiated in 1988 at the funeral of Walter Gabriel, whom he knew well, having grown up in Ambridge when his father worked for Squire Lawson-Hope.

Hebden, Audrey (Bunty)

b. 25 Feb. 1922; 1 son, 1 dtr

Bunty wears the trousers in the Hebden household. No one would ever be good enough for her only son Mark. She was thirty-three when he was born and her protectiveness towards him made her unpopular with Shula, whom he married in 1985. Her tendency to bossiness makes friendship hard to come by, but Jill Archer has managed to get on well with her.

Sheila Allen

HEBDEN, JOANNA

With her ginger hair and brown eyes, Mark Hebden's sister dearly wanted to be a bridesmaid at his wedding to Shula Archer in September 1985. What with Shula not wanting bridesmaids and Joanna being two stone overweight, her chances were slim. Mother has had her on a strict diet since then, we are told.

HEBDEN, MARK CHARLES TIMOTHY

b. 20 Feb. 1955; m. Shula Archer 21 Sept. 1985; d. 17 Feb. 1994

Phil and Jill Archer were surprised when Shula brought Mark Hebden home for supper. This young solicitor from Borchester was very different from Shula's previous boyfriends. Little did they realize that Mark would eventually become their son-in-law.

Mark, an only son, had been brought up in Borchester. A quiet determined man, he had been educated at Shrewsbury School and went on to read law at Durham University. He was always a keen sportsman. He was under-14 Borchester judo champion, school cross-country champion, a footballer and a talented cricketer. On leaving school, he enjoyed skiing, hang-gliding and sky diving. He later became captain, and backbone, of Ambridge Cricket Club, for whom he scored a rare century. (Victor ludorum Marcus!)

In 1980, soon after he arrived on the scene, Mark was brought into conflict with the Archer family over a case of hunt sabotage. The Jarretts, represented by Mark, were accused by the South Borchester Hunt of criminal damage. They, in turn, accused the hunt of assault. Shula sided firmly with the Hunt. The magistrates (one of whom was Phil Archer) found the Jarretts guilty. Mark claimed the bench to be nothing more than 'Borchester's high-class mafia'. Furthermore, in an article for *The Borchester Echo*, he referred to the bench as 'socially accepted amateurs'. Fur flew in all directions. On appeal, the verdict against the Jarretts was reversed. In spite of all this, Shula's feelings for Mark were strong enough for her to say 'yes' when he proposed to her at Brookfield on New Year's Eve.

They bought a cottage in Penny Hassett, but by July Shula was having second thoughts and called the marriage off. Mark was lost without her. He even had the romantic notion of throwing up his career, buying up an old forge and becoming a blacksmith. Luckily these plans didn't materialize, and soon Mark found that his emotions were engaged elsewhere. In 1982 he embarked on a headstrong affair with Jackie Woodstock. Then he became engaged to Sarah Locke. In spite of herself, Shula found that she was jealous of both rivals.

It took his career trip to Hong Kong in 1984 for him to realize that he loved Shula best. When she visited him while he was working there, things weren't easy. But after her return to England, Mark followed her back and proposed to her on Lakey Hill.

In September 1985, Shula and Mark were married in considerable style and moved into a flat in the Old Wool Market in Borchester.

A year later they were in Glebe Cottage, but the marriage had already hit rough waters. Mark was irritated by the constant 'friendly' attentions paid to Shula by Nigel Pargetter. Then, when he went to work for a new law firm in Birmingham, he and Shula saw less and less of one another. They began to drift apart.

After getting involved in a messy antiques venture with Shula's brother Kenton, Mark set up a law practice in Borchester; he had hated the commuting and enjoyed working for himself. So well did he do that he was able to expand in 1991 and take on a partner. Shula was less than amused to find the lovely Usha Gupta working with her husband. Mark and Shula's inability to have children added to the tensions within the marriage. When Shula's younger sister, Elizabeth, became pregnant by fraudster Cameron Fraser, Mark supported Shula in her wish to adopt the baby. Horrified and distressed by Elizabeth's abortion, the couple, in their desperation to have a child of their own, embarked on IVF, seemingly without success.

Then tragedy struck. Just as their marriage had got through the rough passages and entered a calm, secure phase, Mark was involved in a fatal accident. He crashed his car into a tree as he swerved to avoid Caroline Bone, who had been thrown from her horse. He was killed instantly. He was buried in the churchyard at St Stephen's church. He was never to know that, at long last, Shula was expecting their child, for whom it will be up to Shula to keep Mark's memory alive.

Richard Derrington

HEBDEN, REGINALD GEORGE

1 son, 1 dtr

Like his son Mark, Reginald Hebden was a solicitor, until he retired. At home, however, his wife Bunty rules the roost and he rarely gets a word in edgeways. When Mark died in 1994, he was stoical and supported Bunty in her great distress.

HEBDEN, SHULA MARY (NÉE ARCHER)

b. 8 Aug. 1958; m. Mark Hebden 21 Sept. 1985

Shula Hebden is the most quietly determined of Phil and Jill Archer's four children. She has had to be: life has dealt her many knocks.

Shula and her twin brother Kenton were born in 1958. By the age of five they were attending the village school (now closed) where Shula, surprisingly, was considered to be a little backward. But with her usual persistence she made it to Borchester Grammar School where her careers teacher suggested she should go all out to try to become a vet. Shula certainly loved animals but her absolute passion was for horses and riding. Like most small girls she started by riding ponies but such was her promise as a show jumper that in March 1974 she caught the eye of Ann Moore, the champion of the day, who thought Shula had the potential to become a professional show jumper. Shula's life became hectic. She was doing a part-time secretarial and business course at Borchester Technical College, helping Christine Johnson with the Stables and Riding for the Disabled and spending long hours practising in the show-jumping ring. By August she had made great progress but was too head-strong for her own good. Showing off in front of Jack Woolley she injured herself and her mount, Mister Jones. She was unable to compete in the regional finals and by the following spring had begun to accept that she didn't have what it takes to be a profes-sional rider. At Trina Muir's suggestion she took a horse management course; but unfortunately there was no job at the end of it for her. For a while she worked for her father Phil as his farm secre-tary but Shula had soon had enough of working at home. She was relieved in December 1976 when she got a job with the Borchester estate agents Rodway & Watson as a junior office clerk.

Shula and Mark Hebden (Judy Bennett and Richard Derrington)

From her teenage years onwards, Shula had plenty of boyfriends. Relations with her parents were frequently strained as she flit-ted from one seemingly unsuitable boyfriend to another. The boy who would have brought her a box of Milk Tray was Neil Carter: he carried a torch for Shula for many years. He watched from the sidelines as Shula went from Eric Selwyn to farmer's boy Bill Morris, from plummy Charles Hodgson to Jeremy of the soft-top convertible, not to mention Robin Catchpole, Pedro from Spain and Martin Lambert, the vet. But Neil just didn't have that certain something. Simon Parker, a roving reporter with *The Borchester Echo* with a roving eye, evidently did, and in

1977 Shula fell for him in a big way. She was there for the taking – and take her he did, into the cornfields at Netherbourne, where that certain something was lost for ever. Shortly afterwards, Simon moved on to a new conquest. Her next boyfriend, Nick Wearing, caused even more havoc in Shula's life. In need of a complete break, she decided to travel overland with him to New Zealand. Some friend he turned out to be. He abandoned her in Bangkok, where her passport, money and all her belongings were stolen. A tearful Shula rang Brookfield to say that she was coming home. At Birmingham airport her anxious parents were horrified by how thin and pale Shula was. But the experience had helped her to grow up.

In 1980, Shula found her much-loved grandmother dead at Glebe Cottage. She was most touched when Dan Archer told her that it had been Doris's wish that Shula should eventually inherit Glebe Cottage.

By now, Shula had met a promising young local solicitor Mark Hebden, who treated her to a trip in a hot-air balloon for her twenty-second birthday. But their growing romance was threatened when Mark defended some protesters against the South Borsetshire Hunt. A keen hunter, Shula found herself in opposition. Their rift was instantly healed when Mark, to Shula's amazement, proposed to her on New Year's Eve 1980. She accepted. By now Shula was an important member of the team at Rodway & Watson. She and Mark planned to get married, do up a pretty Victorian cottage in Penny Hassett and continue with their separate careers until children came along. Six months later, nagging doubts had crept in and Shula asked Mark for a postponement and time to think.

It took Shula nearly three years to conclude that she wanted to marry Mark. Nigel Pargetter had enchanted and amused her. But Mark's brief engagement to Sarah Locke and his lengthy trip to Hong Kong finally made her heart grow fonder and helped her to make up her mind.

What could have been grander for this couple than for the reception to take place at Netherbourne Hall, thanks to Shula's best friend Caroline Bone's family connections? To crown it all, the Queen's cousin, Patrick Lichfield, an old friend of Lord Netherbourne's, took the photographs.

But theirs wasn't to be a fairytale marriage. Shula and Mark moved into a flat in the Old Wool Market in Borchester and soon settled back into their busy working lives. Some weeks Shula saw more of her old boyfriend Nigel than she did of Mark. The young couple realized that they were going to have to work at their marriage. They moved into Glebe Cottage in 1986 and it seemed an ideal place to bring up a family. But when Shula didn't conceive she confessed her sense of failure to Caroline Bone. Then in 1990 Mark and Shula were delighted to discover that she was pregnant. Unfortunately it was an ectopic pregnancy which had to be terminated. This placed a huge strain on the marriage and at one point they even discussed separation but decided to give the marriage one last chance. Mark wanted to expand his practice and take on a partner, hoping to be able to spend more time with his wife. Shula was less than delighted when she discovered that Mark's new business associate was going to be the lovely Asian woman Usha Gupta.

When Shula heard that her sister Elizabeth

Archer was expecting a child by Cameron Fraser, she asked if she could adopt the baby. She was horrified when, instead, Elizabeth chose to have an abortion. Mark and Shula decided that their only hope of having a child lay with in vitro fertilization. There followed a long round of medical checks and hospital appointments but despite one short-lived pregnancy Shula seemed destined never to have a baby.

On the morning of 17 February 1994 Shula was furious when Mark announced that he might not be home in time to help her with Caroline Bone's pre-wedding supper party, but she was delighted when he called her on his car phone to say that he would be able to make it after all. Seconds later he was dead. He had swerved to avoid an accident and his car had crashed into a tree. A week later, Shula discovered that she was pregnant again. If only she could have shared the joyful news with Mark. This time nothing, but nothing, was going to stop her having the baby.

Shula has astonished everyone in Ambridge with her courage. In the painful process of trying to rebuild her life for her own sake and that of her child, her lifelong Christian beliefs and the support of her family and the Ambridge community have given her strength.

Judy Bennett

HEBDITCH, ERNIE

Hebditch was an excellent pig breeder near Little Croxley who wanted to get out of pig breeding and offered Phil Archer some of his stock in 1991. Phil had rejected Neil Carter's suggestion that Phil should buy from him the previous year, so Neil was furious when Phil decided to accept his offer.

HEBE

On the strength of an undefined relationship with Nelson Gabriel, Hebe sang at the opening of his wine bar, but when she found he couldn't pay her, she happily allowed Jack Woolley to whisk her away to the splendours of Grey Gables to perform there.

Hebe Taylor

HELSTON, MR

In 1952 Dan Archer required capital so that he could buy the smallholding from Jack and Peggy Archer to enable them to move to Cornwall. His bank manager in Borchester, Mr Helston, agreed to allow him an overdraft. He advised Dan on a regular basis and four years later, after the loss of the Brookfield herd to foot-and-mouth disease, helped with the purchase of new stock.

Will Kings

HENDRICKSON, VICTOR

Victor was a live-in groom for a year at the Stables in 1974.

HENSHAW, SIR HARRY

Jack Woolley was proud to be able to tell Mrs Antrobus in 1988 that his very first Grey

THE BOOK OF THE ARCHERS

Gables resident, Sir Harry Henshaw, was none other than the brother to Lucinda Packer of the Packer chocolate empire. His satisfaction was short-lived, however, when he found Sir Harry dead in his bath after a last meal of Pat Archer's organic yoghourt and honey. Jack called the police, ambulance and fire services, but it was left to Dr Thorogood to pronounce death from natural causes.

HENSHAW, MICHAEL

A substantial farmer with 1,500 acres near Waterley Cross, Michael Henshaw was the chairman-elect of the Hollerton branch of the National Farmers' Union in 1974. He asked Phil Archer to stand as vice-chairman and he was duly elected.

HEPPLEWHITE, FLORA

Wilfred Sproggett insisted on taking Flora Hepplewhite with him for protection when he had to accompany Tom Forrest to Mrs Turvey's for New Year's Eve 1956.

HERIOT, ROBERT

Robert Heriot was commissioned to paint portraits of Richard Grenville and Hazel Trentham in 1966. The pictures were later included in an exhibition the artist held in London. While he was in Ambridge, Robert became friendly with Dawn Kingsley, John Tregorran's business partner, with the result that she

became inattentive to her work at the New Curiosities Shop. When she quarrelled with John, Robert sprang to her defence and helped them come to an agreement.

Robin Bailey

HEYDON BERROW

Heydon Berrow is common land to the south of Ambridge, densely wooded around the lower slopes.

HIGGS, JOHN

John Higgs was first employed as chauffeur to Jack Woolley in 1966. Unbeknown to his employer, he used Jack's Bentley to visit his ladyfriends. In 1983 he referred to his current one as 'the High Flier from Little Croxley'. Jack Woolley also expects him to work as a handyman. A job at the garden centre, although at first considered to be beneath his dignity, had interesting results: Higgs discovered a talent for growing plants. He has become indispensable to his employer for such magnificent chrysanthemums as 'Woolley Magic' and 'Woolley Wonder'. Hazel Woolley once had the temerity to pick these prize blooms and, when he reprimanded her, she sacked him. Higgs left Grey Gables in a fury to lodge with the Horrobins, until a craven Jack apologized and begged him to return to work.

There have been differences of opinion between Higgs and Grey Gables' chef Jean-Paul, such as the time when, during a rehearsal for a raft race, they fell into the water and Jean-Paul accused Higgs of wanting to drown him.

HILL, BERNARD

In 1978 Doris Archer engaged Bernard Hill to help her with the garden. An old-age pensioner with twelve grandchildren, he lodged with his son and daughter-in-law in one of the council houses. Jean Harvey wooed him away from the Archers' garden by paying him more money. He had a penchant for pinching ladies' bottoms and snapping their knicker elastic. Doris and Polly Perks both suffered this indignity.

Graham Rigby

HODGE, TERRY

Ruth Archer went to Paradise Farm in Edgeley in 1992 to find out if Terry was interested in the feed co-op she was setting up. She returned home in a rage, describing him as a male chauvinist pig, and wasn't comforted by Tony Archer's wry comment that he knew that already.

HODGES, MICK

A hippy vegetable wholesaler with a business called Zodiac Organics, Hodges came to see Pat and Tony Archer in 1987, with a view to selling their organic vegetables. However, the proposal didn't come to anything as Pat felt that his business practices were dubious.

Stuart Organ

HODGESON, CHARLES

For a short while in 1976 Charles Hodgson was Shula Archer's boyfriend. Proudly named after Prince Charles, he was a member of the South Borsetshire Hunt and chairman of the Young Conservatives. He farmed 600 acres with his father near Waterley Cross and was rather 'county'. Shula was thrilled when he asked her to ride his mare, Swallow, in a local point-to-point. But she fell off. That was it, really: she had had enough of Charles – he was too plummy.

HOLLAND, ELIZABETH

When Phil Archer resigned from his job as Charles Grenville's farm manager in 1962, and moved his family into Hollowtree Farm, the Grenvilles, wanting to give him a farewell present, paid Elizabeth Holland to redesign the kitchen in the Archers' new home. She delighted the children by suggesting that part of the lawn be made into a children's paddock.

HOLLAND, STEVE

Kathy Perks' first husband Steve Holland tracked her down to Ambridge in 1985 and asked her to come back to him. She was afraid to talk to him and asked DS Dave Barry to inform him that she wanted a divorce. Realizing that there was no hope, Steve agreed to start divorce proceedings and returned to find comfort in the arms of his many girlfriends in Chesterfield.

Colin Starkey

HOLLERTON

Hollerton is a small market town six miles west of Ambridge, and with its railway station provides one of Ambridge's links with the outside world. Hollerton Junction managed to survive Beecham's closures and still has a service, even though the trains stop for only a few minutes nowadays. Over the years Hollerton Junction has witnessed all sorts of arrivals and departures, from Jane Maxwell's final leavetaking in 1952 to Susan Carter's midnight return in 1994.

There are many associations between Hollerton and Ambridge that span the generations. Mabel Larkin used to visit her sister Clarice and husband Fred who lived there in the fifties; Walter Gabriel and Mrs Turvey opened a pet shop there in 1960; and Tony Stobeman set up his betting shop there in 1962, to be supervised by Sally Johnson after they married. It was at a concert given by the Hollerton town band at the Free Trade Hall in 1978 that the Archer family first realized how serious Christine Archer was about George Barford. George played the cornet in the band, looking resplendent in his bottle-green uniform with magenta stripes on the trousers, and Christine couldn't take her eyes off him.

Friendly rivalry exists between Ambridge and Hollerton over skittles, darts and cricket matches, and the point-to-points at Hollerton are well attended. It was at one of these that Christine rode the ill-fated Midnight in 1953 and came second, beaten by Reggie Trentham.

HOLLOWTREE FARM

In 1961 the dairy side of Jess Allard's farm was amalgamated with Barratt's Farm and Brookfield to create Ambridge Dairy Farmers, which operated from 5 April 1961. When Jess died in 1962 his son Joe decided to sell the farm to Phil Archer, who resigned as farm manager for the Grenville Estate to join Ambridge Dairy Farmers. Phil, his wife Jill and their three children left Coombe Cottage on 30 August 1962 and began their new life, renaming the farm Hollowtree. On 3 September Phil, Dan and Fred Barratt agreed on the complete amalgamation of the three farms to be known as Ambridge Farmers Ltd.

Their fourth child, Elizabeth, was born in 1967 and they continued to live there until 1970, when Ambridge Farmers Ltd suggested that they should live at Brookfield and gave the go-ahead for the necessary alterations. Hollowtree farmhouse was put up for auction and sold for just over £12,000 to Nelson Gabriel, who converted it into flats and lived there himself for a time. The land is now part of Brookfield and is used primarily as a pig unit.

HOLLY

John Archer's new girlfriend spent the night at Bridge Farm after a party in 1992. John pretended an interest in her that was only partly genuine, in order to deflect his parents' attention from his friendship with Sharon Richards. The following year when she was sixteen, Holly saw much less of John and started working for her A-levels with a view to studying history at university.

HOME FARM

Home Farm is the largest farm in Ambridge. The farmhouse, originally called Ambridge Court, was built on the foundations of the ancient Lyttleton Manor and is principally early eighteenth-century in origin. After the Second World War it was converted by Ralph Bellamy into flats for the workers on his surrounding Estate. Brian Aldridge acquired Home Farm from the Bellamy Estate in 1975 and he and his wife Jennifer converted the flats back into a farmhouse. The farm is mainly arable.

In 1978 the Aldridges installed a solar-heated swimming pool. In the same year Jennifer and Jill Archer joined forces and created the Two Jays Craft Studio in a converted barn on the Home Farm estate. With typical insouciance, Jennifer neglected to put in for planning permission; but she was saved from prosecution by the fact that the Studio didn't make any money and was closed down very rapidly. In 1986 she designed the Home Farm holiday cottages called collectively the Rookeries, and enjoyed finding suitable pieces of furniture, while neglecting such necessities as plumbing until the very last minute.

Over the past few years, Brian has spent many thousands of pounds on diversification projects, observed with great interest by the villagers. He started deer farming in 1987 and so many onlookers turned up to watch the arrival of the deer that ice-cream vans soon followed, and Brian had to tell them all to clear off. He created an artificial lake for trout fishing and set up his off-the-road riding course in 1992, both of which have taken time to become established.

HONEYSUCKLE COTTAGE

Walter Gabriel bought thatched Honeysuckle Cottage with surrounding land in 1957 from the Wainwrights. In 1977 the thatch was wearing thin. The roof started to leak, death-watch beetle was discovered in the timbers and it finally collapsed in a gale. Walter's son, Nelson Gabriel, came to his rescue and paid not only for a thatcher but also for a new pine staircase. Walter was highly satisfied with the results and took the opportunity to whitewash the walls and get rid of a lot of unwanted furniture from his days as a junk dealer.

In 1988 Nelson was staying with his father and sleeping peacefully when the gable-end wall collapsed in the night. Nelson woke up, only to faint with shock, but happily no one was hurt. Walter moved in with Mrs Perkins, enjoying the fuss hugely, but he was destined never to live in his cottage again as he died before he could return.

The cottage was left to Nelson, who put it up for auction in 1989. However, it didn't make its reserve price and he kept it, deciding to live there himself and keep it available as a base for his daughter Rosemary Tarrant.

HOOD, ARTHUR FROBISHER (DOUGHY)

Arthur Hood had been apprenticed earlier to

Ben White and had left the village to become a ship's baker. On his retirement he returned to Ambridge with his nephew Percy and his family in 1956 and took over the baker's shop from Ben White.

Accident-prone, he was once locked inside the church and played an SOS on the bells to summon help; on another occasion he fell down the well and in his absence all the bread was burned.

He adored his assistant Rita Flynn and allowed her to put her caravan behind his shop, even though it got him into trouble with the authorities. He even made a will in her favour, and was extremely annoyed when she became engaged to Michael O'Leary.

Percy's family moved back to Scotland, but Doughy's great-niece, Joan, returned to live in Ambridge, and got a job with Carol Grey at the market garden. Hollerton Bakeries wanted to buy Doughy out and, when he refused their offer, tried to steal his customers. Joan's attempt to help him by sabotaging Hollerton Bakeries' vans only made matters worse. By 1961 his financial situation was so bad that he had to give up baking his own bread and buy it in from his bitter rivals.

Laura Archer became his partner for a while (he was pleased when she stopped making changes to his arrangements) but financial pressures persuaded them to sell the business to Juniper Bakeries in 1965.

Jack Woolley gave him a job at Grey Gables, and he baked bread for the Bull until Juniper Bakeries pointed out that he was breaking their sale agreement. Next Mrs Turvey employed him part-time at her pet shop and Walter Gabriel sought his help in the production of rocking chairs.

In 1968 he went to Scotland to live with Percy's family, but returned five years later looking for property in Ambridge. He was disappointed when Ralph Bellamy refused to sell him Blossom Hill Cottage and moved out of the district once again.

Arnold Ridley

HOOD, BETTY

Married to Percy, Betty Hood is the mother of Diana, Margaret, Joan and Roger. They had previously lived in Ambridge but the family had moved north. On their return in 1956, Doris Archer helped them move into Court Farm.

Betty's eldest daughters got work in Ambridge, but with teenage Joan there were problems. Betty advised her badly, urging her to go out with Dusty Rhodes rather than Jimmy Grange, which proved to be poor judgement. The family moved back north in 1959.

Dorothy Smith

HOOD, THE RT REVD CYRIL, BISHOP OF FELPERSHAM

Cyril, Bishop of Felpersham, is a man of simple tastes, with little time for elaborate robes. When he came to Ambridge in 1987 to carry out a confirmation, the vicar Richard Adamson arranged for him to meet a cross-section of the village community. This included Joe Grundy, Walter Gabriel, Mrs Potter and Sid and Kathy Perks, all of whom the bishop asked to join him later at Grey

Gables. Higgs, Jack Woolley's chauffeur, drove Cyril in the Bentley from Mrs Potter's, to Walter's and thence to Joe's. He chatted with Joe for quite a time, and sampled a glass or two of the Grundy scrumpy. Fed up with waiting, Higgs went off to the Bull, and Joe drove the bishop to Grey Gables in the back of his van – not quite as Jack had planned. Jack had prepared an elaborate feast for Cyril and was taken aback when his guest arrived accompanied by much of the village; by now Nelson Gabriel and Mrs P. had joined the throng. Everyone tucked in while the smiling bishop ate a piece of cheese with some water to wash it down. When he had finished, he benevolently commanded them to take home the left-over food with them. Joe was in his seventh heaven.

Cyril and Jack Woolley have long been friends. Jack asked him to officiate at his wedding to Peggy Archer, to which he was pleased to agree.

In 1993 Jack arranged another dinner for Caroline Bone, Robin Stokes and the bishop. Caroline took a walk round the grounds of Grey Gables and was impressed with his enlightened opinions about, among other things, the ordination of women. His kindly intelligence helped her to come to a positive conclusion about her chances of happiness with Robin. Six weeks later, Robin and Caroline were able to tell him about their engagement.

Peter Howell

Diana Hood (Eileen Barry)

eldest daughter of Percy and Betty Hood. She worked for a while at Fairbrother's as a poultry girl in 1956 and enjoyed a mild flirtation with Phil Archer, but remarked to her sister Joan that she thought him 'too much of a stick-in-the-mud for a husband'.

Eileen Barry

HOOD, DIANA

Diana was the very attractive 23-year-old

HOOD, JOAN

see Burton, Joan

HOOD, MARGARET

Maggie Hood loved horses and had worked with the Hunt where her father had been bailiff. When in 1956 the family moved to Ambridge for three years, she found her ideal job with Christine Archer at the Grey Gables stables.

Jean Lester

HOOD, PERCY

3 dtrs, 1 son

Percy Hood was married to Betty and father to Diana, Margaret, Joan and Roger. Originally from Ambridge, he had left during a farming depression to take a job as bailiff on a northern estate.

On Percy's return to Ambridge in 1956, to Court Farm, Dan Archer was pleased to lend him some milking equipment to help set him up. He did not altogether settle down in Ambridge. Norman Wynford and he had disagreements with George Fairbrother and he lost some cows through yew poisoning.

In 1959 he took another job as bailiff on the Scottish borders, sold the farm and left. News of his death in 1970 reached the village through his uncle, Doughy Hood.

Ronald Baddiley

HOODS' FARM

see Kenton's Farm

HOPKINS, MR

Mr Hopkins ran a fleet of lorries in Hollerton, and in 1975 he bought ten acres at Bull Farm. He wanted to develop the land but was refused planning permission, so rented it to Tony Archer. They came to a gentleman's agreement that should permission be granted at a later date Tony would leave at short notice, but he's still there.

HORROBIN, BERT

4 sons, 1dtr

Bert Horrobin is a lengthman and the father of the Horrobin brood. He is often miserable, and smokes heavily. But then, he is the father of the Horrobin brood.

William Eedle

HORROBIN, CLIVE

b. 9 Nov. 1972; 1dtr by Sharon Richards

Clive Horrobin was put behind bars in 1993 and as far as most people in Ambridge are concerned that is where they would like him to stay. He was sentenced for leading an armed raid on the post office and escaping from remand. While he was on the run he terrorized his sister Susan Carter and used emotional blackmail to get money and clothes from her. When she was accused of seeking to pervert the course of public justice, Clive did nothing to help her defence and was totally unconcerned that because of him she ended up in prison.

But then Clive has never been concerned much about anybody but himself. He abandoned his girlfriend Sharon Richards when she was heavily pregnant, helping himself to her ghetto-blaster on the way. A year later, claiming long-overdue affection for his daughter, Kylie, he tried to move into Sharon's council house. And he had no qualms about informing on his mate Bruno when the police asked him who else had been involved in the raid on the shop.

Alex Jones

Horrobin, Mrs Ivy

4 sons, 1dtr

Ivy Horrobin is used to visiting members of her family in prison; and her attempts to keep her own family on the straight and narrow have met with little success. Of her four sons, Stewart, Gary, Keith and Clive, two have done time inside and Stewart and Gary both wear smart leather jackets which they are rumoured to have stolen from Birmingham. Ivy hoped that she had been more successful with her daughters and was shocked when Susan was imprisoned for seeking to pervert the course of public justice: Susan had always been the one member of her family who had seemed (unlike her sister Terrible Tracy) to have escaped its influence.

Ivy is not averse to telling people what she thinks. She rounded on Christine Barford when she interviewed her for a survey in 1989 on housing needs. What Ivy needs is a bigger house and a lower rent. Sometimes to subsidize her husband's income she takes cleaning jobs.

She enjoys getting out of her own home, in which a large television set and video recorder have pride of place, to babysit for Susan's children and for Kylie Richards, Clive's illegitimate daughter. When she can afford it, she enjoys a game of bingo in Borchester. She's still hoping that one day she will win the star prize.

Cynthia Cherry

Horrobin, Susan

see Carter, Susan

Hoskins, Florrie

In 1990 Jennifer Aldridge came upon an intriguing local tragedy which she recounted to Martha Woodford. Many years ago a young girl named Florrie Hoskins had lived in Martha's cottage. Discovering she was pregnant, she had disappeared on All Hallows' Eve and drowned herself in the village pond. Unfortunately Martha was so afraid of being haunted by Florrie's ghost that she asked the vicar to perform an exorcism, but Jennifer solved the problem by claiming that the cottage was one of the same name in Lower Loxley.

Howard, Douglas

John Tregorran recommended that Robin Freeman should consult his solicitor, Douglas

Howard, when Robin's unstable wife, Zoe, maliciously damaged equipment at the Field Study Centre in 1972.

HOWARD, KEITH AND VERONICA

The Howards, together with their children, Coriander and Guy, were the first tenants in one of Jennifer Aldridge's holiday cottages, the Rookeries, in 1986. It was not completed but they didn't seem to mind, although Jennifer was irritated when they instructed the builders in their work on the next cottage. Disliking her time in the country, five-year-old Coriander spent much of it throwing bricks at the lambs.

HOWELL, ARTHUR

Arthur Howell was the first manager of the market garden, appointed by Carol Grey at the insistence of Charles Grenville early in 1961. He and his wife Margaret left at the end of the same year.

HOWELL, MORGAN

Haydn Evans visited his friend Morgan Howell, conductor of the Llanqraig Choir, to arrange for the choir to visit Ambridge in June 1975 and give a concert in aid of the church funds.
Dillwyn Owen

HUBBOCKS, CYRIL

Formerly a milkman, Cyril Hubbocks retired in 1992 after thirty years with Borchester Dairies. He had been a keen angler all his life and his dream came true when, later in the year, he got the job of Brian Aldridge's fishing manager. The appointment pleased Eddie Grundy, for when Cyril and Tom Forrest got together to reminisce, it seemed all too easy for Eddie to use the facilities of the Home Farm Lake to instruct his son William in the rudiments of poaching fish. But Brian wasn't relying on Cyril for security – he nabbed the poachers himself.

HUGHES, MR

The bell-hanger responsible for rehanging St Stephen's church bells in 1975.

HUXLEY, MALCOLM

A farm worker at Bridge Farm from 1979.

HYLBEROW, LADY

Lady Hylberow's intrusion into the lives of the Archers was bizarre. On her way home from shopping one day in January 1952, Christine Archer restored a small terrier to its owner, only to watch in horror as a careless driver knocked into the dog on a zebra crossing. Christine lost no time in taking down the number of the car and helping the terrier, Foxy, to a vet. What was mystifying was that the owner of the dog, Lady Hylberow, kept calling her Felicity. Eventually Lady Hylberow explained that Felicity was the name of her much-loved daughter who, during the Blitz ten years ago, had gone out to post a letter and never returned. Lady Hylberow liked to believe that she was still alive somewhere and for a moment Christine, who resembled her, had brought the possibility closer.

Lady Hylberow seemed to weave a spell around the normally practical Christine, treating her like her long-lost daughter. She gave her presents, took her out and eventually asked her to go to Ethiopia with her to research a book on ecclesiastical art. All this was viewed with dark suspicion by Christine's family, who found the situation odd to the point of alarming. In the end reality overtook the fantasy and Lady Hylberow was disillusioned when Christine tried to break a theatre date with her to see her boyfriend, Dick Raymond. She told Christine that she'd had enough trouble with Felicity about boys. She wrote a letter to Christine's mother, Doris, saying that she had decided not to ask Christine to accompany her to Ethiopia after all, and that was the end of this odd episode.

Pauline Seville

ILVERTON, MR AND JOAN

Netherbourne smallholder Mr Ilverton sold a pony to Christine Archer in 1953 because he needed more grazing land, but she didn't bargain for the little girl who followed her back to the Stables and was there again next day, sobbing forlornly. It was his daughter Joan. Christine offered to sell the pony back, but he and his wife had realized her distress and were already arranging to buy her another, to be kept at a neighbour's.

Leslie Parker and Ysanne Churchman

IMISON, MR

Though he was a trading standards officer, it was in the guise of an animal diseases inspector that Mr Imison visited Ambridge Farm in 1984. There he found the farm shop selling underweight produce due to faulty scales. He might have overlooked this, but as Mike Tucker had already been warned about not displaying prices and the blackboard was not to be seen – it had been lent to the playgroup

– he felt he was obliged to report him.

Kim Durham

INSLEY, BILL

d. 23 Sept. 1986; 2 dtrs

Bill Insley originated from Derbyshire, where he farmed until the National Coal Board bought him out for £600,000. He was sixty by then and his wife persuaded him to retire early. Suddenly she died and he was lost. His two grown-up daughters persuaded their father to make a clean break and start again, this time on a more modest scale.

So in 1983 Bill bought Willow Farm and 15 acres of land from Phil Archer, and took up breeding rare pigs. He was a gregarious man and the village took to him. Neil Carter advised him about his pigs and Bill, in return, offered Neil his old barn for his hens at a knock-down rent.

He enjoyed Neil's youthful enthusiasm, and he became friends, too, with Martha Woodford. She was piggy-in-the-middle between Joe Grundy and Bill for a time as they vied for her affection. On the spring bank holiday in 1984, Joe invited Martha to see *Mary Poppins* with him. The inside of a dark, airless cinema with the wheezing Joe humming 'It's a jolly holiday with Martha' was hardly her idea of total bliss and she was delighted to be able to tell Joe that Bill had already asked her out. She wasn't so pleased when she discovered that what Bill had in mind was a day looking at various pig breeds. One was much like another to her and they all smelt the same. The village smiled as they watched these two old boys play out a draw.

By 1986 Bill was one of the elder statesmen of Ambridge, ever happy and prepared to be of service. And so it was a sad day when Neil found him dead of a heart attack at home. He left eight acres and the barn to Neil, who was grateful and missed him. Together with Phil and Jill Archer he attended Bill's funeral, as did Martha.

Ted Moult

IPPY

Caroline Bone gave the nickname 'Ippy' to Rustic Oak, the dark bay gelding which she bought after her beloved Ivor had to be put down in 1990. She was devastated when he was stolen from a box at Grey Gables in March 1993, never to be found.

JACKSON, GAVIN

Jackson was the head of personnel at Shires Breweries who sat next to Peggy Archer at the Vintner's annual dance in 1978. He suggested she interview Jackie Smith as a replacement for Nora McAuley at the Bull. Peggy took his advice and Jackie got the job.

JACKSON, MISS

When the Grundys tried deception in a claim in 1989, Borsetshire Farm Insurance sent Miss Jackson to deal with them. As she had been brought up on a farm, their schemes didn't stand a chance. She didn't fuss; she just told them to adjust their claims, then drove off in her jeep.

Joanna Mackie

JARRETT, MR AND MRS

Mr and Mrs Jarrett live in Waterley Cross and are remembered for disrupting the South Borsetshire Hunt in 1980. Phil Archer was on the bench when they were found guilty of breach of the peace and causing criminal damage, but their solicitor, Mark Hebden, appealed successfully against the verdict. Mark's outspoken comments about the judiciary were quoted in the press and caused severe friction between him and Jill Archer.

JASON

Jason is Ambridge's builder. He's good-natured and free with advice, and if his ways of working are very much his own, there are few complaints about the results. Many have employed him, including the Woolleys, the Pargetters, the Aldridges and the church. When young, he had wanted to be an archaeologist – an interest which no doubt helped him to recognize an important shard in the graveyard when he and his apprentice Clint were digging trenches for the new church lavatory in 1992. During the same job several villagers were scandalized to see them playing 'bullfights' with disinterred bones, and unimpressed when Jason pointed out that they were animal bones. Not long afterwards he told Mrs Antrobus that Clint's work was good but he tended to be 'a bit slapdash on the PR front' – a case, she might well have retorted, of the pot calling the kettle black.

Jason's own PR did little to placate Dr Locke when Jennifer Aldridge decided to have alterations made to the holiday cottage where he was staying during 1994 and which he had to leave. But his services remain in demand and the cricket team are delighted with the new showers at the cricket pavilion.

Brian Miller

JEAN-PAUL

Jean-Paul has long been a stormy presence in the background at Grey Gables. A farmer's son from the Dordogne, he wants eventually to open his own restaurant, but meanwhile is content to rule the roost in the kitchens of Grey Gables as chef.

He's partial to the odd Gaulois, and loathes vegetarians and anyone who thinks they know more about cooking than he does. He despises all Englishmen, which puts Jack Woolley at a disadvantage, and it is left to Caroline Bone to pour oil on troubled waters when Jack and Jean-Paul have one of their many misunderstandings.

Jean-Paul (Yves Aubert)

Though quick to take offence himself, he is not over-concerned about the sensibilities of others: he was dismissive of Jack's 'vulgar' Christmas decorations; he binned Kathy Perks's quiche, calling it an insult to the word 'cuisine'; and he punched Dave Barry on the nose when he made the mistake of insulting

Caroline. He unexpectedly showed another side, however, when he laughed on discovering the Tricolore upside-down at the French night at the Bull, and provided Calvados all round.

The villagers, used to his tantrums and threats of resignation, were astonished when he disappeared with all his possessions in December 1991 in the mistaken belief that Peggy Archer was accusing him of stealing wine. It was some time before Jack and Caroline learned that he had been poached by Nelson Gabriel for his wine bar; and it wasn't until Caroline called his bluff by advertising for a new chef that he returned, banishing his temporary replacement from 'his' kitchen – sweet music to Jack's ears.

Jean-Paul keeps his love-life secret, although it's known that he did go out with Hazel Woolley for a while. He named a pudding after Clarrie Grundy, warmed by her love of France, but that is as far as their friendship went, despite her husband Eddie's conviction that they were having an affair.

Something of a dark horse, Jean-Paul lends spice and charm to the very English atmosphere of Grey Gables.

Yves Aubert

J ENSEN, THORKHIL

Thorkhil Jensen was the handsome, blond Danish student who came to work at Bridge Farm in 1991. A hard worker and good company, he spent most of his six months in Ambridge in the arms of Sharon Richards. She was lonely and clinging, and Thorkil was good to her. On his last night in England,

over a candlelit dinner, she begged him to stay with her, but although he said he loved her, he couldn't commit himself. At the airport Sharon tried again, suggesting that she would go out to Denmark with him. Thorkhil avoided making a reply, except to say that he would keep in touch. As Sharon watched his plane getting smaller and smaller in the sky, the doubts came flooding in.

Andrew Wincott

J IMMY

Mrs Turvey's great-nephew came to stay with her in 1955. Tom Forrest and Carol Grey were in the market garden when they caught Jimmy with a catapult in his hand by a broken greenhouse pane. They didn't believe his denials but had to apologize at a later date when Jennifer Archer confessed to the crime.

Dorothy English

J OHNNY

Johnny attended the Riding for the Disabled sessions organized by Christine Johnson in 1976. Walter Gabriel, helping to hold the children on the ponies, excited him so much that he nearly had a nasty accident. However, he was awarded a certificate in riding, which made up for everything.

J OHNSON, CHRISTINE

see Barford, Christine

JOHNSON, FRED

Fred Johnson, owner of a Borchester coach and taxi firm, employed Harry Booker in 1973 to drive a mini-bus from Ambridge to Borchester, serving all the villages between, for as long as the service remained profitable. Harry left the job six months later and the service didn't survive him long.

JOHNSON, HERBERT

Paul Johnson's father Herbert was a successful agricultural contractor during the fifties.

Lewis Gedge

JOHNSON, HILDA

The daughter of a lowly publican, Hilda married wealthy Herbert Johnson and concentrated hard on social climbing. Her son Paul was the apple of her eye but his marriage to Christine Archer in 1956 was not what she wanted at all. This caused a fierce row between mother and son, and Paul told her that he was happy to do without the Johnson cash and her snobbish approach to life. She reconciled herself to the marriage, however, and left her money invested in Paul's promising business dealings. Sadly, the relationship remained strained and in 1960, despite Paul's protests that he was having a difficult time, she withdrew it all to retire to Bournemouth to run a boarding house.

Hilda Birch

JOHNSON, PAUL

b. 10 Jan. 1931; m. Christine Archer 15 Dec. 1956; 1 adopted son; d. 10 May 1978

Paul Johnson came from a wealthy background, and in the 1950s spent his life almost exclusively in the world of horses. He was a regular winner over jumps at local point-to-points, and it was at such an event that he first met Christine Archer, who was a fine horsewoman in her own right. He was smitten, and they were married in December 1956. For the first carefree year of marriage, they were hardly out of the saddle, riding, racing, hunting with a succession of horsey friends.

In 1957 Paul's father died and Paul had to look after the family business. Three years later his mother wanted to take her money out of the business and he sold it to Charles Grenville on condition that he would be kept on as general manager for another five years. But in 1961 he resigned and embarked on a series of business ventures, none of which provided much return or satisfaction; and behind Christine's back he also sought satisfaction of another kind. Christine always stood by him, though, increasingly, she found living with him difficult.

In 1966 they adopted a son, Peter, in the hope of building a happy family life together, but by 1974 Paul was in Germany trying to expand his business concerns while Christine and Peter remained in Ambridge. He returned to work for a firm in London, dividing his work between there and Ambridge, and the next year was out of work once more. He had had an affair with Brenda

Maynard, PA to his boss, but that was over too. It wasn't long before he set out on a new scheme, a trout farm. It failed, losing £20,000, and he had to file for bankruptcy.

He could take no more. He left Christine a note saying that he was going away for ever. Alarmed, the Archer family began a search, and, with the help of the airport police, ran Paul to earth in Hamburg. Chris flew out to him, but he told her their life together was over, he had a job there and intended staying. Phil Archer contacted Paul, reminding him that there was the small matter of the bankruptcy hearing to face. The family would stand behind him, Phil said, and he couldn't run away for ever. To Chris's delight, Paul rang and agreed to come home and face the music. Whether or not he would have done will never be known, for he was killed in a car crash on the autobahn. Because of his death, the court proceedings were dropped, though Christine had to give up their house, the Wynfords' farmhouse, to his creditors.

Leslie Dunn

JOHNSON, PETER

b. 5 Sept. 1965

Peter Johnson was adopted as a baby by Christine and Paul Johnson in 1966. From an early age he showed an interest in music; he was a soloist for the school choir and at one stage was considering a career in music administration.

His reaction to Paul's death in 1978 was quiet, perhaps because his father had been becoming more and more distant from him. When Christine announced that she was going to marry George Barford he was pleased. George had been kind to him, taking him fishing and letting him help with the shoot.

He left Ambridge to go to university and since then has only spent fleeting visits at home.

Simon Cornish

JOHNSON, SALLY

see Stobeman, Sally

JONES, LIBBY

Libby Jones, a milk recorder in her twenties, had just parted from her boyfriend when in 1977 she had a flirtation with Tony Archer while his wife Pat was looking after her sick mother in Wales. The family were scandalized when he took her to the Cricket Club dance and Jennifer Aldridge insisted she stay the night at Home Farm to ensure that she didn't spend the night with Tony. She was convinced that they were having an affair, although her husband Brian said drily that Tony was incapable of it.

Jennifer's antipathy to the girl was surprising, given that Libby had saved Adam Travers-Macy's life when he was bitten by an adder on Heydon Berrow. On that occasion Jennifer had rewarded her with a silk shawl.

Hedli Niklaus

JONES, MARY

see Thomas, Mary

JONES, SID

Sid Jones broke into Coombe Farm in 1959 and stole Phil Archer's gun and binoculars. He was caught by PC Bryden and in Phil's absence Dan Archer was able to identify his belongings.

Lewis Gedge

JORDAN, PERCY AND ELSIE

Percy: d. 13 Aug. 1985

In 1975 Percy Jordan decided to retire from his tenancy at Valley Farm on the Berrow Estate. Since he had no children he asked the estate manager Andrew Sinclair if he could pass the farm on to his nephew. When Sinclair explained that this wasn't possible, Percy was worried that he wouldn't be able to afford anywhere else to live. The problem was solved when Percy was allowed to rent the farmhouse while the Estate farmed the land. His wife Elsie had had her heart set on a modern bungalow as she found the stairs in the farmhouse difficult, but they were happy with the compromise.

After his retirement Percy continued to work part-time for Pat and Tony Archer at Willow Farm. He was a great help when Tony was recovering from tetanus in 1980. Paul Johnson also employed him for a short

while on his ill-fated fish farm.

In 1985 Percy died at Willow Farm while doing the milking. He had had a stroke. At his funeral the mourners remembered his prowess at bell-ringing and in his younger days at cricket, but agreed that he had been rather a dull fellow with no sense of humour. But Percy bequeathed to Walter Gabriel an album of photos of Rosie Wynyard, all taken after her marriage to Piggy Atkins, which gave rise to speculation that to her, at least, he might not have been so dull.

William Eedle

JULIE

b. 1 Apr. 1964

When his wife Polly died in 1982 Sid Perks had the painful task of finding someone to take her place as barmaid in the Bull. He interviewed Julie and offered her the job almost immediately, hoping that having a woman around the place would be good for his daughter Lucy. She accepted.

An attractive eighteen-year-old, Julie was often seen jogging round Ambridge in a bright pink tracksuit; and her black dress with a split skirt caused such a fuss in the Bull that Sid had to ask her not to wear it. As she came from Ladywood in Birmingham, country life was new to her and she wasn't sure what she felt about it. Not only that but her boyfriend, Ahmed, a westernized Muslim, disapproved of her job, and she was afraid that he would drop her, which eventually he did. She had no shortage of suitors in Ambridge, however. Sid was delighted with her, Neil Carter thought she was wonderful, and for a time Clarrie Grundy wasn't sure whether she disliked Julie most because Eddie had a crush on her, or because she called him a creep.

Despite all these excitements Julie grew restless and gave in her notice at the end of the year, telling Sid that she would be working at the Feathers. Neil Carter continued to go out with her and she accepted him when he proposed to her in 1983. They planned an autumn wedding at the Birmingham Register Office, but when she saw Clarrie's wedding photographs she changed her mind and decided to have a church wedding in June, spending a pleasant afternoon in Birmingham with Shula Archer looking for a white jumpsuit to wear for the occasion.

It wasn't only the vicar, Richard Adamson, who felt that Neil and Julie were mismatched, and fortunately DS Dave Barry arrived on the scene at just the right time to bring their differences home to them. He took Julie to the policeman's ball, and the fact that she accepted the invitation and thoroughly enjoyed herself made the couple realize that she was far from ready to settle down. They broke off their engagement, and she left Ambridge to work in London shortly afterwards.

Kathryn Hurlbutt

K

KEEPER'S COTTAGE

A new road was built in 1960 through part of Charles Grenville's land towards Borchester, affecting his game-breeding grounds and some workers' cottages. One of them had been occupied by his gamekeeper Tom Forrest, so he was consulted about the design of the replacements. April Cottage and Keeper's Cottage were built as a pair, and Tom has occupied Keeper's Cottage ever since.

KENNEDY, VIVIAN

When in 1953 Phil Archer wanted to reclaim part of Brookfield's rough acreage on Lakey Hill for planting, he asked Vivian Kennedy, the district officer, to come and take soil samples for analysis. Vivian was likeable and attractive, and when Phil invited him to tea he soon made friends with the rest of the Archers, getting on especially well with Christine, Phil's sister.

Christine was flattered when Vivian tried to date her on a couple of occasions and was surprised when he suddenly started avoiding her. Fate took a hand in the unlikely person of Walter Gabriel, who managed to hit a cricket ball through Vivian's car windscreen as he was driving up to Brookfield. Dan Archer rushed Vivian into the house to have his cut forehead bathed and Christine was all tender solicitude. While she mopped his brow, Vivian hinted that the reason he had been avoiding her was because of local gossip about her affair with her married boss, Basil Grove, but left before she could reply.

He later apologized and wrote to ask her to go out with him for a punt on the river. It was a beautiful summer evening but Vivian was too busy trying to put into words all that he felt about her to admire the countryside. He was so engrossed that he didn't notice the approach of a motor boat and fell out of the punt trying to avoid it, Christine laughing at the spectacle. His ardour dampened, Vivian disappeared from Christine's life.

Gordon Walters

KENTON, GARY

Gary Kenton's main claim to fame is that he fell down the stairs in Arkwright Hall, fighting with Jimmy Grange over the favours of Hazel Woolley. He had come to Ambridge in 1959 when his mother acquired for him the tenancy to Hood's Farm. He specialized in broiler production, but his farming proved to be no more successful than his romancing and he sold the farm to Charles Grenville the following year.

Bryan Kendrick

KENTON, MRS KITTY

Kitty Kenton was a jolly lady who had managed a pub with her late husband. She obtained the tenancy of Percy Hood's farm for her son Gary in 1959 and stayed at the Bull while overseeing the work that needed doing on it. She had an infectious giggle which was often heard when she was in Walter Gabriel's company.

Beatrice Kane

KENTON'S FARM

Some farms have names which outlast many occupants and seem as permanent as towns and villages; others are named after their tenants and change often, like Kenton's Farm which went through four names in a dozen years. Joe Blower, fed up with life in general and farming in particular, negotiated the sale of his tenancy in 1955 to a young

couple named Court. The landowner, Squire Lawson-Hope, was furious at not being consulted but allowed the transfer to go through. The new tenants moved on after only a year when Percy Hood and his family took the farm over on their return to Ambridge after several years in the north. Three years later the Hoods decided to leave again when Percy got a job as bailiff near the Scottish border.

Kitty Kenton took on the farm for her son Gary, but he found the management of the farm too difficult and in 1960 he was thankful to sell the tenancy to Charles Grenville, by then the landowner. The farm became part of the Berrow Estate.

KING, GEMMA

No one was quite sure whether David Archer was attracted to Gemma King, with whom he went out in 1986, because of her father's Jaguar with its personalized number plate. Her volubility chased him away in the end.

KINGSLEY, DAWN

Dawn Kingsley worked in John Tregorran's antique shop in 1961. She became a partner, but, restless, moved to Jack Woolley's New Curiosity Shop and then back to the antique shop. Jack Woolley had faith in her talents and offered her loans of £7,000, which she invested in the Theatre Royal, Borchester, and later repaid. Then she cast about for another enterprise in which she could invest her time and money. While studying to become an expert in china and porcelain, she met the artist Robert Heriot. She grew so interested in him and took so much time off work that Tregorran would have sacked her had she not been a partner.

Peace between the three was restored and the partnership dissolved amicably, but her plans to marry Heriot did not come about.

She was last seen by Polly Perks in 1968 in Borchester looking for another job.

Patricia Bendall

KIRK, JULIET

Juliet worked in the catering division at the Field Study Centre in 1971. On one occasion she was on her way to Arkwright Hall when her car skidded and she landed in a ditch near Ambridge. Fortunately for her, Sid Perks and Tony Archer were at hand, and soon had her back on the road.

Margo Biddle

KNIGHT, JIM

Mr Rodway of Rodway & Watson thought very highly of their employee Jim Knight. He worked alongside Shula, and in 1989 successfully took over the sale of Nelson's antique shop.

KNOWLES, BILL

Brian Aldridge engaged Bill Knowles as his new farm foreman in 1990. Ruth Archer, who was doing work experience on Home Farm, didn't enjoy working with him at all. She thought that he was a chauvinist and took delight in giving her menial tasks. Brian was no help to her until she uncovered Knowles' plan to cheat his employer: he had persuaded a sales representative to supply Home Farm with nitrogen fertilizer at £126 instead of £124 per tonne with the two of them pocketing the difference. Knowles was sacked, and for a while Ruth was able to bask in the warm glow of Brian's approval.

KORTCHMAR, CONN

Wicked Kate Aldridge did some research before she forged a letter to her grandmother's wartime sweetheart, Conn Kortchmar. She found that Peggy Woolley was more than happy to fill in some of the details as she reminisced. She told Kate that she had been stationed at Warpole End Manor, and that together with the other ATS girls she had gone dancing at the Corn Exchange in Cambridge, where they met the GIs. It was at such a dance that Peggy met Conn.

Kate's letter entranced Conn to such a degree that he came over to Ambridge in person, arriving on 26 August 1992. It was intensely embarrassing for Peggy but once he realized what was going on he handled the situation with great tact, reassuring Peggy that he had intended coming to England anyway, to see his son and new granddaughter in Bristol.

Soon Peggy and Conn were talking about the old days – how they danced the night away, how they won a Chinese fan for their jitterbugging, and much more. They talked so long that Conn had to spend the night at the Lodge wearing pyjamas borrowed from the disgruntled Jack Woolley.

Conn came back from Bristol a few days later to stay at Grey Gables, fired with enthusiasm for reviewing some of his old wartime haunts. He tried to involve Jack but he was too busy, and it was left to Peggy to accompany Conn on this heady nostalgia trip. She found herself involved in a whirl of activities, upsetting her family in the process. Jennifer Aldridge was angry, her husband Brian sarcastic, Tony Archer teased her and Jack became fed up and resentful.

Conn moved in with Marjorie Antrobus at Nightingale Farm as her paying guest so that he could stay longer, and raised a flutter in Marjorie's heart. But Peggy confessed to Jill Archer that she found him overpowering. He tried to persuade her to go back to Boston with him, but she refused, and when Jack thought Conn had sent her flowers and was upsetting her he finally took matters into his own hands, and stormed off to tell Conn to leave them all alone. (Ironically,the flowers had been sent by Kate Aldridge, as an apology for the fuss she had caused.) A much chastened Conn returned to Bristol, having left a present for Peggy: his Zippo lighter – a fitting end to a fine romance.

Don Fellows

LAKEY HILL

Lakey Hill rises 771 feet above sea level to the north-east of Ambridge. There are traces of several prehistoric burial mounds. It is a famous landmark in the neighbourhood and the locals say, when there's a red sunset and the sun catches the top of the hill, 'There's blood on Lakey Hill'.

It was owned in the fifties by Admiral Bellamy, who rented 100 acres to George Fairbrother for a rough shoot. Phil Archer, when he was working for Fairbrother in 1953, tried to increase the area under crops by reclaiming some of the higher ground, but found the soil poor and difficult to plough. In 1955 Fairbrother was fined for arson when he burned off gorse and heather without a licence. The summit and southern slopes now belong to Brookfield and the Archers use it mainly for grazing sheep.

Lakey Hill is one of Ambridge's most scenic areas and has given pleasure to many generations. Phil Archer sat at the top of Lakey Hill with Grace Fairbrother on Coronation Day in 1953, roasting potatoes until four o'clock in the morning. Over twenty years later his daughter Shula stayed on the hill till early morning with Neil Carter, watching the string of bonfires set alight in celebration of the Jubilee.

LAMB, FRED

Fred Lamb came from Waterley Cross to help out several nights a week at the Bull in 1983. Easily flustered, he was unable to stand the pace for long.

LAMBERT, MARTIN

b. 1955

Martin Lambert was the assistant vet in Bill Robertson's practice from 1984 to 1989. Soon after his arrival in Ambridge, Shula Archer caught his eye and he went as far as pushing Eddie Grundy into the River Am when he insulted Shula at a bonfire party. When Shula had had enough of him, he turned his attentions to her younger sister Elizabeth.

Martin wasn't thought of as kind, but could be on occasions: he once gave Walter Gabriel a budgie to keep him company. Wanting to live in Ambridge, he tried to rent Honeysuckle Cottage from Nelson Gabriel after Walter's death, but Nelson decided to keep it in the family. Martin did his best to persuade Caroline Bone to let him have a cheap room at Grey Gables but Jack Woolley put his foot down. Unable to find anywhere else to stay he was forced to move in to Grange Farm. Joe and Eddie Grundy, delighted to have a resident vet, tried to get free consultations for their stock. But Martin knew his price and veterinary bills duly arrived. Eventually Joe's gloomy prophecies and sepulchral cough drove him to move into a flat in Borchester.

Scott Cherry; David Goodland; Steve Hodson

LANDER, LADY ISABEL

Daughter of a Field Marshal who had been created an earl for his services to the nation, Lady Isabel Lander came to Ambridge in 1969 to look after her uncle, Brigadier Winstanley. Owner of a house in Sussex and a flat in Belgravia, she acquired even more property when her uncle bequeathed his estate to her while he was still living. She employed consultants to advise on the running of the estate, and disposed of some of it. Nightingale Farm was sold to Hugo Barnaby. The pair of them got on well and she invited him to join her in Sussex for Christmas 1970. After the death of her uncle she moved back there for good.

Mary Wimbush

LARKIN, BOB

d. Feb. 1957

In 1957 Ned Larkin invited his brother Bob to stay because he wanted him to meet Pru Harris who he felt was 'just the nice quiet type of girl to keep him under a bit. 'Cos he's been a rare wild 'un with the ladies.' Sure enough, Bob turned up at the Bull ready for some fun. Finding Pru a bit on the quiet side, he turned on the charm to excite her a bit. She refused to go out with him, which he found an irresistible challenge and he started pestering her. Tom Forrest, her long-time admirer, galloped to her rescue and was very taken aback to learn that Bob, a fast worker, had already proposed twice. Despite all Tom's efforts Pru finally agreed to go out with Bob, probably in a desperate attempt to wake Tom up to a realization of his feelings for her.

Meanwhile, there was a petrol thief abroad in the village, and when Ned woke his brother one morning he discovered a pocketful of money which certainly hadn't been there the previous night. Bob explained that it was money from a bet he'd put on weeks ago.

More petrol was stolen, this time from Tom, and a pair of gloves belonging to Ned were found soaked in petrol in a hedge. Things looked black for Ned, who was very resentful at being called a thief. Ned's wife Mabel, who didn't find Bob any more charming than Pru had, told him that Bob had borrowed the gloves, and when confronted Bob admitted that he had got the sack from his job, and had stolen the petrol. Ned turned him out, but, still anxious to protect his brother, persuaded the police to drop the matter and tried to pay back the money to all the people he had robbed. Incorrigible, Bob rang Pru to ask her out and was surprised that she turned him down with such force.

His story came to a tragic end one February night in 1957 when he went poaching. Tom and Phil Archer were patrolling the woods and caught sight of him. Tom and he struggled, a gun went off and Bob was killed. Tom was arrested and charged with his murder, but subsequently acquitted.

Lewis Gedge

LARKIN, CLARRIE

see Grundy, Clarrie

LARKIN, JETHRO

b. 28 Aug. 1924; m. Lizzie; 2 dtrs; d. 17 June 1987

Typically to be found sitting on a hay bale with Neil Carter, chewing over the events of the day with his sandwiches, flasks of tea at the ready, Jethro was a man for whom the old days were the best days and the old ways the ones you could rely on.

Ned and Mabel Larkin's eldest son, Jethro came back from Dorset in 1966 to be nearer his parents, bringing his wife Lizzie and daughters Rosie and Clarrie. He got a job on the Berrow Estate. The next year he went to work for Phil Archer at the Hollowtree pig unit and the fam-

ily lived at Rickyard Cottage. They moved to Woodbine Cottage four years later.

He was a man of habit: he liked the remains of the Sunday joint in his sandwiches on Mondays and corned beef sandwiches on Wednesdays, and he didn't like outsiders coming into the Bull. He was modest: when he saw Phil Archer's advert for a new man in the paper it took Dan Archer and Phil a long time to convince him that he wasn't going to be given the sack. He never outwardly contradicted his employers, but if he didn't approve of an instruction it just didn't get done. Dan, who knew his Jethro, must have smiled quietly in his beer as he watched Phil's efforts to improve Neil Carter's and Jethro's attitude to their work. Phil optimistically put up in the workshop a chart of the year's work on the farm, asking Jethro and Neil for their comments, but of course they didn't have any. He called a meeting to discuss the plan but Jethro didn't think all this discussing was a good idea and didn't go. Exasperatingly he was sometimes right. Once he told Phil that a field was not fit for ploughing and when Phil persisted the plough got stuck and had to be pulled out with a tractor, to Jethro's high delight.

Jethro was inclined to put off going to the dentist when he needed to. When he had trouble with his gums he kept taking out his false teeth, which drove everyone mad. Finally the pain, and Jill Archer, forcibly drove him to the dentist where he had his seven remaining teeth extracted and had to wait six weeks for the gum to heal before his lower dentures were ready.

In 1978 Jethro was left £4,200 by his Uncle Charlie, which to him was a fortune.

Neil persuaded him to use some of his inheritance by going halves on a car. Against everyone's advice Jethro did so, but the arrangement was doomed from the start and after a month he bought Neil out.

In 1979 Phil, fed up with the lack of interest Neil and Jethro were showing in their work, started to take a firm stand with the pair. A lot of philosophical rumination went on over the lunchtime sandwich after that, and they were much relieved when Phil showed signs of being more reasonable. Then Jethro started having trouble with his feet and took to going to the chiropodist in working hours, which made Phil even crosser. But these considerations were swept aside by the death of Jethro's wife Lizzie, which knocked poor Jethro sideways. He took refuge in his daily round of tasks on the farm until he could get over it.

By this time Clarrie had started to go out with Eddie Grundy, of which Jethro didn't approve at all. He stubbornly refused to give her away at her wedding, and Clarrie walked out of Woodbine Cottage for a couple of nights to show how serious she was before he would change his mind. He was getting on, and thought of leaving Brookfield because David Archer was too bossy and called him 'the aged old retainer', but they made it up and he shared his seedcake with him when David complimented him on his fence-mending. Just retribution as David hated seedcake.

Jethro Larkin (George Hart) and Tom Forrest (Bob Arnold)

The next few years were tranquil, studded with occasional incident. He dropped a bale of hay on Phil's head and thought he'd gone barmy when he found him inside Hollowtree playing a piano left by the Grundys on their way to taking it to the Bull. He saw a naked David Archer climbing out of his sister Elizabeth's bathroom window after she locked him in and nearly crashed the tractor when he saw Elizabeth sunbathing topless in the orchard. He went to Holland for a holiday; and he nearly emigrated to Canada. He won a flying lesson in a sweepstake at the Bull, and hung on to it like grim death when Elizabeth said that it should be hers by rights – only to find that flying was not his forte and that he had to keep his eyes shut throughout the whole ghastly experience.

On 17 June 1987 David rushed into the kitchen at Brookfield to announce that there had been a terrible accident. Jill Archer immediately called the ambulance and Christine Barford went to fetch Clarrie, who sensed that things were serious. Jethro was dead. A branch had fallen on him while he and David were cutting it down, and he had suffered an internal haemorrhage. He left £10,000 to Rosie and Clarrie.

George Hart

L ARKIN, LIZZIE

m. Jethro Larkin; 2 dtrs; d. 18 Sept. 1981

Married to Jethro Larkin, Lizzie, typical of many women of her generation, spent most of her life at the kitchen stove. She was grateful to her daughter Clarrie when she asked Phil Archer to help pay for improvements to the kitchen at Woodbine Cottage (of which they were tenants), although Jethro was furious. In the end Phil agreed to pay half the cost, and Eddie Grundy started removing the old range before the new one was ordered. Eddie pulled a fast one by selling the old one to Nelson Gabriel for his wine bar for £20. In fact the 'new' range was secondhand which annoyed Clarrie, but Lizzie was grateful for small mercies. She didn't have long to enjoy it as she started getting headaches and eventually couldn't eat. She had a stroke and was rushed into hospital, where she died from a subarachnoid haemorrhage in September 1981.

Lizzie had run Jethro's house for thirty years and kept an account book. After her death Jethro looked through it and found unexplained entries amounting to £7 10s. In 1959 Lizzie had asked Doris to look after a little cash box that she put her spare housekeeping into every week for Jethro's Christmas present, a secondhand bicycle.

Once Lizzie and Nora McAuley sang 'The Housewives' Lament' together in a village revue. It's a good epitaph for a gentle lady.

L ARKIN, MABEL (NÉE BRACKEN)

d. July 1983

Mabel was Ned Larkin's wife. They had five children, who all married, and she had an elder sister called Clarice who lived in Hollerton with her husband Fred.

Mabel did odd jobs for Carol Tregorran at the market garden and she also helped Doris

Archer at Brookfield. She was a member of the WI and a staunch supporter of all village fêtes. In 1967 she was proud to be selected as the Ambridge WI delegate for the AGM at the Albert Hall in London. Carol and Doris helped her to buy a special outfit, but it took the combined efforts of Ned and Dan Archer to dissuade her from wearing the hat she chose for herself.

She and Ned moved into Woodbine Cottage just before Christmas 1967, paying Ralph Bellamy 12s. 6d. a week rent. Ned died soon after, and she had to cope on her own. She became Hugo Barnaby's housekeeper and moved into a flat at Nightingale Farm. In 1975 she agreed to be housekeeper for Brian Aldridge for a trial period as she was concerned that the council might be buying up Nightingale Farm. She continued to work for the Aldridges for a time after Brian married Jennifer Archer, but by 1979 she had retired to Manorfield Close, where she died a few years later.

Kay Hudson

LARKIN, NED

d. Dec. 1967

In 1956 Dan Archer's farmhand, Simon Cooper, retired and was replaced by Ned Larkin. Ned and his wife Mabel had five children, all of them married. A family-minded man, he was very protective of his no-good brother Bob, and used an illness Bob had had when young as an excuse for all Bob's shortcomings. This illusion was laid to rest alongside Bob in 1957 when Ned invited him to stay: the visit ended tragically with his accidental death at the hands of Tom Forrest. Tom had caught Bob poaching and in the ensuing struggle a gun went off and he was killed. The case was not clear-cut, and Tom was charged with murder before being acquitted at the Assizes. Village tongues wagged and the fact that Bob had been making a play for Tom's girlfriend, Pru Harris, was not overlooked. It was all hard for warmhearted and loyal Ned to come to terms with and for a while he turned against Tom until he realized the truth: his brother was a bad lot.

Ned was great friends with Walter Gabriel. The two of them got up to all sorts of mischief, none of it malicious and much of it comic, resting as it did on an essential innocence in the character of both men. In 1959 they went to fetch a dresser that Mr Grenville had bought from the sale of contents of Arkwright Hall and were frightened when they heard some strange noises. They were sure it was a ghost, but in fact it was a gypsy called Gregory Selden who'd been camping out at the Hall. He was a petty thief and made the mistake of stealing the biscuit tin full of money that Walter had been saving up for his old age. Eventually PC Bryden caught up with Selden, found the nearly empty tin and arrested him. Ned found the rest of Walter's money up the chimney at the Hall and Walter was so delighted that he gave Ned £35 reward with which he bought a secondhand Austin Seven. The story of Ned and Arkwright Hall didn't end there, for in August of the same year he managed to fall through the floor and discover a hoard of gold sovereigns, estimated by John Tregorran to be worth at least £5,000.

Ned Larkin (Bill Payne)

the numbers. The fact he could led to the arrest of thieves who had robbed Charles Grenville – and another reward for Ned.

Ambridge mourned a popular lovable character when Ned died in 1967, within months of his retirement from Brookfield, and just after he and Mabel had moved into Woodbine Cottage.

Bill Payne

LARKIN, ROSIE

see Mabbott, Rosie

LARKIN, SUSAN

Susan was Ned and Mabel Larkin's married daughter. She lived in Newcastle with her husband Charlie, a long-distance lorry driver, and their two children, Bobbie and Joyce.

When she came to stay with her parents in September 1959, she was depressed. She didn't talk much but clearly her marriage was not a success. Joyce accidentally drank some paraffin that her grandfather, Ned Larkin, was using on his car and had to be rushed to hospital. Susan was so upset that she decided to return home, and Ned obtained the use of Mr Grenville's chauffeur-driven car to take them back in style.

Patricia Gibson

LATHAM, MRS

Mrs Latham's shapely presence enlivened the bookshop Henry Featherstone ran with

Ned had another brush with Ambridge low life, when, unable to sleep with the pain of toothache, he went for a walk late at night. He met Tom and together they discovered a vehicle parked down a farm track with alternative numberplates in the back. Next day Tom and PC Bryden tracked him down to the dentist to ask if he could remember

Roger Travers-Macy in Borchester. She worked there as their assistant in 1967.

LATIMER, REVD DAVID

d. Feb. 1973

David Latimer became vicar of Ambridge with responsibility for the parish of Penny Hassett in 1968. He went down in Tom Forrest's estimation almost at once by asking him and Dan to call him by his Christian name; they compromised by simply calling him 'Vicar'. This should have given him some idea of what he was taking on, but he wasn't put off and he tried to bring about some changes, such as using the church for secular activities during the week. He met with less success, however, when he suggested that the old gravestones should be removed to tidy up the churchyard. He was a kindly man, and although he didn't like marrying people during Lent or Advent he made an exception for Greg Salt and Nora McAuley. His health failed him and in 1973 he died while in Sussex on holiday, staying with his mother.

Arnold Peters

LATIMER, HESTER

Hester Latimer understood her role as wife of the vicar of Ambridge, and enjoyed her life in the country, being an excellent horsewoman. When she and her husband David first arrived in Ambridge, their youngest daughter, Kate, was twelve and still at

school; their son Kit was doing his A-levels; and their other daughter Tessa was at university.

After her husband's death in 1973 she was in the predicament familiar to church dependants of having no home of her own. The diocesan widows' officer, Canon Meridew, called on her to discuss her financial situation and to give her the news that she would have to vacate the Vicarage within three months. She decided, with much courage, that she would have to move in with Tessa and get a job. But life had another blow in store for her. On leaving Grey Gables her car brakes failed and she crashed into Jack Woolley's car. No one was seriously hurt but her car was badly damaged and she needed to sell it to give her some cash in hand. Jack, whose bluff exterior hid the traditional heart of gold, bought it from her.

She was much moved when her husband's parishioners held a sherry party in her honour and she was presented with a cheque for £300. She left Ambridge in May with warm memories of her time there. Two years later she returned for a visit, staying with Peggy Archer. She brought news that Tessa was now married to a social worker.

Penelope Shaw

LATIMER, KEITH

Keith Latimer was a friend of Grace Fairbrother's cousin Guy and an expert mineralogist, so when George Fairbrother needed a survey of his land in October 1951 after ironstone had been discovered on it, he was the obvious choice of surveyor. He estimated that 100 acres were affected by the iron-stone, and wanted to survey Squire Lawson-Hope's adjoining land too, although the Squire was opposed to the idea of mining. Keith told Dan Archer and the Squire that there was anything up to three million tons of ironstone in the seam, which would fetch £40 a ton when manufactured and take thirty to forty years to bring out. He found their concern that Ambridge would become a mining community instead of a farming one totally irrelevant.

Local feeling ran high on the subject. Walking Christine back from an outing to the pictures one night, Keith saw a light in one of the lorries by his equipment and they disturbed saboteurs. The diamond bit for his drill went missing, and he found his drilling rods in the trout stream. Together with Dick Raymond and Phil Archer he lay in wait one night to catch the saboteurs but just as they were about to rush them Keith bungled it by falling over some drilling rods. Later Phil told him that Bill Slater, who had a private grudge against Fairbrother, was responsible for the sabotage, and he agreed to let the matter rest because of his involvement with Bill's tragic death after a fight at the Bull.

Keith stayed to give evidence at the public enquiry into the scheme and at Fairbrother's instigation met Mr Crawford, an industrialist who held the mineral rights to the land. He tried to convince him of the advantages of mining the ironstone, but Crawford fell in love with Ambridge, and refused to co-operate, and the scheme fell by the wayside. Keith showed tenacity and loyalty to Fairbrother and when he left Ambridge in early December he was still convinced that Crawford, Squire Lawson-Hope and their supporters had got it all wrong.

Jack May

LATIMER, TERESA MARY (TESSA)

b. 1949

Though she was the vicar's daughter, Tessa was something of a handful, extrovert, high-spirited and very attractive to Tony Archer, who in 1969 regularly took her out. She went to university and after getting a good degree entered the probation service. After her father David Latimer's death in 1973 and her mother's departure from Ambridge, she lost contact with the village.

Carole Davies

LAUGHTON, MR AND MRS

Mr and Mrs Laughton lived for a short while in the warden's flat at Arkwright Hall in 1961. They worked at the mill in Hollerton.

Helena Williams

LAWRENCE, BOB

In his mid-forties in 1977, when he was employed as manager at Carol Tregorran's market garden, Bob Lawrence was a reticent man, but a good worker. When Jack Woolley set up the garden centre he went to Bob for advice and found his suggestions very helpful.

LAWSON, ELIZABETH

Elizabeth Lawson, a fully qualified nursing sister, was employed in January 1957 to look after the ailing Lettie Lawson-Hope. She did her best to keep Lettie interested in life and encouraged Doris and other women from the village to visit her and keep her up-to-date with local affairs.

Although engaged to a young doctor, Elizabeth soon became friends with Phil Archer. He took her to a Valentine's Day ball and wanted her to be the leading lady in the Ciné Club's first film. On one occasion he took her to the woods to listen to the dawn chorus. She decided that the two of them were getting too close and that it was unfair to her fiancé. She solved the problem by returning to London in May.

Eileen Barry

LAWSON-HOPE, CLIVE

Clive Lawson-Hope came to run the Lawson-Hope estate for his uncle the Squire early in 1952. He spent much of the next year at odds with Tom Forrest over his ways of working on the estate and with Walter Gabriel, whom he tried to have evicted from his farm for inefficiency. He wooed Grace Fairbrother and in the summer of 1953 asked her to marry him, but, angry when she did not immediately respond, withdrew the proposal.

When the following year another uncle, Percy, died and left him a substantial farm in Kenya, he decided that a more exciting challenge awaited him there. Before leaving,

he proposed to Christine Archer, but she was uncertain of her feelings and not prepared to commit herself to a life in Africa. He left for pastures new.

Leslie Parker

LAWSON-HOPE, LETTY

d. 21 Apr. 1958

It was Lettie Lawson-Hope who gave Doris Forrest her first job as a maid. Eventually Doris was to become Lettie's personal maid as well as confidante. When Lettie grew frail and old, Doris went to visit her every day at Glebe Cottage (where she had by now moved from the Manor). Doris confided to Lettie that she wanted her husband Dan Archer to retire and settle down in a small cottage somewhere.

When Lettie died in 1958, Dan's old shire horses, Blossom and Boxer, were teamed together once again to pull her coffin to church on the hay wagon. She was interred in the Lawson-Hope family vault. In her will she had left Glebe Cottage to Doris.

Kitty Scopes; Kay Hudson

LAWSON-HOPE, SQUIRE

Squire Lawson-Hope lived in some style at the Manor. He and his lady wife Lettie employed a housekeeper, a butler and a maid. The family coat of arms, which had been granted to William of Ambridge in the tenth century, was carved above the drawing-room fireplace.

During the time the family had lived in Ambridge, most village folk worked for them at some time or other. At the Battle of Waterloo in 1815 a member of the Archer family fought side by side with a member of the Squire's; and a Gabriel was batman to the Squire's father at the Battle of Vimy Ridge in 1917.

A true country gentleman, Lawson-Hope was disappointed that he didn't have a son to succeed him. His dearest wish was that his nephew and namesake would inherit the family estate, in line with tradition. It wasn't to be: the young Clive Lawson-Hope spent a year running the estate, but decided to choose Kenya as his home. On the death of the old Squire in 1954, the house, the land and the farms were sold and Dan Archer was able to buy Brookfield. All that remains to remind Ambridge of them is the family vault and the Lawson-Hope memorial seat on the village green.

Ronald Baddiley

LEE, BARNEY

In the early 1950s Barney Lee, an old army pal of Jack Archer's, shared a small farm in Cornwall with him. Unfortunately, he wanted to share Jack's wife Peggy too, so the young Archers moved hastily back to Ambridge. Barney pursued them and continued to pester Peggy, who was relieved when he gave up the chase and headed off back to Cornwall.

Twenty-five years later he returned as manager of Carol Tregorran's market garden. For a while Peggy was pleased to see him, but not for long. Like Jack, he was a heavy drinker. Carol sacked him, he got drunk in front of Peggy and to everyone's relief staggered out of Ambridge yet again.

Gordon Walters; Michael Ford; Douglas Ditta

LEGGATT, MRS

In 1992 Brian Aldridge called a temporary truce to marital hostilities when his wife Jennifer was hurt in an unpleasant incident. Mrs Leggatt was an inexperienced rider on Brian's off-road riding course who left her dog in the car for too long. When she finally let the animal out it attacked the Home Farm sheep, and when Jennifer endeavoured to rescue them she was bitten for her pains.

LENZ, EVA

see Coverdale, Eva

LENZ, DR AND MRS

Dr and Mrs Lenz came to stay at Home Farm when their daughter, Eva, who was working as an au pair there, was married in 1980. Although the Aldridges did their best to entertain their guests, they were not easy, and they were relieved when the Lenzs decided to see a Shakespeare play in Stratford-upon-Avon and stay there overnight. Sadly Mrs Lenz couldn't understand a word of the play, nor did they like their hotel, so they turned up at Home Farm in lively mood just as Brian and Jennifer had settled down for the night.

Harold Kasket

LEWIS, PAT

see Archer, Pat

LILY, MARTHA

see Woodford, Martha

LISA AND CRAIG

Lisa, Craig and their baby Scott just appeared, in October 1992, in residence at Rickyard Cottage, to the astonishment of all at Brookfield. Phil Archer wasted no time in consulting solicitor Mark Hebden as to the quickest way of having them removed, to Jill's great relief, but the matter was not to be resolved simply.

The Archer sons David and Kenton were unimpressed by their father's legal moves and set about making life unpleasant for the unwanted occupants. Jill, on the other hand, was taken aback when Lisa introduced herself in the village shop, and found that hearing their side of the story not only allayed her fears about what sort of people the squatters might be, but also gained her sympathy for their plight.

Against the background of Phil's plotting and David's harassment, Jill and Lisa negotiated. Lisa found work at Bridge Farm, while Jill coaxed Phil into an agreement that the squatters could become low-rent tenants; she babysat for them, washed Scott's nappies and offered them food. But tensions within the Brookfield household grew, and Phil drew

the line when she wanted to invite them to Christmas lunch.

In the New Year it seemed that Lisa and Craig would not be able to keep up the rental payments, but for several months they managed and an uneasy truce prevailed. Then, as the end of their first six-month letting neared, they vanished. Jill found a note from Lisa on the cottage door saying that Craig had lost his job as a farm labourer, but it left no clue to their plans and they were not heard of again.

Tracey Gardiner and David Phelan

LLEWELLYN, EWAN AND GWYNNETH

Ewan Llewellyn was a council workman, who lived in Wales with his wife Gwynneth. They were Pat Archer's uncle and aunt, and occasionally came to visit Pat and Tony in Ambridge. Ewan was a champion bowler, and annoyed the villagers when he won a silver cup donated by Jack Woolley in 1975. They allowed him the glory, but not the cup, which remains in the Bull to this day. Gwynneth, talkative and lively, had a tendency to bossiness which annoyed Tony, although in the end he was grateful to her for all the help she gave to Pat.

Dillwyn Owen and Margaret John

LOCKE, DR RICHARD

b. 1963

Ambridge was taken aback when the new GP in 1992 turned out to be more interested in prevention than in cure, and it took time for the villagers to realize that this could be in their best interests. Practical, energetic, unable to suffer fools gladly, Richard Locke has nonetheless shown that he can be a good listener when necessary. Jennifer Aldridge came for a repeat prescription for sleeping tablets and stayed to tell him all about her problems; and Shula Hebden found him conscientious and sympathetic when he counselled her on the subject of the IVF programme she wished to undertake. The learning hasn't been all on one side, however, as Richard would be the first to admit. Never having lived in the country he was stumped when Clarrie Grundy presented symptoms imitating pneumonia and influenza, until Robin Stokes suggested Q fever, caught by inhalation when drying off premature lambs with a hair drier. Robin's diagnosis was correct and Richard was able to help his patient.

Single-minded in his approach to work, Richard has proved elusive when it comes to the opposite sex. When he moved into one of the Home Farm holiday cottages, Elizabeth Archer was delighted to be invited to his housewarming party but found herself playing second fiddle to a video of a rugby game. After that experience she could only warm to Nigel Pargetter. While Richard's chauvinism inadvertently helped Elizabeth and Nigel's romance along, it infuriated Debbie Aldridge, who is certainly

Richard Locke (William Gaminara)

not indifferent to his charms. She had been caught up in the raid on the village shop which took place in 1993, and thought that she was dealing effectively with the traumatic aftermath. Richard begged to differ, angry words were ex-changed, and paradoxically it took the Battle of Hassett Bridge to restore harmony; Richard was a member of the Sealed Knot organization which re-enacts battles from the Civil War, and Nigel consented to hold one of the re-enactments in the grounds of Lower Loxley Hall. Though at first she mocked the event, Debbie couldn't resist joining in, and Richard had the satisfaction of playing swashbuckling hero when she fell off her horse and he carried her to the safety of the Hall. But Debbie didn't let him swash his buckle for long. They have been out together, but are so quarrelsome that even Elizabeth and Nigel have lost patience and begged them to keep apart. This they have agreed to do, and they have come to an understanding which has – so far – preserved their precarious friendship.

For all his hard work and good intentions, Richard is still regarded as a newcomer, and he has some way to go before he becomes fully established as part of the community.

William Gaminara

LOCKE, SARAH

Blonde, sporty rich-girl Sarah Locke became engaged to Mark Hebden in October 1983. He would have married her, but for the fact that her father was summoned to Washington DC, USA, on legal matters and the wedding was postponed until the following September. Mark did not like her parents; nor, by August, did he like Sarah much and the wedding was cancelled – fortunately for Shula Archer (whom he was later to marry).

LODGE, THE

The Lodge is a black and white building at the entrance to the Country Park belonging to Jack Woolley. It is deceptively spacious and has a stained-glass window in the hallway.

Over the years it was occasionally let and used as accommodation by staff at Grey Gables, including Gordon Armstrong and George Barford; but later fell into disuse. Caroline Bone suggested that it could be converted into a new home for Jack and Peggy Woolley after their marriage in 1991. They viewed it and despite its poor condition decided to go ahead with the necessary improvements and move in. They took great pleasure in planning the kitchen and the conservatory, and put in extra windows to create more light.

Now Jack and Peggy are happy together at the Lodge which gives them a comfortable proximity to Grey Gables while preserving their independence.

LOTTERBY, HETTY

Hetty, otherwise known as 'Queen of the Crystal', came from Felpersham, and in 1974 daringly opposed herself to Gypsy Rose Perkins and Martha 'the Mystic' Woodford as fortune-teller at the Ambridge fête.

LOWER LOXLEY HALL

Lower Loxley Hall is the ancestral home of the Pargetters. Their family tree can be traced as far back as the seventeenth century, and the date on the front door is 1702. In 1760 Henrietta Lady Pargetter created the drawing-room and the library in the neo-classical style. The gardens are said to have been laid out by Sir John Pargetter, who made his fortune in colonial India. Peacocks strut on the lawns, which are surrounded by 400 acres of parkland. Spurge laurel has been found in the woods, indicating that some parts are very old indeed.

Nigel Pargetter has done his best to enable Lower Loxley Hall to pay its way and keep it intact. On 7 July 1989 he opened the Hall to the public, offering tours of the house and cream teas. Together with Elizabeth Archer as his marketing manager he launched a corporate open day in 1992 which was very successful. Events at Lower Loxley Hall have included a transport festival, a murder weekend and a Sealed Knot re-enacted battle. Such goings-on are not to his mother Julia Pargetter's taste, but he persists in the knowledge that they are a necessary evil.

LUCAS, ARNOLD

Arnold Lucas was a retired solicitor who lived in the Dower House, which he had rented from the Bellamys. He filled the conservatory with all sorts of cacti, and had the intriguing hobby of making authentic military models. Mrs Blossom, who acted as his housekeeper, kept a maternal eye on him and noticed that his eyesight was deteriorating rapidly, although he refused to accept any assistance. She put his name down on the list for the *Talking Newspaper for the Blind*,

and Jill Archer came to deliver it.

He was proud and cantankerous, but no match for Jill, who gradually won his confidence. She took him to London to see a specialist but as she suspected it was too late. He had acute inoperable glaucoma and the diagnosis was that soon he would be entirely blind.

He took the news well, and persisted in his refusal to go and live in Worthing with his daughter Phyllida and family. Jill bullied him into accepting help from the social services, but he found the mobility officer, Geoffrey Taylor, hard to take. Jill told him he was a self-pitying snob, which sparked him into making an apology to Geoffrey and a decision to go on one of the mobility exercises, which he did very well. Aware of what he owed to Jill, he gave her a brooch, a family heirloom, for her birthday. Eventually he decided to live with his daughter after all and offered Jill one of his antiques as a farewell. She chose a half-moon table which she later sold at auction, donating the money to the Talking Newspaper organization.

George Woolley

LUKE

Caroline Bone was proud of her innovation at Grey Gables in 1988 when she engaged Luke, a pianist from a local music college, to play classical music in the lounge during dinners. So she was rather dashed when Phil and Jill Archer, celebrating their thirty-first anniversary, asked to be moved as the music was too loud.

THE BOOK OF THE ARCHERS

LUMLEY, CAROLINE

Ms Lumley, a retired headmistress, gave Colonel Danby a good game of croquet in 1977 despite her advanced years, but, finding her rather formidable, he didn't much enjoy it.

LYTTELTON, HUMPHREY

When Phil Archer, ciné enthusiast, filmed the fête in 1957, he made sure of capturing on celluloid its opening by the jazz band leader Humphrey Lyttelton.

LYTTLETON BROOK

Tributary of the River Am, running through Home Farm, on which Brian Aldridge has developed his artificial fishing lake.

MABBOTT, ROSIE (NÉE LARKIN)

b. 14 Sept. 1951

Eldest daughter of Jethro and Lizzie Larkin, Rosie left home to marry Dennis, a successful salesman who had once earned his firm a Salesman of the Month award. She had two children, Bess and carrot-haired David. In 1981 the family moved to Great Yarmouth where Jethro sometimes stayed with them. There, in 1984, she had the horrific experience of seeing her husband run over and critically injured as he crossed the road. She sent immediately for help to her sister Clarrie Grundy who stayed with her until Dennis recovered and returned home.

MCAULEY, NORA

m. Greg Salt 23 Dec. 1968

Pretty, impulsive Nora McAuley came from Ulster to join her fiancé, Paddy Redmond in 1966. Jack and Peggy Archer were delighted to see her as they both felt that Paddy was getting too close to their daughter, Jennifer, and hoped that Nora would draw his attention away from her. For a while she did, until Paddy decided to leave his job at Brookfield and move south. Nora declined to go with him: she liked Ambridge and had a good job at the Bull, so she broke off the engagement. A month after Paddy left, Jennifer gave birth to a son. Nora knew perfectly well where Adam's red hair had come from but chose to say nothing.

Nora was soon a vibrant part of village life, helping Christine Johnson with the Riding for the Disabled scheme, running the bottle stall at the fête and organizing a weekend visit from a group of children from Ulster. She was warmhearted and listened to many a tale of woe across the bar at the Bull. It was in this way that she got to know Gregory Salt whose mother had recently died and who was having problems with the rest of his family. He courted her, and they were married on 23 December 1968; but the marriage was short-lived and they divorced four years later.

Then she met George Barford. Theirs was an attraction of opposites: she was bright, talkative and generous, he was taciturn and stubborn. Only Nora could have persevered in the face of the difficulties George brought to her life, and only she could have perceived the worth that lay beneath the surface. He was an alcoholic, separated from his wife and suffered from depression. But none of this deterred Nora. When George tried to commit suicide and refused to see her at the hospital, she was waiting for him at the Lodge when he came home and soon decided to move in with him. Once there, she discovered that his wife Ellen was still writing to him. As usual, George would not talk to her about it and Nora decided that the only way to find out what was happening was to confront Ellen. This she did, and it was only then that she discovered that Ellen was a Roman Catholic, which was why she had never divorced George.

Finally Nora could take no more of the situation. She moved back to the Bull, where Sid and Polly Perks were sympathetic as always. There, she discovered that she was pregnant. She was delighted by the prospect, but realizing that she couldn't live with George decided that she wouldn't tell him the news. She had reckoned without the village grapevine and soon George was begging her to return to the Lodge. Then Nora fell downstairs, and had a miscarriage. During the time of her recovery, she and George came to understand each other better and she moved back in with him.

This time things were happier, but Ellen still refused to give George the divorce necessary for him to marry Nora. She was delighted when George's son, Terry, came to stay with them and disappointed when circumstances subsequently forced his return to his mother.

Then, once again George became depressed. Deciding that she must spend more time with him, Nora gave up her job at the Bull and went to work at the canning factory in Borchester. But she found George's moods too much to cope with and soon fell in love with another man. She told George that she was leaving him and in 1978 moved to Borchester with her new lover.

Julia Mark; Daphne Neville

MACDONALD, NELLIE

Dan and Doris Archer weren't sorry to see Laura Archer disappear down the drive in 1957, on her way to live with her friend Nellie Macdonald in Stourhampton, twenty-five miles away. They were fed up with Laura's perpetual interference in the management of the farm, and Doris remarked that she gave Laura and Nellie a month before they got on each other's nerves. In fact it was three months before Nellie gave Laura a week's notice.

McGUIRE, SHEILA

Mike Daly met Sheila McGuire, the attractive ward sister at Felpersham Infirmary, when he went to visit Phil Archer there after his eye operation in 1952. Chatting about their Irish backgrounds, he claimed that he knew her uncle Rory and took her off to tea.

Kathleen Canty

MACKENZIE, CLIVE

Clive Mackenzie came from Christchurch, New Zealand, where his family had a large sheep station. He came over to England to study at Oxford and earned extra money sheep-shearing during the summer of 1976. He arrived to shear at Home Farm and Brookfield with fellow shearers Bazza and Michele, and persuaded Shula Archer to accompany him and Michele on a touring holiday of Europe a month later.

Marcus Campbell

MACLAREN, DR

Dr Angus MacLaren, a patient, quietly spoken Scot, cared for the health of Ambridge from 1959. He looked after several generations of Archers, dealing with Dan and Doris, Jack's fatal weakness for alcohol, and the dramatic birth of Elizabeth. His passion was fishing. Dr Poole, who came as his assistant in 1974, took over the practice soon after.

Ian Sadler; Duncan McIntyre

MCPHERSON, MRS

Tony Archer was taken aback when in 1975 the dairy adviser who visited Bridge Farm turned out to be a very smartly dressed young woman. He had been warned about sediment in the milk, and Mrs McPherson suggested ways in which he could improve his milking procedures.

Carol Snape

MACY, ADAM

b. 22 June 1967

Adam's birth to Jennifer Archer caused an enormous stir in Ambridge, because he was born out of wedlock and no one knew the name of his father. No doubt some of them guessed when they saw his shock of red hair, just like Paddy Redmond's. He was adopted by Roger Travers-Macy after Jennifer married him and for a while his life became secure. Then at the age of three two strangers, Henry Smith and Chloe Tempest, kidnapped him and took him off to Birmingham to hide him. They delivered a demand for £5,000 to Roger's father, but they were so inept that before Mr Travers-Macy had time to react the police had already discovered Adam's whereabouts and he was on his way home.

By 1976 Roger and Jennifer had split up and Jennifer had married Brian Aldridge. Brian and Adam got off to a bad start until Peggy Archer learned how afraid he was that Brian would leave him, as Roger had, and had a word with Brian. After that their relationship improved, as did his performance at school.

Brian and he shared a passion for cricket. When he was ten he was given a new bat, which delighted him. Unfortunately he had an argument when Brian found him 'out' during a match, but he screwed up his courage to apologize and was rewarded with a trip to the second test match at Old Trafford with Brian.

Riding on Heydon Berrow with some friends he jumped off his pony, landed in a bush and got bitten by an adder. Libby Jones, the milk recorder, was passing by and took him to hospital, but he was seriously ill. A new anti-venom serum was recommended by a leading specialist in tropical medicine and it was rushed to Borchester from Birmingham in time to save Adam's life. It all made excellent copy for *The Borchester Echo*.

After the birth of Brian and Jennifer's daughter Kate, Adam started having bad dreams and problems with his maths teacher. Brian and Jennifer didn't think much of the school and took him to have a look at Stoneham, a boarding school, which he hated on sight. Brian dealt with his maths teacher in a few crisp words, and said that if he wanted to go to St Peter's, a prep school only fifteen miles away, he could, but he would have to pass the entrance test. Adam passed his test with flying colours.

He liked Eva, the Aldridges' German au pair, who had the knack of getting chewing-gum out of his hair. When Eva got married his small stepsister Kate was bridesmaid and wedding guests were taken aback when she stood up and sang an extremely rude song in the middle of the service. They didn't have to look far for the true culprit.

He was a bit of a rebel and more of a countryman than an academic. He enjoyed all sports and riding, and didn't mind early-morning running to get fit for the Pony Club tetrathlon. He managed to get into Sherborne, Brian's old school in 1981, which pleased Brian enormously, though Adam wasn't so keen when he learned that he would have to play hockey. He came home for the holidays and was resentful of John Tregorran, spreading rumours that John and

his mother were having intimate walks with each other, and undermining Jennifer by the discovery of a grey hair in her head.

After A-levels he went off to Canada, returning in 1987 for university interviews to read agricultural economics. He was bronzed and fit and confident, and amused at the attentions of sixteen-year-old Lucy Perks. But Elizabeth Archer dismissed him as adolescent and boring.

He graduated from Newcastle University in 1990 and has been travelling ever since, interested in agriculture in the third world. He keeps in touch with Brian and Jennifer with the odd phone call and postcard and, more surprisingly, has maintained contact with Roger Travers-Macy.

Judy Bennett; Jeremy Whitticase

M ACY, DEBORAH

see Aldridge, Deborah

M ADISON, CLARE

Ralph Bellamy went out with Clare Madison, a dress designer, in 1966. She was estranged from her husband, who wanted to divorce her and threatened to bring a charge of 'alienation of affections' against Ralph, but he turned out to be more than equal to the occasion. He hired a private detective to watch Clare's husband and soon amassed sufficient evidence against him to ensure that he dropped the action. By then Ralph was more interested in Valerie Woolley, and Clare became involved for a brief time with Phil Archer.

MAITLAND, KENNETH

Kenneth Maitland was a bit of a mystery. He seemed to know all about horses but never rode one. When he arranged Grace Fairbrother's horse-management course in Ireland in 1953, Reggie Trentham took exception to Kenneth's high-handed attitude about horses, especially as Kenneth didn't ride himself. Convinced he was a sham, Reggie challenged him to a race and Kenneth accepted. Reggie bet £250 on himself to win. He lost the bet. But the race had obviously taken it out of Kenneth. Pale and tired, he suddenly disappeared from Ambridge without settling his account at the Bull. His belongings were examined in the hope of tracking him down and among them were found Reggie's cheque, torn to pieces, and papers which made it clear that he had been forbidden to ride for two years following a spinal injury in a riding accident. Within a few days another cheque arrived in the post for what was owing at the Bull. Reggie Trentham was forced to eat his words.

Lewis Gedge

MALCOLM

When Jethro Larkin broke his leg at Brookfield in 1975, Malcolm, a social sciences student, came to help out at Brookfield in his absence. He was an unmitigated disaster, managing to damage the tractor, give calf feed to the cows and spill four tons of corn across a field. Phil Archer had no choice but to sack him and hope for Jethro's speedy return.

Jim Hooper

MANOR COURT

This eighteenth-century gentleman's house was the home of Admiral Bellamy, Ralph Bellamy's father, who lived there until he died in 1964. Carol and John Tregorran bought it soon after they married in 1967, and used it as a display centre for John's antique business as well as a home. Manor Court was sold when they moved to Bristol where they now live.

MANOR HOUSE

Manor House was the sixteenth-century ancestral home of Squire Lawson-Hope, and has the family coat of arms carved over the fireplace. When the Squire sold his estate in 1955 Manor House was bought by Dr Cavendish who founded a 'Health-by-Nature' Home which proved unsuccessful. He sold it to George Fairbrother, and it formed part of the Fairbrother Estate purchased in 1959 by Charles Grenville, who lived there until his death in 1965. He left the Manor House to his wife Carol who reluctantly sold it to Jack Woolley in 1968 for £24,000 when she married John Tregorran and moved into Manor Court.

MANSON, STEVE

After the death of his father-in-law in 1989, Steve Manson decided to move to Norfolk and run his market garden instead of staying on as Brian Aldridge's foreman. Jennifer

Aldridge was furious when he gave in his notice, as Brian was in hospital recovering from an accident and she was managing the farm on her own. Steve offered to remain until after harvest, but foolishly Jennifer turned him down.

MARGARET, HRH THE PRINCESS

Jack Woolley was thrilled when Grey Gables became the venue in June 1984 for the Borsetshire NSPCC centenary fashion show, attended by the patron, the Duke of Westminster. His pleasure redoubled when HRH the Princess Margaret, president of the NSPCC, made an impromptu visit to the event.

MARKET GARDEN

Until 1954 this piece of land at the north end of the village was a smallholding. Jack and Peggy Archer ran it until 1952, when they sold it to Dan Archer for £1,150 and left for Cornwall. Dan had Simon and Bess Cooper look after it for two years before Carol Grey bought it and turned it into a flourishing market garden. In association with George Fairbrother, she expanded her business with the purchase of adjoining land from the Partridge sisters and Doughy Hood. By 1959 Charles Grenville had bought out George Fairbrother and the market garden became part of the Grenville estate, and at Charles's insistence she appointed Arthur Howell as manager in 1961. Jack Woolley and Ralph Bellamy bought the Grenville Estate in 1965, and three years later, after her marriage to John Tregorran, Carol bought back the market garden with an additional 50 acres of orchard. The couple stayed in Ambridge for nearly twenty years before selling up and moving to Bristol. The market garden has since been closed down.

MARNE, TIMOTHY

Sid and Polly Perks liked Timothy Marne, a middle-aged man from Dublin with a smooth tongue, who worked for them as barman in the evenings at the Bull. They were on the point of offering him a permanent job, in 1978, when he suddenly said that he had to leave because his mother had died. In fact there had been a moment of mutual recognition between him and George Barford. George was once a policeman and Timothy was familiar to him as a conman with several aliases. By the time George and PC Drury returned to the Bull Timothy/Thomas/Trevor had gone.

Alan Barry

MARSHALL, RUPERT

When young Richard Grenville started pilfering at his boarding school in 1975, this kind and sensitive housemaster took pains to ensure that it stopped without recourse to any drastic action, believing that the boy was disturbed by the absence of his stepfather, John Tregorran, in America.

Simon Carter

MARTIN, JOHNNY

b. 1951

Tom and Pru Forrest first discussed the possibility of fostering children after they enjoyed looking after Susan Blake in 1960. They visited a local children's home and with the advice of the child welfare officer, Miss Weldon, chose Johnny. He stayed with them for several weekends before arrangements were finalized, but then disappeared from the home. Tom found him hiding in the windmill at Heydon Berrow with his friend Peter Stevens, and Johnny persuaded Tom and Pru to foster Peter as well. Their upbringing was not easy, Peter being particularly troublesome. Johnny pursued a more conventional path, passed the 11-plus and went to Borchester Grammar School. He went to work on the Bellamy Estate in 1967, and Ralph Bellamy arranged for him to do further forestry training for a year on Lord Felpersham's estate, where he afterwards remained. Both young men have now left Ambridge and apart from the occasional Christmas card have lost touch with their foster parents.

Peter Hempson; Philip Neads; Brian Hewlett

MARTIN, MR

The owner of Bull Farm, Mr Martin, decided to sell up and emigrate with his son and married daughter in 1974. The auction was held at the Drum and Monkey in Borchester and Phil Archer bought 35 acres of the land adjoining Brookfield.

MARTINDALE, MR AND MRS

When Jill Archer started running farmhouse holidays at Brookfield in 1990, she awaited her first guests with trepidation, not least because they were bringing their baby, Astley. They proved to be delightful, and Phil Archer spent a pleasant half-hour discussing church organs with Mr Martindale.

MASTERS, VINCE

Vince Masters, married with two children, was taken on as a garage mechanic by Haydn Evans in 1975. He lacked experience with farm machinery, though, and was unreliable, so after a year he had to go.

MATTHEWS, PETER

Jack Archer met Peter Matthews, an architect, at the Casino at Borchester, and recommended him to his brother Dan Archer. In 1970 Dan asked him to design the alterations needed at Brookfield before Phil Archer and his family moved in to the farmhouse.

MAXINE THE MOHICAN

At a circus in 1990, Eddie Grundy chatted up the circus girl Maxine the Mohican. She seemed to him no less exotic when she revealed that she came from Hull. He was secretly delighted that his wife Clarrie was going on holiday and, after seeing her to her bus, returned to the circus. Enthralled by Maxine's long black hair and leather-fringed costume, he tripped over a guy rope but, undeterred, asked her home for sausages and chips. Fortunately, Joe Grundy's disapproval kept her at bay until Clarrie's return.

MAXWELL, JANE

Phil Archer engaged Jane Maxwell in 1951 as poultry girl on Fairbrother's Estate as a little bit of spite. He wanted to attract the attention of Grace Fairbrother who was paying far too much attention to Alan Carey, and to remind her that he could have other interests too. Jane certainly made the point, with her tall willowy figure, bright blue eyes and peaches-and-cream complexion. Not only that, but she had attended Harper Adams college and was extremely efficient at her job. Grace didn't like her at all, and all her worst suspicions were confirmed when she found Phil and Jane cuddling late one night. In fact Jane had been working late and fallen asleep, and Phil had just put his arm round her to help her up when Grace entered. Grace later apologized but there was an element of mutual distrust underlying the later friendliness of the two girls.

She started to go out with Dick Raymond, and together they did a bit of detective work and discovered that Bill Slater was responsible for sabotaging Keith Latimer's drilling equipment. But when Phil told her that Grace had virtually proposed to him, he and Jane were stunned into an awareness of how much they meant to each other. Phil was soon involved in a tug-of-war as Grace and Jane fought for him in their different ways. Jane wanted him

to leave Ambridge with her and find another job but he was reluctant to move.

Jane moved out of the Bull and took a room at Mrs P.'s for 25s. a week including full board and laundry. She was constantly jealous of Grace and squabbling with Phil, and in the end decided that second-best wasn't good enough for her. She handed in her notice and drove to Hollerton Junction in a hired car rather than wait for Phil and Grace to take her. She left a note of explanation for Phil with Sam Saunders at the Bull, and that was the last he heard of her.

Mary Wimbush

MAYNARD, BRENDA

When Paul Johnson went to work in London in 1975, Brenda Maynard was personal assistant to his boss, and she and Paul had an affair. The following year he confessed all to his wife Christine and resigned from the job. Brenda followed him to Ambridge where he and Christine had the difficult task of convincing her that the affair was over.

Jane Rossington

MEAD, FRANK

Polly Perks's father Frank Mead died in 1975 in the county mental hospital, where he had spent the last years of his life, having become a compulsive arsonist. Before fire-raising, he had run a smallholding and sometimes worked for Phil Archer. He is buried in Penny Hassett, his home village.

Graham Rigby

MEAD, LIZZIE

Following the death of Frank Mead in 1975, his daughter Polly Perks wanted her mother Lizzie to give her and her husband Sid Perks some financial help towards buying Rose Cottage in Penny Hassett; in return, Polly offered her the cottage to live in during her retirement. But Mrs Mead was unimpressed and uninterested in the whole idea. Instead she became a lonely, rather bitter old lady, eventually living with her widowed sister Joan and her revolting cat in Edgeley.

Peggy Anne Wood; Joy Davies

MEAD, POLLY

see Perks, Polly

MERIDEW, CANON

The vicar of Ambridge was ill in 1972, so Canon Meridew came out of retirement to officiate at the wedding of Joby Woodford and Martha Lily on Christmas Day. He was in Ambridge again the following year in less happy circumstances when it fell to him to advise Hester Latimer after her husband's death.

Norman Shelley

MERRYMAN, MISS

After an early retirement due to ill health, Fred Barratt found that time hung heavily on his hands. He started to drink, and delighted in spreading malicious gossip. When Jack Woolley and Carol Tregorran began to receive unpleasant anonymous letters in 1968, at a time when Jack and his wife Valerie were drifting apart, it was natural that they should think that Fred was responsible. Jack was in the habit of confiding his troubles to Carol and the letters implied that they were more than just good friends. To Jack's great distress he learned that the letter-writer was in fact his secretary of many years, Miss Merryman, and so he had to sack her.

MEYRUELLE

On 15 September 1994 Ambridge was twinned with Meyruelle, a small town in the Languedoc Roussillon. The idea originated with Clarrie Grundy, and was developed, if not taken over, by Jack Woolley when he spied commercial possibilities. The French delegation – the Mayor of Meyruelle, M. Touvier and Mme Beguet – scored a great success when they visited Ambridge in June 1993. Jack and Peggy Woolley returned the visit with Clarrie Grundy, to the annoyance of Lynda Snell who had lobbied long and hard for the nomination but was unable to go due to illness.

MICHAELS, DR

A young doctor who briefly helped Dr MacLaren in 1973 before being offered a preferable practice elsewhere.

MIDNIGHT

Dan and Doris Archer bought the horse Midnight from Reggie Trentham to give to their daughter Christine for her twenty-first birthday in 1952. Christine trained with Reggie and despite her father's fear that she would have an accident rode the horse at point-to-points with some success. When fire broke out in the stables at Grey Gables in 1955, Grace Fairbrother died in her gallant efforts to save the horse. Christine was still riding Midnight in 1959.

MILLER, SANDY

In 1974 Neil Carter went to a party at Sandy Miller's place in Borchester which was raided by the police. She hid her 'reefers' in his pocket and he was charged with possession of drugs. Desperate to keep out of trouble with the law, she begged him not to inform on her, and, despite being found guilty and put on probation, he didn't. He was devastated when, despite his sacrifice, she made it clear that she didn't want to see him again.

Elizabeth Revill

MISTER JONES

Phil and Jill Archer wanted to give their daughter Shula a present after she had finished her O-levels in 1973. She asked for Mister Jones, a difficult horse owned by Lilian Bellamy. When Lilian wouldn't sell, Shula refused to have a horse at all and was given a saddle instead. But Lilian allowed Shula to ride Mister Jones at the riding stables whenever she wanted to, and arranged for her to meet the champion rider Ann Moore, who confirmed her potential as a show jumper. In August 1974 Shula qualified on the horse for the regional final, but landed badly at a five-barred gate while showing off in front of George Barford and Jack Woolley. Suffering minor injuries herself, she was more concerned for Mister Jones who was also hurt. Both horse and rider recovered but, to Shula's intense disappointment, too late for the regional final.

MOORE, ANN

Champion show jumper Ann Moore came to Ambridge in spring 1974 to see Lilian Bellamy's new indoor riding school, where she remarked on Shula Archer's evident promise as a rider. Shula took Mister Jones to her stables and worked there with her. Several months later she went again, but Ann had to say that she suspected that Shula was too headstrong to make it to the top.

MOORE, DONALD

In 1975 Christine Archer and Trina Muir were exercising their horses when a dog dashed from the hedgerow, causing Trina's mount Red Knight to panic. Donald Moore, a car salesman driving past at the time, could not avoid hitting the horse, which had to be put down.

Morgan, Basil

Basil Morgan ran the sports centre at Borchester. He was attractive, and had been divorced from his wife Joyce seven years previously. He wooed Jackie Smith away from the Bull to serve behind his bar in 1979.

Peter Brookes

Morley, Mr

In 1977 Polly Perks was told by Mr Morley, her gynaecologist, that she couldn't have any more children.

Morris, Bill

Bill Morris, farmer's boy from the Welsh borders, was eighteen when he took out Shula Archer in 1975. They had met at college on an NCA course and Shula thought that her parents would like him. When she brought him home to Brookfield to show him off, over dinner this big-headed young know-all told her father Phil Archer that he considered Ambridge farmers to be old-fashioned. Phil was not amused and Shula was on her father's side.

Jim Hooper

Mrs Archer

One of Eddie Grundy's favourite ferrets, so named because it was a jill.

Muir, Trina

Lilian Bellamy employed Trina to manage at the riding school in 1973. She came from Edinburgh, and used to do competition riding until a bad fall left her lame. She settled in well with her job, but didn't have much of a social life until Gordon Armstrong came on the scene. They started going out with each other and she began to like him so much that she was upset when he casually mentioned that he had an interview for another job away from Ambridge. She was nice enough not to gloat when she learned that not only was he turned down for the job but also that he had been robbed. He had gone for a drink to drown his sorrows, met a girl who relieved him of his wallet and had to hitchhike home. Trina enjoyed keeping him at arm's length for a while after that, but relented in the end and let him take her to a St Valentine's dance.

Trina was impressed with Shula Archer's riding potential and they were good friends until an accident occurred when Trina was riding one of Shula's favourite mounts at the riding school, Red Knight. A dog dashed out of the hedgerow, causing the horse to panic as a car approached; the next thing Trina knew was that the car had hit Red Knight and one of his legs had broken. The vet had to put him down, and although it wasn't Trina's fault Shula blamed her (but she cheered up when she was told that she could choose and train a horse to replace Red Knight from the insurance money).

Trina's on-off relationship with Gordon was wearing, and he persisted in saying that marriage was not for him. There was nothing else to keep her in Ambridge and when she went home for Christmas in 1978 she rang Christine Johnson, who had by then taken over the riding school, to say that she had found a new job there and would not be coming back.

Judith Carey

MUMFORD, JOHN

Blacksmith who worked on the other side of Edgeley in the 1980s.

N

NELL

Working dogs are part of the scene at any farm, there to do a job and never as pets; however, affection inevitably grows between man and animal during years of association and there have been many instances in and around Ambridge of the bending of the rules. Dan Archer got his last dog, Nell, from Sammy Whipple at Home Farm in 1977 and trained her to work the Brookfield sheep, though by then Dan acknowledged that he no longer had the patience he once did. Phil Archer kept her on at Brookfield after Dan's death and long beyond her useful working life; and when in 1991 she was found dead in a snare illegally set by Brian Aldridge's keeper, Phil's fury revealed the attachment he had to the dog and to his memories of her at work with his father.

NELSON'S WINE BAR

In 1980 Nelson Gabriel developed an old warehouse in West Street, Borchester, reno-vated it in the American bar style of the twenties known as 'speakeasy' with a picture of Al Capone on the wall, and put up a sign outside saying 'West Street Wine Bar'.

By 1983 he had a change of heart, stripped the interior, repainted it and put a black and gold sign outside saying 'Nelson's'. He served cocktails and introduced 'happy hours', which went down very well with his younger clientele, but were not sufficient to save him from insolvency in 1984. His father Walter Gabriel stepped in to help, and once again the decor was transformed.

This time Nelson sought an art deco effect with chocolate-brown paintwork, potted palms and a huge mirror on the wall. Outside, the word 'Nelson's' was written in gigantic silver letters across each pane of the dark-brown windows, and Nelson co-opted the services of a singer, Hebe. Unfortunately the bailiffs turned up on her opening night and Jack Woolley took the opportunity to lure Hebe to Grey Gables. Once again Walter turned up trumps and bailed Nelson out until he made some money from the sale of property he owned in Lanzarote. Nelson then took the business back in hand.

No further redecoration took place until 1991 when Kenton Archer bought some furniture from a local country house which Nelson liked and which enabled him to redecorate in his own version of a gentleman's club style. Caroline Bone designed a colour scheme to go with it, and a new sign was put up which read: 'Nelson's Wine Bar'.

NICHOLAS, ALAN

Dan Archer and Jack Woolley gave a lift to Alan Nicholas on their way back from a long journey to Scotland to fetch the railway locomotive Jack had bought for the Country Park in 1972. Alan was a post-sixties hippy with long hair and a guitar, singing for his supper wherever he went, with a great deal of charm. He spent the night in the clubhouse and was giving the engine a good clean when he met Tom Forrest for the first time, and sang him a song about railway engines that he had just made up. There is no record of Tom's reaction.

Sid and Polly Perks allowed Alan to play his music in the Bull and he camped out at Rickyard Cottage with Tony Archer. A couple of girls spent the night there too, although Tony swore that all they'd done was discuss literature.

Alan was so likeable that when he made plans to leave for London Sid begged him to stay, asking him to be chef for the Steak Bar in spite of the fact that he couldn't cook. Alan accepted, but he couldn't cope with a proper job. He was unreliable, unpunctual and, even worse, he sang an anti-hunting song one evening, which annoyed Ralph Bellamy. He fell for Frances Graham, in charge of the mobile library, and was sad to find out that she was already married. He made a half-hearted pass at Trina Muir; and he felt so guilty when Haydn Evans accused him of giving Angela Cooper ideas about leaving home that he decided the time had come to move on.

Raymond Skipp

NICHOLSON, LESTER (NICK)

b. 7 June 1946; m. Lilian Archer 26 May 1969; d. 18 Mar. 1970

A Royal Canadian Air Force officer, Nick Nicholson came to Lilian Archer's stables one day to hire a horse. He invited her out to dine and a loving relationship began. An ear infection forced him to leave the RCAF and he became a private pilot to a wealthy businessman. Lilian and he exchanged letters and they married in 1969. In 1970 Nick and Lilian went to Canada so that he could receive medical treatment but he sustained a fatal fall in hospital there.

Hayward Morse

NICHOLSON, LILIAN

see Bellamy, Lilian

NICK

Nick was an old tramp whose unkempt appearance made him look far more frightening than he was. He knew most of what was happening in Ambridge and in 1951 it was he who guided Grace Fairbrother to Heydon Berrow when she was searching for Alan Carey.

Will Kings

NIGHTINGALE FARM

Nightingale Farm belonged to Brigadier Winstanley's estate, inherited after his death by his niece Lady Isabel Lander. She sold it to Hugo Barnaby in 1970 and a year later Barnaby opened an art and craft centre there, living in a flat above, with Laura Archer as assistant curator. By 1976 Barnaby had disappeared to America and his cousin John Tregorran was left to organize the removal of his possessions and look after the Centre in his absence. The local council was interested in purchasing it but sufficient funds were not available, and the Youth Club had the use of the building for some years.

Neil Carter moved into the flat, which he shared with Michele Brown, New Zealand sheep-shearer. He continued to live there after Michele's departure and his marriage to Susan Horrobin. In 1984 Barnaby wished to sell Nightingale Farm and offered the Carters

£4,000 to leave, which they did.

When Shula Archer, working for the estate agents Rodway & Watson, showed Marjorie Antrobus round Nightingale Farm in 1985 the property had fallen into disrepair and the driveway was full of holes. However, as a breeder of Afghan hounds Marjorie's prime concern was for her 'gels'. The fact that the buildings were set well back from the road and that half an acre went with the farmhouse was quite enough to persuade her to buy it. She restored the farmhouse to its original state and converted the outbuildings into kennels. She takes in lodgers from time to time, most recently Dr Locke.

NOLAN, MR

In 1977 Mr Nolan, the Irish foreman of an asphalt team, persuaded Haydn Evans that his garage forecourt needed resurfacing. Haydn paid him handsomely and the work was done. But all too soon the weeds were coming through the delicate smearing Mr Nolan had put down and as they continued to grow the Irishman was nowhere to be found.

David Jackson

OAKLEY, JIM

Jim Oakley worked for Paul Johnson when he set up his fish farm in 1977, until it failed.

OAKLEY, STEVE

A stockman's son from Shropshire who had been made redundant, resourceful Steve Oakley set up as a freelance. He worked on the Home Farm harvest in 1994 and, though Brian Aldridge didn't share his trenchant views on land use and modern agriculture, he found him an excellent worker.

Matthew Morgan

OGLETHORPE, MRS

In 1958 Mrs Oglethorpe's net curtains had been busy twitching. Walter Gabriel was the first to hear about the number of times she had seen Paul Johnson's car outside the house of her neighbour June Whitworth. Mrs Oglethorpe had 'drawn her own conclusions'.

O'HARA MR

Aged seventy and just recovering from pneumonia, Mr O'Hara did his best with the installation of Pat and Tony Archer's new kitchen in 1989, but he wrecked the electricity system, which it took the combined efforts of Robert Snell, Bert Fry and Brian Aldridge to put right.

O'LEARY, MICHAEL

As foreman of a road-working team in Ambridge in 1960, Michael O'Leary made a big impression on the locals. Doughy Hood, jealous of Rita Flynn's interest in O'Leary, was delighted to see him go, but Jack Archer organized a farewell party in Hollerton. A few months later he was back and engaged to Rita, whom he took to Ireland the next Easter.

Michael Collins

OLIVER, ALAN

see Red Link

P., MRS

see Perkins, Polly

PADBURY, ELLEN

Ellen Padbury and Neil Carter became friends at a Young Farmers' scavenger hunt in 1977 when Shula Archer had forsaken Neil for Simon Carter. As well as being pretty, Ellen liked riding pillion on his motor-bike, which multiplied her attractions in his eyes. To his delight she won the 1977 Miss Ambridge competition at the village fête. But when he learned that Shula and Simon had fallen out, Neil's interest in Ellen quickly faded.

PAGE, JOCELYN

When in 1973 two pages of an old book were found in the Bull, it was Jocelyn Page, assistant in the County Records office, who phoned landlord Sid Perks with the news that they were from a 1587 edition of Holinshed's *Chronicles* and contained scribbles in the margin which raised the possibility of a Shakespearean connection. Sadly, her optimism proved unfounded.

Ysanne Churchman

PAGET, TINA

When Tina Paget, nineteen-year-old daughter of a university colleague of John Tregorran's, came over from South Africa in 1960, she stayed in Carol Grey's cottage. Joan Hood tried to involve her with her friends in Borchester and arranged a date for her with Ricky Boyd at the Borchester Palais. Tina, on Carol's advice, stood him up. Ricky tracked her down to John's shop, where he threatened her angrily, but she showed her mettle by retaliating with an antique paperweight. Carol and John were relieved when the time came to take Tina to meet her parents at Hollerton Junction and see the family off on their holiday.

Karen Perkins

PALMER, CHARLES

The Deputy Chief Constable of Borsetshire, Charles Palmer, was a good golfer and in 1989 Jack Woolley was flattered by his attendance at a golfing weekend at Grey Gables.

PALMER, MR AND MRS

Sid and Gladys Palmer were tenants at Glebe Cottage when Letty Lawson-Hope died in 1958, leaving the cottage to Doris Archer. Having expected that it would be left to them, out of pique they spread malicious rumours about Doris which the village ignored.

Betty Taylor

PARGETTER, ELIZABETH (NÉE ARCHER)

*b. 21 Apr. 1967; m. Nigel Pargetter
29 Sept. 1994*

There is only one person who is allowed to call Elizabeth Pargetter 'Lizzie' and that is Nigel Pargetter. To everyone else she remains uncompromisingly Elizabeth. The last of Phil and Jill Archer's four children, she was the baby of Brookfield until her niece Pip arrived on the scene in 1992. Even then at the age of twenty-four she was still finding it difficult to get used to not having entirely her own way.

Her birth caused a great deal of anxiety. She was born with a hole in the heart and it wasn't until after two major operations and subsequent half-days only at primary school that she had anything like an ordinary childhood. But by then she was used to being the centre of attention: a place she was determined to keep. The daughter of a livestock farmer, she caused a gratifying amount of chaos in the Brookfield kitchen by announcing that she had become a vegetarian.

When she failed to get into Borchester Grammar School because she didn't work hard enough to pass the 11-plus exam, her parents decided that the best thing for her would be to send her off to be a boarder at Cherrington Manor. She quickly became the naughtiest girl in the school and certainly the only one to arrive back at the start of term accompanied by a gorilla – Nigel in his favourite costume. In 1984 she was caught drinking under age in a public house and the school had no option but to expel her. Having faced her parents' wrath, she realized that she would never have any sort of glittering future without A-levels and enrolled at Borchester Technical College to study English literature and environmental science. But Elizabeth still found studying a problem. It interfered far too much with her social life, which in turn interfered too much with the cosy pattern at Brookfield. She would spend hours in the bathroom preparing for her dates with Terry Barford, Tim Beecham, Nigel Pargetter and anyone else who asked her out. Finally her father Phil gave in to her request for a bathroom of her own – a privilege which she zealously guarded. She was furious one evening to discover David using it to prepare for an evening with Sophie Barlow and locked him in. A naked David was forced to climb out of the bathroom window.

Once she had got her own bathroom, the

next thing she needed was a car. Determined to get 'wheels' as soon as possible, she applied herself to driving lessons and passed first time. She wheedled Phil again, this time to buy her a red Metro. Phil wasn't pleased when, within a few months, she crashed into Eddie Grundy's Capri.

Like her elder sister Shula, when she first left school Elizabeth found it difficult to decide where her future lay, but one thing was certain: she needed to make enough money to pay for her expensive social life. To this end she spent the summer of 1986 working as Mrs Snowy, ice-cream vendor. There was great competition between her and Mr Snowy: for this appearance in Lizzie's life, Nigel dressed in white overalls with a straw boater. Then, despite the fact she mimicked her lisp to annoy David, Elizabeth embarked on a hectic foray into the fashion world with his girlfriend, Sophie.

Eventually she decided that journalism was the career for her. Armed with her one A-level pass in English, she approached Jack Woolley, owner of *The Borchester Echo*, for a job. Journalism suited her well. She had a flair for it, even though she missed the scoop story of the exploding marrow at the Derrington flower show, because she was too bored to stay until the judging. Her experience at the *Echo* gave her enough confidence in her ability as a reporter to apply for and get a job on the *Birmingham Evening News*. Elizabeth moved out of Brookfield and into the big city in July 1990; but a year later she was back, suffering from glandular fever. Jill tucked her into bed and cosseted her, and soon Elizabeth was back on form.

She soon discovered that Cameron Fraser had broken up with Caroline Bone and, determined to impress him, Elizabeth, who had not ridden for years, accepted his invitation to go cubbing. She fell from her horse, was rescued by Cameron and their affair began. It ended when he abandoned her, pregnant, at a motorway service station. Humiliated and heartbroken, she hitched back to Ambridge. The next thing she knew, the police were questioning her as to Cameron Fraser's whereabouts: he was wanted for criminal fraud. Even though Shula and her husband Mark had offered to adopt the child, Elizabeth felt that her only option was to abort the pregnancy. This shocked Jill, who was longing to welcome her first grandchild, legitimate or illegitimate, and so hurt Shula that it was a long time before she could even bring herself to speak to her sister. Elizabeth, in grief herself but sure that she had made the right decision, for the first time recognized other people's pain and needs.

Nigel, as ever, loyally supported Lizzie. He had generously made her the marketing manager at Lower Loxley Hall during the height of her affair with Cameron. When she told him she had been deserted by Cameron, Nigel had offered to marry her and bring the baby up as his own but Lizzie had turned him down. For some time the two of them worked side by side at Lower Loxley, building up the business and trying to keep Julia Pargetter from causing too much havoc.

Lizzie and Nigel had been friends since she was seventeen. They had always had a lot in common, especially their sense of humour. Together they had enjoyed a long adolescence. Nigel had previously asked Lizzie to marry him and she had asked him when he was going to marry her, but in the end neither felt ready to make the commitment. Then Nigel realized that they were both older and wiser. He proposed to Lizzie again and she said 'yes'. They decided to keep the engagement secret until after Robin Stokes and Caroline Bone's wedding. But the wedding was postponed after Caroline was hurt in the tragic accident in which Mark Hebden was killed. Lizzie watched in agony as Nigel rallied round to help Shula. She found it hard enough to cope with her future mother-in-law without having to struggle with her jealousy and came close to breaking off the engagement. But Nigel reassured her that it was Lizzie and Lizzie alone that he wanted to marry on 29 September 1994.

At last, Elizabeth's life seems to have fallen into place.

Judy Bennett; Nicolette Gorton; Alison Dowling

Pargetter, Julia

*b. 17 Aug. 1924; m. Gerald Pargetter;
1 son, 1 dtr*

Julia Pargetter is a snob, and though not a member of the aristocracy she would like to be. She has always claimed that with her blue eyes, golden hair and long legs, she could have been, given the chance, the débutante of her year. Her marriage to Gerald Pargetter brought her a life of elegance and sophistication and the chance to become mistress of Lower Loxley Hall. She had two children, Camilla and Nigel, who were brought up by a nanny. One of the few failings to which Julia has ever admitted is being 'not very good with children'.

When her husband died in 1988, Lower Loxley and the estate were in a state of financial crisis. It became clear that if something wasn't done quickly everything would have to be sold. At first Julia made a half-hearted attempt to help Nigel get the place back on its feet; but she found economy tedious and soon decided that she would rather leave things to Nigel and spend her time abroad. Eventually her money ran out and she was forced to return to Lower Loxley.

She was appalled by the steps Nigel had taken to save Lower Loxley: she thought the Bank Holiday extravaganzas 'common' and could not bear the thought of the hall being used for business conferences and wedding receptions. Lower Loxley was her home and she didn't want the general public there, even if they were prepared to pay for the pleasure. She was disgusted by the fact that Nigel had chosen Elizabeth Archer as his business manager and insisted on calling her 'that Archer girl'.

Determined that Nigel should marry a woman with money, she set her sights on Debbie Aldridge as a potential daughter-in-law and tried to manipulate the two of them into an affair. She sent them away on business trips together and invited Debbie to dinner at Lower Loxley. Debbie wore a bracelet that Julia's expert eye recognized as paste. She was delighted when she discovered that Debbie had borrowed it from Elizabeth. Eventually Julia realized that her matchmaking wasn't going to work; but that still didn't make her behave any better towards Elizabeth.

Always looking for amusement, Julia turned her attentions towards Nelson Gabriel. He was flattered. Nigel encouraged Nelson to take Julia out for trips so that he and Elizabeth could get on in peace at Lower Loxley. (On one occasion she complained of a 'hideous evening' spent with his dealer colleagues.) Nelson was charmed by Julia's urbane wit and hurt when he discovered that she didn't care for him as much as he cared for her.

Gradually Julia's behaviour became more and more erratic. It became clear that she was an alcoholic. Nigel tried hard to stop her drinking but to no avail. Eventually there was nothing for it but for Julia to enter an addiction clinic. After one false start she began to come to terms with a life of sobriety. Soon she was back at Lower Loxley, bouncing with health and full of good intentions to help Nigel and Elizabeth, who told her they were engaged to be married. Julia gulped and congratulated them but excused herself from attending the engagement dinner Jill Archer gave at Brookfield.

After several fiascos in the offices at Lower Loxley, Nigel and Elizabeth decided that they must encourage Julia to do something that would keep her out of their hair; so they were delighted when she began to show an interest in horticulture. Julia felt that here was something which fitted her image of herself and Lower Loxley, though it remains to be seen if it will be as short-lived as some of her other passions. In 1994 Julia's sister Ellen Rogers revealed that her real name is Joan and that Julia was the name she took when she broke away from her background as a greengrocer's daughter for a career as a singer and dancer in popular wartime revues.

Jo Kendall; Mary Wimbush

Pargetter, Nigel

b. 8 June 1959; m. Elizabeth Archer 29 Sept. 1994

On 15 November 1983, a gorilla bounded into Brookfield Farm, beating its chest and growling. Nigel Pargetter had arrived to take Shula Archer to a fancy dress ball.

Nigel was the heir to a 2,000-acre estate at Lower Loxley. In his childhood years he was brought up by a caring nanny who even tied his shoelaces for him. His mother, Julia, would never have stooped so low. Julia has described her son Nigel when a child as 'soft, always bringing home crippled hedgehogs and half-dead reptiles'. He had a nursery full of beloved toys, but his favourite was a bear called Tiddles. Nigel and his father loved playing with toy trains. The idyll ended when Nigel was sent away to Rugby School as his father had been.

Before he inherited Lower Loxley Nigel had a variety of short-term jobs. When employed to sell swimming pools, he would celebrate in grand style before any contract had been signed. He even took Shula to dine at the Connaught Hotel in London before one such deal fell through. Threatened with the sack he thought he would make a last attempt to sell a pool to Jack Woolley. During their discussion Jack had half an eye on his chauffeur Higgs, who was on the kitchen roof clearing out blocked drains. Suddenly Jack spotted that Captain, a dog of little brain but much curiosity, had followed Higgs out. The next thing Nigel knew was that he was perched precariously on the

Nigel Pargetter (Graham Seed) and Elizabeth Archer (Alison Dowling)

splashing about in an over-heated pool, using up all the heating oil.

Nigel wooed Shula for about a year. Once, desperate to impress her, he prepared an elaborate meal, using two bottles of his father's Taylor's '50 port for Cumberland sauce. On another occasion, ever the gentleman, he escorted Shula home from a hunt ball and was left by her to sleep on the sofa. Later he crept upstairs and into what he thought was Shula's bed. But, to his horror, he was soon cuddling up to Phil Archer. A ban on overnights at Brookfield was immediately enforced. After another dance in 1984, a drunken Nigel couldn't find his car and took what he thought was Tim Beecham's. The car, in fact, belonged to Mr Cunningham, and Shula and Nigel had to spend a night in the cells. Nigel was found guilty of taking and driving away. Mark Hebden defended Shula, and Nigel, recognizing their growing attachment, began to cast his gaze in the direction of Shula's younger sister Elizabeth.

The gorilla suit made another appearance at Brookfield when Nigel arrived to escort Elizabeth back to school for the start of a new term. He was soon a willing accomplice when Elizabeth played truant, and it was Nigel who bought the celebratory drinks

kitchen roof with Jack who, in a vain attempt to rescue the stolid Captain, made a spectacular leap into the flowerbeds below, leaving Nigel to restrain Captain from following him. His bravery clinched the deal but it was a decision that Jack may have regretted when he discovered Captain, Nigel, his friends and the entire staff of Grey Gables

when she was eventually expelled.

In despair, Mr Pargetter sent him off to stay with an uncle in Zimbabwe. Frequent postcards were received at Brookfield by everyone except Phil. Soon his uncle too had had enough of Nigel's excesses, and he was packed off back to Lower Loxley in disgrace. Elizabeth was delighted to see him again. But they were soon at war, driving rival ice-cream floats as Mr and Mrs Snowy. Mrs Antrobus's dogs were nearly driven mad by Nigel's incessant 'Teddy Bear's Picnic' chimes.

Determined to make his son face his responsibilities, Mr Pargetter sent him to work at the Stock Exchange. This didn't last long: Nigel was better at spending money than investing it. In March 1988, Nigel's father died and he inherited Lower Loxley Hall. It had been sadly neglected over the years. One day, whilst swinging on a banister, a large lump of wood came away in Nigel's hand. He realized that huge sums of money were going to be needed to save his ancestral home – and that it was time to grow up.

In July 1992, Lower Loxley Corporate Entertainments was launched, with Nigel as director. He had shrewdly invited Elizabeth Archer to be his marketing manager, insisting, however, that she train and qualify properly for the job. This says a lot about Nigel's generosity of spirit, since by then Elizabeth had fallen desperately in love with Cameron Fraser.

The company has proved to be more successful than many people anticipated, no thanks to Julia's determined opposition and her resentment at the commercialization of her home. Nigel and Elizabeth have hosted a series of spectacular events, such as the Battle of Hassett Bridge and the local 1994 point-to-point race.

Nigel is a consistently kind person, always willing to lend a generous (if not always expert) hand with meals-on-wheels, rescuing animals, haymaking or restarting cars. When Elizabeth was pregnant with Cameron Fraser's child, Nigel was compassionate and sympathetic. He has been a most caring and attentive friend to Shula Hebden since her husband Mark's death.

After several 'secret' engagements to his long-loved Lizzie, in May 1994 he officially asked Phil for her hand in marriage. Jill and the rest of the family were delighted and the marriage took place in St Stephen's on 29 September 1994.

Graham Seed; Nigel Caliburn; Graham Seed

PARKER, SIMON

Simon Parker was a reporter on *The Felpersham Evening News* before Jack Woolley offered him the job as editor of *The Borchester Echo* when Mr Hapgood-Harman retired in 1976. Simon was thirty-six, a heavy smoker and an individualist. Jack gave him a free hand as long as he followed Jack's advice, but Simon pursued his own course, and he had ambitions for the paper. He wanted circulation increased to 10,000, the London agent changed to improve the national advertising they needed and, above all, some fresh blood on the staff.

He had his own standards, which didn't always please his readers or employer. He knew Shula Archer well but still printed a negative story about her hunting while on the dole. Phil Archer cancelled his order for the *Echo* immediately. He wrote up a corruption story about one of Jack's friends, Councillor Tyrell JP, which made Jack furious and, unrepentant, quit his job before he was sacked. He was vindicated when Tyrell resigned from the Borchester council, which proved that there was indeed truth in the rumours, and Jack had no choice but to reinstate him.

Simon was victorious in his love life too, pursuing Shula and deflowering her in a Netherbourne cornfield. He was an unpredictable lover, turning up when it suited him and expecting Shula to be there, which she found irritating. He asked her to join him skiing with some friends but it looked as though the trip would never take place when he started going out with a girl he'd met, fascinated by her purple-painted fingernails. He and Shula were reconciled just in time for their holiday.

During the May Day celebrations in 1978 Simon casually told Shula that he'd been offered a job in London which he intended to take, and she was very upset. Hapgood-Harman had to come out of retirement until Jack could find a new editor. The last Shula heard was that Simon was on his way to Kathmandu.

Alaric Cotter

PARTRIDGE TWINS

Known simply as Partridge One and Partridge Two, Eddie Grundy's friends have never revealed their real names. Eddie thinks the names may be biblical, along the lines of Zebediah or Ezekiel, but as they communicate only through grunts, his theory may never be confirmed.

PASCO, LYN

Tony Archer advertised for a general farm worker in 1978, but turned Lyn Pasco down when she applied for the job, as he didn't think she was suitable. She was a student at a local agricultural college looking for a year's practical experience on a farm, and had already had an off-putting time in a previous job when her married boss made advances towards her. When no other candidates were forthcoming Tony had little choice but to take her on. She got off to a bad start when while cleaning the drains she got the rods stuck, but she soon proved to be so useful that Brian Aldridge cast a predatory eye in her direction. He engaged her to help with the lambing at Home Farm, for which she showed an excellent instinct, and when she returned to college for her final year she continued to work there most weekends. To make amends for poaching on his preserves Brian offered Tony the services of Ricketts, one of his own farm workers.

Jane Galloway

PATCH

When Robin Stokes took up residence in the Vicarage at Ambridge in 1991 he brought with him Patch, his Old English sheepdog. Tragically, while roaming the countryside Patch ate a poisoned egg and died. After some weeks of investigation Robin discovered that gamekeeper George Barford was responsible for putting down eggs in order to kill corvids that were threatening his game birds. Robin agreed not to report George, provided that he surrendered the poison. Robin was greatly cheered when Caroline Bone gave him a Jack Russell, jokingly referred to by Mark Hebden as JR – a name which stuck.

PATILLO, ROGER

see Travers-Macy, Roger

PATTERSON, JILL

see Archer, Jill

PEACHES

Peaches was the shapely barmaid at the Cat and Fiddle in 1986, as sweet as her name and much adored by Tim Beecham.

PEARSON, DICK

When Dick Pearson, the landlord of the Cat and Fiddle, was ill in 1983 he had to engage a relief landlord. Eddie and Joe Grundy couldn't be seen for dust when they learned that Dick's replacement used to be in the army and ran a boxing club in Leeds. They didn't reappear until Dick's return a couple of months later.

PEDRO

Shula Archer met Pedro in Spain when travelling in Europe in 1976. Later in the year he came to England and surprised Shula with a visit to Brookfield. She showed him Ambridge and took him hunting, after which he departed for London, leaving behind him a red rose in farewell.

Norman Painting

PEEL, JOHN

Eddie Grundy was extremely excited in 1991 when he learned that BBC Radio One was to hold its disc jockeys' Christmas lunch at Grey Gables. Caroline Bone had met Johnny Beerling, controller of Radio One, as she sailed down the Zambezi on a raft, and he remembered her that Christmas when his catering arrangements fell to pieces. A quick fax to Grey Gables and all was solved, giving Eddie the chance of seeing one of his idols, John Peel, and demonstrating his many talents.

John slipped in to see Bert Fry's production of *Aladdin* and was so taken with Eddie's impressions of Radio One disc jockeys that he invited the Grundy clan to join him at the Christmas lunch. He not only paid for their meal but took away a couple of Eddie's tapes to listen to, and promised to be in touch. Eddie thought his fortune was made, so he was shattered when some weeks later the tapes were returned, accompanied by a standard letter from the BBC saying that the songs were not suitable for broadcasting. Eddie still believes that John Peel missed the chance of a lifetime.

PEGASUS

see Snout, Mr

PEMBERTON, GUY

b. 1931; 2 sons

Guy Pemberton, a distinguished widower in his early sixties, bought the Berrow Estate in 1993 and decided to farm it himself. Coming from a long line of yeoman farmers, he previously owned an estate in Suffolk managed by his eldest son Andrew. He sold up after Andrew's tragic death in a car crash and moved to Ambridge to be closer to his younger son Simon, who works in Leamington Spa.

Guy successfully ran the gauntlet of meeting his tenants and even managed to deal with Lynda Snell in full flood at the welcome party given in his honour by the Woolleys. He continued to have Estate business handled by agents Rodway & Watson, which brought him into close contact with their employee Shula Hebden and he had the good sense to value her experience. His gentle manner cloaks a sharp intelligence and he quickly grasped the complexities involved when Shula explained set-aside regulations to him. He has already proved to be a loyal employer, as Susan Carter found out when he spoke up for her at her trial.

When Peggy Woolley put the Bull up for sale, Guy went into partnership with Sid Perks and they bought it together. Guy has shown as keen an interest in this investment as in all

Mrs Antrobus (Margot Boyd) and Guy Pemberton (Hugh Dickson)

his other work. Ambridge may yet discover that his velvet glove hides an iron fist.

Hugh Dickson

PENNY HASSETT

The nearest village to Ambridge is Penny Hassett, beyond Lakey Hill to the north-east. It is a little larger than Ambridge, and its main claim to fame is the annual pancake race held on Shrove Tuesday, a long-standing tradition upheld in recent years by the WI. St Saviour's church has a fine Jacobean pulpit, but is in poorer condition than St Stephen's in Ambridge, and is less well attended.

PERKINS, ARTHUR

m. Polly Perkins (Mrs P.) 1959; d. 4 Dec. 1968

Four years after Grace Archer's death in 1955, George and Helen Fairbrother decided to have a stained-glass window designed in her memory. Arthur Perkins was the stonemason who came to install it in St Stephen's church.

Mrs P. met him when she waited on him for his first meal at the Bull, where he was staying, and once they got over the coincidence of their surnames they had a long chat. He was a widower, and this was to be his last job before retiring and taking a trip abroad. Mrs P. liked him, and was so impressed by the fact that he didn't drink much that she invited him to her cottage, where they enjoyed several suppers. Walter Gabriel was very put out, and when he saw Arthur digging Mrs P.'s front garden took it upon himself to ask him his intentions. Arthur was so annoyed at this intrusion that he told Walter that he'd probably marry her – which, when Walter told her about it afterwards, gave Mrs P. a great shock. But Walter had succeeded in putting ideas into her head and shortly afterwards she accepted Arthur's proposal.

The Perkins went off to live in Arthur's house in London and had some happy years there. In 1965 Arthur had a heart attack and they returned to Ambridge, living in Rickyard Cottage. They went to Italy with Jack and Peggy Archer, and planned to go to Scotland with Dan and Doris Archer; but Arthur's health wasn't good and Mrs P. was so upset about the news of her granddaughter Jennifer Archer's illegitimate baby that they returned to London in 1967. Arthur was too ill to attend Jack and Peggy's silver wedding party in July of the following year and he died in December.

Bernard Fishwick

PERKINS, MRS POLLY (MRS P.)

b. 6 March 1905; m. Albert Perkins; 1 dtr; m. Arthur Perkins 1959; d. 3 May 1991

The redoubtable Mrs Perkins came to Ambridge in 1951, aged forty-six, at her daughter Peggy Archer's insistence. Her first husband Albert, a railway worker, had just died. The village was never to be the same again.

Sharp-featured, bespectacled, with a predilection for wearing black, Mrs P. (as she was always known) had a strong code of moral values. She never flinched from doing her duty, however painful to herself or others; she once bashed a stranger over the head with her umbrella for mistreating cattle at the Borchester market. What Mrs P. didn't know about the goings-on in Ambridge wasn't worth knowing. Her advice was always practical and to the point, though sometimes unpalatable. She advised Peggy to starve her husband Jack for a fortnight: an object lesson on how much of the housekeeping money he had been spending on drink.

Though she polished the brasses and was a pillar of the church, she was also extremely superstitious. As 'Gypsy Rose Perkins', she jealously guarded her right to read the tea-leaves at local fêtes, successfully fighting off the likes of Martha Woodford. Once she refused point blank to help with the make-up for the village play when she discovered that it was to take place on Good Friday.

Mrs P. was a great person to have on your side. Her granddaughter Jennifer Archer got an earful from Granny P. when she confessed to lying to her mother about trouble at school, but it was Mrs P. who later put on her coat and sorted out the teacher. Her fierce exterior hid a warm heart; although she never quite got over Jennifer having an illegitimate baby in 1967 she forgave her in the end. She could be generous with money: Walter Gabriel as well as members of her family benefited from loans.

Mrs P. had no shortage of suitors. Joe Blower, Doughy Hood and Walter Gabriel all wooed her in their disparate ways; but it was Arthur Perkins who succeeded in capturing her heart and in 1959 she married a Perkins for the second time and they went to live in London. After Arthur's death in 1968, she came back to Ambridge where Walter Gabriel was still waiting for her. He always held a special place in her heart, a truth obvious to all the village, but one carefully preserved from Walter himself. She turned him down when he eventually proposed in 1970, and was so furious when he kissed her in 1976 that she refused to go to a New Year's Eve party at the Woodfords when she knew that he would be there. Undaunted, he continued to pursue her until the end of his days. It was an erratic and colourful courtship.

Mrs P. claimed to dislike having a fuss made over her, but she was sometimes lonely. At Christmas 1987 she felt so left out that she disappeared without telling anyone where she was, leaving them frantic with worry; typically she was babysitting for the Tuckers, and was wryly amused at the family's concern.

A remark not long before her death summed up the fatalism underlying her philosophy of life: 'There's not much you can do about it, is there?' When Jennifer and Peggy arrived for lunch on 3 May 1991 they found Granny P. sitting peacefully in her chair. She had passed away quietly. She was buried in the churchyard at St Stephen's.

Pauline Seville

PERKS, KATHY (FORMERLY HOLLAND)

b. 30 Jan. 1953; m. Sid Perks 24 Apr. 1987

When Kathy arrived in Ambridge in 1983, she was still married to Steve Holland. But she was determined to get away and start afresh.

She got a job teaching Home Economics in Borchester. Rose Cottage was available for rent, and the landlord was the Ambridge publican, widower Sid Perks. Kathy was form teacher to Sid's daughter Lucy.

As he showed her round, Sid was attracted to Kathy and asked her out for a meal. She found his company pleasant enough, but her eyes were soon to be for someone else. When a video recorder was stolen from the school, Kathy met Detective Sergeant Dave Barry. They met again when, out driving, she had a puncture and he mended it for her, so she invited him for tea. He had begun to steal her heart.

In 1985, Steve Holland turned up in Ambridge. Kathy was too frightened to speak to him, so asked Dave to tell him on her behalf that she wanted a divorce. A furious Steve went back to Chesterfield. By August her divorce had come through, and she and Dave were having a steamy affair. Dave urged her to move in with him, but something made Kathy hold back. His old-fashioned male chauvinism infuriated her.

She confided in her friend Pat Archer, and also, later, in understanding Sid, unburdening herself to him one night at the Bull. They went to the Mop Fair in Borchester together and on the Big Dipper, to their surprise, they shared a lingering kiss. Greatly encouraged, Sid began to lay siege to Kathy, taking her out all over the place, swimming, to restaurants and nightclubs. Finally, he proposed marriage to her. At first Kathy turned him down, but he persisted, and in the end she gave in. On the one hand she still wanted Dave, but, on the other Sid was kind, loyal, sympathetic, the archetypal Mr Nice Guy. She decided to settle for the latter.

The wedding took place at Borchester Register Office on 24 April 1987, with Tony Archer as best man. But Sid soon began to display a possessive streak. He disapproved when, with Jill Archer, Kathy joined the South Borsetshire Villages Choir to sing Handel's *Messiah* at Felpersham cathedral. And when she applied for the job as head of her department at school, he was less than keen on the prospect of her spending yet more time away from him. To placate him, Kathy busied herself planning a vivid new menu for the Bull. Clarrie Grundy and Susan Carter, the regular pub helpers, resented what they saw as her bossiness, and went on strike. She just couldn't win. Kathy began to devote more of her time and energy to school life and was delighted when she got the job of head of department.

In 1989, Borchester Free School was to amalgamate with Worcester Road Comprehensive. Kathy was opposed to the plan and felt, too, that she was unlikely to keep her head of department post. To add to these troubles, she was not getting on well with Sid's daughter Lucy. They rowed about anything and everything. Kathy realized that Lucy was taking her rage and grief at Polly's death out on her. She put it to her straight: no way was she going to try to replace her mother in Lucy's life. Couldn't she perhaps be a good friend instead?

The schools' amalgamation was confirmed, and Kathy was eager for new challenges. Sid just wanted them to work in the Bull together. She told him that she might set up her own business. One evening, when she went with a girl friend to a jazz session in Nelson's Wine Bar, Dave Barry bought her a drink and she turned to his sympathetic ear. And was he ready to listen; in fact he was prepared to go to any length to lure confused Kathy away from unsuspecting Sid. When Sid came to pick her up later, they were tête-à-tête. Sid was livid. Then on New Year's Eve 1990, having drunk far too much, Kathy stayed downstairs in the Bull after the party and she and Dave made love. In the cold light of the following day, she tried to avoid Dave. He told her that, drunk or not, she must have known what she was doing. She finally gave way and began a secret affair with Dave. Sid took her away for a weekend in Devon, and she feigned tiredness to avoid lovemaking. Sid was very unhappy. At first, Kathy enjoyed the secrecy, even found it exciting – the making of excuses, the going to First Aid classes in Borchester, and the fish, chips and more with Dave Barry on the way home afterwards. They went away for weekends together, Kathy pretending she was going to a girl friend's. When Dave gave her some chocolates in Nelson's Wine Bar on Valentine's Day, she lied to Nelson and said that she'd bought them for herself.

But soon feelings of guilt overwhelmed her. Pat Archer, at this time, was a true friend. She arranged some counselling for Kathy and supported her after she met Dave at the end of April to call the whole thing off. Kathy wanted nothing more than for her life to return to normal, but Dave was not the sort of man to take rejection lying down. He took to hanging around the pub, dropping snide remarks and drinking to excess, but by August he seemed to have accepted the situation and got a transfer back to his home town of St Albans. Kathy should have felt relief but instead felt only emptiness, especially as she had handed in her notice at school and didn't have her teaching to occupy her. Fortunately Caroline Bone offered her work at Grey Gables health club but there was still an underlying tension at the Bull.

Christmas and New Year passed, but on

left to right: Kathy Perks (Hedli Niklaus), Sid Perks (Alan Devereux) and Tony Archer (Colin Skipp)

Kathy's birthday in January 1991, a card arrived from St Albans and on Valentine's Day a bottle of perfume with the same postmark, and a card which Sid pretended was from him. That night, Sid stormed out of the bar and disappeared. Kathy and Lucy were frantic. Lucy confronted Kathy about the affair, saying she'd known all along, and, once more at odds, they had to carry on as best they could. Peggy helped out until she learned the real reason for Sid's dramatic departure. Nelson Gabriel gamely came to the rescue behind the bar.

Sid returned six weeks later gripped by a new resolve. He told Kathy, in front of all the regulars, that he wanted her out of the Bull, for ever. Once again Pat provided refuge and Kathy lived at Bridge Farm for a while. Caroline offered to make her job at Grey Gables full-time, with accommodation provided, and there Kathy made her base while she tried to put her life back together. Her attempts during the next few months to effect a reconciliation with Sid were unsuccessful and he seemed set on divorce. He wanted Kathy to sign a confession admitting adultery. So she did, storming into the Bull and slamming it down on the counter in front of a packed bar.

This unhappy situation persisted until Sid burned his hand on Bonfire Night when Kathy was on St John Ambulance duty, and they began to realize how much they were missing each other. Sid later came to her for a talk about Lucy's problems adapting to university life. When Mike Tucker had his breakdown in 1991, Kathy found him crying alone at Willow Farm on Christmas Day and telephoned his wife Betty at the Bull,

where she was staying with the children. Sid brought her to him, and after seeing the touching reunion, Sid and Kathy went off for a walk together in deeply thoughtful mood.

In the New Year they started to put the pieces back together. Sid acknowledged that he was far from perfect; Kathy was truly sorry for the past. He wanted her to return to the Bull and when she finally did he welcomed her back as publicly as he had rejected her all those months before. Lucy, however, couldn't cope with Kathy's return and was rarely seen at the Bull. Her decision in 1994 to marry in New Zealand, though deeply distressing to Sid, was a relief to Kathy.

When Sid eventually bought the Bull from Peggy Woolley in 1993 in partnership with Guy Pemberton, it was with the idea that Kathy would, in time, leave Grey Gables and help them set up and run a restaurant. This was delayed when Caroline's accident meant Kathy taking over her job. But the plan offered a new challenge and a way for her and Sid to work together and build a partnership for the future.

Hedli Niklaus

Perks, Lucy Judith

see Gemmell, Lucy

Perks, Polly (née Mead)

b. 15 May 1943; m. 27 Sept. 1966; 1 dtr; d. 10 Feb. 1982

On 27 September 1958, with Jennifer

Aldridge and Lilian Bellamy as bridesmaids, spinster Polly Mead married bachelor Sid Perks, cut the wedding cake and hoped fervently for a life of contentment. Her early years had not been secure or happy – she'd endured a lonely childhood with her mentally ill father and irascible mother – and now she determined that she would work as hard as she knew how to make things go better.

The next two years were full for Polly. She won a competition in *The Borchester Echo* and went with Sid on a day trip to Boulogne, then had a lucky win of £1,000 on a premium bond which she was able to use as a deposit to buy the village shop and post office. A month later she was delighted to tell Sid that she was pregnant, but tragically two months later she and Walter Gabriel were attacked by a young man when she refused to hand over the post office takings and she had a miscarriage.

However, in 1971 she gave birth to their daughter Lucy, who was six months old when Peggy Archer offered Sid and Polly the tenancy of the Bull. It was an inspired choice, and with Jack Woolley buying the shop, it could not have worked out better. Sid and Polly made a great success of the pub, good cheer abounded, and soon the Borchester Hunt were meeting there regularly for their stirrup cups. The only drawback was that Polly had to be licensee since Sid had a criminal record, but Sid soon forgot to feel humiliated in the pleasures of being 'mine host'.

In 1974 Polly had an ectopic pregnancy, and when she returned to the Bull she found Peggy enjoying being in charge and reluctant to hand over to Polly again. But she soon recovered and took her rightful place, and in 1976 her customers voted her into the Publican of the Year contest. She was thrilled when she came second. With the £25 prize money she treated Sid to dinner at Redgate Manor, their favourite haunt.

Polly persuaded Sid that one day they would need a home of their own, and they discovered Rose Cottage, in Penny Hassett. Since Polly's mother refused to lend them any money, Peggy stood as guarantor for a loan. They let it until the day they could live there themselves.

Polly found it was hard work getting the right people to help out at the Bull. Nora McAuley was a find, helping to develop the bed and breakfast side of the business, as well as coffees and teas. Polly was sad to see her go in 1977, and for a while she had trouble replacing her. It was a difficult time. Peggy was thinking about selling out to the brewery, Sid started to worry, drinking more than usual, and Lucy was talking to an imaginary friend, a puppy called Crackers. But Peggy decided not to sell out after all, Caroline Bone came to work for them and Lucy could play with Leo, the Great Dane Caroline was looking after for a friend. Large slobbery dogs do not as a rule attract strangers into pubs; but the problem was solved when Walter Gabriel fed Leo some of his granny's embrocation and the gigantic canine slept while Caroline pulled pints.

Caroline gave in her notice and Clarrie Grundy took her place. Lucy did so well at school that her teachers thought she might win a scholarship. Sid and Polly thought about going on a canal holiday, but found they'd left it too late. Then in February 1982, Polly, driving to the cash-and-carry with Pat

Archer on the muddy road to Borchester, slid out of control into the path of an advancing milk tanker. Pat was unharmed; Polly died instantly. After the funeral, held on 15 February, grieving Sid placed a bunch of roses on Polly's grave.

Hilary Newcombe

Perks, sid

b. 9 June 1944; m. Polly Mead 27 Sept. 1966; 1 dtr; m. Kathy Holland 24 Apr. 1987

A raw young lad from Birmingham, Sid Perks was sent to an approved school at fifteen for breaking and entering. On release in 1963, it was his good fortune to meet Jack Woolley, a fellow Brummie, who sensed that, given the right chances, Sid could make a success of himself. He gave him a job as chauffeur and general right-hand man, and Sid repaid Jack's kindness by never letting him down. He moved to Ambridge with Jack in 1963.

During the following summer Sid became a regular at the Bull, as much attracted by the barmaid Polly Mead as by the beer. Polly came to know about Sid's murky past and for a while held him at arm's length; but when she had troubles of her own she turned to Sid, and he was kind and sympathetic. Their relationship deepened, and they got engaged, and then married in September 1966. Jack Woolley generously arranged a honeymoon house in Cornwall and a car to get them there.

The early years of married life were make-or-break for Sid. He stopped working for Jack, found temporary work under Phil Archer at Hollowtree and a part-time job for a 'Mr Brown' on a pig holding. When Sid discovered that the pig holding was all a front and that 'Mr Brown' and his brother were in trouble with a protection money gang, he got out fast, and for two years worked for Paul Johnson at the garage. Then Polly's good luck in the premium bonds enabled them to buy the post office and village shop from Jack Woolley. Sid's criminal record meant that Polly had to be postmistress, while he went on working at the garage.

He was also prevented from holding the licence of the Bull, when in 1972 after the death of Jack Archer, his widow Peggy offered Sid and Polly the tenancy of the village pub. It was the perfect job for them, and the right time. By now they had a daughter, Lucy, whom he adored. For ten years the Bull went from strength to strength. The folk of Ambridge felt comfortable with Sid and Polly behind the bar. They organized trips, including one to Amsterdam, and rekindled enthusiasm for the Ambridge cricket and football teams.

But there were personal crises. Polly had an ectopic pregnancy and was unable to have more children and Sid, like many publicans, had a period of alcoholic overindulgence. In 1976 little Lucy Perks was found in a coma. She had swallowed what she thought were sweets at her grandmother's. They were sleeping pills. After several terrible hours at the hospital they were told that she would recover.

In 1975 Sid and Polly bought Rose Cottage in Penny Hassett as an investment for their future retirement. But on 10 February 1982, Sid's world collapsed. Driving on the wet, muddy road to Borchester Polly smashed into the side of an oncoming milk tanker and was killed. Sid bravely opened up the Bull the day after the funeral. He was advised by Mark Hebden that he could now hold the licence in his own right and somehow he soldiered on with the help of his daughter Lucy. The tragedy drew them closer together.

Two years dragged on for Sid. But then Kathy Holland, Lucy's form teacher, needed a roof over her head and rented Rose Cottage. He was instantly attracted to her. At first, Kathy's interest lay elsewhere, with DS Dave Barry. But in time, she warmed to Sid. He was there as a shoulder to cry on when her relationship with Dave was going badly, and things developed from there. They have been married now since 1987. To begin with it was hard for Sid to deal with Lucy's jealousy and feelings of exclusion. He didn't much like the idea of his wife having an independent career and would have preferred her, like Polly, to spend her time behind the bar at the Bull. There were tensions in the marriage that were difficult to resolve.

Sid and Kathy nearly came to divorce in 1990 over Kathy's affair with Dave Barry. Ironically Sid found out about it only after it was over, when Dave sent Kathy some perfume on Valentine's Day, 1991. The shock sent Sid to Wales for six weeks to think things over. When he came back, he unceremoniously threw Kathy out. For some time he refused to have any discussion with her, and began divorce proceedings on the grounds of Kathy's adultery. He seemed determined to drag her name deep into the mud. But on Bonfire Night he burnt his hand and it was Kathy, on St John Ambulance duty, who tended to him. Gradually, and with time, they were able to talk things over, heal the wounds and rebuild their relationship.

Lucy didn't find out about the reconciliation until she took her father an early morning cuppa and found that two cups would have been better than one. Furious, she stormed out. But the battle was lost. For the first time since Polly's death Sid put his own happiness before that of his daughter, as Lucy was quick to realize. She returned from university in the summer merely to sting her father for money to pay off her debts. Since then Sid and Kathy have hardly seen her. The news in 1994 that she had failed her exams, and that she intended to marry and settle in New Zealand without even introducing him to her boyfriend, hurt Sid bitterly.

However, Sid is a stronger, more decisive person now. The marriage seems settled and secure. As he grows older, he commands the affection and respect of his customers at the Bull. He was happy to buy the Bull in partnership with Guy Pemberton and he and Kathy are united in their efforts to make it a going concern.

Alan Devereux

PERRINS, MISS

Miss Perrins was the careers mistress at Borchester Grammar School who in 1973 suggested that Shula Archer should become a vet.

PERRY, LES

When Neil Carter was interested in starting a youth club in Ambridge in 1976, 24-year-old Les Perry did his best to help him. He himself was already a youth club leader and taught PE at Borchester Technical College.

When their application to hold the club at the village hall was turned down because the hall was fully booked, Neil and Les viewed a narrow boat at Bramworth. For a glorious moment they envisaged buying it, doing it up and cruising along the canals. Fortunately John Tregorran offered them the use of Nightingale Farm for a trial period, and they were able to set up the Youth Club there, where it remained for several years. In the meantime Les got married and began spending less time at the Club.

John Bull

PETERS, ALICE

Alice Peters, wife of Sam, became caretaker of Hollowtree flats when Sam was forced to leave his job as a cow man for Ralph Bellamy after his illness in 1974.

PETERS, MARIANNE

Marianne Peters was the daughter of an old schoolfriend of Paul Johnson's. In the holidays Paul would sometimes stay with her family in Paris, where her father worked for the British Embassy. For some time Marianne carried a torch for Paul and years later, briefly, in 1960 the torch burned brighter following a chance meeting in a café while Paul and Phil Archer were in Paris. But the wick was not turned up and the flame went out.

PETERS, SAM

In 1974 Sam Peters worked as a cow man for Ralph Bellamy, until ill-health forced him to give up. This necessitated Sam and his wife Alice moving out of their tied cottage. Having refused the post of car-park attendant for Jack Woolley, and caretaker at Hollowtree flats, Sam was fortunate to be offered the job of milk tester at Borchester Dairies.

Graham Rigby

PETRIE, JANE

Jane Petrie was in charge of the Art and Craft summer school at Arkwright Hall in 1972. She confided to Walter Gabriel that she had been involved in a miserable love affair and had been cited in a divorce case. Tony Archer became so smitten by her that he was sacked by Ralph Bellamy for neglecting his work. She left Ambridge in August 1972.

Ursula O'Leary

PHELPS, TOMMY

PC Bryden caught Mrs Scroby's nephew Tommy Phelps calmly wheeling Christine Archer's bike through the village in 1955.

PHILPS, MISS

Miss Philps was housekeeper to the Lawson-

Hope family at the Manor until they left Ambridge in 1954.

PLANT, AMOS (MOSSY)

Amos started out as gardener's boy for Carol Tregorran in 1968. By 1972 he was in charge of the vegetables growing in her market garden.

Harry Soan

PLATER, TED

d. July 1993

Ted Plater was a tenant of Nigel Pargetter's at Woodside Farm. When he died in 1993 his widow, Phyllis, left the farm to live with her younger sister in Tamworth.

POOLE, DR JOHN

Popular Dr Poole came to Ambridge as assistant to Dr MacLaren and succeeded him in the seventies. After Colonel Danby had unwisely eaten three deathcap toadstools, he quickly employed a stomach pump, probably saving the Colonel's life.

PORRITT, DAWN ELIZABETH

Dawn arrived at Home Farm on 3 January 1988 as a surprise present for Jennifer Aldridge. After the birth of Alice, Jennifer was desperate for help so that she could get back to her own life as soon as possible.

Aware of the danger signals, her husband Brian hired Dawn as a nanny from an agency in Birmingham. Jennifer was happy to take her on, though not as happy as Brian, who rated her three out of ten for temperament but ten out of ten for looks.

Dawn was very good with Alice, which compensated for her 'dirty vowels', as Jennifer put it, unused to a broad Midlands accent in her own home. However, as a qualified nanny Dawn wanted a proper contract, which upset the Aldridges who preferred to rely on a system of trust – which meant that they took advantage of her whenever it suited them. They were rapidly disillusioned when Dawn wouldn't allow them to get away with this kind of treatment, especially if it put her to personal inconvenience; in addition, Jennifer was apprehensive about Brian's roving eye. Despite Dawn's efficiency it became clear that she was not destined to last long in the Aldridge household.

Dawn had become friendly with Jack Woolley, who offered to mediate with Brian on the vexed subject of the contract. When it still wasn't forthcoming she decided to leave Home Farm until she got one. She's still waiting.

Rachel Wright

PORTER, TRUDY

Although Caroline Bone has remarked that Trudy is not the brightest girl in the world, she would be sorry to lose her from the staff at Grey Gables, if only because she would have to train someone else. Trudy is cheerfully incompetent, preferring disco music and her boyfriend to concentrating on her work. She has been at Grey Gables since 1976 and has worked her way up from waitress to receptionist.

Portia

Portia is one of Mrs Antrobus's favourite pedigree Afghan hounds. She has a tendency to go missing and in 1987 escaped the day before she was due to be mated. When she was eventually found at Grey Gables, she was lying alongside an extremely smug-looking Captain, Jack Woolley's bull terrier. Mrs Antrobus's worst fears were realized when two months later Portia produced nine impeccable mongrel pups, all taking after Captain.

Portia was in trouble once again three years later when she took up residence on Ruth Pritchard's bed at Nightingale Farm, with her litter of four pups. All sorts of attempts to remove her failed and Ruth had to content herself with sleeping on a lilo on the floor. Lynda Snell took pity on the runt of the litter with a bad leg, and took him home, naming him Hermes.

Postles, Mrs

Mrs Postles was Walter Gabriel's home help in the early eighties.

Potter, Mrs

Though dependent on her walking frame and not seeing too well, Mrs Potter remains very lively for one of Ambridge's oldest inhabitants. She lives in Manorfield Close.

Pound, Ken

m. Mary 8 May 1935; 1 dtr; d. 17 Nov. 1983

Ken and Mary Pound were tenants of Ralph Bellamy on the 150-acre Ambridge Farm for thirty years. Nothing went smoothly for them. In an effort to produce high-quality milk, Ken crossed Friesian and Jersey to little avail. They changed from free-range to battery hens in an attempt to improve their egg yield. Their antiquated henhouse scraper broke and they had to muck out by hand – on one occasion helped by Walter Gabriel, who inadvertently raked out the eggs with the rubbish. Ken and Carol Tregorran went into partnership with a farm shop, housed, to Carol's chagrin, in one of Ken's old barns. Planning permission had not been obtained and so they were harassed by bureaucracy. Two years later Carol withdrew. When Harry Booker, husband of their daughter Marilyn, opened a Sunday market on their land, customers poured in although a distraught Mary discovered that they were not only breaking the terms of their lease but were also liable for prosecution for selling prohibited goods on a Sunday. They were fined £120.

The Pounds worked as a team, but Mary was the strong one. She found time to preside over the WI, enter ploughing competitions, play in the ladies' football team and nurse Ken when ill-health dogged him.

Life was not all bleak. There was a famous family New Year celebration at their house with the Grundys. (Mary was always kind to Joe and saved him from several disasters.) She regularly asked for socks and a pink cardigan at Christmas, and wore with pride the woolly 'tea-cosy' hat that Walter Gabriel once gave her.

Ken's health went into decline. Mary's strong shoulders finally gave way in 1982 and she handed in their notice to quit the tenancy of Ambridge Farm the next Lady Day. Their move revived old rumours of an affair between Mary and Silas Winter in the year before Marilyn's birth.

Eight months after their retirement Ken died, bequeathing his stuffed vampire bat to Mike Tucker. It was his dying wish that Joe Grundy and Mike should become good neighbours and Mary solemnly organized the shaking of the hands after the funeral. Not long afterwards she moved to a bungalow in Edgeley.

Michael Collins; Garard Green

POUND, MARILYN

see Booker, Marilyn

POUND, MARY

see Pound, Ken
    b. 1918; m. Ken Pound 8 May 1935; 1 dtr
    Ysanne Churchman

PRESCOTT, ANN

see Grenville, Ann

PRESTON, SIR TIMOTHY

Colonel Danby and his friend Sir Timothy Preston regularly went grouse shooting together until Sir Timothy's straitened circumstances forced him to cancel the arrangement in 1977.

PRESTWICK, MYRA (MIMI)

The formidable Myra Prestwick has left her mark on several Ambridge folk through her work as a magistrate and is regarded by fellow JP Phil Archer as a model of decisiveness. In 1982 she was on the committee of the Borsetshire Conservation Trust, which was due to consider objections to Phil's controversial proposal to drain and plough Palmer's Meadow. In the face of Jennifer Aldridge's opposition and the prospect of undergoing Myra's tough scrutiny, he withdrew the plan and left the meadow undisturbed.

Shirley Stelfox

PRICE, JIM AND MRS

The Prices ran the village shop and post office in the sixties, he fretful over the confusion caused by her inability to distinguish between the shop and post office tills, she, oblivious to any problem, forever chatting to all and sundry. They retired in 1968 and moved to Cornwall to be nearer their son and his family.

Leslie Bowmar; Gordon Walters

PRICE, MAGGIE

Maggie Price met Shula Archer at Borchester Technical College. They became friends and in her spare time Maggie was happy to help out at the stables. Neil Carter rather fancied her and took her on holiday to Devon, but Maggie was quick to point out that they were just good friends. That was in 1975.

In August, Kenton Archer took her to the pictures, but as the words 'The End' appeared on the screen, so did all further knowledge of Maggie Price.

Rachel Newman

PRITCHARD, RUTH

see Archer, Ruth

PRITCHARD, SOLLY AND HEATHER

Solly and Heather Pritchard are the parents of Ruth Archer and live in Prudhoe. Solly manufactures toilet paper. Although reputed to be 'very proud and quiet', he made a most amusing speech at Ruth's wedding to David Archer in 1988. The Pritchards were pleased to entertain Ruth, David and their daughter Pip for Christmas in 1993.

Richard Griffiths

PROTHEROE, MISS

Seeing Jennifer Aldridge tense and taking tranquillizers, Brian Aldridge insisted that they should have a nanny to help with Alice while he was recovering from the accident in 1989 that had left him with a form of epilepsy. Stern and dressed entirely in black, she proved to be another of the succession of the Aldridges' unsuitable helps and was with them for only a matter of weeks.

PULLEN, MR

Mr Pullen, one of Ambridge's pensioners, has become a constant anxiety to any organizer of events for the Over Sixties. In particular, planning for their coach trips has to allow extra time for frequent unscheduled stops needed because of his unfortunate bladder complaint.

R

RADFORD, PENELOPE

Nelson Gabriel brought his very refined girl-friend Penelope Radford to Ambridge on a brief visit in 1980. Her attraction for him may not have been entirely unconnected with the fact that her father was a successful wine merchant.

Angela Rippon

RANDALL, PC GEORGE

PC Randall was the village constable in 1951. Problems he had to deal with included a rick fire at George Fairbrother's, the breaking of the Betting and Lotteries Act when Christine and Philip Archer were selling raffle tickets around Ambridge, unsolved break-ins and a car accident involving Grace Fairbrother. He served Dan Archer with a summons for shooting a racing pigeon. In 1955 he was promoted to sergeant and left the district. PC Bryden was to be his replacement.

Raymond Baseley; Chriss Gittins; John Hobday; Edward Higgins

RAWLINGS, PETER

Peter Rawlings was a patient of Dr Cavendish in 1955 and an alcoholic. His desire for drink, which drove him to steal Mrs P.'s handbag and Carol Grey's whisky, warred with his desire for Joyce Richmond, who worked at the stables. Any setback – the breaking of a date, or Cavendish's refusal to lend him money to hire a motor-bike – had him reaching for the bottle. He wanted to leave Ambridge with Joyce and under her influence and Cavendish's efforts he suddenly became violently teetotal, pouring the contents of the doctor's drinks cupboard down the sink. His friends tried to persuade him to be less extreme but it was a hopeless battle.

RAYMOND, DICK

A reporter on *The Borchester Echo* in 1951, Dick Raymond soon found that his best sources of information were the vicar for births, marriages and deaths, and the Bull for everything else. He was a devil-may-care, attractive young man, with a good line in banter. Once he met Christine Archer it didn't take him long to persuade her to act as his special correspondent on the dispute over George Fairbrother's intention to mine ironstone on his land. Their relationship would have deepened more rapidly had it not been for the machinations of Grace Fairbrother who was anxious to pair Dick with Jane Maxwell and keep Phil Archer for herself. Her scheme failed, and Dick was the first to learn of Phil and Jane's engagement. Phil also told him of Grace's duplicity, enabling him to make it up with Christine, who invited him to tea at Brookfield the following day.

While at Brookfield he overheard an interesting conversation when he picked up the telephone to contact his office. Two men were talking, and it became clear that they were planning to sabotage Keith Latimer's equipment for surveying Fairbrother's farm. He and Phil agreed to tell Keith, then lie in wait for the saboteurs by the rig and catch them red-handed. It didn't work out entirely as hoped. Dick tried to bring down one of the men with a rugby tackle and received some nasty blows to his face, but the man got away, together with his partner.

Dick suspected that his assailant might have been Bill Slater, Mrs P.'s nephew and lodger. This was confirmed unexpectedly when he took Mrs P. and Jane Maxwell home (Jane was then living at Mrs P.'s) after a party. He went outside to fetch some coal, only to discover a missing diamond drilling bit belonging to Keith in the coal-house. The matter was clinched entirely when he matched a button he'd picked up after being attacked with one missing from Bill Slater's working jacket hang-

ing on the scullery door. Not knowing what to do, he gave Phil the diamond bit and let him decide but Bill's tragic death took place before Phil could take any action. In the end he returned the bit to Keith, who promised to keep the identity of the saboteur a secret.

Meanwhile Dick had problems of his own. Chris took exception to the tone of an article he'd written in the *Echo*, and he made the mistake of listening to Walter Gabriel's advice to sweep her off her feet. He waylaid her, Chris slapped his face, whereupon he recoiled and ended up sitting in a bucket of water. But they soon made it up and were often seen together. However, his job proved to be an enemy to romance, for he moved to London to work on a paper there. Then he went off to Malaya, and some time later Christine heard that he had got engaged to a rich planter's daughter. He wrote her a letter breaking it all off, saying that he couldn't hold her to a boy-and-girl romance, and that they should treat the whole thing in its true light, as 'a warm and pleasant friendship with no strings, on either side'. Some tears were shed in Brookfield that night.

John Franklyn

REDDING, GLORIA

Gloria Redding's husband Alfred was 'in furniture' in Birmingham before they retired in October 1973 to one of the Hollowtree flats. Her efforts to be sociable weren't well received by Doris Archer and Martha Woodford, as their conversations with her seemed to return with awful inevitability to her many operations.

Eileen Barry

RED HOUSE FARM

Red House Farm, 80 acres of land to the south-west of Ambridge, was one of the five farms retained by the Berrow Estate when Ralph Bellamy sold up his property in 1975. On the retirement in 1992 of Len Roberts, for many years the tenant, Cameron Fraser (then owner of the Estate) offered Phil and David Archer a five-year lease of Red House Farm. The short term gave rise to rumours that he was planning to sell it to developers, in which case Joe Grundy was certain it would become a theme park.

However, after brief but difficult negotiations Fraser agreed to sell to Phil, only for the agreement to become void on Fraser's subsequent disappearance. When Guy Pemberton bought the Estate, the farm continued to be worked as part of the Estate and the farmhouse remained unoccupied.

RED LINK

When Chris and Paul Johnson recognized what an outstanding horse they had bought from Tony Stobeman in Red Link, they engaged the champion rider Alan Oliver to ride him in several events, the most important of these being the 1957 Horse of the Year competition at Badminton where they gained second place. Paul, unhappy that he and his business interests were playing second fiddle to her show jumping, persuaded her to sell the horse at the end of the year to Oliver.

REDMOND, PADDY

1 son by Jennifer Aldridge

Paddy was a bright young Ulsterman who came to work at Brookfield in 1965. He was a persuasive character of many talents, from piano playing to motor-cycle scrambling. His easy charm captivated young Jennifer Archer, to the disapproval of her family, who felt that he had a wild streak they instinctively distrusted. This was confirmed when he returned from a sudden holiday back home with the news that he was engaged. Two months later his fiancée, Nora McAuley, arrived from Belfast to work as barmaid at the Bull.

His engagement was short-lived, as Paddy wanted to leave the Archers and work for himself, but Nora felt it was too soon to move. He went down south, leaving behind him a disappointed Nora and very pregnant Jennifer. He wrote to Jennifer but she refused to see him. Nothing more was heard of him for fourteen years.

In January 1981 a soft-spoken, prosperous-looking man dropped into the Bull looking for Nora McAuley. It was Paddy on his way to a farm manager's job in Ulster, having managed farms abroad and done very well for himself. Jennifer, now married to Brian Aldridge, saw him with Nora and panicked. She was sure that he knew nothing about his son, Adam, and she was determined that they shouldn't meet. It was left to Nora to tell him the truth, whereupon he telephoned Jennifer immediately and persuaded her to bring Adam to the Feathers in a few days' time so that he could meet him. Brian took matters in hand at that point, told

Paddy Redmond (John Bott)

Jennifer to stay at home and introduced himself to Paddy in her place. He gave him short shrift and threatened him with legal action should he make any attempt to see Adam.

Poor Paddy had never wanted to make trouble and in any case was going to fly to Ulster in two days' time. With the predictable luck of the Irish, he bumped into Jennifer and Adam by accident before he left, so at least he had a glimpse of the son and wife he might well have called his own had his life turned out differently.

John Bott

REEVES, MR

The bank sent their farm finance expert, Mr Reeves, to see Tony Archer in 1976 with the bad news that the they were not prepared to lend enough for him to be able to buy Willow Farm.

REYNOLDS, PAULINE

Carol Grey was visited in 1960 by her friend Pauline who, since their days at horticultural college in Wye, had acquired a husband and three children. Her advice to Carol was to give up all her hard work and get married.

Julia Lang

REYNOLDS, PHILIP

Reynolds replaced Robin Freeman as warden at the Field Studies Centre in 1974, but by then the activities were already becoming less intensive and the grounds were absorbed into the Country Park, so he was required for only a short time.

RHODA AND ROSIE

The Tuckers' pedigree goats Rhoda and Rosie were bought by Betty in 1975 in order to create a small milking herd and produce milk for sale to the health food shop in Borchester.

RHODES, FRANK (DUSTY)

In 1958 Dusty Rhodes befriended Joan Hood and made a good impression on her parents. They were deceived. This young man became involved in a series of petty thefts in which he tried to implicate their daughter. Next he stole the Youth Club funds from Joan, but the Borchester CID caught up with him. During an uncomfortable interview, he made a rapid exit and drove off. When Jimmy Grange and Joan discovered him in the Hoods' barn, he threw a brick at them, ran away and fell into the river. He broke his ankle in the fall and was unable to swim, but Jimmy rescued him. The courts put him on probation.

Bryan Stanion

RICE, ANNEKA

For three days in 1993, Anneka Rice rushed into Ambridge and helped co-ordinate the locals into redecorating the village hall kitchen. Her mission accomplished, Anneka, in her skin-tight Lycra, was off to work wonders elsewhere.

RICHARDS, KYLIE

b. 26 Oct. 1989

Kylie Richards was named after her mother Sharon's favourite television personality. She was born in 1989 at the Vicarage, where Sharon had been given accommodation by Gerry Buckle. Her father Clive Horrobin abandoned them and she was registered under her mother's name only.

When Sharon got a job at Bridge Farm, both Mrs Antrobus and Martha Woodford offered to look after Kylie and became unfriendly rivals for some time. Martha fed her fudge and coconut ice; Mrs Antrobus entertained her with educational toys. But Kylie's favourite babysitter was Brian Aldridge whose services Sharon had bid for at an auction of promises; for a while, every time she

saw him, Kylie called him 'Daddy'.

Kylie was three when her father was involved in an armed raid on the village shop but though she was upset by tales of the raid it took her a long time to realize that Clive was responsible.

She helped Tom Forrest plant a tree on the village green, for National Tree Week (her mother was delighted by Tom's speech about Great Oaks and Little Acorns).

RICHARDS, SHARON

b. 7 Mar. 1972; 1 dtr by Clive Horrobin

Sharon does not have very high expectations of what life has to offer – and with her background and experience it's not hard to understand why. The eldest of four children, she was brought up in a Borchester council flat but was thrown out by her parents when she became pregnant by Clive Horrobin at the age of seventeen. Sharon gave up the YTS hairdressing course she was halfway through and she and Clive took refuge with the Horrobin clan for a while, then accepted the Carters' kind offer of a room. Sharon's and Clive's unwillingness to lend a hand around the house soon led to friction and they moved on again when Jerry Buckle offered then a room at the vicarage, where baby Kylie was born prematurely on 26 October 1989. During the pregnancy, Sharon had carried on smoking, complained bitterly about losing her figure and refused to see the doctor, so any hope that she would experience an upsurge of maternal feeling after the birth soon proved ill-founded. In the early months, several people in the village worried about Sharon's apathy and lack of affection towards the baby. She was not helped by Clive's desertion of her when Kylie was just a couple of months old. Several villagers rallied to her support, though, and Kylie was soon being wheeled round the village by a proud Sharon.

Only Sharon could have regarded the offer of the caravan at Bridge Farm as an improvement to her circumstances and when she moved in, in May 1990, it was with the arrangement that she could provide casual labour at Bridge Farm as well as the occasional hairdo for Pat Archer. Pat's social conscience may have been salved but she was less keen when her son John, then fifteen, developed a crush on Sharon. Sharon did nothing to encourage him – indeed, when he set off for Brymore School in September 1990 her only regret was that he would no longer be around to empty the chemical toilet – and early in 1991 she got involved with a Danish student, Thorkhil Jensen, who was helping out on the farm. By this time Sharon's life was starting to take on a more settled quality: she began working in the Bridge Farm Dairy and at the end of March was offered, with the help of parish councillor George Barford, one of the council houses on the Green. She moved there in April with odd bits of furniture donated by various people. Jerry Buckle had instructed that £100 from the proceeds of the sale of his possessions when he left Ambridge be given to her. She bought herself a comfortable bed with it.

Feeling more secure, she sent Clive packing when he came back to Ambridge and tried to move in with her. Her happiness with Thorkhil was short-lived, though, for he had to return home in August 1991 and on his part it was a case of 'out of sight, out of mind'. Again Sharon felt abandoned and alone. In November 1991 she began working with the 'twilight shift' at the canning factory to make some extra money but was incensed when she discovered that male workers were being paid more than female. She took the complaint to solicitor Usha Gupta, who wrote a stiff letter to the canning factory, with the result that negotiations over pay took place. But Sharon felt that the incident had marked her out as a troublemaker and she was one of several laid off when seasonal work dried up.

Sharon can often be prickly and difficult and she never hit it off with Lisa, Jill Archer's unwelcome tenant at Rickyard Cottage, who briefly worked at Bridge Farm. Her relationship with John, however, seems to go from strength to strength. Pat breathed a sigh of relief when, after a fling with Sharon in 1993, John found a more suitable girlfriend. The chemistry between John and Sharon is obviously potent, however, because in 1994 their passionate affair was back on. Sharon's proprietorial attitude towards John does not go down well with Pat, and which of the determined women in his life will win the battle for his affections remains to be seen. As Sharon's life so far has proved, she is certainly a survivor.

Celia Nelson

RICHMOND, FRANK

Michele Brown first aroused Jack Woolley's suspicions at the end of 1976 about Frank

Richmond, his manager at Grey Gables. Frank left after accusations of fiddling with the drinks measures and keeping tips belonging to other staff. PC Drury reported the following March that Frank had been remanded in Liverpool, pending further enquiries.

RICHMOND, JOYCE

Joyce Richmond came as a working pupil to Grace Fairbrother's stables in 1954. She was very taken with Jack Archer and infuriated Grace with her extravagant praise of him. Then Peter Rawlings caught her eye and she tried to help him overcome his alcoholism, telling him that his fate was in his own hands. When he asked her to leave Ambridge with him, she turned him down. She worked at the stables for about a year.

Judith Hackett

RICKYARD COTTAGE

One of several outbuildings at Brookfield, Rickyard Cottage was once used for storage but in 1954 it was altered for the Coopers to live in, since when tenants have been numerous. In 1992 Jill Archer refurbished it as a holiday cottage. Her plans came to a standstill when Bert Fry discovered that it was being used by squatters, Lisa and Craig. There was much dissension among the Archer family as to the best way to deal with the situation, but in the end it was resolved when Lisa and Craig disappeared as quietly as they had arrived, and Jill was able to readvertise the cottage for holiday lets.

RIDLEY, REVD JOHN

Jack and Peggy Archer weren't too impressed when they found their lost daughter Jennifer chatting to Ambridge's new vicar in 1951. He had arrived a week before his official induction to give himself a chance to get to know some of his parishioners, and met Jennifer on her way home from school. While her parents were searching for her everywhere Jennifer was having a lovely time, sharing a bar of chocolate and being taught how to fish.

He was in his mid thirties, had been a chaplain in the last war and still walked with a slight limp, having being wounded in Normandy. In spite of his disability he loved sports, enjoying riding and fishing, and was horrified when he found out that there was no soccer team in Ambridge.

Phil Archer described him as a live wire, which proved to be the case. He was a great believer in getting to know people and showed none of the pomposity often associated with his profession, laughing as heartily as everyone else when he overheard Walter Gabriel's impersonation of the Bishop of Borchester. He asked Doris Archer to recruit more women for the choir and had the nerve to tell George Fairbrother and Squire Lawson-Hope to make up their differences at Christmastime. He went to help Peggy with the pigs when she needed help, and she was touched, telling him that the fact that he practised what he preached meant more to her than all his sermons.

Shortly after officiating over Phil and Grace Archer's wedding in 1955, Ridley exchanged places with the vicar of a small

London parish, Norris Buckland, who needed a rest. He returned just after Christmas and continued to work in Ambridge until 1961 when he was succeeded by Matthew Wreford.

Harry Stubbs

RITA

Hazel Woolley met Rita at the Borchester Settlement in 1972. Her mother had died a year before and her West Indian father struggled to make ends meet by driving long-distance lorries, so Hazel invited Rita to spend Christmas with her.

Elizabeth Adare

ROBERTA

Roberta assisted Lilian Bellamy at the stables from 1967 until she went to work for Lady Isabel Lander in 1974. For a while, Tony Archer took an interest in her and spent a weekend in Shropshire with her and her friends.

Patricia Greene

ROBERTS, JACK

In the late seventies, Jack Roberts worked at Home Farm. Not a success. He was sacked, and even punched, by his employer Brian Aldridge, and the union was called in. However, assault charges were not brought, and eventually he vacated his tied cottage and moved on.

ROBERTSON, BILL

Bill Robertson became a vet like his father, Ian. As a young man he thought about leaving Ambridge for America but decided that he wanted to go to university in Britain. After he graduated he went to work with his father and was soon doing most of the veterinary work in and around Ambridge.

Bill fought a constant battle against the ignorance and obstinacy of many of the local farmers. He tried to convince Tony Archer that regular visits from the vet would save him money in the long run, but Tony was not so sure. And Joe Grundy did not take it kindly when Bill censured him for not ear-tagging his cattle. When the sheep at Brookfield were suffering from pasteurella pneumonia it was up to Bill to reassure Phil Archer that the cows would not catch the infection.

Bill married Sally Arnold in 1976 and they were sad to leave Ambridge when two years later her father bought Poston Hall for them and their baby daughter, though he was often back for visits in his professional capacity.

Geoffrey Hutchings

ROBERTSON, IAN

Ian Robertson was the vet always called by Dan Archer, who admired his efficiency and veterinary skills and became a good friend. He diagnosed milk fever in a cow and swine fever in a pig; and at a suspected outbreak of foot-and-mouth disease at Brookfield in

1956 he sent at once for the vet from the Ministry of Agriculture – both he and Dan knew that an outbreak of the disease would mean that the herd had to be slaughtered, but recognized that there was no other way of stopping its spread. He took his son Bill into the practice and transferred his work to him during the early seventies.

Lewis Gedge; Robert Sansom

ROBERTSON, SALLY (NÉE ARNOLD)

Sally trained as a riding school instructor. She married the local vet Bill Robertson in 1976. Two years later she gave birth to a baby girl. She wanted to continue to work and her rich father bought Poston Hall so that she would have enough land to breed horses. Sally and Bill left the village, though she was happy to return and run the riding stables for Christine Barford when she and George were on their honeymoon.

ROBINSON, MRS

The contractors building the Borchester bypass sent Mrs Robinson to address the parish council meeting about their concerns in March 1989.

ROBINSON, MRS

Sid Perks tried using Mrs Robinson as a provider of cooked food for the Ploughman's Bar at the Bull at Christmas 1974, but found that she and her husband couldn't maintain a good standard, as they were overstretching themselves trying to supply too many pubs at once.

RODGERS, MR AND MRS

Rodgers was taken on by George Fairbrother in 1956 to look after his Hereford herd. He and his wife moved into Coombe Farm, and Mrs Rodgers frequently helped Phil and Jill Archer with their children at Hollowtree Farm and then at Brookfield until the Rodgers left Ambridge in 1970.

Helena Williams

RODWAY, MR NORMAN

Partner in Rodway & Watson, the estate agents for whom Shula Archer began working in 1976. Despite his reputation as a hard man and occasional confrontations between him and Shula, she learned from his experience and advice.

Michael Bilton

ROGERS, ELLEN

Nigel and Elizabeth Pargetter learned why Nigel's Julia never contacted her sister Ellen Rogers when she turned up at their wedding. The Pargetter facade was shattered by her revelations of Julia's real name, Joan, and by her colourful past. Merry widow Ellen owns a profitable club/bar in Spain and lives it up as part of the ex-pat scene.

Rosemary Leach

ROGERS, JOLENE

Eddie Grundy and 'the lily of Layton Cross' could have been a match made in heaven, had Clarrie Larkin and Wayne Tucson allowed them to get together for long enough. Jolene's real name was Doreen; she was the daughter of a butcher at Layton Cross and Wayne's girlfriend. But her mock Country and Western accent, ample bosom, false golden curls and swinging fringes made her well nigh irresistible to Eddie. However, Clarrie claimed his wandering eye in the end and Wayne snapped up Jolene.

In 1985 Jolene was six months pregnant and she and Wayne married. She later gave birth to a daughter they named Fallon.

When, six years on, Eddie turned forty, he managed to track Jolene down to invite her to his birthday party, only to discover that she had split up with Wayne years before and was living with a bass player in Huddersfield. Clarrie viewed her reunion with Eddie with dark suspicion, but Eddie knew which side his bread was buttered on and his loyalties remained with his wife, even if his fantasies sometimes didn't.

Elizabeth Revill

ROSE

Pat Archer got to know Rose when they both attended CND meetings in 1983 and they became good friends. Rose wore dungarees, and had spiky hair and an unpleasant boyfriend called Chris, who threatened to leave her. She was so unhappy that Pat asked her to stay at Bridge Farm to give her a break. Unfortunately Peggy Archer, who was staying there too, took an instant dislike to Rose, convinced that she was on drugs, and Tony Archer was equally unwelcoming. Even Sammy, Peggy's cat, made poor Rose sneeze. She decided that being by herself was a preferable option so returned home on Christmas Eve. Pat has kept in touch and still sees her from time to time.

ROSE COTTAGE

An enchanting seventeenth-century cottage of Cotswold stone several miles out of Ambridge, bought by Sid and Polly Perks in 1975. One of the first things that Polly did was to plant pink rambler roses round the front door. It needed a thorough overhaul but by the end of the year it was completed and advertised for letting in The *Borchester Echo*. Their first tenants never paid them any rent and when served with a summons they did a moonlight flit, taking with them everything but the hall carpet and a couple of pieces of furniture. The Perks soon realized that a good tenant was hard to find.

Kathy Holland, one of Lucy Perks' teachers, rented the cottage in 1984 and became Sid's second wife. They sold Rose Cottage when Sid bought the Bull in partnership with Guy Pemberton.

ROSENTHAL, DAVID

John Tregorran's friendship with David

Rosenthal was briefly tested when a brass candlestick he had brought to John in 1972 for an opinion of its worth was stolen. John found that it had been sold by the thief to Nora Salt and, although they couldn't determine who the culprit was, he bought it back from her and returned it to David.

ROSIE

Walter Gabriel made many surprising acquisitions over the years, but none more so than Rosie the elephant. He bought her to appear at the 1965 summer festival and got even more than he'd bargained for when she arrived with a baby which Walter named Tiny Tim.

RUSSELL, MR

Rural dean who recommended Carol Deedes to officiate at the wedding of Ruth and David Archer on 15 December 1988, when Ambridge had been without a vicar for several months.

RYLAND, DENISE

When Grace Fairbrother and Christine Archer first created the riding stables in 1952, they had no competition, but three years later Reggie Trentham brought them the unwelcome news not only that Denise Ryland had opened new stables at Walton Grange, near Hollerton, but also that she was considerably undercutting their prices. Grace and Christine went to ask her to charge realistic prices but she was uncooperative. Matters worsened when she started seeing Christine's boyfriend, Paul Johnson. She invited him to a party and he got so drunk that he proposed to her, much to Christine's fury, although Denise denied it later, saying that she had made the whole thing up. The girls were not sorry when they learned that Denise had over-reached herself and bankrupted her business in the same year that she had opened it.

Brenda Dunrich

RYMER, PEARL

When Jackie Smith left the Bull in 1979 she was replaced by Pearl Rymer, whose twenty-five years in the trade should have taught her how to manage better. In the space of three weeks she succeeded in upsetting the regulars, annoying Tom Forrest and alienating Sid's daughter Lucy Perks. Sid Perks gave her a week's wages in lieu of notice and they were all thankful to see the back of her.

Joyce Latham

St Stephen's Church

St Stephen's is built on the site of an early seventh-century Augustinian church and was consecrated in 1281. It is an attractive church with elements of late Norman, early English and Perpendicular styles. In 1959 George and Helen Fairbrother added a stained-glass window in memory of George's daughter Grace Archer.

A flower festival was held in 1981 to celebrate the dedication of the church 700 years before. The Lawson-Hope chapel was decked with roses and carnations symbolizing martyrdom, and in the evening a medieval concert took place, using traditional instruments, including a krumhorn, a psaltery and a fifteenth-century spinet.

Like all other churches St Stephen's has struggled to raise funds to cover essential repairs. Matters came to a head in 1984 when there were so many mice that Tom Forrest tried to kill one with a hymn book. Undeterred, the remaining mice ate through the leather and felt organ stops, with the result that Phil Archer could no longer play the organ. Nigel Pargetter's sponsored parachute jump and Tom Forrest's sponsored diet helped raise the £2,000 needed to put it right.

The vicars at Ambridge have never been above encouraging gentle rivalry among the wealthier in their flock. Jack Woolley and Cameron Fraser vied to pay for mending the church clock in 1990. When the clock was repaired, its chime was heard for the first time in years. Sadly, when it was rededicated, and Bert Fry wound it up, the weights crashed through the floor, nearly killing William Grundy.

Building work for a new loo in 1992 uncovered evidence that the church foundations were older than previously thought. The floor was taken up once more in the church tower and carbon dating revealed the timbers to be Saxon, dating between AD 540 and AD 560. Interested students and journalists filled the church and the vicar, Robin Stokes, wondered where he was going to find the money to pay for the excavation. But the archaeologists decided to cover up the hole and leave everything as it was, for fear of causing more damage. Since then St Stephen's has been at peace.

SALT, CAROLINE

m. Greg Salt 1972

Greg Salt's divorce from Nora Salt was rushed through late in 1972 so that he could remarry when it was found that his girlfriend Caroline was expecting a baby.

SALT, GREGORY

m. Nora McAuley 23 Dec. 1968; divorced Oct. 1972; m. Caroline 1972

In 1964 Gregory Salt was twenty-three. He came from a farming family in Heydon and worked for Phil Archer at Hollowtree, lodging with Ned and Mabel Larkin at Glebe Cottage. Two years later his father was taken ill and he had to go home to look after the farm. He decided to go in for milk production and retailing as Borchester Dairies had stopped delivering in the district, and his landlord Brigadier Winstanley gave him some useful advice. No sooner had he started his milk round than his mother unexpectedly died. His father had to be taken to hospital and as he didn't get on with his brother John, Greg threw him out. The Brigadier advised Greg to stay on in the farmhouse but give up his dairy retailing and work for someone else.

In 1968 he started work for the Archers as dairy man, wanting to be near Nora McAuley, who had visited him with sympathy and a hot meal after his father's death. He proposed to her in May but although she accepted, their courtship was erratic and Nora found him uncompromising. He wouldn't accompany her to Ireland at short notice for a holiday as it would have meant leaving Dan Archer short-handed, which made her cross. He didn't enjoy visiting her in her room at Grey Gables, which made her crosser. It was no surprise when she returned her engagement ring to him – or when they got married two months later.

Gregory wasn't particularly happy at Hollowtree and went to work for Borchester Dairies. But by 1972 he had left the Dairies and wanted to leave Nora. They didn't have enough in common to make the marriage work, and he told Nora that he had a girlfriend, Caroline. The decree absolute was rushed through as Caroline was pregnant and that was nearly the last Nora heard of him. Four years later he wrote to say that he had lost his job so could no longer pay her the £30 a month maintenance they had agreed upon privately before the divorce. By then Nora was living with the even more uncompromising George Barford. Taking a dim view of the arrangement, George told her that she had been breaking the law and was to give all the money back. The nicest thing Greg ever did for her was to refuse to accept the total amount.

Gerald Turner

SALT, NORA

see McAuley, Nora

SAUNDERS, SAM

Sam was landlord at the Bull for twenty years

until his retirement in 1952 when he went to live with his niece Millie in Felpersham. He was pleased that Jack Archer was going to take over the pub and suggested that Jack help him behind the bar for a few evenings, to learn the trade. He left the Bull on 1 January 1953.

Leslie Bowmar

SAVAGE, ROBERT

Clarrie Grundy liked Robert Savage, the vet from the Ministry of Agriculture who came to inspect the Grundy sheep for scab in 1988. His deep voice made her tingle. Joe Grundy didn't like him at all because he confirmed that the sheep had scab and would have to be dipped, and that Joe was under threat of legal action because he'd got them from an undipped pen.

Philip Sully

SAWYER, BILL

Bill Sawyer was chairman of the parish council in 1951. It had taken him over twenty years to build his farm, which he rented from Admiral Bellamy, into a thriving dairy concern. A lesser man would have been devastated when the Admiral asked him to leave in 1952, but he decided to give up farming and started breeding dogs with equal success. In 1961 he formed a partnership with Walter Gabriel and Mrs Turvey to buy a pet shop in Hollerton, and together with Mrs Turvey he bought out Walter's share in 1963.

Kenneth Garratt

SCHOFIELD, VIKKI

When Nelson Gabriel held a party to celebrate the opening of his wine bar in 1980, the glamour of the occasion sparked a romance between his assistant Vikki Schofield and Neil Carter. Vikki's father had died when she was little and she lived with her mother who was very possessive. Neil was sure that Vikki's mother disliked him, and when invited to spend Christmas Day with them he had an uncomfortable time, particularly when Vikki refused to eat the brace of pheasants he brought with him, because she disapproved of shooting game.

Their relationship petered out, and by 1982 Vikki was at Borchester Technical College and out of touch with Ambridge.

SCROBY, MRS

Mrs Scroby was a domestic help in the village. Her rates were 2s. per hour. Doris Archer's family urged her to avail herself of Mrs Scroby's services in 1955, but she refused. Interested in things medicinal (she loved to talk about hospitals and operations), she suggested to Mrs P. that the best cure for rheumatism was to dissolve a teaspoon of mustard in a pint of beer, heat it up and drink it as hot as possible. She was about to prescribe her own cure for adder bites to Carol Grey, but was prevented by Dr Cavendish. In 1957 Mrs Scroby was instrumental in persuading like-minded villagers to form an accident prevention committee.

Vera Ashe

SCROGGIN, ALDERMAN

Alderman Scroggin was chairman of the County Education Committee in 1971 when the closure of the village school was a hotly debated issue, and he represented the county at a meeting on the subject in Ambridge.

SELDEN, GREGORY

Selden was a broken-nosed gypsy who camped out in Arkwright Hall in 1959. When Walter Gabriel and Ned Larkin went to the Hall to pick up a dresser Mr Grenville had bought from the sale of contents, they heard some strange noises. They thought it was a ghost, and when they told John Tregorran about it he and Carol Grey decided to go ghost-hunting. But John never made their date, and much later was discovered with a nasty bump on his head in a secret room near the fireplace in the 'haunted' room. Once it was established that the 'ghost' was all too human, PC Bryden came to investigate. In his eagerness to find John's attacker he tripped down the stairs and fell before he could catch a glimpse of any intruder. The theft of Walter Gabriel's biscuit tin full of money trapped Selden in the end and provided evidence against him: he was caught with the incriminating tin by Tom Forrest and PC Bryden, and found to have been responsible for a local bout of petty pilfering. He was offered legal help by John Tregorran in Borchester prison, but he refused it.

Lewis Gedge

SELFORD, HENRY

Jack Woolley's three-year-old horse Grey Silk was trained for hurdles by Henry Selford at his stables on the Worcestershire/Herefordshire border. After indifferent results in his first races, Woolley decided not to persist with the horse and sold him at the end of 1976.

SELWYN, ERIC

Shula Archer's family were concerned from the outset when she started to take an interest in Eric Selwyn after meeting him at Borchester Technical College where he was pursuing his passion for hi-fi and jazz. Rick, as he liked to be called, was thirty-five, and Shula only sixteen. Shula became more and more secretive about their meetings, until she was forced to face the impossibility of the relationship when he admitted to her that he was married.

John Corvin

SEYMOUR, MR

When Mary Weston wrote to Tony Archer in 1974 to break off their engagement, she had already fallen in love with her boss, Mr Seymour. They were married that same year.

SHANE

Shane has worked faithfully for Nelson Gabriel at the Wine Bar for many years. He is famed for his quiches, his seasonal decorations and his self-effacement. He was nervous when Caroline Bone asked him to cater for the 1989 Grey Gables staff party, together with Jean-Paul, but he need not have feared. Jean-Paul granted him a great accolade when he announced to one and all that Shane would make a good assistant chef.

SHAW, LIONEL QUINTUS

Lionel Shaw was a retired company director who settled in Ambridge with his wife and two children in 1955. Walter Gabriel was delighted to meet him, recognizing that Shaw's ignorance of country life could be to his advantage. Soon he persuaded Shaw to allow him to graze his cattle on Shaw's pasture, and then charged him £3 an acre for the privilege. John and Carol Tregorran had a friendly word with Shaw who had the last laugh when he left all his gates open, with the result that Walter's cattle got out. Several days later he bought a gun from Walter, which showed that he had still not learned his lesson.

Will Kings

SHELDON, JANET

see Tregorran, Janet

SHELDON, MRS

After Walter Gabriel gave up his one-third interest in the Hollerton pet shop, Mrs Sheldon took over his share. She was, however, never closely involved in the running of the business, and returned to the north in 1966.

SIMKINS, WILLY

Jennifer Aldridge entered the bidding for her own sheep when it became apparent that Simkins was likely to be successful at an auction in 1988. He was notorious for exporting livestock in bad conditions, and she was determined that such a fate shouldn't befall any animals from Home Farm. Brian, furious, sold the flock later in the week at a loss. In fact, her expensive gesture was unnecessary as Simkins hadn't been buying for export at all.

SIMMONDS, BARRY

Tony Archer took on Barry Simmonds to work at Bridge Farm in 1992. Tony's enthusiasm for cricket may have been in Barry's favour, for he had been a useful batsman and medium-pace bowler for Edgeley and was soon in the Ambridge team.

SIMMONS, MR

Ambridge was puzzled by the mystery of a woman's shoe and handbag found by George Barford and Tom Forrest in the Country Park in 1975 and handed to PC Drury. Theories of foul play abounded and Drury kept watch on the area. When Simmons returned to pick up the incriminating evidence he was apprehended, but his explanation was an anti-climax to the story. He had been staying at the Bull on his travels as a sales rep, and the items had been lost when he'd met a lady friend in the Park. He had come back in the hope that he could return them to her before her husband missed them.

Colin Skipp

SIMPSON, MR

Jethro Larkin's fall through the loft over the calf-pens at Brookfield in 1975 broke his leg and brought Mr Simpson, the local safety inspector, to determine whether there was a case for Phil Archer to answer. The rotten state of the floor was known to Phil and he had warned Jethro about it. The inspector decided that there would be no prosecution.

John Baddeley

SINCLAIR, ANDREW

m. Dorothy Arnold 25 Nov. 1964

Andrew Sinclair, a Scot, took over as Charles Grenville's farm manager when Phil Archer left to work at Brookfield. He worked hard, but his management sometimes brought him into conflict with villagers and tenants. There was a public outcry when he had the trees at Beecham Bank felled – to no avail, for Andrew pointed out that what he was doing was perfectly within the law. So much did Grenville admire Andrew that he and his wife Carol asked him to be godfather to their son Richard.

Within a couple of years of moving to Ambridge, Andrew had wooed and won Dorothy Arnold and they were married in St Stephen's church. When their son was born, Andrew insisted that he was given the suitably Scottish name of Hamish.

Sinclair continued in his role as farm manager after Grenville's death in 1965. He did not get on so well with his new employer, Ralph Bellamy, and the two often rowed but when Bellamy left Ambridge in 1975 he offered Sinclair the job of estate manager for the newly established Berrow Estate, which he accepted. He continued in that position until he retired in 1986, when his job was taken over by Shula Hebden.

James Grant

SINCLAIR, DOROTHY

m. Andrew Sinclair 25 Nov. 1964

Dorothy was the sister of Ted Arnold, new manager at the market garden in 1961. After he stole money from Laura Archer and Jack Woolley in 1963, she worked hard to repay it to them through her dressmaking and hairdressing. She supplemented her income further by working at Doughy Hood's bakery in the mornings. She was thrilled when Ann Grenville made her manageress of a gown shop in Borchester where her brother was by then living while on probation.

Dorothy's knight in shining armour had red hair and a Scottish accent: she fell in love with Andrew Sinclair, manager of the Bellamy Estate, and married him in the parish church in 1964. Although there was now no need for extra money, she made

Doris Archer's suit for a garden party at Buckingham Palace in 1965. Then her hands were full dealing with their son Hamish when he was born two years later and they enjoyed a happy family life.

Joan Anstey

S KINDLE, SID

Doris Archer was pleased to sell Dan Archer's father's old chair to Sid Skindle, the travelling dealer, for 30*s*. Dan wasn't so happy with the deal, however, as he had declined an offer for it from the doctor, who had been prepared to pay £15.

S LATER, BILL

d. 15 Nov. 1951

Bill Slater was Mrs Perkins's nephew and an orphan. He was twenty-five when he came to live in Ambridge, hoping that working in the country might help his asthma. He lodged with Mrs P. but was too fond of a tipple and a wager to please her.

He wasn't a country lad, and was impatient with his own ignorance of skills like topping sugar beet and pleaching, but he was a dab hand with machines. He had a go at repairing George Fairbrother's big tractor and had a major row with him when the tractor's engine cut and died in the process of flattening a hummock. Bill was furious, especially when it was later discovered that there was nothing wrong with the tractor but that the hummock was in fact ironstone. He made a

bad enemy, losing no opportunity to stir up village feelings against Fairbrother's proposal to mine the ironstone, and threatening to take rotten eggs and tomatoes to the public meeting Fairbrother called in the village hall. He managed to stop the meeting most effectively when he burst in with the news that one of Fairbrother's hayricks was on fire.

Bill had a soft spot for Molly Oakley and reacted dramatically when he discovered that Keith Latimer's assistant Bert Mathews was taking her out. The rumblings of his anger ebbed and flowed, but climaxed one evening when he saw Bert and Keith having a drink in the Bull. He started to argue about the ironstone yet again, and when Keith told him it was a waste of breath because it was all *sub judice*, Bill told him nastily not to swank just because he'd gone to a school where they taught Greek. 'It's Latin, you clot,' returned Bert laughing, and Bill swung a punch.

They were thrown out into the yard, but Bill wouldn't let the matter go and in the subsequent struggle fell and hit his head on the old mounting block. Keith took him home as he was feeling dizzy and complained that his head hurt. Mrs P. took one look at him and prepared him her panacea for all nocturnal ills, a cup of cocoa. He drank it, was violently sick and the next day he died. It was found that he had a very thin skull and the slightest knock might have had the same effect. After his death, Keith discovered that Bill had been behind the sabotage of some of his equipment but, uncomfortable with the part he had played in Bill's death, agreed to keep the matter secret.

John Franklyn

SMITH, BAZZA

Bendigo born and bred, Bazza Smith was one of the team of antipodean shearers who arrived at Brookfield in 1976. He entertained the regulars in the Bull with his version of 'Waltzing Matilda' and other Aussie favourites.

Leon Tanner

SMITH, HENRY

When Henry Smith and Chloe Tempest decided to kidnap Adam Travers-Macy in 1970, they reckoned without Sid Perks. Tempest chatted to Sid while Smith snatched Adam, but Sid kept such a close eye on the pair that he was able to direct the police to their whereabouts. The kidnappers asked £5,000 from the Travers-Macy family but were picked up in Birmingham before any money changed hands, and Adam was safely returned home. The two kidnappers were taken to court where Smith was sentenced to three years' imprisonment, and Tempest was given a suspended sentence.

John Baddeley

SMITH, JACKIE

Jackie started work at the Bull in 1978 and was such a good barmaid and bright personality that Jack Woolley made several unsuccessful attempts to entice her to Grey Gables.

She was popular with all the regulars and rapidly endeared herself to Tony Archer with her liking for soccer and support of West Ham United. The attraction did not pass unnoticed and when Pat and Tony Archer gave a party to celebrate St David's Day Walter Gabriel mischievously sent Jackie an invitation, supposedly from Tony, which led to a number of misunderstandings. All was cleared up eventually, but Walter thought it prudent to keep out of Jackie's way for a while.

Jackie went out with Gordon Armstrong, and was good friends with Neil Carter, but she didn't feel seriously about either of them. She found Harry Booker's advances a nuisance and in the end she could only call his bluff by threatening to talk to his wife.

In 1979 she met a man called Basil Morgan who ran the Borchester Sports Centre, and suddenly started to talk of marriage. Two months later she gave in her notice and went to work behind the bar at the Sports Centre, living in a bed-sit in Borchester. Subsequently Sid and Polly Perks heard that she didn't much like her job, and that she hardly saw Basil, but by then it was too late to ask her to return to the Bull.

Maggie McCarthy

SMITH, MAJOR JOHN

see Daly, Mike

SMITH, MR

Phil Archer occasionally consulted Smith, an expert breeder of pedigree pigs, in the early fifties at his pig unit at Layton Cross.

SMITH, MR

The possibility of an extension to the national grid in 1960 brought to Ambridge Mr Smith, the way-leave officer of the Electricity Board, to inspect the Brookfield land that might have been affected and address a meeting in the village hall about the implications of the scheme.

Monty Crick; Graham Rigby

SMITH, MR

Shula Archer showed Mr Smith around Mark Hebden's cottage in 1984 in what she expected would be a routine estate agent's task. However, the conversation became increasingly personal. He told her that he was well-off, redundant and separated from his wife, and asked her out, at which she became alarmed and rapidly concluded the inspection. Not surprisingly, no sale resulted.

SMITH, NANCY

Maid to the Tregorrans in the sixties.
June Spencer

SMITH, SAMANTHA

After the birth of Alice Aldridge in 1988, her parents Brian and Jennifer agreed that they needed help in the house. Brian knew of a beautiful girl named Samantha who he thought would be ideal, but Jennifer thought

otherwise and insisted they advertise in *The Lady.*

SNELL, CORIANDER (CAZ)

Caz Snell, Robert Snell's younger daughter by a previous marriage to Bobo, spent Christmas in Ambridge with Robert and his second wife Lynda in 1988. What with Lynda being uneasy with children anyway, the drum kit Caz received from her mother didn't help to create a harmonious or festive atmosphere.

SNELL, LEONIE (LEN)

Elder daughter of Robert Snell by his first wife, Bobo. Len and her sister Caz spent a tense Christmastime in Ambridge in 1988 with Robert and his second wife Lynda, after which Len was glad to return to boarding school in the New Year.

SNELL, LYNDA

b. 29 May 1947

Lynda Snell left Sunningdale for Ambridge in 1986. Perhaps the good people of Sunningdale were too sophisticated for her to dominate; whatever the case, within hours of moving into Ambridge Hall, Lynda had begun her assault on Ambridge. The first local she came across happened to be Eddie Grundy carrying his precious ferret. 'It's a rat,' she cried; 'kill it, quickly.' Only hours later, she was involved in a bitter dispute with Brian Aldridge about

Lynda Snell (Carole Boyd)

man has fled at the sight of it. In her time, she crusaded for almost every cause known to man: she is in favour of community buses, footpaths, getting younger women to join the WI, the Countryside Commission, saving red phone boxes and hedgehogs. She is anti barn conversions, anti smoking, anti by-passes, anti slug pellets, anti straw burning and anti almost every application for planning permission.

In recent years, hardly a play, function or fête has taken place in Ambridge without the stamp of Lynda Snell and her 'ever helpful' advice. Whatever Lynda assists in, petitions for or organizes, within hours everyone is at screaming point. In 1993, such were the tensions experienced by the cast of the pantomime that she was forced to abandon the project for the time being.

Lynda likes to think of herself as being at one with nature. Unfortunately nature doesn't always reciprocate her feelings. The merest whiff of a pollen grain will trigger off her hay fever. When the oil-seed rape is in blossom she is forced to become a virtual recluse. Ever the keen conservationist, Lynda once spotted Joe Grundy pulling up ragwort on Shula's instructions. She complained loudly about this terrible man destroying lovely wild flow-

public rights of way as she rambled across his land. In a single day, Lynda had managed to infuriate the two men furthest apart socially in the whole of the village. Since then, she has succeeded in maddening everyone in between.

Lynda and her clip-board soon became a familiar village feature. More than one strong

ers. Anyone living in the country knows that ragwort is a dangerous, poisonous weed which can kill animals that graze on it; with a shade more caution and humility she could have avoided her *faux pas*. But Lynda totally lacks humility. By making herself the centre of attention wherever she goes, she constantly lays herself wide open to ridicule. When this happens, only her devoted husband Robert is truly aware of the pain and humiliation she suffers. Quietly at her side, he is one of the few people who appreciates Lynda's vulnerability, and understands that she always acts from the most generous of motives and a genuine desire to create a better world. To her sadness, Lynda has never had children (although the constant patter of tiny feet might have driven her to distraction); and her relationship with Leonie and Coriander, Robert's daughters from his first marriage, has always been cool. When they came for Christmas in 1988 she was almost driven mad by the noise (especially by their musical gifts).

Fortunately Lynda has been able to divert some of her maternal feelings into caring for dumb animals. She saved an Afghan hound, the runt of the litter, from being put down and gave him a home. Hermes has been devoted to her ever since. On a trip to the Royal Show in 1989 she bought two goats: not any old goats, of course, but Anglo-Nubian kid goats. She named them Persephone and Demeter. In Lynda's eyes her goats could do no wrong. She refused to apologize to Jill Archer when they decimated the garden at Brookfield. But even Lynda was defeated when her goats gave birth to kids. There was chaos from the start – mess, round-the-clock feeding, kid goats everywhere. At first she was livid with Robert when he got rid of them but later admitted how relieved she was when night feeds were no longer necessary and dinner at Grey Gables was possible once again. She was shocked to think, however, that the delicious red meat on her plate might have been from one of Persephone's offspring. Not so. Robert had taken them to Nigel Pargetter's Pet's Corner at Lower Loxley.

Lynda was a leading force in the twinning of Ambridge with the French town of Meyruelle. It was unfortunate that an attack of ringworm on her face prevented her from going on the initial visit in 1993.

Lynda has a tendency to know it all and treat condescendingly everyone she deals with. But for all her annoying traits, sometimes she comes up trumps. It was after all Lynda who, having revived her precious pantomime, donated all the proceeds to the Mark Hebden memorial cricket trophy. Ambridge would be a poorer place without her.

Carole Boyd

SNELL, ROBERT

b. 5 Apr. 1943

It was in 1986 that Robert and Lynda Snell decided to exchange the golf courses of Sunningdale for the green fields of Ambridge. Robert is in the computer business, and lives somewhat in the shadow of the daunting Lynda. A quiet tolerant man, he watches from the sidelines as his wife strides about the village on her various concerns. His work

Persephone tried even Robert's seemingly endless patience.

Robert is essentially a suburban man, not always comfortable in the country or understanding of its ways, but for all that kind, generous, and unfailingly supportive of his sometimes rather trying wife.

Graham Blockey

SNOUT, MR

For the fête in 1964, Walter Gabriel and Jack Archer bought from Mr Snout of Hollerton a large balloon which Walter christened 'Pegasus'.

SNOW, GRAEME

Mr Snow, a member of the staff of the County Museum in Borchester, organized an archaeological dig in Jiggons Field in 1974 after John Tregorran suggested that it could contain significant remains. The information unearthed proved useful, but there were no spectacular finds.

SPALDING, JIM

When Mrs P. came to Ambridge in 1951, it was at first thought that she should live at Brookfield in Rickyard Cottage, but as the day neared the Archer family had second thoughts at the idea of such proximity and daughter Peggy arranged for her to take Jim Spalding's cottage with her nephew Bill Slater as her lodger.

Robert Snell (Graham Blockey)

takes him away from the village a good deal.

Lynda is his second wife. His first was Bobo, who gave him two daughters, Coriander and Leonie. He hasn't always found it easy to fit in, but still tries to play his part in village life. He is treasurer of the Ambridge Cricket Club, and a keen member of the team.

In 1989 he surprised and impressed many with his impassioned speech opposing the proposed Borchester by-pass. He's a much stronger character than he might, at first, appear. Certainly, while seeming to obey Lynda's every command, he sometimes goes against her behind her back. But there was no escape from Lynda's pet goats. Sleepless nights getting up to feed Demeter and

SPEAKMAN, MR

Dan Archer was invited by Mr Speakman, chief executive officer of the National Milk Publicity Council, to attend the inauguration of the June dairy festival at Mansion House in London in 1961.

SPENCER, JIM

A local solicitor, Jim Spencer was a friend of Mark Hebden and his partner Usha Gupta. Jim's partnership, Spencer & Holden, were the solicitors approached by the Jarretts for representation following their arrest for disrupting the local hunt in 1980. Mark got the case.

SPENLOWE, MRS EMILY

Fortunetellers at the Ambridge fête have usually made no great claims for their abilities, but Mrs Spenlowe was an exception: she kept in touch with her late husband Humphrey through 'the spirits'. She was not the impractical eccentric that this might suggest, however, but a useful member of several local committees, including those for the 1973 Festival of Ambridge and the WI.

June Spencer

SPROGGETT, WILFRED JOHN

Ornithologist Wilfred Sproggett saw more than birds through his high-powered binoc-

ulars: on one occasion he spotted the hiding place of an escaped convict. Unperturbed, he made his careful notes and trained his glasses elsewhere. The information was duly passed on to the police, but in his own good time. He was a true enthusiast and gave whole-hearted approval to Mike Daly's plan to turn part of the Squire's woodland into a bird sanctuary in 1954. Eighteen years later he was made president of the Borchester Ornithological Society.

He remained a bachelor, despite Tom Forrest's attempts to couple him with Agatha Turvey, whom he knew well. Tom encouraged the friendship, hoping that Mrs Turvey would become attained to Wilfred instead of himself, as her attentions had made him a laughing stock in the Bull. He promised to show Wilfred a Montagu's harrier if he would call on Agatha and be nice to her. Unfortunately, Wilfred was too nice and to their dismay she invited both of them for Christmas. It took some clever manoeuvring on Wilfred's part but eventually she went to her sister Marian and they were saved. She managed to have the last laugh, though: on her return the unscrupulous pair turned up to deliver their Christmas presents belatedly and she trapped them into saying they would join her for New Year's Eve. Wilfred took Flora Hepplewhite with him for safety, but Tom had no such luck.

Philip Garston-Jones

STABLES, THE

see Barratt's Farm

STANTON, MAC

When Marianne Peters arrived from Paris in 1960, Paul Johnson arranged for her to work with Mac Stanton, public relations officer at the Imperial Hotel, Nettleton, where he felt she would be able to gain experience and a good qualification.

Hamilton Dyce

STEVENS, PETER

b. 1953

When the Forrests fostered Johnny Martin in 1960, he prevailed on them to take his friend Peter Stevens as well. There must have been times when they wished they hadn't. Neither boy was an easy charge, but Peter gave most trouble; Pru Forrest complained that he was getting out of control. He painted rude slogans on Jack Woolley's garden wall and stayed out all night poaching. However, he was a clever mechanic and developed an interest in stock-car racing, and by 1971 he had steadied down and was employed by Ralph Bellamy at his garage. When Haydn Evans bought it, he retained Peter and even left him in charge when he had to go overseas for a month. Peter found digs in Borchester in 1977 to be near his girlfriend, though he continued to work in Ambridge until 1981, when he found a new job in Borchester. He lost contact with his foster parents, so when he turned up at a surprise party given for Pru in 1987 and announced that he was running two garages, she was

delighted and overwhelmed.

Edward Seckerson; Peter Biddle; Anthony Smee; Paul Henry

STEWART, JENNY

Caroline Bone went to the 1983 Edinburgh Festival at the suggestion of her friend Jenny Stewart who ran the community centre in Kilbreck.

STOBEMAN, SALLY (NÉE JOHNSON)

m. Tony Stobeman Jan. 1962

Sally Johnson became Christine Archer's partner at the riding stables in 1956. Despite her brother Paul's warnings, she married the dashing Tony Stobeman and helped her husband in his various business activities.

Ann Chatterley

STOBEMAN, TONY

m. Sally Johnson Jan. 1962

Tony Stobeman was an old racing pal of Reggie Trentham's. He wore yellow waistcoats and a general air of devil-may-care. He flirted with Carol Grey and tried to encourage her to invest in his commission agent's business, but she wasn't interested. Paul Johnson, another chum, warned his sister Sally against too serious an involvement with this Lothario, to no avail. After two false starts – he postponed their wedding twice –

they were married in January 1962. He opened a betting shop in Hollerton and later, in partnership with Nelson Gabriel, a casino and betting shop in Borchester. He and Nelson quarrelled and Nelson disappeared. To all intents and purposes so did Tony, as he and Sally were never heard from again.

Jack Holloway

S TOKES, OLIVER

b. 1983

When Oliver Stokes heard that his father Robin was to marry Caroline Bone, he was delighted. Oliver was fond of Caroline and had enjoyed being looked after by her when he and his elder brother Sam visited the Vicarage, because Caroline was inclined to spoil them. When Caroline's horse, Ippy, was stolen, Sam and Oliver were determined to get him back for her. They pedalled for miles on their mountain bikes until at last they thought they'd found him. But it was getting dark and they were mistaken. Poor Oliver burst into tears. He was upset once more when he was told that Caroline and his father had decided to split up after her accident in 1994.

James Naylor

S TOKES, REVD ROBIN

b. 12 Oct. 1951; m. Sarah; 2 sons; divorced

If Robin Stokes has one fault, it is a tendency to take on more than he can manage. Working as a vet and a non-stipendiary minister serving the parishes of Ambridge, Penny Hassett and Edgeley he is often at full stretch and finds it hard to make time for himself.

When he first arrived in August 1991, his parishioners weren't sure how they were going to take to a man who was sometimes a vet and sometimes a minister, but Robin's conscientious approach to both roles soon won the day. It came as a shock when they discovered that that same conscientiousness had cost him his marriage to his wife Sarah, and that Robin was divorced with two sons, Sam and Oliver.

Soon after his arrival in Ambridge, Saxon remains were found under the church. A full excavation was necessary. Despite the historic importance of the find, many people were not happy about the arrival of the archaeologists, especially when they discovered just how much the parish was going to have to contribute towards the cost. Robin had to smooth a lot of ruffled feathers. But eventually the money was raised, and several interesting finds are now in the Borchester museum. Robin found himself at the centre of another row over the village magazine, with Lynda Snell and Marjorie Antrobus vying for the role of editor (a contest which Lynda won).

A fine man who has dedicated his life to the service of others, Robin is always ready to offer sympathy to anyone in need. He comforted Shula Hebden after her ectopic pregnancy, then her sister Elizabeth after her abortion; listened to Marjorie and Caroline Bone as they admitted the loss of their savings to fraudulent Cameron Fraser; and counselled Betty Tucker after the raid in the village shop. And what with participating in pancake races, a sponsored auction, a bike race, village entertainment and a harvest supper, no one could accuse Robin of lack of commitment to village life.

On top of all this, he manages to be a good vet. He could often be found attending a difficult calving in the middle of the night, quite unmindful of the fact that he might be taking a service at eight o'clock the next morning. Even he, though, was stumped when called out to examine Lynda's goats and had to consult his veterinary textbooks.

One of the first people Robin met in Ambridge was Caroline Bone. They became friends and, as their involvement and affection grew month by month, fell in love. But their relationship was difficult: Robin's absolute religious conviction was at odds with Caroline's non-belief, their irregular working hours often made it difficult for them to meet and, hardest of all, they couldn't pursue the relationship openly for fear of upsetting Robin's parishioners. Robin found it difficult to come to terms with Caroline's previous relationships. When Brian Aldridge announced that he and Caroline had had a long and illicit affair, Robin avoided Caroline for two weeks. But when Caroline finally ambushed him on Lakey Hill, forcing him to confess why he had been avoiding her, all was put right in a tender moment of reassurance.

Caroline soon felt ready to make love to Robin and she couldn't understand it when he rejected her during an overnight stay in Birmingham, explaining that his faith dictated that sex should be within the sanctity of marriage. This time it was Caroline who was hurt and confused. Then Robin's dog Patch

was poisoned and it was Caroline who helped him track down the culprit. They became closer again, especially when Caroline's horse Ippy was stolen and Robin devoted much of his precious spare time to trying to help Caroline to find her horse, to no avail. They were like love's young dream as they shared the secret of their engagement.

When they got to know her, Robin's children got on well with Caroline and so he did not expect opposition when in spring 1993 he told them of his plans to marry. Sam, though, was furious, still hoping that his parents would be reconciled. Nonetheless, plans for the wedding went ahead. Robin and Caroline went to pre-marriage counselling, booked a honeymoon in Venice and looked forward to an elaborate wedding at Netherbourne Hall. But the preparations for the wedding began to take their toll on Caroline's nerves and she was delighted when Debbie Aldridge suggested a ride together. On their return, suddenly a car overtook them at speed, Caroline's horse reared and she was thrown. While Caroline remained in a deep coma for several days, Robin prayed at her hospital bedside for her survival and recovery. When she came round it was he who had to break the news that their friend Mark Hebden had been killed while trying to avoid Caroline as she lay in the road, and that their wedding had been postponed.

Slowly Caroline began to recover but Robin found her reluctant to discuss wedding plans. Robin did all he could to pick up the pieces and start anew, but finally Caroline told him that she couldn't go through with the wedding. Robin was devastated. It was hard for him to have to explain to his parishioners what had happened and even the ready sympathy of Mrs Antrobus was of little comfort. He needed all his faith to come through this time and sometimes it was tested to the limit. But as Mrs Antrobus pointed out to him when she found him in St Stephen's church shouting at God, at least shouting at God meant that Robin thought that God was there.

Tim Meats

STOKES, SAM

b. 1981

Sam and Oliver Stokes, the sons of Robin, live with their mother, Sarah, and her new partner in Kent. They visit their father whenever they can.

At first Sam liked Robin's friend Caroline Bone. He enjoyed it when she went kite-flying with him and his brother. But when in 1993 Robin and Caroline announced that they were going to get married it was a different story. Sam was so upset by the prospect that he ran away from Kent and made his own way to Ambridge. His father was not pleased, but Caroline tried to comfort him. Eventually he accepted the situation and the two boys, their father and Caroline went camping in Wales. Sam and Oliver were about to set off for the wedding when the news came that Caroline was in a coma and the wedding had been postponed. While she was in hospital Sam sent her cards and letters. But when Robin broke the news to him that the marriage wasn't going ahead after all, Sam was secretly relieved.

Monty Allen

STUBBS, MRS

Mrs P.'s former neighbour in London, Mrs Stubbs, delighted her with a ticket to see the Coronation procession from a seat on the Mall. But when Mrs P. realized how disappointed Walter Gabriel was that she would not be at the party he'd been planning, she gave the seat to Peggy Archer, and sent her off with messages for all her old friends.

STUBBS, PIGGIE

Piggie Stubbs was an undistinguished farm contractor, until in 1984 he achieved fame in the district by running off to Marbella with the Felpersham carnival queen.

STURDY, SIR MICHAEL

Gerald Pargetter engaged the prominent barrister Sir Michael Sturdy to defend his son Nigel when he and Shula Archer were charged with 'taking and driving away' a car after a Borchester dance in 1984. Nigel was found guilty and fined, but a greater penalty was Shula's growing interest in their solicitor Mark Hebden – and solving that problem was well beyond the capabilities of Sir Michael.

William Eedle

SUGDEN, FOXY

Proprietor of the Secondhand Emporium in Borchester in the early eighties.

SUTTON, BERT

Walter Gabriel's plans to set up a transport firm met unscrupulous opposition from Bert Sutton, the Ambridge haulier. He threatened Walter with legal action and tried to blacken his character by spreading false tales of his business practices amongst the authorities. When Walter was unmoved, he suggested a partnership. His efforts were in vain, and Walter's licence was issued in July 1957.

Edward Higgins

TALT, PATIENCE

Patience Talt was a much-married American widow. While doing business with Robert Snell in 1986, she dallied with Joe Grundy. They drank real ale together and she hinted at marriage. When she left Ambridge, Joe was sad.

TARBUTT, EMILY

Mrs Turvey became increasingly dependent on her companion Emily Tarbutt as she grew frailer, but when Emily came down with flu in 1976 she was unable to look after her. For several days no one called to see them and Mrs Turvey died. She left Emily her house, Lakey View, but Emily had no wish to stay there alone and moved in with her cousin Matthew Wreford.

Peggy Hughes

TARRANT, NANCY

1 dtr by Nelson Gabriel; m. Mr Wilson; 2 sons

Nancy Tarrant, who lived in Penny Hassett, was one of Nelson's girlfriends. She visited his father Walter Gabriel in 1967 to tell him that she was pregnant and that Nelson was the father. Walter told her to move out of the district and that he would send her money. She had a daughter, Rosemary, who was put up for adoption, and a son Simon, with a different father, who was also adopted. Subsequently Nancy married an engineer, became Mrs Wilson and moved to Southampton where she had two sons.

TARRANT, ROSEMARY (NÉE GABRIEL)

b. Aug. 1967

There was a stir in the Wine Bar one evening in June 1986 when an attractive young girl walked up to Nelson and said, 'Hello Dad!' He slipped her away so fast that no one had a chance to find out more, but the hum of gossip could be heard in Penny Hassett.

Rosemary was the result of an early union between Nelson and Nancy Tarrant, and a great surprise to Nelson who didn't know that he was a father. She had been adopted by John and Rachel Dean, teachers in Epsom, and had tracked down Nelson through Nancy whose name she had been given by the adoption society. She had a half-brother Simon, now twenty-one, who had also been adopted, but to Nelson's relief he'd had nothing to do with that inception.

Rosemary was surprised by the conspicuous lack of enthusiasm with which Nelson looked upon her training as a police cadet at Hendon. But Walter's ingenuous explanation that Nelson had been 'picked on' by the police in his younger days seemed to satisfy her – which suggests that she took after her mother rather than her father.

She applied for a posting to the Borsetshire area and came to live with Nelson at Honeysuckle Cottage in the spare room he had freshly painted. She persuaded Nelson to accept her police housing allowance to help his finances, but the other addition she made to the household was not so welcome: Winston, an injured dog with psychological problems. Nelson soon discovered the mixed blessings of parenthood when Winston snacked on his black silk sheets, and even when he had the good taste to attack Joe Grundy, Nelson was not sorry to see him taken to the Dog Rescue Centre. However, Mrs P. forced him to see the error of his ways and he brought the dog back, earning high praise from Rosemary who told him that he was 'decent after all'. Winston then proceeded to terrify the neighbourhood, chasing anything that moved, and in the end Rosemary had him put down.

DS Barry was grateful for Rosemary's assistance in an Ambridge crimewave. Someone had dared to vandalize the cricket pitch, and Rosemary had the unenviable task of breaking the news to Brian and Jennifer Aldridge that their daughter Kate was amongst the gang of vandals seen in the cricket pavilion. Dave Barry had another use for her, crying on her shoulder about his love life. Nelson viewed their friendship with a jaundiced eye, and suggested that her ex-boyfriend, Peter, should come and stay, although he wasn't very keen on Peter either. This clever idea rebounded on him, for Rosemary and Peter renewed their relationship and Rosemary went off with him to London.

Nicola Wright

Tempest, Chloe

see Smith, Henry
Eileen Barry

Terry

George Fairbrother took on Terry under the YMCA's 'British Boys for British Farms' scheme in 1951, but took little notice of the boy's abilities. He ignored Terry's liking for cattle and had him work with the poultry, where the attractions of Jane Maxwell sparked some interest, but didn't overcome his ineptitude with eggs. Phil Archer tried to plead his case, suggesting he could be trained to take over from Angus when he retired, but his plea was too late, for in 1953 Terry was called on to do his National Service and did not return.

Theo Bryane

THOMAS, DEREK

Tony and Pat Archer received good advice on organic farming from Derek Thomas whom they met in 1993 through their co-op. He was particularly helpful to Mike Tucker in getting his produce into the Bridge Farm shop, and warned them all about the opposition that they faced in the opening of an organic shop in Felpersham by Howard Friend.

THOMAS, LEN

m. Mary Jones 7 June 1954

Len Thomas was taken on as a farmhand at Brookfield in 1953. He was a surly young man and even Doris could not find out what was his problem. Eventually he confessed to Dan and Phil Archer that he had a wife and child living in Welshpool.

Len had met his wife Marion while he was doing his National Service; the two of them had quickly married and gone to live on his father's farm. After the birth of their son, David, Marion began to crave excitement and soon turned to other men. She and her child were thrown out of the farm when Len's father discovered what was going on. Len was trying his best to support his estranged wife and child, but she was wildly extravagant and it was difficult for Len to make ends meet, even though he was work-ing at Brookfield during the day and as bar-man at the King's Head in the evenings.

Dan and Phil were pleased when Len became friends with Mary Jones. Len wanted to marry her but his wife spitefully refused to give him a divorce. There didn't seem to be anything Len could do. But then fate stepped in: Marion was killed in a car crash. Len was free to embark on marriage with Mary and when David came to join them, they were a ready-made family. In 1955 Mary had a son of her own, Owen Leonard.

Len decided after four years at Brookfield that he wanted to specialize in sheep and went to work for George Fairbrother. He was a union man which, together with his direct manner, meant that he didn't get on with Charles Grenville, who took over the Estate in 1959. Disappointed at not being offered the management of Grenville's Welsh hill farm in 1963, he became more outspoken at work and moodier at home. By 1966 Grenville had had enough and dismissed him, and he and his family left Ambridge.

Arnold Peters

THOMAS, MARY (NÉE JONES)

m. Len Thomas 7 June 1954

Mary was a fun-loving girl who lived with her widowed invalid father in Hollerton. Helen Fairbrother was fond of her and encouraged her further education; she also admired her embroidery skills. When Mary became friendly with Phil Archer in 1952, the Fairbrothers misconstrued the friendship. But Mary wasn't interested in a romance with Phil – she wanted to spend her time dancing and flirting.

Then she met Len Thomas. Introverted and surly, he fascinated her and she fell in love with him. Len had to tell her that he could not marry her as he had a wife still living, and Mary accepted the fact with dignity. When the news came that Len's wife had been killed, Mary avoided him for several days before going to see him. She told him that she hadn't wanted to be in the way while he thought things out, but she still wanted to marry him. The newly-weds set up home with Len's son, David, and Mary's father. Mary was delighted when her own son Owen Leonard was born.

Mary did her best but money was always tight and Len made a difficult, sometimes violent, husband. When his disagreements with Charles Grenville led to his dismissal in 1966 she had mixed feelings: it was a blow, but she hoped that the chance to make a fresh start would enable Len at last to put his troubles behind him.

Noreen Baddiley

THORKHIL

see Jensen, Thorkhil

THOROGOOD, DR MATTHEW

Matthew Thorogood came from a long line of medical practitioners. But life in a quiet English country village must have seemed strange to him after the three gruelling years he had spent as a doctor in Papua New Guinea. As he established himself as the Ambridge GP in 1986, it soon became clear to the locals that he was an understanding man in whom they could place their trust.

Caroline Bone turned to him on the rebound from her affair with Brian Aldridge, but their relationship didn't, in the end, work out. He was solid and reliable, which was what she, at the time, felt she needed. But he could be rather dull, something of a stick in the mud. When Caroline hastily moved into Ambridge Farm with him she found it hard to relax and feel at home. Matthew was apprehensive that his friends and patients might think they were 'living in sin', and the secrecy of his plans to buy Willow Farm in 1987 infuriated Caroline.

A weekend in Florence might have patched things up as Matthew hoped, had he not invited Shula and Mark Hebden to come along too. It was a disaster, after which the affair began rapidly to cool. A further drop in temperature occurred one afternoon the following summer when, arriving home, Caroline found a chain-smoking Nelson Gabriel making tea. He stayed on for several months while repairs were carried out at Honeysuckle Cottage. Soon, Caroline had gone, back to Grey Gables whence she came, and out of Matthew's life.

By October 1991, Matthew felt it was time to move on. He decided to join his aunt's general practice in Somerset. Since the property market had slumped, he accepted a rock-bottom price for the farmhouse from Mike and Betty Tucker, and sold the land to Phil Archer.

His patients had many reasons for remembering Matthew with gratitude. He was very concerned over Emma Carter's bedwetting; he was discreet when treating Brian Aldridge's epilepsy; and showed great tenderness and care during Walter Gabriel's last days. For all that his personal life had been something of a disaster while he was in Ambridge, his general umbrella of care as a doctor meant that there would always be a soft spot for Matthew in many hearts there.

Crawford Logan

TIMMS, MR AND MRS

Mr Timms worked for Ralph Bellamy and lived with his wife Elsie in one of the workers' flats on the Estate. Lilian Bellamy arranged for Elsie to do some housework for Doris Archer and she sometimes helped out at the Bull in the early seventies.

TITCOMBE

Lower Loxley's head gardener, Titcombe, long responsible for the upkeep of the estate's gardens and park, faced a new challenge in 1994 in satisfying Julia Pargetter's passion for a herb garden.

TODD, RICHARD

The Ambridge fête was opened in 1962 by the film star Richard Todd.

TOMPKINS

Tompkins, a delivery man for a firm supplying dry feeds, was arrested in 1972 and charged with assaulting Angela Cooper and poaching Jack Woolley's deer.

Patrick Connor

TOUVIER, GUSTAVE

Gustave Touvier was the major of the French town Meyruelle, who led the town-twinning delegation to Ambridge in 1993.

He couldn't speak a word of English but had no difficulty in making himself understood when he pinched Lynda Snell's bottom and ogled Clarrie Grundy. Eddie was more offended than Clarrie, but Gustave's fellow delegate Marie-Claire Beguet shrugged her shoulders and remarked that the mayor was well known in Meyruelle for his lack of tact. (How he came to be elected mayor remains a mystery.)

Robert Snell promoted more diplomatic relations when he found out that Gustave liked shooting pigeons and took him off into the countryside with his old air rifle.

Claude le Sache

TOVEY, ARTHUR

d. 1976

Arthur Tovey was a solitary figure, friendly only with Walter Gabriel during the time he was manager of the market garden. In 1976, when he was just forty-two, the metal ladder he was carrying struck a power cable and he suffered fatal burns. He left his money to John Tregorran as a charitable bequest to be disposed of at his discretion.

Harry Stubbs

Arthur Tovey (Harry Stubbs) and Carol Tregorran (Anne Cullen)

TOWEY, SEAN

Brian Aldridge employed Sean Towey to help with the harvest in 1985. He could hardly fail to notice the interest that Sean aroused in his wife Jennifer. Sean was taken aback by the telling off he got from Brian supposedly because he slipped home to get his thermos; he threatened to give a week's notice and to his surprise found himself out of a job. Brian later apologized, but Sean would not relent and made his way back home to Co. Cork.

TOZER, JOE

Joe Tozer was a travelling odd-job man. He stole tools from Haydn Evans and sold them to Tony Archer. He was used as a warning to Terry Barford by his father George, who admonished him to note 'what drink could do to a man'. In 1974 Borchester magistrates charged him with being drunk and begging in the wool market.

Patrick Connor

TRAVERS-MACY, ADAM

see Macy, Adam

TRAVERS-MACY, DEBORAH

see Aldridge, Deborah

TRAVERS-MACY, JENNIFER

see Aldridge, Jennifer

TRAVERS-MACY, MR AND MRS

Mr and Mrs Travers-Macy, the wealthy parents of Roger, were not at all impressed with his choice of Jennifer Archer as his bride in 1968, especially as she was the mother of an illegitimate child. His father said that he would withdraw the loan he had given Roger to help him set up his bookshop unless he abandoned the idea. When Roger refused to do so he had a slight heart attack. But Laura Archer went to visit him and spoke so convincingly on behalf of the young couple that he told Roger he could keep the loan and the interest. When he got to know Adam he grew fond of him, and there is no doubt that he would have paid the ransom of

£5,000 demanded from him when Adam was kidnapped in 1970. Fortunately there was no need, as the kidnappers were caught and Adam came to no harm. In the same year he wrote off the loan completely.

Jennifer never got on well with Roger's mother, who wished herself upon the couple when it suited her. Once she brought with her the only copy of the Ambridge mummers' play, last performed in 1909, which she gave to John Tregorran, knowing of his interest in the past of Ambridge, although she might have been less generous if she knew the extent of his relationship with her daughter-in-law. She got on Jennifer's nerves so much that on one occasion Jennifer took her daughter Debbie to the Johnsons for the night rather than sleep under the same roof as her mother-in-law.

Fred Yule and Beatrice Kane

TRAVERS-MACY, ROGER

b. 9 Mar. 1944; m. Jennifer Archer 27 Sept. 1968; 1 dtr; divorced Feb. 1976

Born late to wealthy parents, who already had two older children, Roger Travers-Macy was too much of an embarrassment to be exactly welcome to them. He was sent straight from prep school to public school and was packed off to France during school holidays. He resented this treatment so much that, in later life, he dropped his family name, taking the surname Patillo from their holiday villa in France. It was as Roger Patillo that he first became known to Laura Archer, when he saved her from a car accident out-side the Bull in 1965. Laura fell for his charm and offered him employment as chauffeur. In return, he gave her a good Stock Exchange tip.

Henry Featherstone and John Tregorran had a job going in their bookshop, which they offered to Roger. He took it, hoping to be made a third partner quite soon. He persuaded his father to finance him and set him up first in a flat and later in Blossom Hill Cottage. Featherstone and Roger proceeded to buy John Tregorran out of the shop.

Roger dallied for a time with Lilian Archer, until she became aware of his relationship with Valerie Woolley. Then Jennifer fell in love with him and he decided that it was time to marry. The Archers may have been pleased with this match, but the Travers-Macys were most decidedly not and threatened to cut Roger off without a penny. The indomitable Laura stepped in and persuaded Roger's father not to withdraw his financial support, or to charge interest on the money owed by Roger. In September 1968 the wedding went ahead, and Jennifer's little boy Adam honeymooned with the newly-weds in Ibiza.

They moved into a flat over the bookshop, keeping Blossom Hill Cottage for weekends. Roger was, at first, a good stepfather to Adam. When they received a kidnap threat, he immediately engaged a nurse to look after the little boy. Her vigilance failed. Adam was kidnapped from the Bull by an unsavoury couple who thought that Roger's wealthy father would pay up for Adam's return. They were disappointed. They were soon captured after a tip-off from Sid Perks, and Adam returned home. Roger was a great support to Jennifer during the ensuing trial.

Roger and Jennifer's daughter Deborah was born in 1970. Life continued on a fairly even keel until Roger took a job dealing in antique books which involved him in a great deal of travelling. Within four years, Roger had walked out on his family, sued for divorce, and set up with his future second wife in London. Despite this, when Brian Aldridge married Jennifer, Roger refused to let Adam and Debbie take Brian's name.

Quite unexpectedly Roger popped back to Ambridge in 1991 to wish his daughter a happy twenty-first birthday. He had a new car delivered to her as a surprise present, and he didn't forget Adam, bringing him some books a couple of weeks later. Invited to dinner at Home Farm, he reminisced with Jennifer about old times, in front of a seething and insecure Brian. Jennifer was persuaded into renewing more than memories with Roger, wounding her husband, her children and ultimately herself. Roger was sent away, but came back in February 1994 for Debbie's sake, after the car accident which killed Mark Hebden. Her involvement in antiques and old books meant that father and daughter now had a shared interest. But he couldn't make good his promise of the financial help she needed to go into partnership with Nelson Gabriel. Debbie felt let down and hurt, and the episode underlined the fragility of their relationship.

Jeremy Mason; Peter Harlow

TRAVIS, MAUREEN

When Susan Carter told 'Mo' Travis in November 1993 that they had a lot in common, she didn't realize how much. If Mo had her way, she and Susan's husband Neil were going to be more than just good friends. She had met him two months before when he came to Hill Farm to sell dairy feed. The farmer was out but the farmer's wife had been very hospitable, and when he called again, Mo once more plied him with chocolate digestives and cups of tea. They discovered that their daughters were in the same class at school, and that Mo and Susan were already nodding acquaintances. Mo's friendships with both husband and wife flourished, while the relationship between Neil and Susan deteriorated as Neil learnt the extent of Susan's aid to her brother Clive Horrobin, on the run from the police.

Neil made the mistake of offering to help Mo with the tasks on the farm that her husband Geoff left untended, and a stolen kiss convinced her that she had every chance of winning him. When Susan went to prison, Mo offered Neil help and comfort, making it increasingly clear that she wanted more than comfort in return. She set him up when she knew that Geoff would be away. She asked Neil to help her at the farm, prepared a romantic dinner and insisted that he stay the night; but it merely made him more determined to remain loyal to Susan, whatever she had done.

When Susan came out of prison in March 1994 she found her husband and best friend at odds. It was some time before she learned the truth and longer before she believed it. Geoff was with Mo when the Carters came to confront her about the situation and prevent her from further mischief-making. The

Carters were taken aback to learn that Mo had behaved like this before. Geoff insisted grimly that Mo would make no more trouble for them and Neil and Susan left Hill Farm very shaken but feeling closer than they had for a long time.

Roberta Kerr

TREADGOLD, DOLLY

Eddie Grundy and divorcee Dolly Treadgold became engaged in 1979. She proved to be too flighty for him, but later she was pleased to visit Grange Farm and cook for the men while Eddie's wife Clarrie was away.

TREADGOLD, ELLEN

Ellen Treadgold was Ralph Bellamy's housekeeper, who left him when he married Lilian in 1971 and went to work for the Travers-Macys.

TREGORRAN, ANNA LOUISE (ANN)

b. 23 Sept. 1969

Anna-Louise was the much-wanted fruit of Carol and John Tregorran's union. Her proud godparents were Lady Isabel Lander, Jill Archer and Hugo Barnaby. She travelled with her peripatetic father, but returned to England for school, taking her O-levels in 1985.

TREGORRAN, CAROL (NÉE GREY AND FORMERLY GRENVILLE)

m. Charles Grenville 18 Sept. 1961; 1 son; m. John Tregorran 1 Feb. 1967; 1 dtr

In 1954 this glamorous lady from Surrey came to Ambridge, purchased a smallholding from Dan Archer (previously worked by his son Jack) and started tongues wagging. She drove her car round a bend and knocked John Tregorran off his scooter, giving him a bump on the head and an ache in his heart. He proposed marriage soon afterwards; she demurred. But their relationship was further strengthened when, while he was showing her a rare lizard-orchid one day, she was bitten by an adder and he was all tender concern.

Carol had attended agricultural college in Wye and turned the smallholding into a market garden. She was a demon for work, grubbing in the compost for the organic fruit and veg (though always, one felt, with immaculate fingernails) grown alongside beautiful freesias and chrysanthemums. But the work was hard. One day Dr Cavendish found her in tears among her plants. She was forced to employ help, first from Dan Archer's old hand Simon Cooper, then from Jack Archer. Over the years she gave work to a string of assistants, and the business flourished until, in association with George Fairbrother, she was able to expand it. She opened a farm shop with Ken Pound (despite running foul of the county planning office). She found time to organize the annual flower show and even managed to get Percy Thrower to judge in 1973. She became a member of the usual village societies, repre-

Peggy Archer (June Spencer), Carol Tregorran (Anne Cullen) and Nora Salt (Julia Mark)

senting the Ambridge WI at the Albert Hall.

It seemed as if she and John Tregorran were destined for each other. In his antique shop she saw a picture that shocked and mystified her. It showed a room that she felt she knew but she didn't know where it was or why she should respond so strongly to it. He untangled her past. Unbeknown to her she had been born to artists who were not married. The picture was of her home, painted by her mother Beatrix. When Carol was only two her parents had parted and she had been adopted by James Grey, her mother's cousin. A memory from babyhood had surfaced and John was there to hold her hand.

However, in 1959 Charles Grenville, a pow-erful businessman, bought Fairbrother's estate, including his share in the market garden. He asked Carol to play hostess for him one day after the defection of his housekeeper Mme Garonne. She was shocked when after the pre-prandial drinks, instead of inviting her to dine he sent her away. A bouquet of flowers helped to ease the hurt and to the amazement of all in 1961 she married him. Before the birth of their son Richard she was amused to discover that he had already put down his son's name for his old school.

America then started to play a fateful part in Carol's life. Charles went there on business and never returned. She joined him for a brief holiday and tried fruitlessly to prevent him from selling the Estate to Jack Woolley and Ralph Bellamy. He died there in 1965, leaving her the house and an annuity.

John Tregorran and the bereft Carol finally plighted their troth in 1967. It was a quiet wedding, witnessed by Jack Woolley and his wife Valerie. Carol sold her fine house to Jack, she and John moved into Manor Court and she bought back her old market garden and orchard.

John embarked on a long lecture tour of America two years later. Carol stayed at home. Their daughter Anna Louise was born in 1969. Life became calmer and she and John developed an interest in local wine growing. Plans were made to start a vineyard and in due course the light fruity Manor Court '76 appeared on the Grey Gables wine list at £4.20 (undercut by Sid Perks at the Bull for £2.10).

In 1974 Hugo Barnaby persuaded John to deputize for him on a lecture tour. Carol tried hard to dissuade her husband, but once more America beckoned. When her son Richard started pilfering at school she sent urgent pleas for John to return. But he took his time.

More stress was in store for her in 1976 when she was accused of shoplifting. Doris Archer thought that the problem was menopausal and she and her daughter Chris were called as character witnesses. Walter Gabriel carved her a lily as a symbol of innocence, prejudging Felpersham crown court's hearing at which the verdict was not guilty. The same year her manager Arthur Tovey was accidentally killed when an aluminium ladder he was carrying touched a power cable.

She was further disenchanted by John's behaviour when he allowed gypsies into the orchard. They overstayed their welcome. When he collaborated with Jennifer Aldridge on a local history project and their involvement with each other became a small scandal, Carol sent him back to America, with some relief, to organize antique fairs. This time she and the children joined him there.

1980 saw their return. Daughter Anna was enrolled at Kingsley House School and they took up village life again.

For a time Ambridge believed that John had resumed his affair with Jennifer but it was not the case and in 1990 the family moved to Bristol.

Anne Cullen

TREGORRAN, GWEN

Gwen Tregorran had been married to John Tregorran's brother Bernard until he was killed in a car crash, leaving her with their son Bobbie to rear on her own. John had helped her financially as much as he could, but in 1957 she arrived at Blossom Hill Cottage with some good news: she had met a man called Duncan Livsey and they were to be married. John was particularly pleased because it meant that he could now afford to buy Flavell's antique shop in Borchester.

Ann Kindred

TREGORRAN, JANET (NÉE SHELDON)

m. John Tregorran 29 June 1963; d. 31 Oct. 1963

Janet Sheldon was a pretty, blue-eyed district nurse who was wooed and won, in 1963, by John Tregorran soon after Carol Grey's marriage to Charles Grenville. The four became so friendly that Janet was married from the Grenville house; the reception was at the Bull. Only a few months later, Charles was driving her home to Blossom Hill Cottage after tea one day when the car crashed and she was killed.

Judy Parfitt

TREGORRAN, JOHN

m. Janet Sheldon 29 June 1963; m. Carol Grenville 1 Feb. 1967; 1 dtr

In 1954 a bearded young stranger was discovered living in a gypsy caravan on Heydon Berrow. John Tregorran had arrived suddenly and without explanation. The Ambridge grapevine was soon hard at work. When the Christmas Club money was stolen from the Bull, suspicion fell on him; and when one of the horses vanished from Clive Lawson-Hope's stables, Clive leapt to the conclusion that he had something to do with that too. He redeemed himself by retrieving a horse stolen by gypsies from Christine Archer, who had been giving him riding lessons. In revenge, the thieves destroyed his caravan. Anne Trentham suddenly realized that she had seen John before: he had been a lecturer at her university who, after a lucky win on the pools, had thrown up his job and taken to a life on the open road.

Christine and John became close friends. One day she showed him some ancient stones bored with holes in a field near Ambridge. John, who loved anything from the past, found them fascinating. He soon discovered that they were the remains of the original Manor House at Coombe Farm. The local farmers were furious that the surrounding fields had become sites for potential archaeological excavations.

Christine was only one of John's girl-friends. His other inamorata included Jane Maxwell and Grace Fairbrother. In 1955, John was literally bowled over by Carol Grey as she drove round a bend while he was riding his motor-scooter in the opposite direction. A few months later John proposed to Carol, only to be gently rebuffed. It would be 1967 when they eventually married. By then John was a widower. He married Janet Sheldon, the district nurse, in 1963, but she was killed months later in a crash involving a car driven by Charles Grenville.

John was always a bit of a showman. He organized country fairs, produced a mummers' play, played the harpsichord and appeared in the Ambridge Christmas revue, one year declaiming 'the Green Eye of the Little Yellow God' (as Nelson Gabriel was to do many years later.) John enjoyed cricket, bowls and whist. His ultimate acceptance by the village came in 1964 when he became a parish councillor.

John always enjoyed a drink, and over the years downed many a pint at the Bull with Walter Gabriel and his cronies. On one occasion in 1959 he was cautioned by PC Bryden for brewing beer at home without a licence. But no licence was necessary when he and Carol planted their own vineyard at Manor Court and produced their first vintage in 1976.

A generous man, John is remembered for several good turns. In 1956, when Walter

John's own past caught up with him when in 1967 he finally married Carol. She was by now Charles Grenville's widow, with a five-year-old son, Richard. In 1969, John and Carol's only child Anna Louise was born. The birth did little to cure John's wanderlust. Twice, during the early years of his marriage, he left his family behind and travelled round America lecturing on antiques. Carol was left to cope alone, first with the advances of John's cousin, Hugo Barnaby and secondly with problems caused by her son Richard.

The marriage became still rockier when John and Jennifer Aldridge collaborated on an historical land survey. They quickly became infatuated with one another and when Carol came home and found that Jennifer had taken over her kitchen, she saw red. John once more set off for America, where he sorted out his emotional priorities. He returned to Ambridge and to Carol. Then quickly and quietly he and the family moved to Bristol. All Ambridge has heard from them since is the odd Christmas card addressed to Brookfield.

Basil Jones; Philip Morant; Simon Lack; Basil Jones; John Bott; Roger Hume

John Tregorran (Philip Morant)

Gabriel suffered a reversal of fortune and reputation, it was John who bought him a new suit and encouraged him back into village life. He also helped his sister-in-law Gwen. When she remarried and no longer needed his financial support he was able to invest his spare cash in an antique shop and again indulge his passion for the past in the form of books, furniture and musical instruments.

TRENTHAM, ANN

Ann Trentham was the pretty cousin of Reggie Trentham. She had crushes on Phil Archer, with whom she enjoyed a Boxing Night party in 1953, and John Tregorran whom she thought she had seen somewhere before. Eventually she remembered that he had been a tutor at her university. She was lucky with neither.

Margaret Joynson

TRENTHAM, HAZEL

see Woolley, Hazel

TRENTHAM, REGGIE

*m. Valerie Grayson 21 Jan 1953; 1 dtr;
d. 1964*

Reggie Trentham was a bit of a cad. An excellent rider, he was not above betting on himself and cheating to win. A very good amateur boxer, he paid an old pro called Craggy Sims £1 an hour to teach him dirty tricks. A skilled cricketer, he fractured Jim Cornford's ribs with his wicked bowling. Mike Daly's life was made difficult by Reggie's feuding and false accusations.

He was not all bad. A director of the Country Club at Grey Gables, he was a generous host there. In 1952 he offered Phil Archer £2,000 so that Phil could propose to Grace Fairbrother but Phil wanted to make his own way. Dan Archer found his help invaluable when buying the horse Midnight for his daughter Christine's birthday. (He encouraged Chris in her riding career as much as he could.)

His wooing of Valerie Grayson, whom he had installed as hostess at the Country Club, was not at all smooth, but finally he won her. It was their intention to sell up and travel the world before having a family, but before they did so a daughter, Hazel Anne, was born. The family left Ambridge two years later, but in 1964 Valerie returned with their daughter after Reggie died in the Bahamas.

Peter Wilde

TRENTHAM, VALERIE

see Woolley, Valerie

TREVELYAN, SHEILA

Sheila was a one-time acquaintance of John Tregorran's who booked in at the Bull in 1958 to write a book on village life. She asked John to give her a job, becoming his assistant. To the amazement of John's friends she announced their engagement in October; but it was short-lived and she broke it off the following month when she started in vain pursuit of Tony Stobeman and then left. She completed her book, a satirical account of Ambridge and its inhabitants called *Glasshouse Village*, and returned in 1959 to see how it had been received. They claimed never to have heard of it.

Ann Kindred

TRING, ZEBEDEE

d. Christmas 1973

Zebedee Tring lived on his own, with his dog, Gyp, and a cat called Queenie. He could not abide women. A man of simple tastes, he was content to live off scrumpy and bread and cheese. He enjoyed gardening, and for three years worked at Arkwright Hall. Having retired, he became an odd-job man.

Zebedee died in his sleep just after Christmas in 1973. His only relatives, a cousin and her husband from Tewkesbury, attended his funeral.

Graham Rigby

TRUGG, MATTHEW

In 1958 an old shipmate of Doughy Hood's arrived unexpectedly in Ambridge and stayed in Doughy's spare room to Rita Flynne's disgust. Trugg didn't like Rita any more than she liked him. He told Doughy to get rid of her or he would let Clarice Conway know of Doughy's whereabouts. Doughy didn't yield, and Clarice arrived in pursuit of him. But Rita dealt with her, while Trugg got himself into trouble. He stole Jill Archer's handbag and foolishly tried to sell it to Ned Larkin in the Bull. PC Bryden was informed but took two days to make his move, by which time Matthew had made a hurried departure.

Lewis Gedge

TRUSCOTT, BEN

When Ben Truscott heard that Mary Weston, travelling farm secretary, had mentioned him in a talk she gave at the WI in 1974, he threatened to sue her for slander. Since he was a farmer at Penny Hassett and one of her clients, she feared that he might have a case against her. She wrote to apologize but he took this as an admission of guilt and became even more determined to proceed. Her solicitor advised her to suggest that he settle out of court, and Truscott asked for £250. Mary neatly turned the tables on him when she amassed written statements from those who had attended the meeting testifying that she had never spoken of him by name. He had no case and abandoned his suit.

Philip Morant

TUCKER, BETTY

b. 4 Aug. 1950; m. Mike Tucker 1972; 1 son, 1 dtr

Betty was born in 1950 and at the age of twenty-two married Mike Tucker. When he began working for Ambridge Farmers Ltd, the two of them lived contentedly at Rickyard Cottage, Betty helping out at Brookfield occasionally.

Betty came from a farming background, and in the years before she had children followed the traditional path of many farmer's wives, breeding sheepdogs (with little success) and keeping bees. But she was proudest of her goats. For many years, she supplied the local health food shop with milk and the Bull with cheese.

In 1978, Haydn Evans offered the Tuckers a partnership in the running of Willow Farm, and although this meant that her precious goats had to go, Betty was delighted. The early years at Willow Farm were perhaps her happiest. She and Mike had a small son Roy, they enjoyed village life and everything went well for them. When their daughter, Brenda, was born in 1981 it looked as if all was set fair.

But within two years of Brenda's birth, Haydn Evans decided to sell up and the Tuckers moved to the dark and unwelcoming farmhouse at Ambridge Farm. In her positive way Betty made the best of it; but then in 1986, Mike went bankrupt and they lost their home. Jennifer Aldridge offered to rent them a cottage and gave a desperate Betty a job as a cleaner. She caught Brian's eye – her vulnerability appealed to him – and he was

Mike and Betty Tucker (Terry Molloy and Pamela Craig)

soon paying her compliments and trying to seduce her. Betty fled. She told Mike, and with difficulty stopped him from attacking Brian. It came as a great relief when Matthew Thorogood, who now owned Willow Farm, was prepared to let the farmhouse to the Tuckers.

Doing her best to keep the family financially afloat, Betty worked wherever she could, cleaning for Lynda Snell, helping Nelson Gabriel sort out Honeysuckle Cottage and assisting Pat in the dairy at Bridge Farm. She jumped at the chance of a permanent job when Jack Woolley asked her to run the village shop. Mike was not happy about it, angry that his wife had to work and that her wage made such a difference. The fact that Betty enjoyed the work was even more humiliating for him. He became bitter and resentful. Betty did what she could to reassure him, but Mike sank deep into a mood of self-pity.

Betty believed that the only way they could own their own farm again was to buy property of their own and use it to raise capital. Without telling Mike, she applied for low-cost housing. This, coupled with his loss of an eye in a farming accident, was the last straw for Mike. He became unpredictable, depressed and aggressive. Sid Perks was so concerned that he walked Betty home from the Bull one day to find her kitchen wrecked.

She was so relieved to discover that escaped pigs were the culprits, not Mike, that she started to laugh. She turned to Sid for comfort and a cuddle and they became dangerously close, but her inner voice told her to resist temptation and the moment passed.

Matters didn't improve and just before Christmas 1991, threatened with violence from Mike, Betty took the children and left home for the Bull where Sid offered them rooms. On Christmas Day Mike was found alone sobbing uncontrollably and Betty was summoned to his rescue. She came at once, the family was reunited and finally Mike admitted that he needed psychiatric help. Slowly they began to rebuild their lives together.

Some good luck helped, in the shape of the compensation Mike received for his injury: £33,000. It was enough for a substantial deposit on a house and Betty was delighted. Mike wanted to use the money to invest in all sorts of unsuitable projects, which Betty advised against. She managed to persuade him that it was in their best interests to buy Willow farmhouse from Matthew. By spring 1993, for the first time in years the Tuckers could enjoy life again.

But April had a sting in its tail, in the form of a raid on the village shop. Clive Horrobin and his accomplice forced Betty at gun-point to hand over money and she was held hostage until they left. For weeks Betty was terrified by any sudden noise. Traumatized and in need of tender loving care, for once she had to lean on Mike and he supported her. Betty was not sure about continuing to work at the shop, but realized that until Mike's market garden was providing enough for both of them, she had no other choice.

Betty has been a mainstay of village life and will always lend a hand where she can. She still helps in the Bull in an emergency. She has been a lively member of the WI and a parish councillor, and also played in the ladies' football team. She has encouraged her children Roy and Brenda to get involved too: Roy is a member of the cricket team and Brenda a keen participant in amateur dramatics. Betty is above all a hard worker, happiest when she is busiest, and even now, in her middle forties, she finds it hard to slow down.

Pamela Craig

TUCKER, BRENDA

b. 21 Jan. 1981

Now in her teens, Brenda Tucker played as a little girl with her 'My Little Pony' castle and dreamed of growing up to be Kylie Minogue; but at the age of eight her dreams faded fast as she faced up to the appalling reality of her father Mike's arson attempts and near-suicidal depression. The added shock of his accidental loss of an eye must have made Brenda wonder what life was about.

Brenda played with fire herself for a while when in 1992 she became entangled with the Blossom Hill gang, of which the street-wise Kate Aldridge was the leader. Sensibly, however, she soon got fed up with their destructive company and developed a healthy interest in dressing-up, especially for the Battle of Hassett Bridge, re-enacted by the Sealed Knot at Lower Loxley Hall.

Helen Cutler

TUCKER, MIKE

b. 1 Dec. 1949; m. Betty 1972; 1 son, 1 dtr

On the one hand, it could be said that Mike Tucker has had more than his fair share of bad luck to contend with over the years. On the other, he has always had the tendency to blame others for his problems.

When Mike, with his wife Betty, arrived in Ambridge in 1973 as the new dairy unit manager for Ambridge Farmers Ltd, the future looked promising for them. A strong union man, he soon called a meeting in the Bull, to revive the local NUAAW and got himself elected secretary. When Joby Woodford fell through a loft ceiling at Brookfield, it was thanks to Mike that he got compensation.

Mike and Betty lived in Rickyard Cottage, and in the village he was happy to work and play hard. A game of darts, a pint or two, the odd game of cricket in the sunshine was all he desired – as well, of course, as a dutiful wife at home to cater to his every need.

Betty wanted a family, but Mike preferred things as they were. When she announced that she was pregnant in 1977 he was furious, and accused her of secretly coming off the pill. But he soon came round to the idea of fatherhood. And when Haydn Evans offered him the rental of Willow Farm, he was full of confidence in the future.

Having little capital of his own, he needed a hefty loan in order to set himself up. Haydn was initially disappointed with Mike. He wanted Willow Farm to be fully worked as a dairy, not just doing contract milking, and he was angry when Mike thoughtlessly cut down all the willow trees. Why else, he reasoned, had it been named Willow Farm? But Mike didn't care. He was expanding his business, and the retirement of a nearby farmer Des Drayton enabled him to buy his herd of Ayrshires (an unusual breed in the area). Having installed a bottling plant at the farm, he had now become a true dairy farmer in his own right, with his own milk round.

Mike now had a baby son, Roy, and with Betty's help was steadily improving his business. In 1980, Betty became pregnant again. He was pleased, and also proud to win first prize and the princely sum of £10 for one of his Ayrshires at the Borchester show. Early in 1981, little Brenda was born. Mike felt he hadn't a care in the world. He was a heavy smoker and drinker at this time, usually in the company of Tony Archer. Their wives could keep each other company, so 'what the hell?' was his attitude.

Then after nine relatively untroubled years of farming, things started to go wrong for Mike. The vet called round to do the three-year test on his herd. One cow was found to have bovine tuberculosis. It had to be slaughtered and the herd put into quarantine. It turned out that a cow Mike had bought at a dispersal sale the previous September had been the source of the disease. Four more cows had to be slaughtered, a costly business, but by the end of the year his herd had been cleared.

But problems were mounting for the Tuckers. Haydn Evans decided to sell Willow Farm, but, luckily, Ambridge Farm was vacant at the time, and the Tuckers moved lock, stock and barrel and became tenants of the Berrow Estate. In the next two years, Mike was severely under-capitalized, the milk yielded little ready cash and the size of his overdraft became alarming. In 1985, his whole world fell apart. He post-dated a cheque for £1,000 which bounced and the bank called in his £18,000 loan. He lost everything: stock, machinery, plant. Mike Tucker, aged thirty-six, with a wife and two children, was declared bankrupt.

Mike felt humiliated and bitter. As a union man he'd spoken his mind, people had listened, looked up to him. Now all that had gone. For a time the family stayed at the Bull; then they moved into one of the Home Farm cottages. By 1988 Matthew Thorogood had bought Willow Farm and was happy to lease it to the Tuckers (on condition that they would have to leave if he found a buyer; Mike felt certain that the execrable pong from Neil Carter's adjacent porkers would keep prospective purchasers away). Mike, Betty and the children moved back, as tenants, to the farm they had been partners in six years earlier.

Betty, much against Mike's wishes, took a job cleaning at Home Farm. Both children were at school now, and they needed every penny. Mike's male pride was hurt when she took a job at the village shop. Despite Betty's long hours, he expected her to answer to his every whim. Mike, it seemed, had begun to generate his own bad luck.

Cameron Fraser began to employ Mike fairly regularly on his estate, and, while he was silaging in May 1991, when Jim Ascott started the tractor before its pickup hitch was secured, the hydraulic pipe linking tractor and trailer snapped under the strain and one end caught Mike in the eye. Shula Hebden was near by, inspecting the Estate, and rushed Mike to Borchester General Hospital. Mike's retina had become detached, and he was now blind in one eye.

He took it badly, spending more and more time at the Bull, getting into arguments and even a drunken fight with Tony Archer, one of his few friends. Betty pleaded with him to get professional help, but he wouldn't even go to Matthew Thorogood.

At the end of 1991, Jim Ascott retired, and wanted to rent out his land. Mike jumped at the chance: sheep would be the answer to all his problems. He begged Betty for the last of her savings. But Jim changed his mind, and went for set-aside instead. Something in Mike gave way. Stumbling madly across Jim Ascott's field he headed towards the barn with a can of petrol. Just as he was about to light the match, he was seen by Eddie Grundy, who persuaded Mike to hand over the petrol and the matches.

He still continued to rage. Betty, beginning to fear for her safety and that of the children, left to stay at the Bull, leaving Mike alone at the farmhouse.

On Christmas Day, Kathy Perks bravely visited him. He was a broken man, and wept for his wife and kids. Betty came back to him and comforted him. She made Mike promise that, now, he would seek medical help.

In the New Year of 1992, Mike and Betty began to pick up the pieces. Many people rallied round to help: the vicar, the doctor, the psychiatric nurse. He was given work at Hollowtree, and a share in Neil's egg business, mostly out of kindness, and he began doing the milk round once more. He started to feel lucky again.

Then he received a sum of money in compensation for his eye injury: not the huge figure he had boasted about, but a tidy sum nonetheless, £33,000. He wildly planned all manner of extravagant schemes: a time-share in Spain, a car valeting service. Betty put her foot down. She wanted a house, a home for the family to call their own.

In 1993 Matthew Thorogood decided to sell the house at Willow Farm. Mike and Betty could afford a mortgage on it, but only if Matthew would agree to sell at a reduced price. Matthew, who was leaving Ambridge, and knew how much it meant to the Tuckers, sold to them.

Mike has developed a market garden selling organic fruit and vegetables in the Bridge Farm shop and the organic co-op. With the purchase of Neil's hens he has been able to add his own eggs to the other products on his expanding milk round. At long last the Tuckers have a home of their own and are taking advantage of the chance to make a fresh start.

Gareth Armstrong; Alexander Wilson; Terry Molloy

Tucker, Roy

b. 2 Feb. 1978

Born in 1978, Roy Tucker is intolerant of his father Mike's weaknesses. He is an academically bright, independent boy, mad on pop music and crazy about Aston Villa FC. He has recently become a regular player in the Ambridge cricket team.

Tuckworth, Miranda

In 1990 Caroline Bone had just started going out with the new owner of the Berrow Estate, Cameron Fraser. Cameron lived at the Dower House, and when she called one day and found Miranda Tuckworth there, clearly very much at home, she leaped to the conclusion that she was his girlfriend. In fact, Miranda was the interior designer he had called in to help with redecorating the Dower House.

Tucson, Wayne

Eddie Grundy's friend Wayne Tucson worked as a baker, but preferred to think of himself as a Country and Western star. In 1985 he astonished Eddie by saying that he wanted to get married but the fact that his girlfriend Jolene Rogers was six months' pregnant may have had something to do with it. The couple planned to move into one of the starter homes on the Chestnuts Estate. Their daughter was born in June and they called her Fallon. Unsurprisingly her parents split up soon afterwards.

Turner, Clive

When his assistant, Peggy Archer, returned from a cruise in April 1974, Jack Woolley couldn't wait to take her out to dinner. He was not so pleased when Clive Turner, a widower she had met on the ship, arrived at Grey Gables to return a book he had borrowed.

TURVEY, AGATHA ERMYNTRUDE

d. Mar. 1976

Mrs Turvey was a widow with a commanding presence, who lived in Ambridge for some years with her companion Emily Tarbutt. Tom Forrest did an occasional job for her – a kindly gesture on his part which unfortunately she misconstrued, and she would use any excuse to summon him to her side. There was much sniggering in the Bull and Tom, highly embarrassed, tried to avoid her with varying degrees of success.

She could alarm Walter Gabriel too, but theirs was a love-hate relationship. In 1965 he was the only one to remember her birthday. He did, however, take a secret pleasure in annoying her whenever possible. He bought Parson's Field, which adjoined her garden, and filled it with pigs. When she objected he started breeding maggots, until John Treggoran had a word with him and they were removed. Despite this, in 1961, she and Walter shared a short-lived business partnership in a pet shop in Hollerton. She bought him out two years later.

In 1976 she went out too soon after an attack of flu and contracted pleurisy. She died in March, and left her house and contents to Emily Tarbutt.

Courtney Hope

TWELVETREES, MRS

When Walter Gabriel used a real parrot playing Long John Silver in the vicar's production of *Treasure Island* in 1964, it delighted the audience. Whether Mrs Twelvetrees was equally delighted to receive the parrot as a present after the production is unrecorded.

TYRELL, TOM

Tom Tyrell was a councillor, a JP and a friend of Jack Woolley's. As proprietor of *The Borchester Echo* Jack had some control over its contents, and in 1977 he tried to suppress an article written by the editor, Simon Parker, hinting that Tyrell was guilty of misconduct on the housing committee. While he did not permit his own building firm to put in tenders for work, he was open to bribes from other firms anxious to get sub-contracting jobs. Woolley forced Parker's resignation but had to reinstate him when Tyrrell resigned from the Borchester council, thus justifying Parker's attack.

U V

UNDERWOOD, DEIRDRE

Deirdre Underwood and her mother were tenants of Hollowtree Flats when she first met Tony Archer. She was twenty-five, attractive and well-off, and when she asked him to spend a week with her in Wales in 1972, Tony was tempted. In the end he turned her down as his mind was too full of Jane Petrie.

Eileen Barry

VET

see Gascoine, Jim; Lambert, Martin; Robertson, Bill; Robertson, Ian; Stokes, Robin

VICAR

The vicar of Ambridge left to take up a cathedral post in the autumn of 1951. He played an excellent game of tennis but his first love was books, and he was usually found with his head buried in an abstruse Latin or Greek tome. He was a pleasant man and well liked, but churchgoers in the district hoped that a more forceful personality would take his place.

Ronald Baddiley

see also Adamson, Richard; Buckle, Jeremy; Latimer, David; Ridley, John; Stokes, Robin; Wreford, Matthew

VILLAGE HALL

The Ambridge village hall was set up as a charitable trust with the parish council as trustees, managed by a committee of twelve including representatives from the local organizations using the hall. It was always well supported.

In 1976 an electrical fault caused a fire which badly damaged the building, and it was decided to use the insurance money to convert the former village school into a new hall. The council agreed the plan and the villagers were so enthusiastic that the work was completed by Christmas.

In 1992 Marjorie Antrobus booked the

hall for a nostalgic wartime Christmas concert called *Tickety Boo*, which attracted such a large audience that the licensing officer got to hear about it, asked to inspect the hall and discovered several shortcomings. He told Christine Barford that as licensee she was responsible for all transgressions under the terms of the entertainments licence. Christine immediately panicked and shut down the hall until she could get matters sorted out. It was a drastic measure but had the advantage of awakening village interest. The villagers rallied round, headed by Lynda Snell, who even managed to get television personality Anneka Rice involved. Funds were raised, the necessary repairs were made and finally, to Christine's relief, the hall could safely be reopened.

VYCE, DR ALOYSIUS

Dr Vyce was a shareholder with John Tregorran in the 'Health by Nature' home founded by Dr Cavendish at Manor House in 1955.

Lewis Gedge

WAINWRIGHT, HORACE

Alderman Horace Wainwright was the chairman of the Borchester highways and bridges committee in 1975 when Jill Archer became involved in campaigning for a permanent gypsy site in the area.

The Borchester Echo featured an article in which Horace Wainwright supported the campaign, but even so Jill felt that he had no real sympathy for the plight of the gypsies and that his motives were political. In the event the campaign proved unsuccessful.

WAKEFIELD, FRED

Phil Archer offered Fred Wakefield a job with Ambridge Farmers Ltd in 1976. He used to work at a Hollerton factory and had been made redundant; he also had experience of farm work and proved a useful addition to the staff at Brookfield.

WALKER, MR

In 1976 Mr Walker of Drybank Farm offered Betty Tucker a fixed price for her goats' milk which he would then supply directly to a health food shop.

WALKER, MR AND MRS

Heavily pregnant with Alice in February 1988, Jennifer Aldridge needed someone to help with the cleaning. Mr Walker from Penny Hassett, whom the Aldridges employed as their gardener, suggested that his wife might help them out. She had cleaned for Lady Lockheart at Hassett Hill Manor for twenty-five years until the old lady went into a home, and she also cleaned for Mandy Beesborough. The formidable Mrs Walker gave the matter due consideration and thought she might be able to add one more to her list of clients. She interviewed Jennifer carefully, wasn't too impressed with her c.v., but felt that if Jennifer understood her rules right from the start they might manage to get on. She could give Jennifer only two mornings a week; she wouldn't lift anything heavy, or do landings, ceilings or grates; ironing was extra; and she wouldn't babysit, make beds or load the dishwasher. It says much for Jennifer's state of mind that she was overjoyed and engaged her on the spot.

Mrs Walker arrived like a whirlwind on her moped the following Monday and proceeded to put Home Farm in order. She was bossy but efficient and Jennifer soon learned to have her cup of Camp coffee and a gypsy biscuit ready at ten thirty sharp. Her bark was worse than her bite; although she said she never did overtime she did help Jennifer prepare for a dinner party on one occasion, and showed her how to dress a crab. However, Jennifer was a disappointment to her and not really what she was used to. She started to clean for Nigel Pargetter at Lower Loxley, which was much more in her style, and to Jennifer's great annoyance reduced her cleaning hours at Home Farm in order to fit in extra time for Nigel. She took umbrage when Brian Aldridge got in the way as she tried to dust his study, gave a week's notice and bounced off into the sunset on her moped. She got her come-uppance from the Pargetters when Nigel's mother Julia returned to Lower Loxley and replaced her with another treasure three years later.

Gillian Goodman

WALTON, SAMANTHA

A gentle presence in the midst of the chaos at Grange Farm, Samantha Walton came to help Clarrie Grundy look after her children in 1985.

Their mothers had been friends, and Clarrie remembered babysitting for Samantha when she was five. Now Samantha was studying to become a nanny and her two weeks at Grange Farm formed part of her work experience.

She worked hard and kept to herself, playing classical music on her guitar, and was dismayed when Eddie Grundy made advances towards her. He recovered his senses after she saved their son William from choking and bought Samantha a brooch shaped like a piglet as both a thank-you present and a souvenir of her time with them – a time she was unlikely to forget.

Dionne Inman

WARNER, BENJAMIN ALFRED (BEN)

Ben Warner slipped into Ambridge in 1982. In his forties with a chipped tooth and shaven head, and wearing a kaftan, this strange misfit set the village buzzing. To most people he was aggressive and unapproachable, but both Jackie Woodstock and Shula Archer found themselves drawn towards him for a while, being so unlike any other man they had ever encountered. But generally this loner caused feelings of unease and distrust.

Whether collecting fungus, berries or wood, Ben cared little for the law against trespass. There had been a spate of local burglaries and all eyes looked towards Ben. Early in 1983 Shula disturbed him while he was stealing from Blossom Hill Cottage. He was arrested, pleaded guilty to five counts of burglary and went to prison. Ambridge was better off without him.

Don Henderson

Warren

Warren was one of Kate Aldridge's first unsuitable boyfriends who took her drinking in Borchester clubs. They had a minor crash driving a stolen Alfa Romeo in 1992. They both ran away hoping the police wouldn't hear about it. In the heat of the moment Kate forgot that she had earlier locked William Grundy in Blossom Hill Cottage. When the police became involved in the search for him they questioned Kate and the story came out. Inevitably Warren was soon involved in their enquiries, convinced that she had grassed on him. He was fined and put on probation for twelve months. Kate's parents forbade him to see her again.

Warren, Sue

Shula Archer and Sue Warren were schoolfriends, but their friendship became strained when in 1976 Shula thought that her boyfriend, Bill Morris, was seeing Sue. The girls went their separate ways when Sue left to study at Manchester university, later marrying Godfrey Wendover's son in 1988.

Waters, Bobby

Bobby Waters was an energetic, hard-working farmer who managed Ralph Bellamy's dairy units in 1972. The units comprised Sawyer's Farm and Heydon Farm, where Bobby and his wife Jessie lived, and were retained when Bellamy created the Berrow Estate in 1975.

That same year he had an accident in one of the milking parlours but the damage proved to be muscular, and after a long convalescence he recovered fully.

Alaric Cotter

Waters, Minnie

In 1966 Minnie was employed at the Bull as temporary barmaid.

Brenda Dunrich

Watson, Fiona

When Ralph Bellamy employed Fiona Watson as shepherdess to his 800 sheep, she refused to accept the job description – she was as much a shepherd, she insisted, as any man. She replaced Len Thomas, with whom the contrast could hardly have been greater. She came from a professional family, her father being a solicitor and her brother a student at Cambridge. She lived happily in an estate flat for three years working hard and enjoying flirtations with Tony Archer and Hugo Barnaby, but told Bellamy in 1970 that she was engaged to a farm manager. When they married soon after, they moved away from Ambridge.

Carole Boyd

Watson, Frank

When *The Borchester Echo* ran a competition to find the best publican of 1977, Frank Watson of the George, Borchester, won first prize.

WATSON, MR

Mr Watson was partner in Rodway & Watson estate agents, where Shula Archer worked from 1976. She was not always grateful for his advice and almost challenged him to sack her when he rebuked her for accepting an offer on a cottage too readily. He didn't rise to the bait, and thought sufficiently well of her to buy her a brooch of a horse for her twentieth birthday.

Patrick Connor

WEARING, NICK

Nick Wearing was nineteen when he first came to Ambridge in 1978 for a year's work on a farm before possibly going to agricultural college. His father, an old friend of Phil Archer's, was a wealthy landowner who hoped that one day his son would run his estate; but as yet Nick had shown few signs of interest. It was arranged that he would start work at Bridge Farm, where he lodged for a few weeks before moving in with Neil Carter at Nightingale Farm.

Tall, good-looking, with a light-hearted attitude to life, Nick was the answer to a maiden's prayer as far as Eva Lenz, au pair at Home Farm, was concerned. The Aldridges were less delighted when he broke her bedroom window trying to wake her for a spot of badger-watching. He went out with Eva for a while longer, but he had a low boredom threshold, and was soon pursuing Shula Archer.

He enjoyed himself in Ambridge but decided that farming was too much like hard work. He joined Shula on her overland trip to New Zealand in 1979, leaving her at Bangkok and flying on to Australia to explore new horizons there.

Gareth Johnson

WELDON, MISS

Miss Weldon was the child care officer who visited Tom and Pru Forrest in 1960 to discuss with them the possibility of fostering a child.

Margaret Joynson

WELLS, DAVID

When Jack Woolley held a shooting party in 1976 he invited David Wells, a financial consultant, from London. Although Wells looked the part, he'd never attended a shoot before and from Jack's point of view the day was a waste of time.

Alan Devereux

WENDOVER, GODFREY

When Peggy Archer arrived at the Bull with a ship in a bottle, one summer in 1988, landlord Sid Perks sensed that something was going on. When she turned up a week later with an old ship's bell, he knew that matters had become serious.

In fact, Peggy had struck up a friendship with widower Godfrey Wendover, one time commanding officer in the Royal Navy. He lived in one of the barn conversions on the

Berrow Estate managed by Rodway & Watson, and he and Peggy had met through her work there. When he rang up to discuss problems with the wiring Peggy answered the phone, and sparks flew. She visited him to see what she could do to help, and two days later they visited the Three Counties show together.

Godfrey brought a nautical dash to Peggy's life that enchanted her. For a while she became infatuated with both him and anything to do with the sea. They made an odd couple at the village fête when they manned the treasure island stall dressed up as pirates. Peggy's children became alarmed that Godfrey's intentions were serious: they were convinced that he was after their mother's money. But he confounded them all when Peggy was offered three quarters of a million pounds for the Bull and he advised her not to sell.

The romance waned when it emerged that Godfrey did not share Peggy's love of animals. When he took her out for a belated birthday celebration in 1989, he made the fatal error of laughing when she talked about entering her cat Sammy for the Midland Counties cat show. After that it was simply a matter of time: Godfrey soon faded from her life.

W EST, DAVID

Phil Archer persuaded George Fairbrother to take West on as full time farmworker in 1956.

Ralph Hallett

W ESTMINSTER, DUKE OF

A month before the Borsetshire NSPCC centenary fashion show was due to be held there in June 1984, Redgate Manor burnt down. Jack Woolley prevailed on Caroline Bone to use her influence with Lord Netherbourne, chairman of the centenary committee, to transfer the event to Grey Gables. Which she did; and he was highly delighted when she revealed that the Duke of Westminster, patron of the centenary appeal, would be present. The Duke spoke at the event on behalf of the Society and its appeal. Caroline rose still further in Jack's estimation when he found that she was an old friend of the Duke's.

W ESTON, MARY

There was a touch of the Cinderella story about Mary Weston's entry into Tony Archer's life in 1973. Tony met her at a Young Farmers' dance and thought she was entrancing; but since he didn't know her surname, he couldn't get in touch with her again. A month later she arrived at Willow Farm in her capacity as travelling farm secretary to help him with his paperwork, and this time he made sure he didn't lose her. After a whirlwind courtship they became engaged and were set to be married in July. Then things started to go wrong: they were late for their own engagement party, Mary lost her ring, there was a muddle over honeymoon dates and they had to postpone the wedding. They began to see less of each other, and it was not a surprise when Mary wrote to Tony from her holiday in Majorca breaking their engagement. She married her boss, Mr Seymour, shortly afterwards. Maybe Tony had a lucky escape, for by 1983 Mary was described locally as 'a pillar of the Little Croxley WI'.

Catherine Crutchley

WHARBURTON, FLT. LT. CHARLES

When a jet plane crashed near Five Acre Field at Brookfield in 1952, Charles Wharburton was put in charge of salvage operations. After he and Dan Archer discussed the compensation to which Dan was entitled, he met Mrs P. when she came to view the wreckage with Walter Gabriel. He thought she was a fine figure of a woman and accepted eagerly when she invited him back to her cottage for a cup of tea. Once there he fanned the flames of Walter's jealousy by altering the aerial on her TV set to give her a better picture.

Wharburton's son Jimmy was staying with his uncle and aunt, but he wanted to be near his father and ran away. It was settled that he should stay with Mrs P. until Wharburton could get leave and take him on holiday. Jimmy wanted to take Mrs P. with them, and for a moment she was tempted; but to the regret of both Wharburtons she put duty before pleasure and remained in Ambridge.

Harry Stubbs

WHIPPLE, SAMMY AND JOAN

Brian Aldridge employed Sammy Whipple as shepherd on Home Farm soon after buying it in 1975, and he and his wife, Joan, have been there ever since. Apart from a tense period when Jennifer was trying to manage while Brian was unwell, he has remained generally in the background, very much an accepted part of the farm scene.

WHITE, BEN

Ben was the Ambridge baker in 1952. The quality of both his bread and his manner left much to be desired: he was awkward and aggressive, and once nearly got run over when he stepped off the pavement to avoid Walter Gabriel. He annoyed Squire Lawson-Hope when he started a campaign for the felling of his elms, and irritated George Fairbrother by informing the police when he shot a racing pigeon. He was unscrupulous when it served his purpose and in 1953 was forced to resign his position as clerk of the parish council when it emerged that he hadn't noted an instruction to make further enquiries about a housing scheme. This was because the scheme required compulsory purchase of an acre of land which he owned near Lakey Lane. In 1956 he sold the bakery to his former apprentice Doughy Hood.

Will Kings

WHITE, HARRY

Harry White was the son of Jim White who had worked on the Lawson-Hope Estate for many years. In 1962, nineteen and ripe for mischief, Harry was involved in a robbery at the Grenvilles; when he found a packet of love letters written by John Tregorran to Carol Grenville he demanded £200 from Carol for their return. Carol told her husband Charles all about the letters and they enlisted the help of PC Dryden, who arrested Harry and his accomplice Chuck Ballard when they picked up the money.

Gordon Walters

WHITE, HAZEL

When Hazel White met Jimmy Grange at Borchester Tech in 1960, for her it was love at first sight. Their relationship didn't last: Jimmy wasn't ready for steady relationships. Hazel just put it down to experience.

Mary Chester

WHITE, MR AND MRS

Jim White was taken on by the Lawson-Hope Estate in 1949 and remained there until the breakup of the Estate in 1975.

Jim White; Edgar Harrison; and Elspeth Duxbury

WHITE, MARTIN

Tony Archer employed Martin White to help at Bridge Farm in 1979. Soon after starting, he persuaded Tony to let him take his paid holiday immediately – a concession Tony soon regretted, for Martin never returned.

WHITWORTH, JUNE

Miss Oglethorpe started the rumours in 1958 about Paul Johnson's relationship with his secretary, June Whitworth, after seeing his car parked at night outside her house in Borchester. Paul laughed it off, but his wife Christine was not amused. One night she confronted them there, only to find that they were working late as Paul had claimed.

Judith Hackett

WILLIAMS, GEOFF

The farm manager on the Berrow Estate prosecuted in the health and safety case brought against him by Mike Tucker, who lost an eye in an industrial accident in 1991.

WILLIAMS, GEORGE

National Farmers' Union secretary who proposed Phil Archer as a magistrate in 1976.

WILLOW FARM

Willow Farm was bought by Welsh farmer Haydn Evans for his son Gwyn in 1972. A year later Tony Archer went into partnership with him. When Tony moved to Bridge Farm in 1978 Mike Tucker took over the partnership but had to move on after Haydn sold up in 1983. The land was divided between Brookfield and Home Farm, with Bill Insley buying the farmhouse, outbuildings and 15 acres. He rented an old barn and outbuildings to Neil Carter for his pigs and battery hens, and when he died in 1986 he left Neil the outbuildings and 8 acres of land.

The Tuckers returned to rent the farmhouse in 1988, but it was eventually bought by Matthew Thorogood as an investment – not a very good one as it turned out. By 1993 Matthew was finding it so difficult to sell the property that he had to sell the farmhouse and land separately, and accepted Mike Tucker's offer to buy the farmhouse. The remaining 7 acres were bought by Phil Archer.

After the trauma of their bankruptcy at Ambridge Farm, Mike and Betty Tucker felt that they had been given a second chance. Mike was happy to be farming again even on a small scale. He rented land from Neil and developed an organic market garden, growing ever more exotic vegetables. They heard from the Soil Association that they could call themselves officially organic on 22 July 1993.

WILLS, BRUNO

Bruno Wills was one of the raiders (with Clive Horrobin) of the village shop in 1993. He evaded arrest and when caught would not admit his guilt. He was eventually positively identified and convicted, much to the relief of the village.

Matthew Morgan

WILSON, JEAN

When in 1977 Shula Archer went out with Steve Robinson, manager of a travel agency in Borchester, she got to know Maggie Price and Jean Wilson who worked for him. She was shocked when Jean told her that she was pregnant with Steve's child, and that he had refused to help her. Shula could do nothing for Jean, but she immediately stopped seeing Steve.

Jean Doughty

WILSON, JUDY

When Laura Archer died in 1985 she left her will unsigned, so Phil Archer advertised in New Zealand newspapers for her next of kin. The only response was from Judy Wilson, Laura's younger brother's granddaughter – her great-niece. She inherited Ambridge Hall, which she sold, displacing Colonel Danby. In 1993 Phil and Jill Archer were surprised to receive a wedding invitation from her and went to Sydney, Australia, for the ceremony.

WILSON, LAURA

see Archer, Laura

WILSON, MR AND MRS

Sid and Polly Perks were impressed with the Wilsons, who wanted to rent Rose Cottage in 1977. They needed somewhere peaceful to stay for six months while Mr Wilson carried out work in the area related to his business.

WINSTON

Rosemary Tarrant gave the name Winston to the injured terrier she found in 1989. Neither she nor her father Nelson Gabriel managed to control him, however; and after a series of incidents, including an attack on Joe Grundy and a chase after Tony Archer's heifers, the dog had to be put down. Nelson buried him in the garden of Honeysuckle Cottage under a cairn of stones.

WINSTANLEY, BRIGADIER

Brigadier Winstanley was the last of his name to own one of the large estates near Ambridge. He was a vigorous and generous landlord, full of opinions and advice on both farming and family matters to his tenant Greg Salt.

His favourite pursuits were hunting and shooting. He and Bellamy were joint masters of the hunt. His life was changed dramatically when early in 1969 anti-hunt demonstrators disturbed his horse and he fell, breaking his ribs and injuring a knee. His niece Lady Isabel Lander came to tend him. He decided that he had had enough of the estate and bequeathed it to her, withdrawing himself entirely from its management and refusing even to give advice when she asked for it.

Two years after his injury he fell again at the hunt, but this time his injuries proved fatal.

Godfrey Baseley

WINTER, SILAS

b. 1898; d. pre 1983

Silas Winter had an affair with Mary Pound, and may well have been her daughter Marilyn's real father.

WOGAN, TERRY

After losing his way several times, Terry Wogan eventually found the Grey Gables golf course where he was due to play a celebrity match in 1989. Pru Forrest greeted him with warm words of welcome and a pot of damson jam, and Jack Woolley thought him worthy of the Royal Garden suite. He played an excellent match, and left Ambridge with some regret.

WOODBINE COTTAGE

Woodbine Cottage was long associated with the Larkin family. Ambridge Farmers Ltd had bought the cottage from Ralph Bellamy and it was let to Mabel and Ned Larkin in 1966. After Ned's death in 1967 his son Jethro, with his wife Lizzie and their daughters Clarrie and Rosie, moved in from Rickyard Cottage.

Phil Archer let the cottage to Bert and Freda Fry in 1988. He was annoyed when, a year later, he wanted to give it to his son and daughter-in-law, David and Ruth, and the Frys refused to move. Bert felt that he had a duty to protect his image, as he had become an overnight celebrity after the publication of his country sayings in *The Borchester Echo:* he had been photographed outside Woodbine Cottage and he knew that that was where his followers would expect to find him. Phil gave up and the Frys are still there.

WOODFORD, JOBY

m. Martha Lily 25 Dec. 1972; d. 7 Jan 1983

Joby Woodford arrived in Ambridge in 1967 as a forestry expert. He was a master of woodwork, and made rustic furniture in his spare time, which he sold with great success at the local garden centre. He was forever sawing, planing, driving in screws or nails for the people of the village, whether it was scenery for plays or sockets for the football posts. His proudest moment was when he heard Dan Archer's speech of thanks when he made and donated the new wooden shelter on the green in aid of the Jubilee commemorations.

In 1972 Joby proposed to widowed Martha and they were married in church on Christmas Day. At once, Joby put his foot down: no wife of his would have to work on petrol pumps or clean other people's houses, but a part-time job working in the village shop would be fine.

During their first years together, Joby and Martha, too old to have children of their own, agreed to provide a home for Neil

left to right: Canon Meridrew (Norman Shelley), Tom Forrest (Bob Arnold), Joby Woodford (George Woolley), Jack Woolley (Philip Garston-Jones), Mrs Perkins (Pauline Seville), Martha Woodford (Mollie Harris) and Walter Gabriel (Chriss Gittins)

Carter, a young apprentice shortly to work for Ambridge Farmers Ltd. They stood by him in 1974 when he was charged (falsely as it turned out) with possession of drugs. He was found guilty and placed on probation, but Joby and Martha's understanding saw him through this time until he felt he could cope on his own and moved out.

It was only in the last few years of Joby's life that the village learned that he couldn't read. He had broken his arm whilst tree-felling and was helping Martha in the shop while it mended when Doris Archer came in to buy a card for Tom Forrest's birthday. As she had left her glasses at home she asked Joby to read the message for her. With barely a pause he made up a rhyme and pretended to read it out; she liked it so much that she bought the card. In fact the real verse was about big-headedness, which didn't please Tom one bit, and when Dan found out what had happened, Joby's secret was revealed.

He enrolled at Borchester Technical College, and with the skilled teaching of young Miss Kinshull and plenty of encouragement from his friends, he mastered the basics of literacy. Indeed, he became something of a crossword fanatic. For five happy years, Joby enjoyed reading. Suddenly, at the end of the first week in January 1983, he collapsed and died in the village shop.

Joby had little formal education, like so many of his generation, but he did have a complete understanding of the countryside, of forestry and estate management, and he was a craftsman. He was, too, a man of principle. And, above all other things, he loved his wife, Martha.

George Woolley

WOODFORD, MARTHA (FORMERLY LILY)

b. 31 July 1922; m. Joby Woodford 25 Dec. 1972

Martha was the widow of Herbert Lily, the postman at Penny Hassett, and, after the death of her baby son, she came to Ambridge to work in the Field Studies Centre at Arkwright Hall. It wasn't long before she had a row with Zebedee Tring and was given the sack, and she worked for over a year as a cleaner before becoming pump attendant at the garage owned by Ralph Bellamy. By then she had met Joby Woodford and in early December 1972 accepted his proposal. They were married on Christmas Day. Mrs P. was matron of honour and Canon Meridew presided. She and Joby were to be happily married for over ten years.

Joby didn't want Martha to work full-time, but was happy for her to help out at the village shop. Then Angela Cooper, the shop's manager, eloped with her boyfriend, and Jack Woolley persuaded Martha to take her place. It was a while before she was qualified to run the post office side of the shop, but she succeeded in the end. Soon, the business expanded, with home deliveries, papers on sale and even, to Sid Perks' annoyance, an off-licence. Joby wasn't too pleased either, when Jack persuaded Martha to stay open in the evenings. After all, he reasoned, who was to cook his dinners? Life passed more or less tranquilly, until in 1983 Joby collapsed and died while helping Martha with the stock-taking. She was stunned and bewildered: Joby had to all appearances been as fit as a fiddle. Heartbroken, she sought comfort from Ivy, a spiritualist medium, but without success.

An attractive, mature widow such as Martha is bound to have an appeal to such mature widowers as Joe Grundy and Bill Insley, who by 1984 were in hot pursuit. Nothing was too much trouble: each eagerly vied with the other with helpful jobs and thoughtful favours. Throbbing wires must have crossed, though, when Martha was presented with two bird tables, one from each. After a dinner à trois at Martha's, Mrs Perkins was heard to comment caustically that Joe and Bill 'were after more than her puddings!' For a short time, Martha sought and enjoyed a step up the social ladder by listening and dancing to records with a delighted Colonel Danby.

By 1988, the increasing paperwork and the VAT at the shop had begun to get Martha down. She was no longer a young woman, and errors were creeping in. A year later she slipped a disc while reaching for some mints for Kenton Archer. During her enforced absence, Jack completely reorganized the shop and on her return she could not find anything. She was even more alarmed when Jack described his future plans to her. As she floundered, unsure of her next move, Marjorie Antrobus took pity on her and Martha misconstrued a casual remark as an invitation to stay for a fortnight. Marjorie was too kind to disabuse her, but their friendship was sorely tried.

Martha began to feel lonely. In 1990, she was even frightened of her own home, fearing that it was haunted by the ghost of Florrie Hoskins, who used to live there.

Eddie Grundy and Snatch Foster appeared, as a practical joke, ghost-like at her window. Hearing of her terror on that occasion, Kate Aldridge and William Grundy tried more of the same at Hallowe'en. Kindly Martha invited them in and, over hot drinks and homemade cake, scared the pair witless by declaring her ability to commune with real ghosts. That Christmas, Martha ordered a huge turkey. When asked who she was sharing it with, she calmly replied, with a glint in her eye, 'Why, Florrie Hoskins, of course.'

Martha takes part in every aspect of village life, knitting scarves, gloves and hats for many of the children, working part-time in the shop (with Betty Tucker) and taking part in activities with the Over Sixties. But, strongly disapproving of the proposed superstore, discos at the Bull, screaming peacocks at the same, and the liaison between John Archer and Sharon Richards, she isn't, on the whole, very much at home in the world of the 1990s.

Mollie Harris

Woodstock, Jackie

Daughter of the owner of a gravel quarry, Jackie Woodstock was loud and vastly spoilt. Thought of at Brookfield as an unsuitable girlfriend for David Archer, Jackie became friends with Shula Archer through their political affiliations with Borchester Young Conservatives in 1980. But in her white Triumph Spitfire she lured Shula's boyfriend Mark Hebden away from under Shula's nose. They became engaged, and lived together in the fast lane of life, enjoying hang-gliding and skiing. Jackie, though, continued to flirt outrageously and Mark wasn't prepared to stand for it. The engagement was broken. Jackie cared little, it seemed; but she took on more than even she could handle when she went out with the reclusive Ben Warner, who violently assaulted her. Some in the village would say she deserved it.

Anne Louise Wakefield

WOODWARD, MR

Mr Woodward, an elderly Shropshire farmer, had successfully reclaimed land on the Shropshire borders and, passing through Ambridge in 1952, called on Phil Archer when he learned of Phil's efforts at reclamation on Lakey Hill. 'Under bracken there's gold, under gorse there's silver, under heather there's copper,' were his enigmatic words. He advised Phil to put subsidies into land, not into the bank – advice which Phil understood, even if he could not always follow it.

Will Kings

WOOLLEY, HAZEL (FORMERLY TRENTHAM)

b. 15 Feb. 1956

Hazel was the only daughter of Valerie and Reggie Trentham. As a child she contracted a slight case of polio. After the death of her father she was sent away to boarding school.

When Jack Woolley was courting Valerie, he persuaded her to let Hazel move to a day school near Ambridge. Before marrying her mother in 1966, Jack tried hard to win Hazel's approval (he gave her two dogs) and soon she preferred his company. When she was adopted officially by Jack, she was thrilled to be given a new birth certificate. She chose to stay with him at Grey Gables when her mother left.

At twenty-one, she came into money from a trust fund. She was by then living in London. Her visits to Jack were sporadic and only when she needed more money. On her rare trips to Grey Gables, she behaved badly, sleeping late, complaining that the maids hadn't cleaned her room, kicking Jack's dog Captain, trying to sack Higgs and generally causing mayhem.

In London she had a job as a PA with a film company in Soho, a flat in Richmond, a smart car and a smart boyfriend. She lost all four. A *poste restante* address in Bangkok was the last Jack heard of her. A telegram with her name on it was read out at his marriage to Peggy Archer in 1991.

Hilary Armstrong; Jan Cox; Hilary Newcombe

WOOLLEY, JACK

b. 19 July 1919; m. Valerie Trentham 22 Feb. 1966; 1 adopted dtr; divorced Sept. 1974; m. Peggy Archer 1 Jan. 1991

Jack Woolley, a self-made new-rich businessman from Stirchley, Birmingham, swept into Ambridge in 1962, determined to amass as much land as he could. He bought the Grey Gables Country Club, intending to turn it into a holiday centre for tired businessmen,

Peggy and Jack Woolley (June Spencer and Arnold Peters)

and the Grey Gables stables from Christine Johnson. He added the Walton Grange stables and sufficient acres to create a golf course. He bought premises in Borchester, opened his New Curiosity Shop, had second thoughts and sold it to John Tregorran all in the space of four months. In 1964 he and Ralph Bellamy bought the Grenville Estate together.

After all this, he took off on a well-earned cruise, leaving Valerie Trentham in charge of Grey Gables. In 1966, she became the second Mrs Woolley (Jack's first wife had died some years before). This new marriage was not happy. Childless himself, Jack tried hard to make friends with Valerie's daughter

Hazel, and officially adopted her only months before Valerie left him in 1972. Their divorce was finalized in 1974. When Valerie died in 1983 Jack blamed himself for 'driving her to drink', though most agreed that Valerie had always had problems of her own. Hazel has been a deep disappointment to him: in recent years he has seen her only rarely, when she needs money from him.

Jack has many local interests and owns the village shop and the local newspaper, *The Borchester Echo*. In 1972 he felt a need to play with trains, putting on a smart new station-master's uniform, blowing a whistle and sending his newly-acquired engine the

Empress of Ambridge off on her maiden voyage at Ambridge Park Railway. It proceeded through Bellamy Halt and Woolley Central stations, but not without mishap. The launch champagne exploded, startling Stan Cooper the driver. He jumped, knocked the steam-cock open and scalded his back. At the second attempt, with Tony Archer acting as fireman, the points got stuck and the *Empress* ran into the buffers, damaging her engine. Jack had to relinquish his dream and the *Empress* was taken over by the Borchester Railway Society.

Jack is a man of tremendous energy, with a seemingly endless list of interests and hobbies to throw himself into – though in recent years ill-health has slowed him down a bit. When he fancied the noble sport of fishing, he bought himself any amount of expensive tackle, and got Tom Forrest to teach him. He was outraged when his first lesson took place standing in the middle of a field. But the tutoring Tom gave him must have been effective, for Jack is now a good fisherman, and has even earned Tom's grudging approval. He is a keen golfer. And he's a member of South Borsetshire Hunt, though he doesn't ride to hounds. When once he owned a racehorse, Grey Silk, in partnership with Ralph Bellamy, he organized a coachload of villagers to go and cheer the animal on at the races; Grey Silk came in third out of a field of eight. Jack likes a flutter: once he confessed to Jill that he'd lost £100 at a poker game, and when Nelson Gabriel opened a casino in Borchester, Jack was a frequent punter.

As regular a churchgoer as time allows, he's always taken a close interest in St Stephen's, both financially and practically, and donated both chiming and self-winding devices for the clock. He even took lessons in campanology in Hereford to impress Tom Forrest, unaware that Tom was going on the same course.

He has, since he was a young man, been a keen ballroom dancer, an interest he shares with his present wife Peggy (whom he married in 1991); they can sometimes be seen gliding across the floor at Grey Gables' tea-dances. And he is the proud holder of the Borchester Chrysanthemum Society challenge cup. He boasts wonderful flowers, though it is Higgs who tends them for him in the greenhouses at Grey Gables, when he isn't busy driving Jack around in the Bentley.

When he stood for the post of chairman of the parish council, he dutifully kissed babies – even William Grundy; bought endless rounds of drinks; provided the Over Sixties with a lavish tea prepared by the Grey Gables chef Jean-Paul; and sold them basic food-stuffs at cut prices in the village shop. But he showed his unscrupulous side and determination to win when he suppressed an article in the *Echo* which supported Pat Archer and substituted pictures of himself. He won with 120 votes.

That Grey Gables became a success is a great personal triumph, though Jack would be nowhere without the efforts of his loyal staff, particularly at various times his wife Peggy, Caroline Bone, Kathy Perks and Jean-Paul – a fact which, to his credit, he'd surely be the first person to acknowledge. The restaurant has won a prestigious gourmet award, the Golden Rosette, and Grey Gables was honoured by visits from the Duke of

Westminster and HRH the Princess Margaret.

But there have been bad times, too. Poachers have made a practice of taking game birds, fish and deer from the estate. And in 1973 there was a major robbery in which a great deal of uninsured silver was stolen. Jack was attacked by the burglars, gagged and tied. Peggy Archer found him and ministered to him, and he was admitted to hospital suffering from shock, though, being Jack, discharged himself far too soon. The following year, at the news of Valerie's decision to sue him for divorce, he suffered his first heart attack.

For many years, Captain the Staffordshire bull terrier was his much-loved confidant and over-indulged friend. Captain twice won the cup at the village fête competition for the dog which most resembled its owner, but in spite of desperate coaching from Jack, refused to 'die for the Queen' in the tricks section. After the show was over, of course, Captain performed the routine immaculately many times for anyone and everyone. Jack and Captain took healthy walks together each day, but both their attempts to lose weight were thwarted by Jean-Paul's strawberry tartlets. Jack's mobile phone was permanently programmed with the vet's telephone number so that he could reach him instantly, should anything happen to Captain. At a low point in Jack's life, when he was feeling particularly old and unloved, he bought himself a toupee; but Captain showed more sense and chewed it to bits. One day when Higgs was sent on to the roof of Grey Gables to clear the gutters of leaves, Captain followed him. An anxious Jack, watching them from a lower kitchen roof,

lost his balance and fell. A hair-line fracture and a loss of memory resulted.

On another occasion Jack collapsed at Grey Gables and was given the kiss of life by Lynda Snell, who had come to lobby him about No Smoking Day. Back in hospital, he was fitted with a pacemaker. As a patient Jack enjoyed all the flowers and messages of goodwill and waved to Captain through the window. But on his return home he was hurt to see his pet slavishly following George Barford, who had given the dog some much-needed training and discipline in his master's absence.

Jack pursued Peggy Archer for many years, but always without success. For some time Peggy went out with a rival, Captain Wendover (or Captain Pugwash, as Tony Archer nicknamed him). She finally relented and their wedding, conducted by the Bishop of Felpersham, took place on 1 January 1991. The couple sped off in Jack's open-topped Bentley to honeymoon in St Lucia. But on his return Jack was devastated by the news of Captain's death. Since then Peggy has been a constant helpmeet and ally. Jack even commissioned a rose to be named after her and exhibited at the Chelsea Flower Show: 'The Ambridge Rose'.

Jack collapsed again in 1993 when he was collecting the takings from the village shop and it was robbed by Clive Horrobin and his accomplice Bruno Wills burst in with shotguns at the ready. He spent a short time in hospital, and, more shocked than anything else, he soon recovered.

Jack and Peggy have now moved into the Lodge and Jack is discovering for the first time the joys of being a member of a large family. He's an ebullient man who has survived knocks and learned to rein in his enthusiasm for life somewhat. The ruthless streak he displayed as an ambitious young entrepreneur has mellowed into warmth and consideration, showing that he is a businessman extraordinaire with a heart of molten gold. He is a popular member of the Ambridge community and, by those close to him, much loved.

Philip Garston-Jones; Arnold Peters

WOOLLEY, PEGGY (NÉE PERKINS AND FORMERLY ARCHER)

b. 13 Nov. 1924; m. Jack Archer 17 July 1943; 1 son, 2 dtrs; m. Jack Woolley 1 Jan. 1991

The only daughter of Albert and Polly Perkins, brought up in London, Peggy was never to lose a sense of her city roots, despite her marriage in 1943 to Jack Archer, Ambridge born and bred.

Jack and Peggy ran a smallholding at the north end of Ambridge until 1952, when one of Jack's army friends, Barney Lee, offered them a farm partnership in Cornwall. They sold up and moved away with their three children – Lilian, Jennifer and Tony – but within just four months Jack brought his family back. A weeping Peggy told her sister-in-law, Christine Archer, that Barney had fallen in love with her and that Jack believed she had encouraged him. It looked as though her marriage was over; but eventually Jack was made to see sense and they were reconciled.

Jack applied for a licence to manage the Bull in place of Sam Saunders, who was retiring, and got the job. But on the day of his interview Peggy went down with diphtheria and spent a miserable Christmas in Felpersham Isolation Hospital. Her family was permitted to visit but could only look at her through a glass window. She came home tired and weak, to discover that Jack, unhappy away from farming, had started to gamble and to drink too much. The next few years were difficult as Jack's condition deteriorated, the licence for the Bull was transferred to Peggy and increased responsibility was heaped on her shoulders. The one bright event was when the Bull was put up for sale by Stourhampton Brewery in 1959, and Laura Archer helped them buy it for £5,300, giving them some measure of independence. By then Peggy had set herself irrevocably against the idea of being a farmer's wife and Jack, frustrated, plunged ever deeper into debt and drink. He became ill and died in a Scottish clinic in 1971, Peggy holding his hand.

The following year Peggy asked Sid and Polly Perks to manage the Bull and went to work for Jack Woolley at Grey Gables to run the Country Park, unwittingly taking the first step towards a quirky relationship that was to delight and aggravate her over the next twenty years. Hard-headed and uncompromising in business, Jack was putty in her hands, and she ruled him with a rod of iron. He proposed to her in 1974 and she turned him down, resigning from her post at Grey Gables; but that was by no means the last of their association.

After a holiday in Guernsey where Lilian and her husband Ralph Bellamy now lived,

Peggy worked as part-time secretary for Andrew Sinclair, who was managing the Berrow Estate in Ralph's absence. He was uneasy at first, thinking that she had been sent to spy on him, but they soon became friends.

The birth of her first grandchild, Pat and Tony Archer's son, John Daniel, on New Year's Eve 1975, followed by the news that Jennifer was to marry Brian Aldridge, gave 1976 a bright start – indeed, put her in such a mellow mood that she consented to go back to work part-time at Grey Gables. However, Jack found it impossible not to interfere in her life, glowering at Barney Lee when he paid her an unexpected visit, and giving conflicting instructions to her landscape gardeners, who were working on the Bull gardens. It was hardly surprising that when he offered to go into partnership with her in the Bull she turned him down, telling him that he was too dominating.

When Ralph Bellamy died in 1980, Peggy found herself at odds with Lilian, who refused to play the part of grieving widow and was drinking too much. But this distress was to pale into insignificance a few months later when Peggy shared Dan Archer's vigil throughout the long night after Doris Archer died.

The next years were unsettling. There was a fire at Blossom Hill Cottage, which Peggy had rented from the Bellamys for some years, and she was unable to return to her home for several months. Then Jack Woolley had an accident and didn't recognize her when she went to see him, which was very worrying until she could see that he was showing signs of improvement. Just when she thought she could relax she heard about Caroline Bone's affair with Brian Aldridge and had to help her daughter Jennifer.

With all these stressful events it was not surprising that she became ill. Her shoulders were stiff and uncomfortable and polymyalgia rheumatica was diagnosed, for which she was put on a course of steroids. Unfortunately one of the side effects of the treatment was that she felt constantly hungry; she even found herself stealing her granddaughter Kate Aldridge's chocolate cream eggs.

It was at this vulnerable stage in her life that she met Godfrey Wendover, a retired widower who had once been in the navy. Suddenly life was fun again. She became completely infatuated, to the annoyance of her children and to Jack Woolley's intense jealousy. In the event Jack had much to thank Godfrey for, because it was in comparing the two men that the scales were finally dashed from Peggy's eyes and she began to realize how much she loved Jack. Godfrey made the crucial mistake of laughing when she talked of putting Sammy in the Midland Counties cat show; but Jack understood, because of his affection for his dog Captain. He not only accompanied her to the show but he gave her a slap-up dinner afterwards. She stopped seeing so much of Godfrey and Jack started courting her seriously with more tact than he had shown in his younger days. This time when he proposed in October 1990, she accepted him.

Of her children, only Lilian was pleased when she heard the news; Tony and Jennifer were far too concerned about how it would affect them. Peggy remarked, with characteristic tartness, that Jennifer was only really worried about losing a free babysitter; and indeed she was very put out when her mother was no longer available to look after Alice at a drop of a hat. However, they all behaved well at the wedding and gave Peggy and Jack a proper send-off for their Caribbean honeymoon.

It took time for Peggy to adjust to being married once more, and it helped when the Woolleys moved from Grey Gables into the Lodge, and so had a home of their own. Any hopes for a peaceful retirement were soon to disappear: recent years have been eventful. Her mother, Mrs P., died in 1991, which saddened her greatly. Then Conn Kortchmar, one of her GI boyfriends during the war, unexpectedly arrived in Ambridge and took her on a nostalgic trip of the past. It was both exciting and exhausting, but her main feeling was one of gratitude when Jack gave him his marching orders. The raid on the village shop in 1993 made Jack so ill that he had to go to hospital, which jolted them into an awareness of how precious was their remaining time together. They have since started to ease out of some of their activities and responsibilities.

Peggy realized that it was time to put the Bull on the market, even though 1993 was an uneconomic time to sell. It was hard for her to relinquish such a vital part of her life, with all its associated memories, but she did so with good grace.

As a single parent Peggy showed courage in the face of difficulties that would have overwhelmed a less determined personality. She more than deserves the lifestyle and protection brought to her by marriage to Jack Woolley.

June Spencer; Thelma Rogers; June Spencer

WOOLLEY, VALERIE (NÉE GRAYSON AND FORMERLY TRENTHAM)

*m. Reggie Trentham 21 Jan. 1953; 1 dtr;
m. Jack Woolley 22 Feb. 1966; divorced Sept.
1974; d. 1 Aug. 1983*

Valerie Grayson first arrived in Ambridge in 1952 on the arm of Reggie Trentham. She was a friend of Mike Daly's and had worked in intelligence with him during the war. Reggie installed her as a hostess at the Country Club and, in due and stormy course, married her. Their daughter Hazel was born in 1956 and the three went for a world cruise.

Reggie died in the Bahamas in 1964 and, the call of Ambridge being strong, Valerie returned with the young Hazel to run Grey Gables for Jack Woolley while he was away. She then helped Lilian Bellamy to build up her riding stables. Jack persuaded Valerie to marry him in 1966. Within a short time, she showed little interest in either Jack or the decoration of their new home, leaving it to Carol and John Tregorran to get on with. Nor did she give Jack any support whatever in his business plans.

Always a heavy drinker, she saw herself as something of a *femme fatale*, and when Hazel was safely installed in boarding school, she had affairs with Ralph Bellamy and Roger Travers-Macy. Having made sure that Hazel was officially adopted by Jack, she left him and was reported to be living with yet another man.

When Valerie came back to Ambridge in 1973 to demand a divorce, Jack became so stressed that he had a near-fatal heart attack.

When she died in 1983, Jack blamed himself for driving Valerie to drink, but no one agreed with him. Perhaps her problem was that, having worked in military intelligence during the war, she had a very low boredom threshold.

Ann Johnson; Jenny Lee; Heather Canning

Worth, DI

Detective Inspector Worth headed the investigation into the death of Bob Larkin in 1957.

Wreford, Revd Matthew

Matthew Wreford was the vicar of Ambridge from 1961 to 1968.

John Carlin

Wynford, Norman

Norman was a careless, pleasant young man whose father Thorpe Wynford wanted him to settle down before he got into too much mischief. Thorpe bought Walter Gabriel's tenant farm for Norman in 1957. Norman had some experience of farming and farm management, and planned to keep a small dairy herd, some hens and pigs. All these plans came to nothing when three years later he met a young Hollerton girl called Julie and fell in love. His father violently disapproved of her. Norman wanted to help Julie's parents with £200 as a deposit on a house, but Thorpe refused to help in the vain hope

that he could 'bring his son to his senses'. Norman tried to sell Phil Archer some stock at an absurdly low price in order to raise the sum but Phil wouldn't take advantage of him and lent him the cash instead, to be repaid when the stock was sold. Norman left Ambridge when his father sold the farm, but didn't forget to repay his debt to Phil.

Robert Chetwyn

Wynford, Thorpe

Thorpe Wynford bought Walter Gabriel's farm for his son Norman in 1957. Sadly Norman disappointed him when he decided to marry a girl Thorpe thought totally unsuitable. When Norman refused to give her up, Thorpe washed his hands of them. He saw Phil Archer in Felpersham and told him he was going to sell the farm. Three weeks later they clinched a deal.

John Sharp; Tom Harrison

Wynford's Farm

In 1957, Thorpe Wynford heard that Walter Gabriel had tired of running his tenant farm on the Fairbrother Estate. He offered to lend Walter money so that he could buy the farm outright at the advantageous terms available to the sitting tenant and then sell it on to Wynford. For Walter it was the ideal solution. But three years later serious differences split the Wynford family and the farm was put on the market again.

Dan Archer wanted to buy it, in partnership with his son Jack, but Jack's wife Peggy objected because she didn't want to be a farmer's wife again. Instead Phil Archer bought it as an investment, letting the land to Dan and the farmhouse as a holiday home. In 1963 when Paul and Christine Johnson were looking for a base in Ambridge Phil suggested that they use the farmhouse. Phil decided to accept Charles Grenville's offer for the property before the Johnsons moved in, but Grenville accepted them as tenants. A few years later, they bought the farmhouse and paddock.

In 1973, when Paul was working in Europe and Christine often alone in Wynford's, she was joined by Jennifer Travers-Macy and her children while her husband Roger worked away from home too. Jennifer left in 1976 after her divorce and second marriage. Paul's business difficulties at this time forced them to take out a second mortgage on the house, and to raise further capital for his new fish farm he had to sell the paddock to Phil in autumn 1977. The collapse of the fish farm and Paul's death in an accident in Hamburg meant that Christine had to move into the Stables when the farmhouse was sold on behalf of his creditors.

YELLAND, MRS

When Mrs Yelland received a telegram from the Queen on her hundredth birthday in 1963, Lilian Archer came to pay her respects. She was delighted by the old lady's reminiscences, going back to Victorian times and the letter she produced written by Walter Gabriel's grandmother, Meg.

Margaret Parker

YOUNG, MARVIN

Marvin Young, who lived in one of the council houses, got into trouble with the Pounds in 1975 when he sprayed their shop sign with paint. He showed a greater sense of responsibility the following year when he took on the delivery of the *Felpersham Evening Post* after Martha Woodford stopped selling it at the village shop.

THE ARCHERS' FAMILY TREE

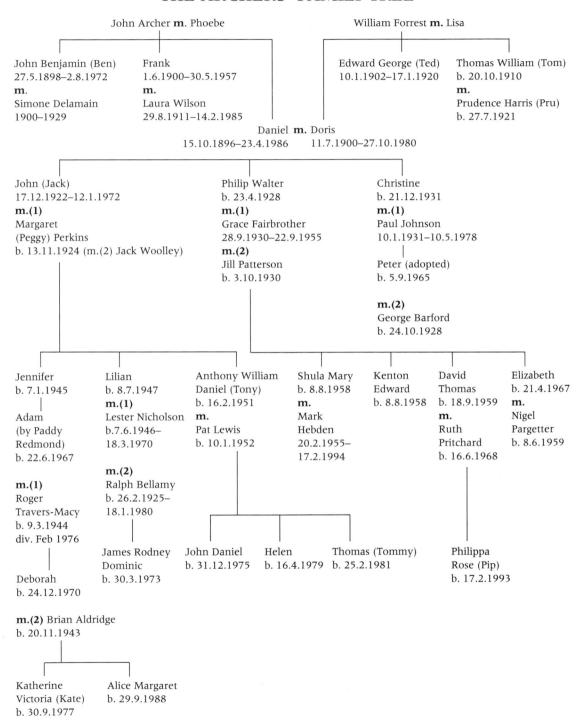

John Archer **m**. Phoebe

William Forrest **m**. Lisa

John Benjamin (Ben)
27.5.1898–2.8.1972
m.
Simone Delamain
1900–1929

Frank
1.6.1900–30.5.1957
m.
Laura Wilson
29.8.1911–14.2.1985

Edward George (Ted)
10.1.1902–17.1.1920

Thomas William (Tom)
b. 20.10.1910
m.
Prudence Harris (Pru)
b. 27.7.1921

Daniel **m**. Doris
15.10.1896–23.4.1986   11.7.1900–27.10.1980

John (Jack)
17.12.1922–12.1.1972
m.(1)
Margaret
(Peggy) Perkins
b. 13.11.1924 (m.(2) Jack Woolley)

Philip Walter
b. 23.4.1928
m.(1)
Grace Fairbrother
28.9.1930–22.9.1955
m.(2)
Jill Patterson
b. 3.10.1930

Christine
b. 21.12.1931
m.(1)
Paul Johnson
10.1.1931–10.5.1978

Peter (adopted)
b. 5.9.1965

m.(2)
George Barford
b. 24.10.1928

Jennifer
b. 7.1.1945

Adam
(by Paddy
Redmond)
b. 22.6.1967

m.(1)
Roger
Travers-Macy
b. 9.3.1944
div. Feb 1976

Deborah
b. 24.12.1970

m.(2) Brian Aldridge
b. 20.11.1943

Katherine
Victoria (Kate)
b. 30.9.1977

Alice Margaret
b. 29.9.1988

Lilian
b. 8.7.1947
m.(1)
Lester Nicholson
b.7.6.1946–
18.3.1970

m.(2)
Ralph Bellamy
b. 26.2.1925–
18.1.1980

James Rodney
Dominic
b. 30.3.1973

Anthony William
Daniel (Tony)
b. 16.2.1951
m.
Pat Lewis
b. 10.1.1952

John Daniel
b. 31.12.1975

Helen
b. 16.4.1979

Thomas (Tommy)
b. 25.2.1981

Shula Mary
b. 8.8.1958
m.
Mark
Hebden
20.2.1955–
17.2.1994

Kenton
Edward
b. 8.8.1958

David
Thomas
b. 18.9.1959
m.
Ruth
Pritchard
b. 16.6.1968

Philippa
Rose (Pip)
b. 17.2.1993

Elizabeth
b. 21.4.1967
m.
Nigel
Pargetter
b. 8.6.1959